Academic Working Lives

Also available from Bloomsbury

Academic Identities in Higher Education, edited by Linda Evans and Jon Nixon
Analysing Teaching-Learning Interactions in Higher Education, Paul Ashwin
Education, Work and Identity, Michael Tomlinson
Identity and Pedagogy in Higher Education, Kalwant Bhopal and Patrick Alan Danaher
Interpretive Pedagogies for Higher Education, Jon Nixon
Rethinking Knowledge within Higher Education, Jan McArthur

Academic Working Lives:

Experience, Practice and Change

Lynne Gornall, Caryn Cook, Lyn Daunton,

Jane Salisbury and Brychan Thomas

Bloomsbury Academic
An imprint of Bloomsbury Publishing Plc

B L O O M S B U R Y
LONDON • NEW DELHI • NEW YORK • SYDNEY

Bloomsbury Academic

An imprint of Bloomsbury Publishing Plc

50 Bedford Square	1385 Broadway
London	New York
WC1B 3DP	NY 10018
UK	USA

www.bloomsbury.com

BLOOMSBURY and the Diana logo are trademarks of Bloomsbury Publishing Plc

First published 2013
Paperback edition first published 2015

British Library Cataloguing-in-Publication Data
A catalogue record for this book is available from the British Library.

ISBN:	HB:	978-1-4411-8534-1
	PB:	978-1-4742-4379-7
	ePDF:	978-1-4411-9970-6
	ePub:	978-1-4411-5302-9

Library of Congress Cataloging-in-Publication Data
A catalog record for this book is available from the Library of Congress.

Typeset by Newgen Knowledge Works (P) Ltd., Chennai, India
Printed and bound in Great Britain

This book is dedicated in memory of:

*Iris Blockwell, Celfyn and Gwen Thomas, Edith Margaret Plant (Peg),
Anna, John and Irene,*

and our friend Dr Steven Harris.

A special dedication to Frank Cook (1951–2012): in his words 'I am so proud of her'

Contents

List of Tables and Figures

Tables

Figures

Acknowledgements

A book about what we do in education and the ways in which people in the public sector add value.

For Dr Roger Cannon who has supported this project and the work of the team and book since its outset, '*Diolch yn fawr*'.

We would like to thank our informants, colleagues, students, friends and families . . . and our patient partners, please read here: Alan, Anne, Roger – thank you all very much. Particular thanks also go to colleagues and mentors including Professors Linda Evans, David Turner and Rob Cuthbert; Professors John Furlong, John Gardner, and Dr Sue Davies (Welsh Education Research Network); Cardiff University School of Social Sciences, Professors Alan Felstead, Sally Power, Brian Davies, Dr Sara Delamont; Professor Rosemary Deem, Monica Gibson-Sweet and University of Glamorgan Business School; Dr David Blaney, Dr Barbara Crossouard; Rebekah Daniel, Iheanyi C. Egbuta, Sian Lewis, Sadie Fentham, Mark Connolly, Eryl Mills, Philippa Coulson, Susy Rogers, Jan Clarke, Professor Helen Phillips; Glynis Bennett and Dr Gina Dolan; Newport Business School and Professor Andrew Thomas, Dr Lyndon Murphy; Chimkwanum Okecha: poet and consultant.

To the staff and students of 'CS', you know who you are, and remembering Brigid Watt – magical years and amazing times. Thank you also to Professor Harry (GH) Jamieson, John O. Thompson, Dr Paul Baxter, Alexis MacKenzie, Doreen Bowsher, John Trevitt, Mr Jack Lord (Netherton Moss), Hilary and Jim Hudson. And Gloria Jones, departmental secretary, who had a lot to put up with.

Lyn, Jane, Brychan and Caryn, as members of the Working Lives team, wish to acknowledge the contribution to this book of the Working Lives team leader and fellow editor, Lynne Gornall, for her driving force, energy and unstinting enthusiasm, without which this volume would not have been possible. She kept each of us anchored and grounded when the going got tough. We are all greatly indebted to her for this.

The Working Lives team as a whole would like to thank Alison Baker, Frances Arnold, Carly Bareham, Claire Cooper, Kasia Figiel and Rosie Pattinson at Bloomsbury Academic and associates Jon Ingoldby and Josh Pawaar for their great patience and support of this publication.

Publishers' acknowledgements

Fig 8.1. Discourses about the role of academics
Doherty and Manfredi (2006) Discourses about the role of academics: Plato's Academy/ The Teaching Factory. Reproduced with the kind permission of Emerald Group Publishing.

Fig 14.1. Academic employability model
Rothwell and Arnold (2007). Self Perceived Employability Model. Reproduced with the kind permission of Emerald Group Publishing.

Fig 28.1. The AI cycle
Cooperrider, in Whitney and Stavros (2008). The Appreciative Inquiry Cycle. Reproduced with kind permission of Crown Custom Publishing, Ohio, US.

Note: Citations and referencing
In this book, we have broken with convention so that citations and references in general run as more recent first, unless for author's reasons of historical or sequential import; we wanted to foreground authors' more *recent* ideas.

Foreword

At a time of deep institutional and professional divisions within and across the higher education sector, any book that reminds us of the nature and purpose of academic work performs an important, timely and critical function. This book certainly offers such a reminder. It does much more than that, however. It drills down into the experience and practice of academic work, and in doing so helps us understand some of the seismic shifts that are currently shaping further and higher education – locally, nationally and globally. Through its insights into academic working lives, their experiences and practices, it enables us to understand some of the deep codes of educational and social change operating across society. This is an important book that speaks to academic workers, institutional managers and policy-makers – and which will undoubtedly impact upon their work at the level of practice, organizational ethos and strategic planning.

The central theme of the book – as its title announces – is 'academic working lives'. 'Work' is the most general word in English for doing something or for something done. Unlike 'labour', it suggests a sense of agency and purpose. The term 'working' carries the added sense of something that is functioning well – something 'in good working order'. The phrase 'working lives' refers thus to that aspect of our lives that is concerned with getting things done, but it carries the added sense of lives that are functioning well and flourishing. A working life – unlike a laborious life – is a life that aspires to well-being and human flourishing; an academic working life is one that acknowledges research, scholarship and teaching as necessary constituents of that flourishing.

That is not to say that an academic working life does not involve the burden of emotional labour. Of course it does, and – as many of the following chapters argue – the current climate of institutional and professional competition adds to that burden. However, this book is concerned primarily not with critiquing current systems, but with providing new perspectives and opening up new possibilities for change. Although the contributors engage with the research-based and theoretical literatures associated with such categories as 'academic professionalism', 'academic identity' and 'academic boundaries', they reframe these categories within a broader framework of ideas, methodologies and insights. One such insight – seminal to the book's central theme – is that change starts with lived experience and working practice. It starts, that is, with the everyday and the ordinary. Education is, at its very best, commonplace: grounded in the reality of our everyday lives.

Notwithstanding the increasing global interconnectivity of human existence, life is lived – culturally, politically and socially – at precise points of interconnection. Globalization is experienced not as an airy abstraction, but as a located reality. Thus, while the following chapters represent an impressively wide range of international contexts and perspectives, each of them focuses on the specificity of working life, practice, changes and experience within a particular context and from that particular perspective. Many of the chapters are based on original research and all are informed by inquiry and analysis. Together they comprise an authoritative and wide-ranging record of academic working lives located within and across national and continental boundaries.

This sense of multivocality – of inclusivity that is respectful of difference and divergence across educational contexts – emerges from the collaborative nature of the ongoing project that has generated this book. All too often, edited compilations are assembled according to a pre-specified structure negotiated between the editor and the publishing house. However, in this case the book has been developed through a genuinely collaborative process in which its overall shape and structure has emerged through discussion between the contributors and in negotiation with the publishers. It is a great credit to the core editorial team – and to the publishing house – that they have managed to sustain this degree of flexibility and creativity.

The most important message I take from this insightful book is that life is about what we *do* – what we practise and how what we do is experienced by ourselves and others. It is our practices that carry our values. Academic workers do not need theories imported into practice; nor do they need accounts of practice that are devoid of theoretical – or generalizable – import. What they need – and what this book provides – is the opportunity to engage in a process of deliberation about the ends and purposes of higher education as these relate to academic practice. This is not a process that can be bureaucratically managed. It can be initiated and – having been initiated – can be sustained through the kind of collaborative, research-based and self-reflective inquiries documented in this original and timely book.

Jon Nixon
Cumbria, March 2013

Working life

Place of suspense and mystery. Off site. For plotting
and incubation, between nourishment and inspiration.
Where dissonance and doubt are plumbed for ideas.

Confinement concentrates attention. Stills and shields.
Out of sight, day shades into night. Seclusion offers
uninterrupted thought. Secret, steamroller production.

Riding the wave of power and danger. That high. We
manage risk, avoid the sudden plunge. Salvage
collaboration, conviviality. Sustain creative agency.

Sharing outcomes. Healing. Making a difference.

Val Walsh
March 2013

Introduction

'Starting the Day Fresh' – Hidden Work and Discourse in Contemporary Academic Practice

Lynne Gornall, Lyn Daunton, Jane Salisbury,
Caryn Cook and Brychan Thomas[1]

The work of 'Working Lives'[2]

In this chapter, as an Introduction to a book on academic working lives, we discuss one of our major areas of work. Other chapters in the book consider different aspects of the 'Working Lives' research, but here we touch on many, if not all, of the themes contained in the volume.

Unseen work as hidden from view

With so much attention, analysis and measurement given to the more visible aspects of academic performance – teaching hours, exam scripts marked, candidates credentialized, funds secured, research as published units – surprisingly little attention is given to the manner and methods by which academics actually do their work. The equivalent of what we know as *teaching observation* or *research impact* assessment seems to be lacking in any schemes for 'preparation observation', 'writing the book chapter observation', 'designing assessment observation', 'drafting the bid observation', 'answering all the emails observation', and so on. In this chapter, the members of the Working Lives team discuss what is 'unseen' in academic working. As one 'critical friend' advises, 'Universities are getting an amazing deal from people [like you] who graft at teaching all day then come home for the second shift and do research or admin'.

The anthropologist Sara Delamont reminds us that sometimes the very 'obvious' and most familiar aspects of occupational life are also the most overlooked (1996, 2002). In this case, the 'how I work' of much academic practice has been 'hidden' from the analytic gaze not because it was *secret* but because it has been considered unimportant. It has not been asked about and hence remained undisclosed. But it has been unobserved too. We thus begin the volume by foregrounding this area. We asked our own 'significant others': 'how do I work'?

You get into a late evening (or early morning) frenzy . . . against the clock, too much to do. Downloading stuff, scanning it, picking out material, several things on the go all at once. Solo work, then you leave it to [the] next person . . . impatient, bored now! Fever pitch working [most of the time].

Colleague

Well you are a messy worker, but you are also playful with ideas and I can see and hear you making lots of parallels with things outside of your discipline . . . metaphors and colourful language . . . I get shocked about how you and colleagues do drafts . . . it seems like a fetish . . . you seem to layer and alter (and you say this improves stuff) . . .

Partner

Of course, the signs and signals of academic productivity, indicated above, are all around: 'untidy' desks, piles of books and papers, the multiple screens open on laptops, the carrier bags of marking and the emails sent/received at all hours of the clock. But the processes themselves are often undertaken in private. This is in part because many of them are conducted away from the 'official' workplace (Cook *et al.* 2009). Yet if the (visible) outputs of our work are important, to be measured and made accountable for (Kelly and Boden this volume), then attention to the nature of the *processes* involved must repay itself in value too. A 'methodology of private places observation' and of 'telling interviews with close informants' might need to be developed. We indicated above the timbre that this 'voice' might have. Here is more:

From what I can see, a lot of work appears to be carried out, and very methodically, especially . . . in the mornings and in the evening. These are before and after the main 'office' [campus] working day.

Partner

How do you work? Random. Huge 'to do' lists so you are always busy, fiddling around to get started, then, hours and hours and hours without stopping . . . probably because of the knowledge of how hard it is to get going again. Creativity actually. Not wholly under control.

Partner

You are very methodical but full of self-doubt. Anxious it won't turn out OK. But you can prepare well . . . get the material together and then make the necessary judgements on screen, deciding what to include or leave out [things others find difficult] . . . changing the wording . . . completing.

Friend

You spread out (in two places) . . . I see you running between two floors [laughs]. As an onlooker, I don't get it!

Partner

Writers Acker and Webber, and Huyton in this volume, also discuss aspects of the 'private lives' of higher education (HE) (Trow 1975), what Walsh after reviewing this chapter, calls 'the secret, steamroller production' of academic work (poem, this volume).

Productivity and performativity

A moment's reflection reminds us why academic working lives have become dominated by the focus on visible effects. These have been discussed by scholars as aspects of 'performativity' (Ball 2003), 'academic capitalism' (Slaughter and Leslie 1997) and 'knowledge work' in HE (Fenwick *et al.* 2012; Delanty 2001). The interventionist political projects of the 1980s, Kogan and Hanney (2000) argue, in an impatience with 'process', inaugurated a working paradigm on the 'black box' principle, that 'what mattered' were outputs. In some ways, it was a relief to all: we could get on with our messy and unformalized modes of production without interference (Abrahamson and Freedman 2006). It didn't matter how we produced 'the goods'; what *officially* 'mattered' was what emerged, the tangible, measurable effects of working processes. It seemed reasonable, modern and professional. It is a context also discussed by key writers and in important studies within the existing HE literature (Ball 2007; Goodson 2003; Bottery 1996 for example). We were mistaken, however, in thinking that 'processes' would be unaffected by the outputs paradigm. There is something about the academic persona, and the conditions of our productive working, that makes elements of privacy, self-organization and the role of autonomy important in creating the effective work environment *as 'self-set'* (Malcolm and Zukas 2009). As one Working Lives member comments, 'Whether I work . . . upstairs or downstairs [at home], is not just a question of whether it is warmer, but my mood too.' Another: 'I am a "thick describer" and need to set up space for how I work, including cutting up and pasting and sometimes being nocturnal . . .', and again: 'The work creates disorder . . . during which coherent but untested ideas . . . emerge.'

This raises the question of whether, as academics and educationists, we need to promote more explicitly and defend our working methods. This is especially so when these informal practices are under threat, as staff are enjoined to 'work' or 'not work' in particular ways (Ball 2003; Dixey and Harbottle; Waring this volume). We respect, after all, that students and others may produce material of excellence in any one of a number of scenarios, ones that would not suit others or lead to positive outcomes. But have we been voluble enough in protecting the spaces and conditions of work for ourselves? Such 'informal' aspects of employment and working arrangements (after Delamont 1996, 2002), are part of a 'psychological' tacit contract of work rather than an official one, more often discussed in the breach, perhaps, than in the observance (Cook and Daunton this volume). But such modalities of work are today in question. Many of our informants said that it was harder now to work away from campus: 'Yes, there is a culture of "presenteeism", of being on campus, that managers prefer to have people available, but people often want their colleagues on hand too' (Working Lives team discussion 2012); '[The problem is] "home" to others represents lounging around, relaxing, rather than hard graft . . .' (informant). But there are real problems for academic work, productivity and output with this culture: 'My work can't be done at a desk' (interviewee, referring to research fieldwork and production). Of course, work that is 'unseen', by its very invisibility, makes it easier to be not just overlooked, but *ignored* too. As one family member commented, 'Hours of work? Don't set me off on this topic!'

Working from home (wfh)

Most of the Working Lives research was conducted around academics' evening hours schedules, their working routines off-campus and outside of the 'campus' day. And yes, this included our own project: 'Working on this research took up all the extra "survival" time I had – evening gaps, the odd "light day" and weekends' (Working Lives team member). The study of working from home (wfh) – using where you live as a place of work (as an employee) – is thus at the centre of this project. Our data suggest that staff work *at* and *from* home in some, most or all of the modes shown in Table I.1.

Table I.1   Working modalities: staff work 'slots and modes' – campus, home and elsewhere

MODE	Temporal slot	Working from campus I	Working from home II	Working anywhere III	TIME of KIND or TYPE OF WORK DONE	NOTES fine tuning the categories
a	Week daytime	Y / T	P	Y / T		AM or PM
b	Week early evening	P / U	Y / T	P		Early or Late
c	Week late / night	U	Y	U		Overnight–am
d	Weekend day	Y / P	Y / T	Y / T		Sat or Sun
e	Weekend evening	U / P	Y	P		Early or Late
f	Weekend night	U	Y	U / P		Overnight–am
g	Public holiday leave	U	Y / T	Y / T		Various
h	Personal leave	U / P	Y	Y / P		Home or away
i	Away: work duties	U	U / P	Y / T		Situational
j	Away: illness	U	U / Y / P	P / U		Various

LEGEND: Y=Yes; T=Typical; P=Possible; U=Unlikely.
Source: Gornall 2012.

Across a '24 × 7' day and year then, the most likely workplace for our team and our informants was *not* the conventional workplace or campus (column I). This is particularly so if we include evenings (rows b, e), weekends (rows d, e, f), and when staff are away from work on business, for example, speaking at conferences, travelling abroad to teach (row i), on research leave or even unwell (row j). Working in or at the 'home workspace' was ubiquitous, and the home was the most likely or regular alternate work venue (column II). But it is important to say here what we are *not* saying – that *all* academics wfh, or all of the time. Some do, quite a lot:

I may only go onto campus to teach [supervise or attend meetings] or to return library books.

It is several days since I was last in [on campus] . . . it's not a problem if I'm delivering the goods.

Female informants, pre-1992 university sector

There may be some status divisions operating, between those in research-intensive groups or departments – it could be as localized as this – and those who are not. Nor should the notion of wfh be taken as synonymous with *working in the day* at home (a-II) within the working week. This is because wfh in the daytime on a weekday is now an exception for many staff. Indeed, research vigilance is needed, as some informants initially said that they 'did *not* wfh', taking this definition as the working day (a-II). But '*of course!*' they do wfh, and at every other time, from evenings (b-II) and weekends (d-II, e-II, f-II) to public and family holidays (g-II, h-II), as described in columns (II) and (III) of our Table 1. And here is the 'workload' made visible: the decreasing affordance and opportunities for working from home during the weekday, trying to cope by using all the other time represented in columns II and III. It is, we suggest, a major source of staff experience of pressure. Today, of course, the pleasant and convivial coffee bars of provincial and city areas (column III in Table 1) are also the 'supervision-free' working environments for many independent and employed 'flexibilized', mobile or simply displaced workers (Elliott and Urry 2010). Whilst not without their complexities for 'how I work', these spaces in a marketized environment do provide a service of sorts (Table 1 column III areas a, b, d, e, g, h, i), and help problematize what it is to *work* outside of a 'work' environment, where boundaries are re-drawn.

The expansion of academic work and the decrease in autonomy

Wfh, we argue, has been a symbol of academics' 'own' work, and *choice* about working space and its set-up. Informants told us that this determination was under threat, however, and 'daytime wfh' was all but eliminated by managerial surveillance, cultures of 'presenteeism', expectations of student access or meetings on campus. One, looking back, commented, 'Time working at home was different, a different kind of time . . . creativity/ creative process, and in a [more aesthetic] environment [that] I had some control of. It was a pleasure in 'doing' that was later virtually outlawed' (informant, written comment).

Some academics retained more wfh capacity and affordance than others, correlated with pre-1992 and research-focused higher education institutions (HEIs) in the unequal and differentiated HE system now extant (White 2012: 41; Ball 2008a). The converse was not true, however, that working in a pre-1992 institution necessarily gave greater affordance for flexible and autonomous practices. And if wfh daytime (a-II) is the mode fastest reducing or disappearing, the mode most expanding was weekday evenings (b-II), and one of the week*end* days (d-II) where the 'day off' could be either day at the weekend – or none.

These informal, self-organized and sometimes idiosyncratic ways of working were not a problem for academics while they were at the heart and the centre of their institutions (Nixon 2011; Ball 2007; Taylor 1999). Then, they were able to manage how they produced the goods – so long as they did; 'outcomes', as Kogan (1983) reminds us, have always been important. Universities too had 'autonomy' and the affordance of self-management until the 1990s, when the move away from self-government and public sector funding was also a 'move away', Cuthbert argues (1996: 15), 'from academic self-management'. Not all agree, and some would see HEIs' greater autonomy as linked to an increased managerialism (Deem *et al.* 2007, see also Gornall and Thomas on policy discourse Part 2, this volume). The 'traditional core' of academic work used to be 'teaching in classes and publishing results in academic journals', according to Musselin (2007: 3), 'while other activities, though 'necessary', were 'not part of the job or explicitly rewarded'. We do not identify in the current discourse about a 'blurring of job or role boundaries' (e.g. Musselin 2007; Gornall 1999: 44) any reduction in academics' work or roles in practice, however. Indeed, a recent report (Barber *et al.* 2013) predicts a coming 'avalanche' for the UK HE sector, in which overwhelmed by student choices, technologies, modes and expectations about educational 'delivery', there are increased concerns for academics as well as those who manage the sector. These and other factors make it critical that attention be given to informal as well as formal modes of working in today's employment: Guzman's (2012) notion of 'two kinds of fragility', that of the employed academic *and* of the institution, though developed in a different national context, seems to apply well here, showing that the two are interlinked.

Reporting on 'experience, practice and change'

The Working Lives team sought to explore and facilitate opportunities for collegial discussion about these issues within a research study. Embedded likewise in the contradictions and dilemmas of academic/HE life, we had designed a series of focus group interviews (Fern 2001) which, from the outset, provided the basis for an exploratory, 'grounded' dataset (Strauss and Corbin 1997; Charmaz 1995; Glaser 1993) as well as a discursive space that prioritized participant 'voice' and actor categories (Goodson 2003). The rationale of the research team was to connect – sometimes reconnect – data and notions of lived experience at work to the ongoing facets of organizational change and policy impact (Sato; O'Byrne; Mears and Harrison this volume). Lecturers in HE and further education (FE) institutions thus came together to spend time in discussion and elicitation sessions in March 2008 for the pilot study. Next, short targeted interviews were conducted with colleagues in the three participating HEIs to ask the same questions and obtain individual responses and detail, away from the group discussion environment. These were succeeded by longer, more focused, individual interviews across the UK and a series of conference debates and discussions. A further set of focus group interviews (2009) was organized to cross-check findings and elicit fresh reactions. A final set of questions on the theme of 'Why did you come into HE?' completed the fieldwork.

Using visual methods: making 'hidden' work visible

Some members of the Working Lives team had used visual media in their work previously, including in research, and it was decided that 'visual elicitation' techniques (Stanczak 2007) would be used in the group interview sessions. This was accompanied by discussion about 'subjectivity', the choice of artefacts and documents to use, and how these were to be presented and 'framed' (Turkle 2007). Pictorial images of mobile phones, job adverts, office desks and classrooms, designed to stimulate discussion amongst the variously experienced participants, were thus utilized. In other fields, ethnographers such as Afonso (2004) have experimented with visual illustrations to gain rich informant material, while Waller (1987), a film-maker of working life, uses vivid dramatized sequences within a historical documentary genre. These approaches access *affective* aspects of experience, as well as eliciting empirical detail. Visual media can provoke strong reactions, of course, and this emotional dimension of everyday working life (Bertani Tress; Salisbury this volume) was borne out in our own reflexive discussion as well as in the primary data-gathering sessions below. The outcomes were that our informant group discussions quickly led to a set of topics that were seen to be related: the micro-detail of 'to do' lists and files, office layouts, presence of colleagues, paperwork, reading and preparation, electronic marking, email and educational administration, and the macro-level changes in 'teaching and learning', 'support roles' and new sorts of jobs – including questions of redundancy, volumes of work, pressure, stress, professionalism and so on. Above all, informants told us about the time it takes to actually do the things around 'doing the job' – what we call the 'meta-logistics' of academic work (Gornall and Salisbury 2012, after Neumann 2009) and the impacts of policy on their lives (Nakabugo, Conway, Farren and Barrett; Jephcote; Larsen, this volume), about which they were explicit.

Talking about administration in academics' work

Many ethnographers and organizational researchers, through their studies, have uncovered and brought to attention the texture and grain of the 'working lives' of others in just these sorts of respects (McDowell 2009; Strathern 2000; Wallman 1979; Wright 1994) and we wanted to explore the 'how, what and where' of academic working life from the informants' point of view. Undertaken every day by academics and as part of an 'assumed' if increasingly burdensome working life, 'administration' was the area that Musselin (2007) says has expanded while other traditional aspects of the academic role have become questioned, more complex. But this has been *less* discussed and explored than teaching, research, enterprise or policy-related aspects of academic work. Its volume, growth and pervasiveness might be registered as a wry expression in corridors or meetings, sometimes as a private 'sigh' working alone at night (Daunton *et al.* 2008), but it has been acknowledged only rarely or accounted for in 'workload' allocations. The very tacit work of administration is also something of an *other* of educational life, necessary but not always celebrated work (Strathern, this volume). Yet it is a critical area of *interface*, connecting academics' roles as teachers, scholars, researchers, with ones of manager, organizer, information-sharer in the educational workplace and sector. Indeed there are as many academics who actively enjoy as dislike this work, taking a pride in a good job, being effective in its undertaking.

Both in the initial individual interviews and in plenaries at later presentations of the empirical work, informants told us that they worked at home regularly, frequently and 'usually', at the weekends *and* in the evenings, on holiday, whether away or at home. They found wfh more productive, using laptops to work in different places at different times, in front of the TV and outside in the garden (Thomas and Gornall this volume). They fitted work in when travelling, whether this was for work or non-work purposes, took it away when on vacation, went into work or checked email even when on breaks, off sick or away. The notion of the 'engaged' but 'extended' academic, the *hyperprofessional*, as someone 'always on' (Gornall and Salisbury 2012), seemed readily to gain assent at conferences and seminar paper discussions from Dundee to Oxford, for staff all too familiar with 'intensive' environments or periods of what we may call *extreme working*. As researchers, however, we wanted to avoid assuming that a pathology was in progress (cf. Rogers, this volume); and yet the very simplest question, of 'Where do you normally work?' (after Felstead 2008) brought a tumble of rich description.

> Normal oh dear . . . Normal means 'typically' yes? Well I work, teach in huge lecture theatres, seminar rooms and my departmental office when I'm supervising research students. I also work on preparation of teaching and marking stuff in my office and research and admin too. But normal – normal space? Well I work at home in a study. So my normal is home and office. Of course patterns of attendance vary across the academic year so 'normally' I work from home more when my teaching loads are lighter. Sorry about this but it's not easy to unpack simply – I guess that'll be the same for everyone you ask!
>
> Informant 12, traditional/research based university

The 'high achieving' aspect of academic work (Gough; Rothwell and Rothwell; Floyd this volume), of continuously improving, getting through major workloads and doing a complex job well (Fanghanel 2012), seems as important to a description of modern professionality as the 'demoralized, overworked and broken down' professional of Raman (2000) and others (Rolfe 2013). However, we recognize and had ample evidence for this latter too, and in focusing on the administrative work that lecturers undertake everyday, the role of technology is clearly also implicated. As well as being a tool 'used to bridge the physical gap between those working at home and the conventional workplace' (Elliott and Urry 2010: 10), it has also 'invaded' both home and work spaces, and contributed significantly to performative and productivity pressures.

Concluding remarks

Much important work in education is, we argue, conducted and achieved in the temporal margins and hidden spaces extra to the academy or employing organization.

These practices and the discussions about them are problematic precisely because they raise the question of just what is 'work time' (Ylijoki *et al.* this volume), or where 'the outer limits' of contracts or norms lie, and indeed the issue of 'where it is' that we as scholars are employed. To apprehend this is also to take account of the assumptions and preferences of the professionals involved. In practice, the views and expectations of others, whether colleagues, managers, institutions or the sector, are too often privileged, as are those of wider 'stakeholders', such as employers' organizations, unions, funding councils and government. Yet they are, as we are, always 'positioned' (Goodson 2003) with 'agendas' in the debate.

But teachers have been at the cutting edge of the uses of technologies at work, using multiple software and new devices ahead of the general working population (Hudson, this volume), indeed often called upon to put on the courses and training to upskill the workforce in these areas (Part 4 this volume). Academics have also been in the forefront of professional and employee flexibility, productivity and adaptation (Ball 2008a; Brown *et al.* 2001; Richards this volume) as well as research and development, knowledge creation, experimentation and innovation, passing on, circulating and sharing with students, colleagues and other partners (Hargreaves and Fullan 2012; Brown and Lauder 2003; Cheng this volume). They have embraced ICT and open methods in their courses as part of a new craft (Ecclesfield and Garnett; Gornall this volume), working in new teams and collaborations (Cook and Gornall in Part 5), in models of reprofessionalized, contemporary work (Laugharne, Carter and Jones; Austin this volume). Institutions thus need to include and recognize these, and also to encompass a notion of the 'whole job' in accounts of workload, or else to allow staff the autonomy to (self) organize and manage their time, judging what is to come first, second, third, and what last. This discussion, particularly in the preview of more flexibilized learning systems (for students – see Rogers this volume; Barber *et al.* 2013), is now pressing.

Here is thus a story about learning and work, and what Nixon (in our Foreword) called the 'deep codes' of change. It is one we wish to share, and not only within education but much wider (Chapman this volume). It includes how we can use our knowledge to work with HEIs in moving towards a more progressive set of employment policies. In particular, those which could take account of the less boundaried work of many academics in HE and FE, since these have produced some of our best – as well as most routine – work. In the Working Lives research, it was often these processes that provided not just a sense of the pleasures of academic working life, but also the sources of 'optimism', which Barnett and others (this volume) see as essential to the sector moving forward.

Acknowledgements

We thank our research associates and advisers: Professors Alan Felstead, Sally Power, David Turner, Linda Evans, Brian Davies; Dr Sara Delamont. For WERN, Dr Sue Davies, Professors John Furlong, John Gardner; members and participants in the Network.

Notes

1 The Working Lives research team (2007–9) comprised:
    Caryn Cook, University of Wales Newport Business School
    Lyn Daunton, University of Glamorgan Business School
    Dr Lynne Gornall (project leader), University of Glamorgan
    Dr Jane Salisbury, Cardiff University School of Social Sciences
    Dr Brychan Thomas, University of Glamorgan Business School

2 Working Lives was launched following the award of a successful Welsh Education Research Network (WERN) bursary in 2007. WERN was co-funded by ESRC and Welsh Assembly Government. We are grateful to WERN, ESRC and the Welsh Assembly for support, and to our three HEIs and colleagues: University of Glamorgan, University of Wales Newport, Cardiff University.

Part One

Transition, Identity and Routinized Work

Introduction

Jane Salisbury

Important core themes which permeate across the volume are foreshadowed in Part 1 which also supplies illuminating research evidence on hitherto neglected areas – the college and institutes sector, the post-compulsory 'Cinderella' sector of further education (FE) in the UK.

The contributors in Part 1 use qualitative data to explore empirically the ways in which institutional and sectoral structures and policies have the power to shape the day-to-day work and emotional lives of lecturers in FE and higher education (HE). These comprise a set of narratives on the themes of transition and becoming, of identity and change. Collectively, however, the chapters show lecturers as 'agents' whose actions and resilience can and do mediate the impact of structural forces.

The lecturers analysed in **Carol O' Byrne's** research on an *Irish institute of technology*, for example, were all operating in the same institutional context, yet they did not all pursue or prioritize the same projects. Indeed, structural changes led to new or questioned identities and roles, as well as revised work. For some, it created opportunities, others were not so readily reconciled to the change. *Performativity* is a key theme in the next group of chapters, many of which report on how, in an era of managerialism, front-line staff, as lecturers and tutors, have to 'perform' at the 'customer and client interface', where the student is a 'sacred' commodity. This introduces a *body of work from researchers, teachers and lecturers in Wales*. FE has become pivotal to educational policy in England and Wales, with the post-compulsory sector (PCET) being central to strategies that strive to raise educational standards and also to widen participation and inclusion in FE/HE. This sector has long been celebrated for its rich diversity – not only in its students, but also in the teachers, trainers and tutors – working within it, many of whom have come to teaching through non-traditional routes. Four chapters touch on the policy thrusts to increase and widen the participation of 'hard to reach', often recalcitrant learners.

Martin Jephcote sets the scene with the complexities of *being and becoming a teacher in further education today*. He discusses the professional formation and occupational socialization of FE practitioners in Chapter 2, showing not only how the policy context affects lecturers' work, but also that this too can be a site of struggle.

Philippa Dixey and Lyn Harbottle draw reflexively on journal entries written as teacher participants in a two-year study *exploring learning and working in the FE sector*. Their account is revealing of the impact of the policy imperatives each was required to jump to in order to meet punitive targets for recruitment, retention and student results set by their respective FE institutions. Frustration, alienation and emotion comes through powerfully in their frank descriptions of their work as FE teachers.

This is followed by a second directly voiced study, by **Judith Larsen**, a former head of access studies in a college serving a multicultural locality. In a reflective first-person account from South Wales, she illuminates not only the policy initiatives of the *Access Movement*, but the development work of those teachers who championed it. Larsen shows how a teacher's own career became correlated with such projects, and so too, with their transitions, transformations, changes of focus and directions. What endures, she knows, are the achievements of students.

Jane Salisbury discusses how the *emotional labour of FE teachers* can become routinized, and their emotional dissonance becomes a salient norm as they support some of the most challenging and needy learners. Ethnographic fieldnotes and teachers' journal and interview extracts help render visible this emotion work coupled with a strong ethic of care. The potential consequences of synthetic compassion and feigning and faking feelings, it is argued, can lead to what has been described as 'pernicious psychological consequences' (Ashforth and Humphrey 1993).

Finally, **Trevor Austin's** study of in-service trainee lecturers in an English university, *becoming a teacher in HE*, shows how professionals from other sectors choose to engage with particular curricular elements of their pedagogical training. Later, they may interpret new situations through the lens of a previous background, as they transition to the new status.

1

Structure and Agency in an Irish Institute of Technology

Carol O'Byrne

Introduction

This chapter examines how academics are shaped by, and shape, their working context. Research on academic working lives and identities in the UK (including Archer 2008; Clegg 2008; Becher and Trowler 2001; Harris 2005; Henkel, 2000) and elsewhere (including Churchman 2006; Enders 2001; Tight 2000; Walker 1998, 2001a) suggests that academics' experiences and professional identities are significantly influenced by the context in which they operate. National and institutional policies and structures shape what individual academics can do, as well as what they can be or become as professionals (Walker and Nixon 2004; Walker 2001a). This study explores how both macro- (i.e. national) and meso- (i.e. institutional) level structures, policies and pressures influenced the experiences and professional identities of academics in an Irish Institute of Technology (IoT).

Background and context of the study

Ireland has a binary higher education (HE) system, consisting of seven universities and 13 IoTs. The latter started life in the 1960s as regional technical colleges (RTCs), which were established to provide sub-degree level applied vocational education in science, engineering and business, operating under legislation enacted in 1930 to regulate the provision of second-level vocational training and controlled by the Department of Education. The RTCs initially offered two-year National Certificate programmes leading to third-level awards. These awards were made by the National Council for Educational Awards (NCEA), which was set up in 1972 to oversee the non-university third-level institutions.

Over time, and in response to stakeholder demands, the RTCs began to operate outside this limited remit, providing degree and postgraduate qualifications in a wide range of disciplines, including humanities and social sciences, and engaging in research and consultancy work as well as in teaching and teaching-related activities.

Legislation enacted specifically for the RTCs in 1992 ultimately legitimized some of these 'new' activities, including research. The colleges' expanded role in the HE system was acknowledged by their re-designation as IoTs in the late 1990s. Then, following the 1999 Qualifications Act, a process was established under which the Higher Education and Training Awards Council (HETAC) – the successor to the NCEA – could delegate awarding authority to individual institutes. The 2006 IoTs Act finally removed the institutes from the direct control of the Department of Education and Science (DES) and placed them alongside the universities under the authority of the Higher Education Authority (HEA).

The 2006 changes, although broadly welcomed by the academics of the IoTs, conferred no meaningful increase in operational freedom on the institutions. The majority were delegated awarding authority, but the Awards Council HETAC retained the power to withdraw this authority at any time. Institutional budgets still have to be approved by the HEA and, unlike the universities, institutes receive no baseline funding for research. In addition, all academic appointments and promotions continue to require sanction from the DES, and academic contracts continue to be negotiated at national level by the DES, sectoral management and the Teachers Union of Ireland (TUI), a union that represents both IoT lecturers and secondary-level teachers. Despite insisting that HE institutions play a part in the development of a national research infrastructure and a 'smart' economy (e.g. Department of Enterprise, Trade and Employment 2009), the government continues to limit support for activities other than teaching in the IoTs, and stark warnings about the dangers of 'mission drift' abound in official reports on Irish Higher Education (e.g. OECD 2004, Higher Education Strategy Group 2010).

The research study

Sixteen academics from four different discipline areas (business, engineering, humanities and science) in one IoT participated in the research. It was conducted using a life history approach (Goodson and Sikes 2001). Eleven of the participants were male and five were female. The longest-serving academic in the group had taken up the lecturing role in 1978, having had significant experience in industry before moving into academia. The newest recruit was fresh from completing a primary degree in 1999.

The study sample included academics who had joined the institution prior to the passing of the 1992 RTC Act (referred to here as *pre*-1992 participants) and academics who had been appointed in the post-1992 period (described as *post*-1992 participants; note that these are different from UK definitions). This allowed for a deeper investigation into any of the differences between these two 'generations'. The Tables 1.1 and 1.2 provide a profile overview of the project participants whose experiences, lives and stances form the basis of this chapter.

Individual professional life stories gathered through audio-recorded biographical interviews were set against a contextual backdrop constructed from interview data with institutional managers and an analysis of policy documents. This empirical material was ultimately interpreted using the conceptual tools provided by Archer's

Table 1.1   A summary profile of the pre-1992 study participants

Pseudonym	Gender	School	Recruited in	Early or late pre-1992 group
Kieran	Male	Engineering	1978	Early
Mark	Male	Science	1979	Early
Owen	Male	Business	1979	Early
Simon	Male	Humanities	1981	Early
Betty	Female	Business	1982	Late
Joseph	Male	Engineering	1983	Late
Emma	Female	Science	1985	Late
Laura	Female	Humanities	1985	Late

Table 1.2   A summary profile of the post-1992 study participants

Pseudonym	Gender	School	Recruited in
Francesca	Female	Humanities	1992
Ben	Male	Science	1993
Tom	Male	Engineering	1994
Seán	Male	Science	1996
James	Male	Engineering	1999
Alexandra	Female	Business	2000
Ronan	Male	Business	1998 part-time 2000 full-time
Timothy	Male	Humanities	1999 part-time 2002 full-time

(1995, 2000) work on the interplay of structure and agency as well as her work on the reflexive formation of personal and social identities (2000, 2003, 2007).

Learning from lives

Overall, the research suggested that significant changes had occurred between 1970 and the early 2000s, both in terms of what academics in the IoTs did and in terms of their sense of what it meant to be an academic. The pre-1992 participants, who had developed as lecturers in the RTC environment, were characterized by predominantly teaching-focused professional identities, by 'concerns' (Archer 2000: 313) with student and staff well-being, with connectivity between the academy, the 'real world' of industry, and with impact at institutional level. The post-1992 participants, by contrast, seemed to have developed more complex and multi-layered professional identities. These were built around a combination of roles in teaching, research and administration, and dominated by concerns that were largely individual, rather than institutionally-focused.

Structures and the power to shape: How participants and their projects were affected by their operating context

Archer's social realist conceptualization of the relationship between 'structure' and 'agency' suggests that the structures in which individuals operate possess the potential to either constrain or enable the different 'projects' (2007: 7) that they choose to pursue as they go about forming personal and social (including professional) identities. The research indicated that the 16 academics did indeed find themselves constrained and/or enabled in various ways by structures and policies, as they attempted to pursue the various 'projects' – teaching, research and administration, liaison with industry, external consultancy, pastoral care and others – which are generally pursued by those seeking to establish professional identities as academics (Kyvik 2000). All of the projects that participants either had to, or chose to, engage with were affected by constraints and enablements; but what follows considers the two main 'projects' pursued by the study participants, namely teaching and research.

The 'project' of teaching

The project of teaching has traditionally been broadly enabled: the RTCs were originally established as teaching institutions and the official remit of the IoTs still retains a strong teaching focus. While teaching in general is enabled by policy, individuals' efforts to play the teaching role in particular ways can and do activate constraints. However, most participants thought that third-level teaching – which they defined as teaching in post-compulsory education as opposed to teaching in the compulsory second-level sector – should involve passing on knowledge of and passion for a discipline to a coming generation of academics or professionals. Lecturers from business, science and engineering were able to pursue this project without significant obstruction. Humanities colleagues, however, faced challenges in this area.

The official definition of the IoTs' mission clearly limited them to providing applied vocational education; IoTs were generally not sanctioned to offer courses in the liberal arts. Students who enrolled on applied programmes could choose to take some humanities subjects, but they do not apply to IoTs to specialize in these areas. As a result, the humanities lecturers found themselves constrained, rarely getting to teach their specialism to student specialists or to be the kinds of teachers they wanted to be. A historian who was originally asked to teach communications because she had English in her degree commented:

> Up until about seven or eight years ago, I didn't teach history. There are very few opportunities in this place to teach history ... the tourism skills programme has developed a degree that requires people to be familiar with Irish history for example. It's hilarious actually, Irish history from earliest times to the present in forty lectures ... the ultimate overview with all the difficult bits cut out.
>
> Laura, humanities, pre-1992

Another humanities academic, in the modern languages area, highlighted the extent to which rare opportunities to teach in specialized fields were coveted:

> I'm actually teaching literature in fourth year now. I almost had to claw back that hour ... and I'm aware that there are people hovering over my shoulder wanting that hour.
> Francesca, humanities, post-1992

Lecturers from the other disciplines did encounter some obstacles to the development of 'specialist' teaching identities too. The Regional Technical Colleges were originally established to provide sub-degree qualifications. There was an assumption held by those in government, in the Department of Education, in the universities and even by some managers in the RTCs themselves, that sub-degree teaching did not require significantly more specialism in the subject area than second-level teaching. This meant that RTC lecturers were essentially obliged to be generalists.

> I think that in the institutes, and it's one of the big things that marks us out from the universities, you have to be a generalist ... teach a little bit of everything. And that taxes you in that ... you've got to spend a lot of time reading textbooks and recapturing knowledge or gaining new knowledge that you never had in order to be able to go in there and do the job ... If you teach in a university, you teach in your area of speciality ... [y]ou're rarely asked to teach something that is slightly out of your area of expertise.
> Tom, engineering, post-1992

Both pre-1992 and post-1992 participants vividly recalled having to teach in a variety of areas, including some in which they felt they had very limited expertise, at the beginning of their careers. One business lecturer still remembered being shocked:

> [when I saw the timetable] ... what did it include, but five hours of [teaching] marketing, to languages and marketing students. I was hired to teach accounting ... I had done only one year of marketing, in college in year 2, but that was in 1972 and this was 1982!
> Betty, business, pre-1992

Despite 'meso'-level efforts to ensure that lecturers taught in their specialist areas, individuals' capacity to develop specialist teaching identities were also constrained by contracts that required them to teach up to 18 hours per week. In many disciplines, there were simply not sufficient teaching hours available in particular specialist areas to allow people to divest themselves of teaching commitments that required a more generalist perspective.

While teaching is still seen as the primary function of the institutes, what is involved in the teaching dimension of the role has changed over time, and the participants' stories suggested that many of the changes acted as constraints rather than enablements. The pre-1992 participants in particular hankered after the days when groups were smaller and students more focused.

Policies introduced since 1970, viewed as a whole, have transformed Irish HE from an elite to a mass system (OECD 2004). These policies have brought a higher percentage of school leavers, and larger numbers of mature and other 'non-traditional' students, into the system, and this has impacted on the teaching role. For some participants, this translated into an increase in class sizes, obliging lecturers to take a more formal approach in the classroom, something not welcomed by those who felt that 'good teaching' involved getting to know individual students and being able to pay attention to their progress. Classes also became more heterogeneous, and all participants found themselves having to deal with a wider range of ability and interest than before. While this new diversity was welcomed, some lecturers did comment on the challenges of dealing with groups that belied their assumptions about the characteristics (including basic manners and an interest in learning) of those who choose to engage in HE: 'I think a lot of the students we're getting in the last few years don't have basic social skills and at a time when we're trying to develop the holistic student, that's making our lives harder' (Betty, business, pre-1992).

The introduction of modularization and semesterization – both outcomes of national policies – also shaped teaching. The restructuring of programmes and individual subjects was not greeted with enthusiasm by either 'generation' of participants. Modularization was viewed as a constraint by individuals who saw learning as an incremental process. Lecturers in disciplines where the incremental development of practical skills was seen as central to the learning experience were concerned that the 'stop-start' nature of the new system would prevent them from bringing their students to the level of competence attainable under the old system:

> The current wisdom in my own field would be against it. The pedagogues in my area would argue for a kind of gradual development model, which the modular system doesn't really suit too well.
>
> Simon, humanities, pre-1992

> I would be on the record as arguing quite vehemently against modularization . . . we still try to provide a lot of skills and skill takes time, practice and time. You can't just go home and read about a skill in that way.
>
> Kieran, engineering, pre-1992

Others were fearful that dividing up the material to be covered in discrete 'modules' that might appear, at first glance, to be unrelated, would make it difficult to integrate the learning into the coherent overall knowledge package that they felt should characterize graduates.

The 'project' of research

Unlike teaching, the project of research was clearly constrained in the early years of the RTCs' existence. These colleges were established primarily to train technicians, thus activities such as research, which seemed to distract lecturers from that core mission, were actively discouraged. Over time, the notion that the Regional Technical Colleges might develop a research function gradually came to be accepted. In the late 1980s and early 1990s, national-level funding schemes to support research in science and technology were opened up to the RTC staff. At institutional level, structures started to be put into place to support those engaging in research in these areas. The 1992 RCT Act gave the colleges the right (though not the obligation) to engage in applied research, and subsequent developments, including the introduction of the Technological Sector Research (TSR) Scheme in the mid-1990s, provided an enablement to institutions and to individuals who were interested in research and operating in suitably 'applied' discipline areas.

Research in the Institutes of Technology currently, is at least theoretically, enabled by macro-level policies and structures (Higher Education Strategy Group 2010). Indeed, the institution where the study was conducted clearly wanted lecturers to engage in research and appeared willing to support this engagement, yet many participants felt that the support available was, in real terms, simply not sufficient to allow them to pursue research properly. Ten participants were actively involved in research at some level.

The major hurdle facing those wishing to engage in research was the lack of time. When this study was undertaken, lecturers were contractually required to spend at least 16 hours per week on teaching-related activities. Thus, very limited time was available for the pursuit of research, with no formal time allocations existing for this. The 10 'research-active' academics (all eight post-1992 participants as well as the two pre-1992 humanities lecturers from the 'RTC' era) had thus developed somewhat disaggregated and time-related professional identity sets: they saw themselves as *lecturers* during the day or during term, and as *researchers* in the evenings, at weekends or in holiday time. They felt that they were operating on the 'Cinderella principle' (Alexandra, business) whereby they only got to pursue the projects they wanted to, namely research, when their other 'housework', chiefly teaching, had been completed.

The 10 informants who were involved in research all stressed how difficult it was to find the necessary time for this aspect of the role. Most acknowledged that managers were often quite creative in their interpretation of rules, in order to create time for lecturers to research, and most appreciated the efforts made to support them as researchers. But these efforts seemed to fall short of what was needed. 'Research days' (Francesca, humanities), free of scheduled classes, were of little benefit when the full complement of teaching hours still had to be crammed into the remaining four days of the week. Granting time allocations for postgraduate supervision, and extra weighting for hours taught on postgraduate courses, could free up some time for individuals to pursue their own research. However, as one participant pointed out, the time allocated for these activities was actually needed for the *supervision* activities themselves, and thus, in most cases, lecturers could not devote it to their own work.

> When you get a masters student and you're supervising that person, you get two hours allocation on your timetable . . . or forty-eight hours during the year . . . You spend far more [time] than that . . . supervising – and you probably spent far more than that writing the proposal in the first place to get the student!
>
> Seán, science, post-1992

Lack of an appropriate reward structure for those involved in research was also mentioned as demotivating. Researchers were given no credit for their extra efforts, and while their research records were of some use in competition for limited promotional opportunities (usually to management posts), generally their own career progression involved climbing the same incremental pay scales as their non-researcher colleagues. The research-active participants tried not to allow this to dissuade them from engaging in research, but many (chiefly among the post-1992 participants) clearly felt that they were making sacrifices not expected of non-researchers. Though they felt that they were contributing to something the institution deemed important, some wondered about and questioned the value of these sacrifices:

> I feel penalized as a researcher. There are lots of people going home after a good week's work teaching, but if you are a researcher you have to turn around after your week's teaching and start on your parallel work.
>
> Francesca, humanities, post-1992

Agency in action: How participants react to the constraints and enablements activated by their professional projects

All 16 lecturers involved in the study operated within the same macro- and meso-level contexts, but their individual stories suggested that the policies and structures in which they operated did not impinge on everyone in the same manner, or indeed to the same extent. How then can these different experiences of a common context be explained? Archer's (2003) analysis is helpful here and stresses that, while social forms have the power to constrain or enable, this power remains unexercised until it is activated by agents' projects. Although the research participants all operated within the same national context, they did not necessarily all pursue or prioritize the same projects, nor did they pursue the projects they were all obliged to pursue in the same manner. Individual participants chose to emphasize particular dimensions of their role and to downplay or de-emphasize others, in order to pursue those projects that they considered personally to be important. Conversely, they avoided those that would not contribute to the development of what they saw as desirable professional identities. The potential to constrain or enable, inherent in particular policies and structures, was therefore activated by some individuals but not by others.

Archer (2003) asserts that reflexive engagement with the various constraints and enablements that an individual encounters leads them over time to adopt a particular stance towards these, which 'represents an overall pattern of response to the totality of structural powers' (2003: 342–343). Thus, some individuals adopt an evasive stance, while others react in a broadly strategic manner, and still others take what could be described as a subversive stance. All three stances were represented in the study, with particular stances predominating among certain subgroups of participants. In general, they seemed to reflect the institutional and national contexts experienced by these participants at the beginning of their academic careers.

An *evasive stance* was strongly in evidence among the four earlier recruits in the pre-1992 group, particularly in relation to perceived constraints. These individuals from the 'RTC' era tended to engage largely in activities that did not activate significant constraints, pursuing relatively humble projects that were congruent with the mission of the sector and institution, and with the official definition of the 'lecturing' role. They also appeared to deliberately avoid activities perceived as constraining. One participant provided an example which highlighted how the evasion of constraints could be a deliberate strategy rather than a coincidence – by ceasing to work on a PhD begun before entering lecturing. The rationale was that research was 'discouraged' in the sector in the 1970s. It attested to a conscious choice to avoid courses of action that seemed likely to lead to conflicts:

> There was no push for research in those days. In fact in some ways it was frowned on, because you were taking up resources, you were taking up time, you weren't focusing on your job, so it was not encouraged. For the first few years that I was here, there was a definite non-encouragement of research. So it lapsed, and I haven't done anything about it since.
>
> Owen, business, pre-1992

By contrast, the four later recruits in the pre-1992 group adopted a more *subversive stance* towards constraints. Their projects often activated constraints, and they reacted by ignoring or actively resisting these, and seeking out ways to pursue their projects despite the obstacles thrown in their paths (explored also by Waring, this volume). One engineer (Joseph), chose to ignore the ban on external work in his initial contract, continuing to work part-time in his profession while lecturing. Similar high levels of resilience and creativity in the face of obstacles, and an unwillingness to give up on what they considered important, were also seen in the views of other members of this generation.

> This might sound rather rebellious but I wouldn't have a great track record for doing what I'm told. I've never broken a rule ... but I wouldn't be overly compliant. If somebody tells me I can't do something I find a way around it. I think that sometimes we hear far too much that we can't do this because of that ... I'm not very familiar with the words 'you can't' or 'no'.
>
> Laura, humanities, pre-1992

Thus while those in the earlier cohort of pre-1992 lecturers tended to accept the policies and structures that shaped their working context, the later recruits in that 'pre-1992' group were far more likely to speak their minds and to be critical of these structures, as well as to work, either individually or with others, to challenge these constraints. All four of the later pre-1992 academics had served on an academic council, three held course management roles and one was also a union official for a time.

Among the post-1992 academics, appointed after the 1992 RCT legislation, a *strategic stance* towards constraints predominated. Like the later pre-1992 recruits, they did not avoid activating constraints, but unlike their longer-serving colleagues, when faced with obstacles, they sought to circumvent them rather than plough through them, and to progress rather than protest. In the face of the constraints on research, they took quite a strategic approach. Accepting that resources for research were limited in the IoTs, Ben and Francesca, among others, entered into collaborative projects with university colleagues to increase their chances of securing funding. Realizing however that their jobs were likely to continue to be defined in terms of teaching hours, they explored and exploited mechanisms for getting out of the classroom. Such tactics ranged from using research funding to buy out cover for their teaching, to taking on activities with 'good' hours allocations such as postgraduate supervision, in order to buy time for their own research.

In relation to enablements, the response of the pre-1992 participants was some-what more nuanced than their response to constraints. They were selective in terms of which enablements they chose to access, focusing on those that allowed them to develop those dimensions of the lecturing role that they considered important. As committed teachers who were determined to prepare their students thoroughly for the workplace and to provide them with appropriate academic and personal support, they were quick to avail themselves of chances to develop the necessary expertise and experience to allow them to pursue these projects.

Other enablements tended to be met with a slightly different reaction however. What was striking was that these lecturers had largely taken an *evasive stance* in relation to efforts to enable research. Only the humanities lecturers actually became research-active: Simon completed a PhD and published a book based on his research, as well as presenting widely at both education conferences and conferences in his own field. Laura brought in grants for historical research, something not normally funded in the IoT sector. The remaining pre-1992 participants simply decided to ignore the encouragement (coming from both macro and meso levels) to pursue a research agenda. Though national policies and structures provided some level of facilitation for those who chose to pursue research projects, these were enablements that all but two of the pre-1992 participants were quite happy to evade.

By contrast, the post-1992 participants were more likely to be strategic in their approach to enablements, taking advantage for example of the opportunities to do research. In relation to teaching, they were more likely to seek out and take advantage of opportunities to expand their teaching portfolios than pre-1992 colleagues, seizing any chance to teach in their specialist areas or on advanced programmes. Several were instrumental in creating more opportunities, took advantage of the increasing acceptance that IoTs should be allowed to expand their range of provision beyond sub-degree technician training, and proposed and developed degree and postgraduate programmes in their own particular fields of expertise.

> At one stage I went to our head of department, suggesting that we needed information systems courses within the department. This was probably after I'd done my MBA . . . I thought that we needed taught masters programmes and I would probably have suggested information systems given the areas I had studied up to then.
>
> Seán, science, post-1992

The post-1992 participants were also more likely than their pre-1992 counterparts to be involved in more loosely-structured activities, such as postgraduate supervision, something that had come to count as 'teaching', but which did not involve the kind of work traditionally associated with weekly undergraduate lecturing. The members of this generation took advantage of potential enablements to carve out a teaching role for themselves that was both interesting and more varied. Such initiatives also allowed them to establish at least some connection, namely between a project they were contracted to pursue – teaching – and a project they wished to pursue, namely research.

Concluding remarks

Whilst the study demonstrates clearly that structures and policies do have the power to constrain the activities of individual academics, the empirical data also show that agents and their actions can and do mediate the impact of structural forces. In a positive way, this gives those thousands of us employed as academics in the post-compulsory sector of education a sense that we retain at least a degree of control over our professional destinies. In a context increasingly characterized by a range of challenges, perhaps there are grounds here for some professional optimism too!

Acknowledgements

I acknowledge the valuable assistance of the 16 academics and the institutional managers who shared their perspectives. This research was undertaken for a professional doctorate at the University of Sheffield, and benefited from the generous support of staff from the Sheffield EdD (Dublin) team. Particular thanks also to Professor Melanie Walker. This paper was first presented alongside the WL team at SRHE 2010 in Newport.

2

'Getting on with the Job' and Occupational Socialization in Further Education

Martin Jephcote

Introduction

This chapter considers the occupational socialization of teachers employed in colleges of further education (FE), which in the UK, cater typically for students aged over 16. Since 2005, post-compulsory education and training institutions also have a remit for 14–19-year-olds on vocational pathways (Lumby and Foskett 2005). This chapter brings together two analytic themes: that of being a teacher in changing times, and informing accounts of FE teachers' professional identities (Jephcote and Salisbury 2008, 2009). Underpinning these two themes or perspectives is the importance of the 'duality of context', that is, that the contextual history of the period in which current teachers' identities have been shaped needs to be understood along with a knowledge of the interplay that exists here.

FE in the UK has been in a constant state of change over the last three decades and these changes impact on the lives of those who teach and work in this sector. To be a teacher in FE, therefore, takes on different guises at different times, depending on what is expected, and many of the changes over the last 40 years have been imposed. They are illustrative of what Stronach and Morris (1994, see Yeomans 2002), have termed 'policy hysteria', or 'knee-jerk' reactions to real and pressing problems, some of which are long term, and over time, appear to be intractable. Professional identities are not, however, formed out of single education policies and government imperatives, but are shaped by the cumulative effects of what Ball (2005: 5) refers to as 'policy ensembles'. Uppermost has been the need to align the education system to the needs of employers and the economy, in effect to solve the problem of unemployment, especially youth unemployment, and to ensure a constant training and re-training of the adult workforce.

More broadly, this sector of education has been regarded as both the 'cause and cure' of a spectrum of social issues, including anti-social behaviour and crime (Social Exclusion Unit 1999). Over this period, a key government policy goal has been to increase the numbers of young people entering FE. Yet participation and enrolment at a college of FE may not be congruent with actual learning, and the securing of qualifications or credentials (Bloomer and Hodkinson 2000). Nevertheless, decade by decade, numbers in post-16 education have risen, from 10.4 per cent in 1949/50, to 19.2 per cent in 1959/60; from 34.3 per cent in 1969/70 to 55.2 per cent in 1989/90 and from 71.8 per cent in 1999/2000, to 81.5 per cent in 2008/9 (DBIS 2012). However, getting this age group to remain and stay engaged with learning remains more problematic.

Recent research (Jephcote and Salisbury 2008, 2009; Salisbury this volume) suggests that with this constant state of change, FE teachers do not ignore the different imperatives, but accommodate them within an 'ethic of care'. So, although they acknowledge the importance of their contribution to economic policies which demand 'flexible workers', for example, they continue to give importance to their role and contribution in the development of 'human flourishing' (Carr 2000). Some of the 'contradiction' in this reflects the complexity of being an FE teacher today. First and foremost, they get on with the job, which is prioritizing and putting learner needs and interests first. For O'Connor (2008: 117), such caring is:

> primarily defined as those emotions, actions and reflections that result from a teacher's desire to motivate, help or inspire their students. Whilst caring can be connected to teachers' pedagogical or classroom management strategies, it also exists and is demonstrated within the broader social context of teacher-student interactions in and out of the classroom situation.

So, looked at in the short term, as FE teachers struggle to cope with each new initiative and policy shift, their roles and identities can appear to become fragmented, and many teachers experience work intensification and stress (see Salisbury; Dixey and Harbottle this volume). However, over time, there is a more enduring character to being an FE teacher, which is about developing *resilience* to some of these external pressures (Colley *et al.* 2007).

Attending to the needs and interests of students extends further the remit of the teacher and the complexities of the job. 'Extended professionality' is the term coined by Hoyle and John (1995) which captures appropriately this particular stance of 'going the extra mile'. Additionally, students bring their own dispositions to learning, their own knowledge, beliefs and capabilities, and the impacts of their own social backgrounds which, in different ways, may facilitate or impede learning. Taken together, learning takes place as a 'negotiated regime' (Jephcote and Salisbury 2008), that is, in the ways in which learners' biographies and identities are coupled with teachers' biographies and identities. Attention, therefore, has to be given to these wider contexts as well as the *social processes* of learning in FE. Teachers cannot be 'trained' for these aspects of their routine work; they are *acquired* experientially, through processes of occupational socialization in the workplace.

The changing landscape of FE

As a sector that is inextricably connected with the provision of courses leading to qualifications, it is of little surprise that these have been at the foreground of a 'changing FE landscape'. Indeed, the period of the mid-1980s to the mid-1990s might be characterized as a decade in which the focus of reforming the FE sector was by using the lever of new programmes and new qualifications to drive change. Sometimes these initiatives had different and competing aims (Higham and Yeomans 2007). For example, from 1983, the Technical Vocational Education Initiative (TVEI) and the Certificate in Pre-Vocational Education (CPVE) of 1986 were aimed at 'vocationalizing' both the school and college curriculum across the 14–18 age group. This was a response to claims by politicians that schools and colleges had failed to adequately prepare young people for the 'world of work' and in consequence, the UK economy was lagging behind those of its international competitors (Hodgson and Spours 1999). Subsequently, the debate switched to raising the status of vocational courses and qualifications, marked by the introduction of General National Vocational Qualifications (GNVQs) and Advanced GNVQs in 1992, of which the former were then phased out by 2007, and the latter replaced by Applied (work-related) Advanced ('A') level qualifications (on the 'AS-A2' model) from September 2005.

If the remodelling of qualification structures has been in the foreground, then in the background has been increasing politicization of education in general. In this respect, the period that also saw the rise and fall of the TVEI and the rise and fall of GNVQs is a good case in point. This transformation can be understood in terms of contemporary power shifts, underlying political ideologies, and how these translate into curriculum design, development and assessment for colleges and teachers on the ground. Yeomans (2002) has usefully mapped the continuities and discontinuities between the TVEI and GNVQs, pointing to the discontinuities as 'manifestations of policy shifts' (p. 1). 'Continuities' included diagnosing the 'shortcomings' of vocational education in terms of an 'economic discourse', an emphasis on a more 'practical' curriculum, and a focus on 'progressive education' in the development of 'real-world' problem-solving skills, especially through enterprise education schemes. The roots of discontinuities, it is argued, lay in divisions between and within government departments, each with their own political ideologies, agendas and historiographies (Chitty 2009; Ball 2008a). The ascendancy of the TVEI was achieved because of initiatives from leading Conservative politicians who, by routing the initiative via the Department of Employment, circumvented so-called 'education professionals' at the Department of Education (and Science) (Higham and Yeomans 2007). A decade later, the GNVQ had more mixed political, industrial and professional origins, but unlike the TVEI which was curriculum-led and used existing assessment systems, the GNVQ was an assessment-led and competency-based scheme. Moreover, whereas the TVEI, at least in hindsight, involved teachers in its design and implementation, GNVQs were imposed. As we now know in the face of mounting public attention and research evidence, GNVQs were in fact short-lived, with high drop-out rates, uneven delivery patterns and narrow course content (for e.g. Wolf 2009).

Externally-driven agendas such as these can begin to erode teachers' autonomy and sense of professionalism, as they are expected to deliver more and more courses that meet external requirements. For politicians and employers, this might be no bad thing, as the retraining entailed will, in their terms, contribute to a more skilled workforce, appropriate to the needs of the economy and local labour markets. Paradoxically, in the

UK's positioning itself as a 'knowledge economy' in the 1990s, a higher value and emphasis was placed on 'learning how to learn'. In turn, the terms 'teacher' and 'lecturer' were considered by some as outdated, to be re-cast as 'facilitators and counsellors' (Parsons *et al.* 2001), leading some to call for colleges to be redefined as 'counselling and guidance colleges' (Guile and Lucas 1999).

It was also the *marketization* of FE in the mid-1990s that had most impact on the FE sector and on teachers' work and identities, where former 'professional-ethical regimes' were replaced with 'entrepreneurial-competitive' ones, according to Ball (2005: 6). The 'incorporation' of colleges of FE in 1993 began to make its mark, especially in terms of the advent of 'new managerialism', driven by a new funding regime. This led to a widening separation of the roles of teacher and manager (Jephcote and Salisbury 2007; Shain and Gleeson 1999) and to the associated pressures of 'efficiency' in the form of a move for increased 'recruitment, retention and (students') results' (see Dixey and Harbottle this volume). This inaugurated an era of increased external accountability, regulation and control, including the prescription of teacher 'standards'. For some, these have resulted in FE teachers' de-skilling and de-professionalization; for others it is more a matter of re-professionalization.

Such descriptive statements (and chronologies) do not portray the experiences of being a *beginning* FE teacher (McNally 2006) however, or reflect the variety of backgrounds and heterogeneous roles evident across a diverse FE sector (Salisbury 1994; Lucas 2007). As Hargreaves (2000) found in the case of standards for school teachers, these fail to recognize how, against a background of almost continual reform, teachers maintain a commitment to the needs and interests of their learners. In the next section, empirical material from a selection of FE teachers' journals is used to illustrate approaches to and perspectives on 'getting on with the job'.

Teacher identities: 'out with the old, in with the new'

Changes have taken place ... out with the old, in with the new! ... we are still very willing to work hard, and try new things if they are in the students' best interests. We share any problems we are having with students and rally together.

Tom, Journal 4

The ways in which the changing FE landscape impacts on teachers' work and identities is well illustrated in their own narrative accounts, as shared with the research team in various interviews and journal entries. Here such accounts are taken from qualitative data gathered during an Economic and Social research Council (ESRC)-funded research project which employed a variety of methods, including interviews, journals and ethnographic observation (Salisbury *et al.* 2009; Salisbury this volume). The project took place over a two-year period and followed the 'journeys' of 27 selected teachers and their students on full and part-time courses in three colleges of further education. The following extracts come from a journal entry elicited shortly after the start of a new academic year, and during the second year of their participation in the study. Individually and collectively, the accounts illustrate well the pressures that teachers face and how they manage to accommodate them (or not). At that time, Charlotte, a basic skills and numeracy teacher, revealed how different demands on her time were causing stress:

> Changes this term involve us going from 28 students to 43. A massive increase, with no extra teaching staff. This has led to some stress amongst us and some of us are involved in a performance-related pay incentive which involves a heck of a lot of paperwork, as if we haven't got enough already!
>
> Charlotte, Journal 4

Wynn, an engineering teacher and acting head of department, whose college had introduced 'the 50-minute hour,' (to increase the volume of sessions the staff would have to teach), reflected on funding and efficiency in his journal entry:

> The FE system has already gone through significant change, primarily when the funding arrangements were amended. FE fell into a whole new ball game. The approach from management has been to look closely at [the] productivity of staff, to increase hours of contact with learners, to cut back on resources and to generally crack the whip on academic staff in the interests of finances of the college. The funding system has led to uncertainty [and] cuts in the money available encourages management [to] look at how they can save money, resulting in a reduction in quality of delivery of learning for students.
>
> Wynn, Journal 4

For Deirdre, a teacher of health and social care, the impact of funding cuts and the laying off of part-time evening staff were having an impact, with the result that she and others would have to increase dramatically their teaching contact hours. At the same time, she continued to give pastoral care and attention to her students:

> I have spent approximately four hours on a bullying issue [gives examples]. That's an average of 3.5 hours per week on three students alone, done in my preparation and marking time ... The bottom line is WE CARE about the students – and will do anything we have to, to ensure their well-being.
>
> Deirdre, Journal 4

The need not just to recruit a viable cohort of students to a programme but also the pressure to retain those students on courses was evident in the descriptive account of Deirdre. She recounts how the induction of a late enrolee was done in her own non-contact time:

> [One] student's father ... was verbally offensive to me in the middle of reception. This student joined the course late, I saw her on an individual basis ... on two separate occasions to facilitate what she had missed in induction and also spent time with her undertaking initial assessment testing, a further two hours ... [student later withdrew]

Despite this, the retention rate for the group is high and feelings are positive:

> [O]verall a good start to the academic year ... Life in college with support from line managers is a life more enjoyable and one which leads to heightened motivation and dedication.
>
> Deirdre, Journal 4

In a journal entry about 10 weeks later in the spring term, Penny, a computing and business teacher was also acutely aware of the competing pressures on her time. She drew a clear and somewhat critical distinction between 'education that is results driven' and 'education that prepares students for later life and university'. As she went on to argue:

> There is a distinct focus on attainment and results, particularly in the FE sector ... We are encouraged to embrace new and valuable initiatives ... key skills, bilingualism, entrepreneurship, sustainability, cultural identity, Welsh Baccalaureate ... [But] results themselves do not necessarily equip students ... [and] ... a large proportion of educators go well beyond their contractual duties, not for results, or praise or money – but for the learner.
>
> Penny, Journal 6

'Non-contact time' and 'time' in general and how it was used – or 'gifted' to students, 'colonized' by middle managers – was a permeating theme across the interview transcripts and written journals. It appeared etched into the occupational norms and expectations of these FE teachers and was clearly an important element of their ongoing occupational socialization within the workplace/college setting.

Concluding remarks

The last 30 years have witnessed significant ongoing change in the UK FE sector. The journal extracts provided above illustrate some of the interplay between the context of these changes and the teachers' sense of identities and professional stance. The system, its imperatives, pressures, norms and values are part of an enculturation and wider occupational socialization process for those teachers who come into this challenged and challenging sector. The drive for efficiency of provision, value for money and greater accountability in FE, has resulted in work intensification for staff with consequential impacts upon the ways in which teaching and learning is transacted. And yet at the same time, FE teachers' journal accounts demonstrate an ongoing commitment to meeting the needs and interests of their students within the exercise of an 'ethic of care'. This is a significant part of 'getting on with the job', 'becoming and being a teacher' in the contemporary FE sector. The next chapter, by Philippa Dixey and Lynette Harbottle, illuminates both FE teachers' day-to-day experience as well as their co-participation in the Teaching and Learning Research Programme (TLRP) project.

Note

'Learning and Working in Further Education Colleges in Wales' is a project that began in 2005 funded by the ESRC and Welsh Assembly Government, as part of the extension of the TLRP to Wales. The overall aim of the project was to explore the relationships between students' learning journeys and teachers' working lives, set against changing institutional and external conditions, in three FE colleges in Wales.

3

Teacher Narratives of Performativity and Change

Philippa Dixey and Lynette Harbottle

Introduction

This chapter draws on material from learning journals that were kept by participants – ourselves, now as authors – during a two-year research project that focused on 'Learning and Working in Colleges of Further Education (FE) in Wales'. We were core teacher participants in the Economic and Social research Council/Teaching and Learning Research Programme (ESRC/TLRP) project (Jephcote *et al.* 2008), working in separate FE colleges some 40 miles apart in two contrasting localities of South Wales. Along with 27 other participating FE teachers, we were regularly observed in our routine teaching duties and interviewed. During the two-year life of the project, we also completed some seven journal entries in response to particular questions and writing frames posted out to us by the research team (see Salisbury this volume). In the sections that follow, we utilize and reflect upon some of these journal entries and use extracts from them to highlight typical experiences and pressures arising from a culture of accountability and performativity in FE today. We write from the lecturer's point of view having (between us) worked in the sector for some 36 years, to share with readers insights into 'working lives' on the front-line in FE.

Working in FE

Within the learning cultures of FE, lecturers' daily workloads must assume many differing juxtapositions to meet a variety of changing course and college aims. This is set against an agenda of financial constraint, large groups of students and increasing cohorts of learners with considerable pastoral needs, many an 'inheritance' from earlier school experiences and 'feeling a failure'. Coffield *et al.* (2005) describe the routinized work of FE teachers of analysing and classifying students' individual learning styles and their requirements, and approaching these within the confinements of substantial group sizes; their institutions then measure 'favourable' outcomes from a mixture of data on retention, assessment, accomplishment of goals and the criteria established within the external inspection frameworks.

In their daily work, lecturers continually strive to present and create a challenging but 'doable' learning experience for their students, tailored to meet differing learning styles and needs. They act altruistically in order to meet this goal, often working late and providing students with home telephone numbers to assist in contact out of normal college hours. Yet as FE teaching staff, we have both experienced the steady rise of 'managerialism' in our day-to-day work. As commentators such as Randle and Brady (1997) and Gleeson and Shain (1999) have discussed, this includes the

> re-organisation of the practices and work of lecturers following the application of managerial control techniques. This has intensified lecturers' work and reduced their autonomy and control over the teaching process. In addition, quality standards that were formerly based on 'processes' are now gauged on 'performance indicators or outcomes, based primarily around recruitment, retention rates and . . . results.
>
> Shain and Gleeson 1999: 452

Recruitment, retention and results – the three 'Rs'

Educational institutions must thus provide 'hard evidence' of student outcomes rather than recording teacher 'inputs'. Such an emphasis has shaped the inspection criteria used by Estyn (Wales' equivalent of Ofsted in England). These measure retention and attainment against targets, determining subsequent institutional funding policy; courses will not receive funding from the Welsh Assembly Government if graded below a quality threshold, that is, grade 4, which is deemed unacceptable. One of us commented on the temporal patterns of student drop out:

> This is the time of year, January–February, when students drop-out of your course; no work is being submitted . . . This leads to disciplinary panels [which] can take anything from 45 minutes to two hours . . . [Y]ou get concerned about your retention rate . . . students are leaving, targets for retention have been set . . . a stressful time. You know you're doing everything you can to support your students, but still they leave.
>
> Lynette, journal extract

Spours *et al.* (2007) have commented on the often inconsistent messages about student retention that lecturers receive: feelings of adversity if students leave, feelings of antagonism if they are retained but fail to achieve. On occasion, retaining students has had a deleterious effect on a particular learner and upon resources, as the individual may become tumultuous and difficult. We can both recall frustration at institutional preoccupation over student retention, coupled with the resulting need to offer significant support and promote student welfare, engaging resources and a great deal of a lecturer's time that is unacknowledged in annual analyses of workload.

Although students' attendance at college is not a legal requirement (unlike pupils aged 5–16 years), institutions are still expected to retain students and for these to attain their qualifications. If both retention and attainment targets (set annually) are not met, courses are 'reviewed' by college management, and if improvement is not evident, they are withdrawn. Such radical action is to prevent negative grading outcomes from an external Estyn inspection.

One journal entry reported how a recognition of the importance of recruitment and student diversity was crucial for managers to recognize:

> [R]etention and attainment can be very contentious and the quest for student attainment can be taken too far [. . .]. The work's validity can be questioned
>
> Philippa, journal extract

Teachers can feel pressurized into ensuring that learners reach pre-specified course attainment targets, and doing so may be detrimental to real learning. As experienced lecturers, we both recognize that if support is effective and students are responsive, there is a reasonable likelihood of the person remaining on the course and eventually succeeding. Since writing these journals and participating in the research project (2005–2007), there has been more emphasis placed on technology as a course delivery and support tool, including the uptake of suitable *Learn Direct* online modules, which benefit learners and college finances (WFEPC 2010; see also Rogers this volume on learner retention in online courses). Various 'life issues' often impact on mature 'returner' students, especially economic and domestic matters (JISC 2011a, also see Larsen this volume), in particular, those enrolled on Access to Higher Education courses in FE. In some cases, they are so desperate to get into HE that they cheat or copy assignments, creating sensitive problems for the tutor to deal with. Enrolments for Access to Higher Education courses present special difficulties, where learners have been out of education for a long time and there is considerable diversity within a group:

> [O]ne class may consist of . . . students who have been away from formal education for a long time . . . [s]ome may have formal qualifications, including 'A' Levels and in rare cases degrees or equivalent level professional qualifications. They are studying the Access course to show evidence of 'recent learning' or need certain subjects, including biology to enter nursing; others may not have achieved GCSEs but have life experience.
>
> Philippa, journal extract

Interview and selection procedures, better initial course information and numeracy/literacy testing can contribute to preventing these problems, but 'differentiation' in the classroom remains the challenge for the tutor.

Collaborative, joined-up working for a 'Learning Country' and tensions in the marketplace for students

The Welsh Assembly Government's document *The Learning Country: Vision into Action* (2006b) discussed raising educational standards in Wales and referred to a necessary upskilling of the nation, the role of lifelong learning and collaboration between schools, colleges and universities (see also Welsh Assembly Government 2001, 2006a). Inter-institutional collaboration was further reinforced in the 'Webb Review', published in 2008.

Our own FE colleges undertook such collaborations and compacts with local '11–18' (age range) comprehensive schools. This arrangement paved the way for the formal '14–19 Learner Pathways' policy currently established (Colleges Wales 2011; WFEPC 2010). Institutional Memoranda of Understanding involved the provision of 'school link' courses with FE for vocationally-orientated 14–16-year-olds. These students would be seeking for example to enter auto vehicle studies or hair and beauty programmes, or the college could supply Advanced Subsidiary (AS) and Advanced Level (A2) courses for subjects which local schools could not deliver themselves. The latter, whereby school students from sixth forms attended college campuses for lessons delivered after school, was hugely problematic for one of us. The general difficulty was a lack of communication and cooperation between the different providers, which led ultimately to serious problems with retention and attainment. One of us identified school-college link problems in a journal entry which described how:

> Some prospective students are misinformed about the courses on which they wish to enrol [so] I always try to advise and recruit with integrity . . . to provide a realistic picture of a course – yes warts and all . . . Some may then decide to try another course which may be more suitable.
>
> Philippa, journal extract

Time, assessment and evidence of teachers' work

Here we illustrate some of the issues involved in assessment work, evidence-building for student attainment and how this underpins lecturer performativity. The typical FE teacher's situation is complicated and a reduction in the number of teaching hours allocated to courses, consequent on fiscal considerations and course profit margins, magnifies this – and yet, institutions need to prepare students for forthcoming learning (Bransford and Schwartz 1999). Ecclestone (TLRP 2005: 11) confirms that lecturers are now receiving 'low levels of contact time', and a number of questions are raised from this, including the type of pedagogy engaged in, to teach underpinning knowledge to students:

> There is ever-increasing talk of 'evidencing', 'tracking and signing off targets', 'cross-referencing evidence', 'plugging the gaps in the criteria' and 'delivering achievement'. The terminology dominates teachers' ideas about teaching and learning, while many students expect to pass and to be coached to do so.
>
> TLRP 2005: 11

Consequently, students often achieve their qualification and complete their course of study but at a cost to the acquisition of pleasurable 'learning'. Teachers like us are now so concerned with 'evidencing' that employing differing pedagogical approaches is to a large extent second place – which we both feel has removed many of the elements of enjoyment for students. As lecturers, we 'lived' and also brokered these processes and mechanisms described in the report, and are pleased to recognize them reported in a major national research publication. However, as one of us comments,

> It isn't undertaking the formative assessment with the students [that creates the copious paperwork] but ensuring you have evidence to prove it ... I would like to undertake more practical work with my students ... learning activities that are effective and fun!
>
> Lynette, journal extract

Time to mark and 'internally verify' student work are important issues in the FE sector. Our experiences of marking work within the two-week internal verification (IV) cycle allocated, involving cross-sectional sampling for moderation and scrutiny, frequently took an inordinate period of time to be returned to the first marker. This resulted in lecturer frustration, generated by student dissatisfaction with the non-return or late return of work. Indeed, a JISC study (2011b) confirms that assessment is an area that students articulate great discontent over, compared to other factors; it is also very important to perceptions of learning success.

We both believe that the IV process often thwarts our effective use of assessment *for* learning. For learners, as JISC point out, it both moulds their comprehension of curricula as well as actuating their potential for progression: '... assessment and feedback form a significant part of practitioners' workloads and, with increased numbers, reduced budgets and higher learner expectations [this] continue[s] to be a matter of concern' (JISC 2010a: 7). Not every student appreciates the hours staff spend providing detailed written feedback and advice, and obviously the greater the motivational needs, the more guidance a student will require. Lecturers continually strive to enable students to succeed on their chosen courses. A journal entry captures the unrelenting cycle of formative assessment:

> [I am] marking work, marking resubmissions and work 'referred' and seeing students in tutorial, returning work, setting new hand-in date, and re-marking work ... Even on a second re-submission, work does not meet the required criteria – so oral questioning is undertaken ... and then we fill in a form – 'tutor witness testimony'.
>
> Lynette, journal extract

In the college setting, student retention targets inevitably shape assessment practices, as the TLRP report recognizes:

> ... concern about targets and the need to help learners achieve – often at almost any cost – are leading teachers and institutional managers to turn assessment methods into 'coaching' to raise grade achievement and keep students motivated. Everything is subordinated to the need to hit the target.
>
> TLRP 2005: 10

It is widely acknowledged (JISC 2010a; Ecclestone and Pryor 2003; Ecclestone 2002) that assessment of students' work is carried out under constraints of time and progressively challenging restrictions. Within the last 10 years however, the connection between 'learning, assessment and feedback' has been better understood (JISC 2010a: 8; see also Ecclefield and Garnett this volume). Advances in pedagogy and research on evidence-based practice also enable teachers to help students acquire the skills to monitor their own progress, to become involved in peer assessment and 'deep learning' experiences. Teachers are central to this endeavour, as JISC assert:

> Practitioners with a clear understanding of the principles underpinning good assessment and feedback practice are demonstrating the value of integrating a wide range of technologies into their practice, enabling learners to experience more varied and appropriate assessment and feedback strategies at all stages of their learning programmes.
>
> JISC 2010a: 9

Digitally-literate teachers working in well-resourced classrooms with contemporary technology alongside students – some of whom are more accomplished in technology use than staff – could help circumvent some of the issues around assessment (Banwell *et al.* 2004; BECTA 2006).

FE staff live out the tensions and pressures generated by policy and government imperatives, which are mediated by our respective institutions. We perform and comply with expectations to turn numerous student coursework drafts around, to be audited on the 'three Rs' and to apply 'digital' literacy in student learning. In doing so and jointly with our colleagues, we construct the learning sites that comprise the 'FE sector'.

Concluding remarks

This chapter afforded an opportunity for revisiting journal entries originally written in a research study. Neither of us underestimates the therapeutic value arising from discussing critical incidents and 'talking it through' (Finch 1984) in this way, and we find some considerable comfort too in knowing that recent research has rendered our work situations visible (Salisbury *et al.*, 2009; ESRC/TLRP 2008; Jephcote *et al.* 2008; James and Biesta 2007). Here however, we have 'edited ourselves', augmented the ideas, and by taking ownership contributed two authentic FE teacher voices to this ongoing work. We also participated in some of the Working Lives research sessions (2008/2009) and value the opportunity to be part of this wider network and publication.

Note

Colleges of FE in the UK are similar to institutes of technical and further education in Australia and, to a lesser extent, community colleges in North America.

4

An Insider Perspective on a College 'Widening Participation' Initiative

Judith Larsen

Introduction

This chapter documents not only the policy initiatives of the 'Access to Higher Education (HE) movement', but also the routinized working of some of those teachers who championed it. The chapter is my own reflective account as a head of access studies in a college serving a multicultural locality in South Wales. The establishment of the Access Programme, and the ways in which it was operationalized in association with 'compact' relations to local HE institutions, is described here. Incremental changes in the structure and composition of the programme, and its gradual change to vocational pre-eminence are also discussed. The chapter outlines the policy dynamics favouring widening participation at the time, but also those of a 'devolved Wales'. Gaps and caveats in implementation of such policies, it is argued, thwarted continuity and progression for students on the programmes. These became the typical day-to-day challenges that staff involved in Access work had to negotiate. The chapter draws on professional reflections from an FE course leader's experience of over 20 years; it also provides insights into the life of a teacher–manager, whose work was underpinned by a belief in the transformative capacity of the Access Movement, to positively change students' lives.

An 'Access Programme' and how I became involved

In the UK, an Access course is typically designed to prepare mature students with few or no entry qualifications for an HE course. Typically, it is skills-based, and such courses have been characterized from the outset by their focus on learners disadvantaged by previous educational experiences, as well as those traditionally under-represented in UK HE. At the same time as 'access' has involved enrolling older students – because of age discrimination, the bar of 'over 21' no longer applies – and a commitment to widening participation in HE, it has also meant targeting women and members of minority ethnic groups as well as those from working-class backgrounds (Dunn *et al.* 2007; Archer 2002).

My first introduction to Access in HE was during a wet November evening in Cardiff in 1989. The venue was County Hall and the Labour Party Woman's Education Group had invited a speaker to explain the concept of Access. At the time, I was about to be redeployed as a result of the falling rolls and the closure of a school where I had taught history and sociology for a number of years. I had high hopes of being selected to teach at the local further education (FE) college (Severnside) and was interested in all areas of post-16 and adult education. However, I could not have known then how big a part 'Access to HE' would play in my future working life. The speaker on that rainy night was somewhat partisan – she was a feminist and saw education as a way forward particularly for women – yet the message of the *transformative* capacity of Access, and its potential, captured my attention.

Access courses developed in the UK (and Wales) during the 1970s, as a result of policy drivers to widen participation in further and higher education (FE and HE) by the then Labour government that also, under the leadership of Jennie Lee, Minister for the Arts, pioneered the development of the 'university of the air'. The Open University went live in 1971 and like Access to HE programmes, it has been a beacon of hope, removing barriers to qualifications for many less traditional students (Open University 2012; Spours *et al.* 2007; Tunstall 1974). However, many of the original/initial courses were local, small-scale initiatives with partner higher education institution's (HEIs) until in 1989, a national framework was developed by the Committee of Vice Chancellors and Principals (CVCP) and the Council for National Academic Awards (CNAA). This led to the establishment of Authorised Validating Agencies that were designed to provide quality assurance and nationally-recognized 'kitemarking' systems for the courses. Access courses could thus in future attract funding via the UK funding councils for further education – in Wales the FEFCW, and in England the FEFCE. This support, and the 'kudos' of HE sector involvement, was integral to the success of the early years of the Access programme's development in the UK.

That first introduction to the notion of 'Access', amid the initial wave of publicity and rising visibility of the movement, was to shape my ideas about adult education for many years to come. In fact, totally unaware of it at the time, it was to form the basis of my career in the FE sector for the next 20 years.

From school teacher to college lecturer: Tales from an FE Access curriculum manager

By September 1989, I was transferring the skills I had learned as a secondary school teacher to the newly-formed tertiary college which I had joined as a lecturer. The original college had been established in 1989 to serve a large multicultural locality and had two main sites and a number of outreach centres. As with any new combination of staff and a brand new corporate identity to establish quickly, people were encouraged to put forward ideas to promote the college. In an early meeting with new colleagues I asked the question, 'Why haven't we got an Access course?' and promptly found myself with an hour's teaching remission to design and organize a course for the college. This was not a task for one person alone and I sought out interested colleagues fairly quickly to attend a few initial meetings – thus the 'Access team' was soon formed. It comprised a varied group of ex-secondary school teachers and Severnside technical college lecturers, some of whom had also been adult learners themselves. On reflection and with hindsight, the one thing that melded the group in particular was the idea of social justice and a motivation to build mechanisms that might help to transform the lives of others, especially adults who had missed out on a first chance at FE in the past. Together, we worked with a sense of common purpose, and the basic outline of the course was decided upon quickly. Three permeating themes, of race, equality and gender, would be addressed and delivered through four main subject areas – history, legal studies, sociology and English literature.

The formal letter of intention that preceded the finalizing of the programme outline was followed by an intense period of activity:

> … I confirm that Severnside intends to offer an 'Access to HE' course from 1991 (September) and intends to seek Consortium validation in the summer term 1991. The title will be 'Access Course in Humanities'.
> (Extract from letter dated 6 March 1991 from the Director of Studies to the Access Development Officer for the South East Wales Access Consortium)

Looking back, this was one of the best times in my working life. Severnside's Access course in Humanities was validated after a very searching set of discussions with an expert validation team. After the rewriting of certain key areas, we were ready to go live. Taking advice from the adviser appointed by South East Wales Access Consortium (SEWAC), we made sure that all applicants undertook a written task to establish their level of written English. There was also a face-to-face interview within the selection process. We wanted to make sure that the application process was fair, but also rigorous, and that the individual would have a good chance of succeeding in their hopes of gaining a university place. The one thing to avoid was raising and then dashing people's hopes and dreams of a different future.

By late August 1991 we had 20 'mature students' (over 21 years old) whose ages ranged from mid-twenties to mid-forties. In fact, that age profile mirrored closely the ages of the lecturers with whom they would be working very closely! This suggested a new era in teaching practice too.

The new Access course begins

In September 1991, Severnside Access course commenced. It had 19 students, 13 women and six men, all of whom were in receipt of a variable grant from the local educational authority (LEA) in South Glamorgan. This undoubtedly enabled their attendance and participation; it was the first and last time that financial help was available in this form. Regrettably, it was still not enough for one student, who dropped out quite quickly as the money allocated (approximately £4,000) was not adequate for his studies and maintaining his family. This was a sign of the financial difficulties that mature men in particular could have when studying full-time, and this drop-out pattern was to be replicated during the following years (McGivney 1999, 2004). Lack of finance was later one of the main reasons cited by students for not completing their programme of study (Martinez and Munday 1998). Of course, staff would always try to persuade an individual to consider becoming part-time, taking a slower route to HE, rather than dropping out altogether. Learning about all of this, including student finance, was an unexpected outcome of my becoming a core tutor on the Access course in Humanities at Severnside.

The Access course on the college's main campus was held in its own designated room. This was a former music room with odd brown material for sound insulation on the walls. This unique space was an important resource, in that it separated the Access students from the rest of the student body in the hope that this would let them develop a supportive peer group culture. As the personal tutor to the group, I was responsible for guiding students when they began applying for university – the point of the whole programme. This meant knowing a good deal about nearby and local universities as well as HEIs further afield. Some students were not geographically limited by family or other commitments, but many *did* want to attend the local university. Thus I too was on a steep learning curve. Fortunately, we had sent the outline of the Severnside Access course to several relevant departments at local universities and received supportive comments from academic and Admissions tutors there. The next challenge was getting the students onto the HE course of their choice.

In 1991/1992, the UCAS system allowed every student to identify six course choices, but on our course, not one student was offered a university place based on their written application alone! In fact, each was invited for formal interview by the HEI departments, and then, with relief, offers based on the satisfactory completion and passing of the Access course were subsequently received. Rejections also arrived however, and these did have an effect. Students often were not confident and were easily crushed by interactions with HE admissions tutors. At this time, and in my pastoral and guidance role, I initiated many discussions with HE admissions staff, making frequent telephone calls both before and after selection interviews, dealing with their queries and keeping people on board. In order to build up a database, I also started to compile a list, by university, of Higher National Diploma (HND) and degree courses that had accepted our completing students. This was augmented annually and lasted for 10 years until acceptance of Access qualifications by HEIs was universal; by then, the list comprised 14 pages with some 55 HEIs identified!

The destinations of the first cohort of Severnside Access students were: Cardiff University, to study Sociology and History; the University of Glamorgan, to study, variously art, history, English, sociology, and a combination of subjects; Swansea to study history, London to study sociology, and Middlesex to study law. In all, 16 students completed the very first course, though with only three (males) completing and receiving the Access certificate itself. One of these went on to gain his sociology degree, and later to gain a prestigious Economic and Social research Council (ESRC)-funded PhD studentship in a highly-rated Russell Group university. This former Access student's published scholarly work (Stroud 2012, 2001), some of which concerns itself with inequities and life chances, confirms a belief in the powerful affordances of the Access Programme. I am proud to have been acknowledged in this doctoral thesis (Stroud 2000). The tangible success with the Access to HE programme at Severnside also provided me with the confidence to explore the idea and practicalities of another emerging initiative coming to be known as 'credit-based learning'.

Upwards and upwards

In 1992 I was the project worker for the Welsh Joint Education Committee's (WJEC) new initiative *Modularisation: Towards a Flexible Further Education System in Wales* (WJEC 1992). The major tasks included modularization of the Access course and investigating the impact of modularization on existing college structures. As a by-product, the project included an examination of flexible learning techniques, which in turn became an element of distance learning in the Access course development. The units developed during the time at the WJEC became part of the CREDIS system (Reynolds 1994) and the number of subjects available for study at Severnside was extended to include urban geography, economics and psychology. By this point, the flexibility of the Access course was a critical factor: careful, sensitive timetabling was needed, to enable students to follow individual, tailored schemes, including the offer of a mixed day-and-evening programme. Thus one participant, now a qualified social worker with a successful career, but who then worked days and evenings in a greengrocer's shop, was able to take a 'mix and match' course that she passed in one academic year.

During 1993, I accepted a partial secondment from my college role to join the SEWAC team as Access Development Officer. The demand for Access was growing and the courses were now expected to be modular and credit-based; it led to an 'Access to life science' course at a local college, the first credit-based Access course in SEWAC. Validations and lots of staff training then became part of a typical work schedule. At the same time, I was developing a pre-Access course for Severnside college and this concept of a 'Return to Learn' course started in a community setting in 1994. Many such initiatives were developed in the margins of staff time and roles: earlier significant efforts on course modularization and accreditation were achieved with just a small amount of remission from teaching duties; at SEWAC, I was in reality doing two jobs, and decided to rebalance my working life and return to being college-based.

An indication of how quickly the Access movement had developed, and how far-seeing it was, is contained in the future plans which Sonia Reynolds, head of the Wales Access Unit, announced in an article: 'FE college developments: towards a modular curriculum from which full implementation of an All Wales FE Credit Framework [have] been initiated by FFORWM' (the body representing the FE sector in Wales) (Reynolds 1994).

Changes – discussed at meetings both locally and nationally – kept the work fresh and interesting, and the next five years could be measured by growth in the number of Access students at college, where different departments developed their own provision, using the model provided. Student issues were also surfacing: financial concerns, the cost of child care, the reality of the amount of work needed to complete an Access course, and the role of personal time management, all were raised. Staff responded by writing study skills workbooks and providing 'down to earth' accessible information at interview. Meanwhile, SEWAC had become an open college, and so the South East Wales Open College Network (SEWOCN) became the body awarding Access certificates, while the credit-based nature of the certificate helped many students with the flexibility of units of study. Students were also awarded the specific study units they had passed, which was a major advance on the old pass/fail FE/HE system of annual examinations. If anyone failed to gain a full Access certificate, they were then able to return to complete units and elements in order to achieve the full award at a later date, thus alleviating the problem of reinforcing failure, where hitherto, students who dropped out were left with nothing.

More and more change . . .

In my own career there were a number of developments which were set against the background, in 1993, of the 'long shadow of incorporation' of FE colleges (Jephcote and Salisbury 2007). The effects of this significant structural change were felt acutely by all staff, and the impetus for expansion and development resulted in a surge in the numbers of mature Access and also 'A level' students. As the curriculum manager for humanities and Access in the general education department, I welcomed an internal restructuring which resulted in a new line manager who was keen to encourage and support my ideas and work for Access. This productive relationship facilitated the development of Access to nursing and Access to social work courses as well as new community-based courses. The latter met the 'widening participation' policy agenda, such that locally-based provision placed the student at the centre of learning and avoided obstacles, such as a one-hour bus journey to get to the college campus. The nursing route included sociology, psychology and human biology, and attracted students who then went on to study these as degree subjects at university. The nursing pathway itself was developed as a result of an excellent relationship and help from a local HEI admissions tutor: this led to the provision of a 'February to February' course that met the demands of the annual March intake for nurses. Moreover, a compact agreement with this HEI meant that students without current qualifications, but who had applied for places in nursing, could study a 'bundle of appropriate units' and thus enter Nurse training directly. The report from SEWOCN in 2001 certainly agreed:

> the availability of [an] individual learning programme is a radical step forward and a good practice that could be shared with other providers.
>
> SEWOCN provider review manager

When the Access to nursing course came up for revalidation, it was in very good shape, with four full-time courses and a part-time evening course available. Students were accepted not only into local HEIs (Cardiff, Swansea and Glamorgan) but also into a variety of English universities. It was a demand-led programme, and had quickly established itself as part of the UK trend of the 'vocationalization' of Access.

My continued enthusiasm for championing the Access movement resulted in a new role as chair of the Access tutors' forum within SEWOCN, and duties as a moderator for other FE Access courses. I attended Access training events and firmly believed involvement outside the college would not only allow me to disseminate good practice, but also to gain new ideas for implementation at Severnside.

In 2005, the merger of the three regional Welsh open college networks (OCNs) created a new body called Open College Network Wales. I joined the Board to represent the FE sector. Video-conferencing, given Wales' geographical challenges and the distance between its 23 college campuses, was the norm, and a very interesting part of all meetings. For four years, I was the official chairperson of the Access to HE Committee, until Open College Network Wales metamorphosed into *Agored Cymru*. The change in name and structure of this awarding body reflected the pace of change within the FE sector in Wales, which was also part of the wider changing UK scene of merging organizations.

At this time, the financial imperatives within Severnside College were becoming greater, with minimum class sizes rigorously enforced and the costing and pricing of courses – plus their cancellation if minimum student numbers (initially, 12) were not met. Even this threshold began to slowly edge upwards, so classes were merged, students re-timetabled and the priority became 'that no financial "losses" should be incurred'. Scrutiny of 'recruitment' and 'retention' data also appeared to be more important than learning and student attainment. In quality review meetings, the feeling that we were 'crunching numbers' rather than discussing real people quickly grew. At one particular session, when asked how the retention on a particular course could be improved in the next year, I had to point out that as four students had become pregnant, unless we were going to insist on birth control there were limits on what could be done! Flexibility and the part-time day study facility ceased, and students could no longer change courses or units. It was the era of the accounting balance sheet (see Kelly and Boden this volume, for HE) and of the rise of 'management information systems' in FE.

A personal review

The tensions of being a 'middle manager' in the sector were recognized by others (Gleeson and Shain 1999), as the Access initiative became 'just another course' and part of the mainstream. Almost inevitably, a further internal restructure occurred. It was the end of the *development* phase of Access for me, but it also coincided with changes within Wales, and the refocusing of the Welsh government onto development of the '14–19 Learning Pathways' Initiative. Funding would now follow the strategy for reducing the 'skills gap' (Welsh Assembly Government 2008, 2001; Webb 2008). I was dismayed at the lack of imagination evident, and could anticipate the impacts for adult learner uptake once the *flexibility* of Access programmes had been reduced so dramatically. But I was not entirely disenchanted with the way that things had developed, especially when I think about the individuals that the programmes have helped: the self-confidence and upward mobility, the self-belief of the teachers, lecturers, social workers, town planners, nurses, midwives, operating department practitioners, lawyers, and hundreds of other useful members of society.

These have been the major rewards of my working life. It seems fitting to conclude with the words of a former student, someone from the 1991 cohort, who is now also employed as an Access course leader – the role I once occupied – but in an FE college in North Wales: 'The Access to HE course gave me a level of fulfilment that I hadn't experienced before' (Sue Nelson MSc, cited in QAA 2010). Her story is in a sense my story, as well as a belief in a job that could use the transformative capacity of the Access to HE Movement to positively change peoples' lives. This did not apply only to the students. Today, I help teach and assess trainee teachers, encouraging discussion about access, as well as reflexivity, in personal and professional development as educators.

5

Emotional Labour and Ethics of Care in Further Education Teaching

Jane Salisbury

Introduction and background

This chapter discusses teaching work based on data from a research project funded by the Economic and Social Research Council (ESRC) as part of the major UK Teaching and Learning Research Programme (TLRP) (ESRC/TLRP 2008). The research project investigated the experiences of 'Learning and Working in Further Education (FE) Colleges in Wales' and followed for two years the learning journeys of 27 teachers and 45 students from across seven campuses, which together comprised three FE colleges. The research did not specifically set out to examine teachers' emotional labouring work, yet it became clear during the analysis of the initial interviews, subsequent observational fieldwork and from journals written by both teacher and student participants, that this work was a significant dimension of their day-to-day employment as teachers (Salisbury *et al.* 2009; Jephcote this volume).

Whilst emotions have been a focus of interest to psychologists and sociologists for some time (Clark 1992; Hochschild 1983), the matter of people's display of emotions in work has become a topic of greater interest to organizational scholars over the past two decades or so (Van Dijk and Kirk Brown 2006; Ashforth and Humphrey 1993; Fineman 1993). Most empirical work on the concept of emotion within organizations has tended to focus on employees such as cashier and checkout operators (Rafaelli 1989), flight attendants (Taylor and Tyler 2000; Hochschild 1983) and theme park workers (for example, Van Maanen 1992). 'Emotional labour' as conceptualized by Hochschild (1983) involves techniques of emotion management, or emotion work, to control the emotions that must be expressed as part of a particular process of labour. This is labour that 'requires one to induce or suppress feeling in order to sustain the outward countenance that produces the proper state of mind in others' (Hochschild, 1983: 7); it involves 'effort, planning and control needed to express organizationally desired emotions during interpersonal transactions' (Morris and Feldman 1996: 986).

Hochschild over 30 years ago claimed that teachers in schools, colleges and universities emotionally labour(ed), yet it is evident that at a time when a large proportion of what teachers do is subject to scrutiny and audit, the emotional and less definable elements of teaching have also increased. These aspects of teachers' work remain relatively unrecognized (Jenkins and Conley 2006) and under-examined (Isenbarger and Zembylas 2006; Jenkins and Conley 2006; Constanti and Gibbs 2004; Ogbonna and Harris 2004; Avis *et al.* 2003).

It is now acknowledged that emotional labour is present at different hierarchical levels and among many occupational groups (Fineman 1993), though very few studies have explored the nature and consequences of emotional labour among higher-level professional groups. Scholars have expressed concern that the emotional dimension of teaching is overlooked by policy-makers (Gewirtz *et al.* 2006) arguing that teaching is an emotional practice that cannot be reduced to technical competence or clinical standards (Hargreaves 1998). Similarly, Day (2005: 8), in a study of over 300 teachers, describes teaching as 'an intensely emotional activity characterised by love ... and care, surprise and joy, anger, sadness and fear, excitement and pleasure in students' progress and achievements'.

Teachers manage both their own hearts (their feelings and emotions) and, in some respects, those of their students (emotional well-being, self-esteem and anxieties), in order to manage their students' motivations and engagement in learning. Those teachers with 'holistic focus' embrace the view of FE as a client-centred service and attach prominence to forming and maintaining relationships with learners. I argue here that emotional labour, far from being a marginal feature, is increasingly a central component of teachers' work in FE. Observational field notes, journal and interview data are used to illustrate a particular ethic of care and show the ways teachers' emotional labours are deployed across different situations in their day-to-day working lives. The sheer volume of emotional labour teachers report under the rubric of 'pastoral support' or 'personal tutorial' but which also occurs outside the official timetable (making it *invisible* in managers' workload tariffs) indicates that this labour forms a crucial but under-acknowledged part of the programmatic endeavour for FE learners.

In FE, teaching staff carry out a wide range of disparate tasks including teaching, assessing, mentoring, administration, management, student counselling, marketing and research. Each requires varying degrees of emotional display over an extended period. Empirical material in the following sections will show how certain dimensions of teachers' labour are incorporated into embedded professional and institutional relations.

Teaching as an emotional activity

Monday mornings are hell because you come in ... and there's ... 'so and so's been in a fight' or 'so and so's mother's thrown them out'. Or 'so and so thinks she's pregnant' ... 'so and so's fallen out with their boyfriend'. ... it's all Monday mornings. *Guaranteed*! Before half past nine, right ... 'something catastrophic's happened' ... somebody can't get any grant money ... [or] the bus driver didn't pick him up ...

Teacher interview, Mary, animal care teacher, College B

At interview and in their journal entries, teachers described the emotional struggles and the range of positive and negative emotions they experience. These emotions provide evidence of the complex relationship of teaching and caring: irritation and frustration with students who arrived late, who are ill-equipped or who have not brought in their coursework and who have missed submission dates; sadness about those who drop out or experience tragedy, health scares or personal, domestic difficulties, and joy at how individuals respond to encouragement and demonstrate achievement or progress:

> 10.50 am. Arrive back in my office to find one of my second years in tears ... [a] complicated issue concerning mental health ... cannot inform parents – no counsellor is available ... middle management are unavailable as is the head of student services. 2.5 hours later and still with the student ... emotionally drained. No marking done.
>
> Teacher, Journal 2, Helen, College C

When emotions are underplayed, overplayed, neutralized or changed in order to advance educational goals, teachers perform 'emotional labour' (Hargreaves 1999). It may involve faking, enhancing and/or suppressing emotions to modify one's emotional expressions (Hochschild 1983). Just as flight attendants or call centre employees are paid by organizations to display *positive* emotions towards customers, irrespective of their current feelings and even in unpleasant situations, teachers must do likewise. The students (seen as 'customers') must be made to feel valued, significant and tailored for; teachers must always remain interested in talking to them and supporting them. Metaphorically, this emotional labour is the equivalent of the 'smile down the phone' by staff in service centres (as also described by Bertani Tress this volume).

Hochschild's (1983) early work is well recognized for its analysis of the ways employees 'perform' emotions in the workplace and how these emotions are often commodified for organizational profit. She also used the term 'emotion management' to describe how individuals control and manage their emotions to make sure these are expressed in a way that is consistent with social norms or expectations. Such *management* becomes emotional labour, because emotion becomes 'processed, standardised and subject to hierarchical control' (Hochschild 1983: 153).

In the classroom setting, much emotional labour is routine and predictable. It consists of monitoring communication styles, gauging and assessing the students' moods and orientation to work, subtly or more directly shifting the focus of the encounter so as to achieve particular outcomes. Across settings in the study as diverse as engineering workshops, art studios, IT suites and traditional classrooms where sustained ethnographic observations were undertaken, the teachers regularly engaged in the management and control of emotional encounters in order to develop students' knowledge or technical skills. Their understandings of who they are, what they are doing and why, were underpinned with beliefs about establishing and maintaining relationships.

The learner-teacher solidary relationships to support the whole student

In order to fulfil their duties, teachers labour emotionally, routinely and regularly, establishing trust and confidence, comforting and consoling their students and finding ways to advise, cheering them up, motivating them and acting as a stable source of support. Students across the age range appreciated their teachers' efforts and often drew sharp contrasts with school experiences (Salisbury and Jephcote 2008; Roberts *et al.* 2006). The attention paid to the interpersonal abilities and personal qualities of FE teachers by student participants underscores their manifest concern to work with person-centred teachers.

> I like the more personal relationships in college – we call teachers by their first names and this seems to make it easier to ask for help. Everything seems more open and less reserved. I think you can speak to teachers in college in private, on your own more easily; they are more available to you than teachers in school. In school, any queries or questions that you had always had to be made in public in front of the class.
>
> Student, Journal 1, Melissa, health studies, College A

Whether dealing with challenged single parents who were returning to learn, students suffering constitutional ill-health problems, those anxious about impending assessments or young people in anguish about their sexual identity, teachers consistently engaged with learners in ways that facilitated their encounters with the world of 'college'. This emotional labouring on the part of teachers served to generate and maintain what are understood as 'solidary relationships' (Lynch 1989) and interpersonal rapport, and acts as a symbolic expression of emotional concern and caring; it enables students to feel at ease and to trust their teachers' motives and actions. Indeed, the formation of a specific type of relationship with their student clients was viewed as a necessary component of teaching roles, and considered the crucial vehicle for initiating change in learners' behaviours as the following interview extracts demonstrate:

> The student has to feel that there's a strong relationship. It's the key to getting them motivated and involved in their own learning.
>
> Teacher, Elaine, general education, College B

> Over four years you really get to know them.
>
> Engineering teacher

> They come in as boys and leave as men.
>
> Computing teacher

> Thirty per cent of class time is . . . social – *they* need it, I need it!
>
> Electronics teacher

Teachers reported how they worked at relationships and engaged in lengthy difficult pastoral work outside of contact hours, revealing a strong emotive concern for their students as individuals with lives outside of college, as well as learner identities inside subject departments. A complete lunch break was thus a rare luxury, and both male and female staff commented on the issues students bring into college on Monday mornings, as described earlier.

The teachers also knew a lot about their learners therefore, and some of this knowledge does perhaps contribute to routinized teacher expectations (Jephcote and Salisbury 2008; Jephcote *et al.* 2006). Nevertheless, such 'knowing' generated about and through interaction with individual learners and specific groups, may be a significant feature of FE practice. Students reveal a great deal to teachers, who accept this as part of their job and intervene, offering help or sometimes bringing in the counselling service or arranging medical referrals. One teacher commented:

> A lot of my students, say, have got . . . big problems . . . horrendous personal situations which I would rather not know about.
>
>   Teacher interview, Cheryl, key skills, College C

Teachers explained how they used weekly group tutorials and, increasingly, individual one-to-ones in their non-contact time and lunch breaks to address students' personal and course-related needs:

> Some of those kids . . . (t)hey've been truant, so for me to keep them here and for them to come every day and to have the best attendance ever when you look at their attendance records from school, that is *real* achievement!
>
>   Teacher interview, Jeff, health and social care, College A

Reflecting their concerns with the 'whole' person, some teachers took on and defended students against demanding parents and employers whose intrusive phone calls into lessons disrupted learning and formal assessments:

> [S]tudents . . . can be pulled out of class because . . . they've got to go home to look after a two-year-old. And I'm thinking, don't they [parents] realize they're taking [their] education and chance away . . . ?
>
>   Teacher interview, Carys, business/IT, College B

Anticipating, enabling and negotiating: Emotional labour as routinized practice

The rhythms and routines of FE classroom life are not always smooth, and teachers from across all the three colleges studied spoke of the curriculum time they spent resolving student 'issues'. Observational fieldwork however revealed that emotional labour in the educational setting was often routine and predictable. Many classroom practices are thus the result of teachers *anticipating* and weighing up how they think their students will respond to different teaching and learning strategies, or the way they set up or organize the physical learning setting. One mathematics teacher, for example, truly appalled by the limited numerical skills of her entry-level 1 students (and some of their vulgar behaviour), nevertheless maintained neutrality, disguising her real feelings, and being acutely mindful not to expose the vulnerability of the students with poor numeracy. She strives very hard to make sure that her maths classroom and numeracy sessions are comfortable, as she says, building up the relationship and their trust to make them feel '*safe* in maths' (Charlotte, numeracy class, College C).

Teachers skilfully and diplomatically ignored difficult moments or rude, crude comments from students who were 'acting up' and often were able to manipulate individuals and groups to achieve goals or priorities for the session. Many teachers were observed engaging in 'ego work' involving praise and flattery in order to create a context in which students would participate, comply with instructions or simply accept offered advice.

Researcher fieldnote extract: Level 1 numeracy session with social care students and teacher 'Charlotte', College C

[. . .] Charlotte asks for quiet and speaks loudly from the front of the class reminding the 18 female students that 'we all should all be working on MODE, MEDIAN and RANGE using the data on children's height.' She tours the inside U of tables stopping to repeat and remind individuals what tasks they are doing, she physically flicks through their files and locates relevant sheets for them. [. . .] At the white board and with a blue marker pen and neat print she re-explains it using figures from a sheet. Only about four girls tune in and listen but there is a lot of noise and calling out from others: 'I need a calculator! Who'll loan me a calc?' 'I dunno what I'm supposed to be doing here, I'm totally f**ked – sorry I mean lost!'

Two thirds of the students refuse to be taught collectively and engage in incessant social chatter. Donna, when not describing what she did with her boyfriend – 'pr**k like a donkey' – last night, sings the verses of the modern festive song 'Little Donkey' much to the amusement of her mates. 'Can somebody gag her?' [. . .] Eventually, the teacher visits Donna and looks at her completed tasks: [Teacher] Charlotte says 'Lovely, your file is super Donna, would you like to show it to Jane [researcher]?' The student, Donna, is on her feet in seconds to join me and seems delighted to talk through the meticulously presented file, well indexed and each sheet protected with a plastic pocket [. . .] After about 10 mins and another tour of those who demand help, teacher rejoins us to say how pleased she is with Donna's coursework file explaining, 'Yes, because Donna's file is beautifully presented it's going forward as a sample later after Christmas.' [. . .] Teacher later explains that 'Donna needs a gently, gently approach – she is volatile, has a mouth like a sewer and needs careful handling,' adding [. . .] 'I try to model civility to these girls and to stay calm – but at great personal cost'.

Teacher participants in the study gave accounts of their more challenging students, with increasing workloads and also reported longer working hours, having increased pastoral and administrative duties (see Jephcote this volume). Frustrations with the never-ending task of improving their students' results year-on-year were evident, as recorded by Dixey and Harbottle also in this volume. Many felt that there were unrealistic expectations for certain students, with the result that some teachers experienced anxieties, guilt and depression at being unable to achieve the targets imposed by others. The consequences of interactive work like this can generate powerful feelings of 'inauthenticity and depression' (Erikson and Wharton 1997; Van Dijk and Kirk Brown 2006).

Researcher fieldnote extract: [Teacher] course review, targets and guilt

[. . .] Debra has had her annual review meeting and today . . . [s]he waves a printout . . . Her students have not *all* been positive. There are other datasheets too on student retention, attainment, performance and she is clearly upset . . . 'I work so damned hard with them. I'm always patient – even when I feel furious inside; I prepare really detailed notes and model answers and exam materials for them. Sometimes I could scream when they don't bother to bring their books to class or haven't looked at the course work guidance. But you can't can you?'

Teacher, Debra, general education, College A

Lewig and Dollard (2003) maintain that emotional labour can lead to 'emotional dissonance', an incongruence between feeling and action that can lead to alienation from work. Teachers may be exposed to high levels of 'emotional dissonance' when they are required to display positive emotions which are inconsistent with those genuinely experienced in certain situations (Morris and Feldman 1996). The increasing utilization of student evaluations to assess and control teachers' performance by college management appears to be driving 'student focused' emotional labour. Debra, quoted earlier, is a teacher who has clearly engaged in what Hochschild (1983) has described as 'surface acting' with her classes. Van Dijk and Kirk Brown (2006) have evaluated the mediating role of emotional dissonance in emotional labour and, not surprisingly, identified the links to negative job outcomes. The most commonly described form of acting was a conscious attempt by teachers to arouse or repress emotion. This management of emotion was, in part, a result of FE teachers' caring orientation.

Ethics of care: Principled stances towards FE students

The growing literature on caring in teaching acknowledges the association between caring and good teaching (Noddings 1992; Nias 1999; Jenkins and Conley 2006). 'Caring' is a term open to different interpretations but many FE teachers referred to their obligation to care for students, indicating that 'caring' is an important part of education. In contrast to an ethic of justice, an ethic of caring emphasizes receptivity, relatedness and responsiveness rather than rights and rules. Considering and caring well for the students who are enrolled on specific courses, for example, involves much more than ensuring that learner rights are upheld and that no discrimination occurs in classrooms and across wider college life.

Researcher fieldnote: Teacher and students in vocational access department, Theresa, College A

The staff looking after the vocational access students and helping them through the [life skills] course units are a warm and friendly bunch . . . There is a homely . . . feel about this section of the college and usually the smell of fresh toast, which I asked about. Theresa ... explained why every morning staff and students made toast together; 'at least half of them leave the house without a hot drink [or something to eat] ... you can't learn anything on an empty stomach can you?'

Gewirtz *et al.* (2006) describe teachers as active ethical agents who have to negotiate the extremely dilemmatic terrain of contemporary educational practice. Many FE teachers have to find ways to somehow reconcile conflicting ethical commitments, for example, between interdepartmental collegiality and the survival of their own particular courses and student groups. One IT teacher struggled when her line manager directed her to double up her already sizeable computing group to cover for the long-term absence of a colleague:

> I have never felt so stressed in all my life ... a colleague off ill [whose] classes have now been divided up so that we each have additional students [who we don't know] ... resulting in huge difficulties and endless backtracking to accommodate [them] ... now, I have serious concerns over the attainment of others in [my] group due to the negative impact that the additional students is having.
>
> Teacher, Journal 2, Penny, College B

Discussing the divisions of labour and tasks in education and health work, Cribb (2005: 7–8) argues that the dilemmas professionals face are chronic and serious because there is no simple translation between institutional obligations and ethical obligations, between 'doing my job' and 'doing the right thing'. Indeed, FE teachers reported that some aspects of the job involved doing things demanded by managers that they found ethically distasteful. One example was recounted by Debra, who felt 'uneasy' (ethically) about her management team's instructions to be 'vague' with part-time pupils from a school sixth form about what options they could continue with, when she knew very well their twilight after-school A level provision at the college might be withdrawn. It was awkward for her as well as ethically difficult – 'people need to know ... because they need to plan!'

Teachers respond imaginatively to try to reconcile conflicts between the performative demands of monitoring systems and what they feel to be in the best interests of their students. Mindful that an individual's attendance data on class registers is compiled centrally and on a daily basis, as evidence for their Educational Maintenance Allowance (EMA), teachers did their best to generate data which would ensure that a 'needy' student got their £30 per week.

Researcher fieldnote: teacher (Jeff), health and social care session, College A

Eleven students sit in a horseshoe arc of tables getting out their files and chatting while teacher completes the register [...] 'Before we make a start, can somebody find out what's happening with 'Josie'? Get her to text me asap.' Two girls enter into whispers as one uses her mobile phone to text the missing student. On the wall directly behind where the teacher sits is a laminated poster which lists the college's classroom ground rules: 'Mobile phones should be switched off during timetabled sessions'.

Teachers colluded with class members in their sending text messages from inside lessons, to locate missing students, wake them up or remind them to 'ring into the office or personal tutor', occasionally even making the text messages themselves. Like the New Deal college coordinators reported by Salisbury (2004), teaching staff were reluctant to 'play God' and provide damning attendance data that would reduce or cancel benefits. These were frequently observed-features of FE classroom life (see also Gleeson 2005; Gleeson *et al.* 2005), as FE teachers continually made decisions about compliance and when to subvert institutional rules or to adopt a stance of 'principled infidelity' (Wallace 2005).

Concluding remarks

Teachers as knowledge workers are fully engaged in mental labour; at the same time they are also service workers engaged actively in supporting learners in order to achieve institutional ends. This involves the management of both their own and students' emotions so that knowledge and skills can be taught and acquired, and risky behaviour curtailed.

Contemporary educational goals place increasing emphasis on conferring recognition and building self-esteem for people deemed to be marginalized or vulnerable. Ecclestone (2004) has described the growing political and professional support for the idea that state-sponsored education must build individual and communal self-esteem. FE teachers in the study had clearly bought into this notion, and their concerns with the 'whole student' at times appeared to displace matters of teaching and learning. Teachers spoke frequently of their own sense of reward from 'turning someone round' – getting them 'to believe in themselves' and such remarks appeared to support the Government 'widening access and participation' agenda. Some demonstrated a strong sense of agency and positive sense of having done a good job, and the most emotionally resilient teachers appeared to cope with emotional dissonance, and tended to have a firm sense of moral purpose about their work.

Clearly, emotions are an institutional resource that can also be utilized by different actors to achieve sociocultural and educational ends. Some forms of emotional labour were governed by the expectations of teachers that it was associated with 'profession-alism'. I suggest that the intensification of FE teachers' work and increased manager-ialism have resulted in negative consequences for them (Clow 2005). The stress reported by teachers of course cannot be attributed solely to emotional dissonance. Nevertheless the potential effects of synthetic compassion, feigning and faking feelings can lead to what Ashforth and Humphrey (1993) describe as 'pernicious psychological consequences'. Understanding better the impacts and the consequences of the emotional labour that FE teachers undertake – and indeed those teachers from other sectors – is an important matter for policy-makers and institutional managers and remains a highly relevant focus for future research. The emotional demands of teaching may go unrealized by managers and this may have important implications for teacher supply to and exit from the FE workforce. Yet the powerful impression from two years of sustained fieldwork in this sector was of the *resilience* of the teachers in the FE college settings observed; despite frequent problems and setbacks, in the main, they returned to their classes to teach and support the diverse groups of students enrolled in their subjects, courses and programmes.

Note

'Learning and Working in Further Education in Wales' was funded by the ESRC as a project within its TLRP programme (www.tlrp.org). See Salisbury *et al.* 2009 for a fuller methodological account.

6

Becoming a Teacher in Higher Education

Trevor Austin

Introduction

Whilst there are strong traditions of exploring and conceptualizing the socialization of teachers in schools, the picture in post-compulsory contexts is more uneven. What then does it mean to 'become' a teacher in further or higher education (FE/HE)? Skelton (2012: 23) notes how 'under-researched' the notion of a teacher identity is in these sectors, and particularly today, when this includes the many 'late entrants', who bring to their teaching an experience of other professions outside the academy. This chapter reports a recent empirical study exploring the perspectives, strategies and transitions of a group of 'late entrants' to HE teaching (Austin 2011). The discussion includes the ways in which these informants from 'different perspectives' experienced and managed the process of becoming an HE teacher. This is illustrated through the 'voices' of three case studies, from the fields of health, education and learner support and which exemplify the experiences of a larger sample. The role played by teacher education in these broader processes is a key area of the study.

Background: Becoming a teacher

There are various perspectives put forward on what it is to 'become' a teacher (Huberman 1991; Lacey 1977; Lortie 1975) that provide compelling accounts of survival, shifting identities and transition. Some suggest that the defining features of 'becoming' are those of 'struggle', 'baptisms of fire' or journeys – consisting of 'separation', 'transformation' and 'return' (McNamara *et al.* 2002). Such processes are also seen to be re-played in other sectors. Salisbury (1994: 128) refers to novice teachers in FE as 'in at the deep end', and Hodkinson and Taylor (2002: 256) describe how new lecturers in universities are 'initiated' and subsequently 'normalized', through participation in accredited programmes of teacher training. In much of this work, 'becoming a teacher' is viewed as passing through an 'ordeal' or being 'stage-like' in character.

Later studies see identity-formation itself as part of the process of 'becoming'. Here, novice teachers are not only active agents in their own socialization, but the processes of identity formation itself forms part of the dynamic. 'Identity', however, is not something 'taken on', nor is it a series of bounded 'stages' through which novice teachers pass (Cooper and Olsen 1996). Woods (1981), Samara and Luce-Kaplar (1996) and Day (2004) all reinforce the notion that 'becoming a teacher' involves a transient, sometimes fragmented and changing sense of a 'teacher self'. However, these studies take relatively little account of the problematic and complex nature of *changing* an existing identity and the extent to which these might be re-made, consolidated, maintained or renewed, across different kinds of professional activity (Austin 2011).

The construction of such dual or multiple identities, and their interaction with more formal roles, has been described by Castells (1997) who noted the 'stress and contradiction' (p. 6) inherent in such processes. Such dissonances appear to be most clearly played out in FE and HE, since here, many new teachers are taking a professional role into a new educational and occupational setting. However, it seems probable that the 'dual and multiple identities' work in different ways, with existing identities being sometimes a source of dissonance as well as a resource. Jephcote and Salisbury (2009: 427) have noted how teachers' former occupational identities and their recent or relevant industrial experience can provide many professionals with a sense of credibility and may act as a touchstone to the occupational worlds for which they are preparing students (see Salisbury 1994). They also note how a work-based identity often underpins and shapes dispositions and orientations towards teaching and learning too. However, the evolution and development of new identities also creates dissonances, in the way that Castells suggests. Murray (2005) notes how new lecturers from teaching, nursing and social work have all encountered difficulties, arising from meeting the imperatives of HE and their original occupational fields. MacNeil (1997), in an earlier study, thus identified a 'troublesome duality' which was seen to cause role ambiguity for those trying to be a 'nursing practitioner' as well as a 'lecturer', while Boyd and Smith (2010) have also described how new nurse educators in HE were often unsure of their credibility, both as nurses and as teachers.

New teachers and new professionals

A purposive sample of 10 novice teachers was drawn from a larger cohort of participants undertaking a Postgraduate Certificate in Academic Practice (PGCAP) in 2008–9. This was at a single post-1992 HE institution in England, and the study represents an analysis of the key accounts provided by informants. Participants were new to HE teaching at the start of that academic year, and were drawn from a range of fields including osteopathy, nursing, teacher training, learning support and business studies. The sample typified the staffing profile of an institution heavily committed to a curriculum 'for the professions', with a regime of student support and a continuing recruitment of non-traditional HE students. In common with staff from other similar institutions from the post-92 group of universities, the sample were employed and contracted as lecturers primarily to teach. Whilst academic contracts required some

Table 6.1 Composition of the study sample

	Pseudonym	Age	Vocational area/workplace
1	Peter	41	Senior lecturer in education/university
2	Linda	32	Librarian/university
3	Abigail	49	Careers adviser/university
4	John	61	Lecturer in business studies/university
5	Juliet	45	Sports development officer/university
6	Clare	54	Library manager/university
7	Katrina	47	Lecturer in nursing/university
8	Craig	36	Lecturer in osteopathy/partner institution (other HEI)
9	James	42	Lecturer in osteopathy/partner institution (other HEI)
10	Jane	26	Lecturer in osteopathy/partner institution (other HEI)

research activity, staff surveys conducted just prior to this study (HESA 2008) reported that academic staff in HE typically spend some 86 per cent[1] of their work time undertaking activities related to teaching and the support of their students in the year prior to the study. Conversely, only about 10 per cent of their time was reported as being spent on research (HESA 2008).

Table 6.1 provides a profile overview of the project participants' vocational area and workplace. Their experiences, ideas, talk and stances form the basis of this chapter. The study sample was also typical, as it contained a number of staff already working in the university in a 'support' role – library, careers and sports development staff – those who were being incorporated into course delivery through the institution's education strategy. Gornall (2004, 1999) has described such groups of 'New Professionals', in teaching and learning, and on whom there is an increasing reliance (and see Hudson this volume). Bellard (2005) also comments on the role of such staff, as part of the overall student experience, while Chevallier (2002: 304) notes that 'providing students with the kind of education they expect ... has become crucial for the survival of institutions'.

Collecting the narratives: Methods

Three sets of semi-structured interviews, sampled across an academic year, were used to explore the experiences, emotions and perspectives of the study participants undertaking the PGCAP. Data-gathering sessions began with a 'baseline' interview to establish prior experience and individual pathways into teaching. The two further interviews took place in December 2008 and April 2009, to allow for the accrual and development of views and experiences. All interviews were audio-recorded and transcribed. Participants produced rich accounts amenable to narrative approaches in the analysis and the reporting (Webster and Mertova 2007). The following sections present key findings from this empirical study under three analytical categories. These are: narratives of the professions, narratives of commitment and identities in transition.

Narratives of the professions

In the first of these perspectives, the ways in which prior professional backgrounds of the research participants could affect and be affected by the processes of becoming a teacher in HE are explored. As Denzin (1989: 73) states, '[N]o self or personal experience story is ever an individual production, [but] derives from a larger group, cultural, ideological and historical contexts'. When the participants' interview transcripts were analysed, certain patterns emerged. It seemed clear that the professional backgrounds were shaping emerging ideas about pedagogy and also the development of a (new) teacher identity. These prior backgrounds and experiences appeared to function in a number of significant ways – to motivate, constrain, protect and, more profoundly, to *disturb* the participants. There were also feelings of elation, but of disorientation too, especially when interacting with students.

For the osteopaths and nurses comprising the health practitioner group, there was a strong focus on seeing parallels between themselves in relating to patients and also in relation to students. These health narratives upheld the standards of their original professions. These were not simply 'narratives of care' (Ellis 1999) or of 'healing', but of issues of 'control', as the new practitioners recognized that students could not be managed in the same ways as could their former patients. Kodner (2002: 3) notes that caregivers traditionally demand that their patients be compliant, that is, follow their instructions. Thus, each of our participants was also seeking to understand and cope with their teaching role with 'patients', providing a way of making teaching familiar and more relevant.

The learner support group, consisting of librarians, a sports developer and a careers adviser, like the health practitioner group, were still practising their main university roles. However, their professional backgrounds seemed to play an entirely different set of functions. Whilst not conforming fully to Gornall's (1999: 44) 'New Professionals', they, like her examples, did 'other' themselves in terms of their teaching roles. That is, they initially defined themselves as 'not' teachers or 'academics'. They also got caught up in the wider institutional discourses of 'employability' and 'information literacy', as the study university sought to establish appropriate support for its 'non-traditional' student body (Bellard 2005; Leathwood and O'Connell 2003). This involved teaching large established groups of students and using approaches that were unfamiliar to them. But it was contrary to the ideas and principles they encountered and developed on the PGCAP, which tended to contradict their own more 'collaborative' models of teaching and learning. Encounters with students appeared to reflect wider anxieties concerned with finding their way around the academic curriculum too. The new lecturers also had some reservations about pedagogy, which sometimes led to 'reverting back' to their established techniques, linked to their professional backgrounds. Thus, narratives from the learner support group suggested some different and more problematic transitions for these practitioners.

Narratives of commitment

By setting aside the research participants' occupational group and analysing the particular vocabularies that they used, a second analytical perspective was taken. This was based on the words, phrases and contexts used by participants, and draws on the work of Wright Mills (1940) and Adelman (1981), to produce a typology of 'talk'. These 'types' represented a range of talk, thinking and action, which were seen to portray a range of commitment to students, to the PGCAP programme itself, and to the more general processes of becoming a teacher in HE. To derive these 'types', the interview transcripts were re-read intensively to identify and allocate codes. In this process, as Fairclough says, 'the formal features of the text act as cues which activate the interpreters' resources (1989: 141). This was not an easy or objective process; however, with practice, it was possible to 'see' differing commitments in the language itself. The following examples seek to illustrate some of the differences noted (see Table 6.2).

Table 6.2 Illustrations of talk 'types'

Type	Sample extracts
Missionary	People should feel safe with you . . . my aim is to deliver the best care and I look at everybody as part of my 'family'. To do this I started to look around for opportunities in teaching.
Pragmatic	You just deal with whatever comes up. The [PGCAP] allows me to pigeon-hole things as a range of things come up . . . it's given me permission to develop my own style of teaching.
Caring	I didn't like to just take over [a student's problem] so I began to share her experience . . . I needed to actually help her and see what she needed . . . to nurture a greater confidence in herself.
Passivist	I do see myself as becoming more of an actual teacher, whereas I don't see myself as a teacher now. I hope to be comfortable in seeing myself as a teacher and possibly to engage a bit more.
Credentializing	I needed a tool that I could use to ensure that I was along the right track and to correct me. I came to formalize my apprenticeship in teaching.
Conscript	I see myself as support staff rather than an academic lecturer, we are pushed to do the teaching and it's become part of our remit.

The analysis in this way, fell upon the vocabularies used by the participants to describe their emotions, experiences and behaviours. These 'types' of talk were then considered in relation to each other, to construct a typology which is described in Figure 6.1. The typology indicates a range of possible commitments to a teaching role: thus, 'credentializing' and 'conscripted' talk at one end suggest less commitment, and

Missionary [high]	Pragmatic	Caring	Passivist	Credentialising	Conscript [low]

Decreasing commitment ⟶

Figure 6.1   Types and range of talk

'missionary' talk at the other, much higher commitment. Although these do not 'belong' to any specific individuals or any particular group, 'missionary' talk tended to occur more in the health practitioner group and 'passivist' talk to occur more in the learner support group. The majority of participants also used 'pragmatic' talk, regardless of background, with 'pragmatic' and 'missionary' talk occurring relatively frequently together. In viewing these varieties and modes of commitment in informants' talk, it became clear that these different types and degrees of commitment allowed the participants to variously 'buy-into', 'play at' or even 'resist' the processes of becoming a teacher in HE.

The analysis now turns to focus on the way in which encounters with learners contributed to a shift in how participants perceived their teaching, and how this further developed an emerging 'teacher identity'.

Identities in transition

Encounters with students seemed to be central to changing teaching behaviours and ways of thinking about teaching. The emergence (in the transcripts) of progressively more 'pragmatic' talk reflected these shifts, but also deeper emotional and pedagogic challenges. These were seen in descriptions that reflect Denzin's (1989) notion of 'epiphany', and Tripp's (1993) concept of the 'critical incident'. These provided 'turning points' – moments of realization and recognition for the participants of their new role-identity of 'self as teacher'. Three stages were identified in the analysis (Austin 2011) – the 'loosening of professional bonds', 'shifting orientations', and 'retreating/reverting back'. Of course, whilst these stages may have arisen as a result of the participants' switching between different 'modes', close scrutiny of the empirical material revealed a sequence common to all of the participants. Initially, individuals struggled with issues of power and control: Craig (osteopath) compared students and patients, the latter as 'more surrendering . . . we lie them down on the plinth . . . that's the first stage of the battle won . . . whereas students come back at you'. Katrina (nurse) is more explicit: 'It's a control issue. I do like being in control. That's the thing about being a nurse. You are very much in control at times.' For Juliet (sports development), power and control are manifested differently, and control issues, including routines as part of fitness and safety, start before the session: 'I had been asked to get involved . . . very last minute and not a great deal of preparation. I sort of knew what to expect . . . but I didn't realize it was going to be me explaining it.' Here Juliet realized that she needed to appear authoritative and in control of the situation, but the timing, her contribution and the preparation needed, were decided elsewhere.

Secondly, there were periods of 'immersion' in new pedagogies and new 'realities', when encounters with students produced those moments of epiphany or critical incidents. It is in this stage that the case study individuals can now 'see' teaching in HE as a kind of 'truth'; they perceive its form and significance for the first time. Linda (university librarian) recalls an encounter with two mature students who,

> after a period . . . [and] I hadn't thought of myself [as] doing teaching [they started to] ask really good questions, and that made me think. 'that's the first time I've ever done this [teaching] properly'.

Craig described how, away from the clinic and in other teaching situations, students were 'off the hook and start applying their critical faculties to *you*'. He was also 'shocked' by the challenge of holding students' attention. His students were 'not like' he had been as a student. Craig's background, as an osteopath, 'works' in most clinical teaching situations, but the further he is from the clinic, the tougher he feels it becomes. For Katrina (nurse) this 'truth' became a struggle to make her sessions 'interesting', especially with the 'drier' material: 'I give them the stuff, as they tend to like "doing" but it's really difficult when there are so few people in the group to get any kind of noise going, and it's just you.'

Juliet (sports developer) is trying to position herself between two *styles* of teaching, one familiar from the past, the second built whilst on the PGCAP course. She is striving to find where her 'true' style is, between what she regards as 'instinctive' or in contrast 'academic', and reflecting, recognizes from her approaches that she now 'falls between' these.

The mode of 'retreat' or 'reverting back', also the forms of 'epiphany' and 'critical incident', produced dissonances, but also now became additional resources. 'Reverting back' does not necessarily mean a return to foundations, more a selective and purposeful use of both past and new resources. These might be termed a 'dance of improvisation' (Wenger *et al.* 2009), where teachers apply and adapt their practice in a new landscape. Juliet's interview, for example, evokes this when she speaks of 'opening up horizons, about what it means to be a teacher and how you can teach'. Of the PGCAP course, she added, 'but it doesn't tell you how to teach it . . . you can take things from it . . . you can navigate a path through'. It is as social actors within these processes that the case study individuals start to 'become' teachers in HE.

Narratives of resource and dissonance

Further analysis of the interview data from the full sample revealed two further kinds of narrative – one of 'resource' and the other of 'dissonance'. In practice, these appeared to operate within and across both identity formation and pedagogic development. The 'resource' narrative comes from the way in which participants' former vocational identities worked to provide a range of ideas, standards and experiences. This is akin to Bernstein's 'narratives of the past', which were used to generate 'retrospective identities' (2000: 78) or constructed from past exemplars, criteria and experience. A number of the dataset narratives were shaped in this way. Bernstein has also highlighted how those from vocational disciplines such as nursing or business studies – the 'new university pedagogic regions' – tend to project knowledge from their outside practice into the region itself. Such fields, according to Bernstein (2000), continue to regulate practice, but also 'identity'.

'Resource' narratives crossed into pedagogy through the PGCAP programme, and into the participants' teaching experiences. All of the participants viewed the course primarily as a resource. From the beginning, it was a source of ideas, possible approaches to teaching and a forum for exchanging experience with peers. It also constituted a space within which reflective activity could take place and be developed. The PGCAP was additionally, a forum where participants could meet those who supported teaching, for example, 'New Professionals', such as learning technologists (Hudson 2009; Beetham *et al.* 2001), as well as librarians and traditional learning support staff in the academy.

But narratives of *dissonance* also emerged across identity formation and pedagogic development. This dissonance did not come only, as in other studies, from the 'transfer problem' (Fanghanel 2004), but also derived from identity change itself. This has been described by Castells (1997: 6), and also Murray (2005) and Boyd and Smith (2010). Similar dissonances were observed here, with both pedagogic skills and identity formation complicated by 'transfer' issues (Evans *et al.* 2011). Past practices of teachers in vocational settings as continuing to be 'another kind of professional' also had an influence. However, for the PGCAP participants, past practices and 'other' identities were no longer a clear guide to future thinking and action. This suggested that there might be limits to what 'retrospective' identities and actions could achieve in an HE or new context. The standards, exemplars and values that held in the workplace remained as a guide, but they could also contradict some of the new practices. Figure 6.2 seeks to capture visually these features.

Narratives of the past did seem to provide 'standards' however. These were those of the original professions themselves, but they also performed additional functions, in

	Resource	Dissonance
Identity	Vocational life as a guide to practice as a teacher–standards, ethics, motives and experience	Vocational life – experience has limits in HE and complicates the adoption of a teacher identity
	Retaining main identity	Acquiring a dual identity
Pedagogy	PGCAP– skills, ideas, approaches, peer experiences Workplace peers	Past teaching and past experience as a guide to teaching does not work
		Transfer of skills

(Arrows indicate time)

Figure 6.2 Identity and pedagogy as 'resource' and as 'dissonance'

helping the participants to cope with the new demands of teaching in HE, as Bernstein (1996: 78) has described. For example, the patient-centric views of the health care group helped to make teaching 'feel familiar' and therefore easier to control. For the learner support group, identity maintenance appeared to protect them from, or to 'play out', a teacher role amidst new discourses and approaches to teaching.

Becoming a teacher in HE

Fanghanel's (2012: 6) recent account of teacher identities in HE continues to underscore the notion that these are 'constructed and relatively fluid', are 'influenced by personal biographies' and also 'individual emotions, beliefs and understandings'. The data from our informants resonates with Fanghangel's account, but also goes further, in emphasizing the extended struggle that accompanies the processes of 'becoming'.

Vocational identities appear to need to be 'loosened' or challenged by particular events and encounters. Such occurrences invariably, were cast as problematic or challenging to the participants, and encounters with learners played a central role in this. In turn, these dissonances could be shaped directly or indirectly by identity itself, and seemed to work in two ways. First, directly, in the way that Bernstein (2000) describes, with experience, past standards and exemplars being brought forward and then being challenged by new teaching experiences. But second, identity also worked indirectly too. The various commitments participants made to teaching affected the way that dissonances could be experienced. These commitments appeared to be a key part of the processes of 'becoming' in identity-formation as HE teachers. These are highly complex sets of interactions between past experiences, new encounters and shifting orientations which, for most of the participants, worked to disturb their identities and shape the situations they were in. Those who 'bought in' to teaching, such as Craig and Katrina, seemed to feel – or at least articulate – the deepest disturbance. This related to pedagogy but, more profoundly, to identity itself.

The term 'prospective identities' is used here to describe how disturbances and dissonances were reduced, in a period when the participants sought to control and develop their positions. Most of the participants eventually recognized that teaching in HE was profoundly different to workplace practice, and a practice in its own right. However, they continued to draw on other experience and their other identities. They recognized that there must be some adaptation to their new situation. There was also a view that they needed to 'grow into' their teaching role. This coincided with the increasing pragmatism evident in their 'talk'.

In the process of 'becoming a teacher' in post-compulsory education, participants could be seen to 'hold on' to some of their background but 'let go' of other aspects, as 'prospective identities' that continue to 'use yet rest upon narrative resources' (Bernstein 1996: 79). Hence, whilst prospective identities are essentially 'future-oriented', they also draw on earlier and other identities, but more selectively than the 'retrospective' identities referred to earlier. This was part of the participants' search for an authentic sense of 'self'. However, such processes and experiences were not shared in the same way or to the same extent by all of the participants. Whilst most of them began to re-synthesize aspects of past and present, others put their experience to work as it stood.

Conclusion: The role and significance of the PGCAP course

Whilst Knight's (2006: 5) observation that 'professional formation as a teacher in higher education is substantially affected by doing the job' would be hard to refute, it was clear that the participants in this study drew significant benefits from the PGCAP. Although the participants' viewed the course primarily as a 'resource', and teaching as a 'craft' to be acquired, they valued the interaction with peers and the formal exposure to research on teaching and learning. Some individuals were content to 'bolt on' techniques to established approaches or saw teaching as a means to an end, a way of 'sharing' their profession, others recognized that teaching in HE was a practice in its own right – although this recognition was invariably 'conditioned' by their vocational experience, as a means, for example, to 'defend' their profession. Whilst the challenge of transferring generic teaching ideas led many participants to stay with 'safe' approaches, this had more to do with individual levels of agency and institutional stances than the 'usefulness' of the PGCAP. At heart, their struggle lay in their ability to adapt, to draw on previous resources, but also to incorporate the more interactive, task-focused and broadly constructivist approaches that were advocated on the course. It was not clear whether they would maintain a commitment to developing the skills of teaching itself, and clearly, this would be better evidenced through an ongoing and longitudinal study. For now, Knight's (2006: 5) assertion, that 'the benefits of PG Cert [in teaching] courses may most strongly disclose themselves some time after completion, especially when graduates are in a position to re-design [such courses]', has to be the last word.

Acknowledgements

A presentation to the Working Lives Seminar Series in May 2010 at the Cardiff School of Social Sciences forms the basis of this chapter. I wish to thank audience members for constructive discussion on the presentation.

Note

1 These figures were supplied by the study institution to the Higher Education Funding Council (HEFC) for England to account for staff use of time over the final quarter of the 2007–8 academic year.

Part Two

Leadership, Management and Human Resources Issues

Introduction

Lyn Daunton

Part 2 opens with **Chapman's** contribution and a *policy-led discussion* that ranges beyond purely academics' needs and interests. The author adopts a *societal perspective* to explore links between health, economy, family, gender and environment, and how academics' work through research and educational courses can contribute to a nation's economy and civic good. **Cook** and **Daunton**, members of the Working Lives team, consider academics' understanding of the *'contract' between staff and employers*, and how this may reflect different institutional contexts and sets of interests, raising issues about both personal well-being and professional autonomy. Research on *heads of departments* reported by **Floyd,** suggests tensions between the role of manager and active scholar. The three heads in this study discuss how, as 'caught in the middle', they combine and resolve some of the dilemmas and ambiguities of the role. **Kelly** and **Boden** document some of the financial and accounting changes in the sector, applied to the evaluation of academics' work. They focus on a single aspect, *externally funded research*, in a scenario where individual initiative and productivity is overtaken by an uncomprehending and intervening bureaucracy, and a negative value on a staff initiative. Using empirical studies, **Waring** is also a critic of higher education (HE) managerial regimes, in this case the 'HR' function. He examines the *'rewarding and developing staff'* initiative in HE in the context of manager-faculty relationships. **Gornall** and **Thomas** also consider the context of professional work for lecturers as employees, but at a policy and *'meso' level, highlighting the discourses about 'reform'* that shape the management of change and relationships in the institution, including academic pay. **Nakabugo, Conway, Barrett** and **Farren** report on *research capacity-building* in an even wider, pan-institutional development, involving a collaboration between HE institutions (HEIs) and organizations in Ireland and four African countries – Uganda, Mozambique, Malawi and Tanzania. Staff experiences had much in common across borders and continents. **Rothwell and Rothwell** want to work with institutions to improve scholarship, engagement, *professional development and academic employability,* emphasizing the continuing needs for academics and lecturers to consider 'employability' for themselves, as key stakeholders in the own career potential. Part 2, which focuses on the leadership, management, institutional and policy contexts of academic work, is followed by a set of chapters (in Part 3) on dimensions of the academic role itself.

7

A Policy Perspective from Wales on Employment and Working Life

Christine Chapman

One of the first intake of elected Assembly Members (AMs) taking up their seats in the National Assembly for Wales was Christine Chapman, who has had an inside view of government and policy-making since that time. Christine is AM for the Cynon Valley and has twice held office in government. She has served on the Committee of the Regions in Europe and has chaired several Assembly committees. With a detailed knowledge of political and constituency work, Christine also brings experiences of postgraduate study to the Working Lives commentary, where as a student and researcher in Welsh higher education (HE), she has gained her own qualifications and voice. In February 2010, Christine delivered the keynote address to the inaugural event, in a year of seminars and discussions organized by the Working Lives research team. In this chapter, she discusses some of the thinking around policies which the Welsh Government has put forward to tackle the challenges facing a post-devolution Wales.

Introduction: the past in the present

Wales is a nation of strong communities and values, with a history of industrial success and social engagement, and a country of outstanding natural features. However, the size of the task facing 60 new Welsh AMs in May 1999, at the start of a new devolved political institution, should not be underestimated. The responsibility of shining a spotlight on, and then effectively tackling, the challenges facing Wales was great, given their deep-rooted nature. Many were long-term, shadowy fragments of a Welsh past that have, in many cases, been exacerbated by the industrial policy of the 1980s, and the global economic turmoil of more recent years. These challenges included economic inequalities leading to unacceptable gaps in health and educational attainment, a resulting intergenerational poverty, and poor general skills levels that in turn have contributed to a persistently high unemployment level and an environment scarred by the legacy of an historic reliance on heavy industry in many parts of Wales. The Welsh Government needs academics and HE institutions to partner with it in addressing many of these issues, through their teaching, research and external engagement.

Welsh devolution and a new policy opportunity

The arrival of Welsh devolution meant a fresh approach could be taken. It also signalled the freedom to adopt a specifically *Welsh* solution to tackling some of these Welsh problems. Although initially Wales may not have possessed the right tools for the job, the recent referendum on further legislative powers (Jones and Scully 2012) has rectified this. And, since every Welsh Government from 1999 has included the Welsh Labour Party, either in a single party government or as the largest partner in a coalition administration, this has given Welsh Labour a unique opportunity to shape the political agenda in line with its own priorities and aspirations.

The political reality and the fact that Wales is a small country of only 3 million people has necessitated a different approach to that of the pre-devolution days. With close HE links, much policy-making has been informed by research from academic teams, and its impact documented in studies and analyses. Thus, the Welsh Government's relationship and partnerships with institutions in civil society, business, HE and the social sector has been very important. However, the reality, that the private sector is not strong enough in Wales, has resulted in the Welsh Government taking a more interventionist approach within economic development. Thus, for example, it has targeted particular sectors and growth zones, supporting workers at risk of redundancy, and offering support for micro and small businesses, which at 98.3 per cent, are the mainstay of the Welsh economy (Welsh Assembly Government 2012c).[1] Much emphasis has also been placed on the relationship that the Welsh Government has with its partners in the business and social sectors as well. There are positive developments here: exports from Wales in 2011 were up by over 13 per cent on the preceding year, and there is an increasing focus now being placed on creating a green and sustainable economy, one in which Wales has some leading entrepreneurs and company bases. Health inequalities in Wales, and legacies of industrial and general ill health, have meant a greater emphasis on preventative initiatives and structural change to improve health outcomes. This has had to be achieved within very tight budgetary constraints, including the recent added pressures of recession – but this too has been underpinned and informed by academic policy review work and expert input (Norton *et al.* 2012). The conviction (itself an outcome of research) that what happens early on in life can shape an individual's life chances, has also shaped the Welsh Government's continued support for early years action, focusing on both health and education measures.

The importance of HE to the Welsh economy – and some challenges

The HE sector in Wales, and individuals working within it, are a significant feature in our public landscape. Since the advent of political devolution, priorities for the HE sector in the Wales have built on the traditional Welsh reverence for scholarship, and focused on providing learners with the skills and experiences to equip them for life. They have also aimed to further widen participation within the sector, to promote both internal and external collaboration and to ensure Wales has the very best academic reputation. The roles of HE as both catalyst to enhance economic performance, and as cement to hold together a civilised, democratic polity, have been key themes since devolution.[2] However, the recession and the arrival of a new Education Minister increased the pace and urgency for the Welsh HE sector to respond structurally.

Firstly, the very tight constraints on budgets as a result of the UK Government's economic plan has meant that Welsh HEIs need to be sustainable and ready to play an effective role in tackling the problems facing Wales. The Welsh Labour manifesto for the 2011 Assembly elections pledged to create 'a smaller number of stronger universities' that would be able to develop the 'critical mass' that is an essential prerequisite to achieving true excellence in terms of teaching and research, and which would enable Welsh HEIs to compete successfully within the global knowledge economy. In addition, the policy approach for Welsh HEIs would be in sharp contrast to the more market-driven English model, as described in the Browne Review (2010), and which set out a vision of unlimited tuition fees and inexorable expansion of popular university courses to meet demand. Whilst it is inevitable that any process of change will in the short term bring some disruption and uncertainty and prove a testing time for individual academic staff, change should mean a stronger sector in the long term, and this has been endorsed by sector bodies such as HE Wales and the HE funding council (HEFCW). Change could also lead to academic staff having a stronger role within the running of the HE sector, as the Welsh Government has stated in a White Paper from July 2012.[3]

Secondly, if the Welsh economy is to grow, then the active contribution of HE towards this goal is not simply desirable but essential, and this poses another challenge for academics in terms of their work. There is a delicate balance to be struck: we must never ignore the intrinsic value of learning for its own sake, and its contribution in terms of personal and intellectual development, and we must also protect the independence and freedoms of academics. However, equally, HE must not be seen as remote from the wider world, and HE's contribution therefore must also help to provide the right environment to encourage potential entrepreneurs to flourish.

A powerful argument in favour of this was contained in the report into the Economic Contribution of Higher Education in Wales (2009) carried out in the Third Assembly by the then Enterprise and Learning Committee. One of its recommendations argued that:

> entrepreneurship needs to be embedded more effectively both in the higher education curriculum and within the professional development of research staff: programmes should be established so that Masters and PhD graduates and research staff receive training on commercialisation and on handling relationships with business.

Differences of opinion around the aims and purposes of HE exist amongst academics (Barnett 2011b), and such an approach would undoubtedly involve a radical shift, however.

Raising the stakes in the scientific field has also been a priority for the Welsh Government, as shown by the publication of its Science Strategy (2012c), where it was noted that a 'sound and vibrant scientific and technological base has substantial potential to boost the economy, through advanced ideas, skills and developments and an effective translation through innovation to more high quality jobs'. In this, the Welsh Government makes productive links with course development in universities and also the formation of applied research partnerships. It has also made grant funding available for 'proof of concept' and 'proof of prototype' activities, providing the safeguarding for intellectual property that is essential for the development of new and innovative products. The goverment in Wales has also committed itself to forming a national innovation strategy board.

The extent to which academics have demonstrated their strengths in collaboration, working across boundaries and innovation, is shown by a number of 'best practice' models. Wales' entrepreneurial activity has not in the past matched that of other European Union (EU) regions and it had a lower business start-up rate. There is thus a role for HE in bringing new solutions to these challenges in a variety of rising sectors – the digital economy, the low carbon economy, health and biosciences and advanced engineering and manufacturing. One notable example of this is the Graduate Teleworking Initiative (GTi), delivered by the University of Glamorgan through European funding, whose success I have witnessed first-hand in my constituency. GTi supports business start-ups for graduates and encourages entrepreneurialism, translating this support into positive results for the Welsh economy, and linked to support from the university, in partnership with business and enterprise organizations.

Thirdly, the argument that education is the most effective mechanism by which a more egalitarian society can be forged has been a compelling one for Welsh Labour since the advent of devolution. This has been augmented by a range of studies and reports which clearly map out the critical role of education in improving social justice and participation. As Wilkinson and Pickett (2010) argue in *The Spirit Level*,

> People with more education earn more, are more satisfied with their work and leisure time, are less likely to be unemployed, more likely to be healthy, less likely to be criminals, more likely to volunteer their time and vote in elections.

The challenge for Wales is that there has been too high a level of disengagement from education, and the Welsh Government has therefore laid down expectations on HE that it should maximize participation. These aspirations have been supported by a number of specific measures, such as the retention of the Education Maintenance Allowance, a fairer fees policy for Welsh-domiciled students, better progression routes for post-16s, and an improved provision of courses – not least in the parts of Wales where, as in the Heads of the Valleys area, participation has not been so great. Emphasis too should be on promoting the attainment of relevant qualifications, particularly on a part-time basis, which will help provide students with higher employment skills and opportunities. It is clear that the principle of social justice runs through the strategy adopted in Wales. Furthermore, such democratization demonstrates that 'higher education matters for all of us, whoever we are', as the education minister pointed out in a speech to the Bevan Foundation shortly after taking up his post. The challenge for academics within this climate is the delivery of high quality teaching and the provision of even greater support for students.

Fourthly, devolution has certainly given Wales a greater international profile. The relationship between Wales and Europe has grown closer since the successful application for Structural Funds, which have played an important role in stimulating some of the poorest parts of the Welsh economy. But closer relationships with our European partners, including their educational institutions, also offer distinct opportunities for Welsh universities, and for their students and academics to work closely and productively together. There is scope for the adoption of a truly transnational approach, and I welcome as an example of best practice the workshop established by the national university representations of Austria, Germany and Poland to exert influence on the future direction of EU cohesion policy. The financial aspects of these relationships are also undeniable, with the EU granting a budget of €80 billion to its research and innovation programme, Horizon 2020.

Research innovation

Some Welsh universities have enjoyed success in accessing the funding set aside by European institutions for the purposes of innovation or research, but Welsh-based universities have not seen the successes in research, consultancy and project collaborations that many HEIs in England have achieved. Thus partnership between HEIs, both within and outside Wales, is critical, and it is clear that more must be done to create strong and responsive links. We must be realistic about the challenges involved in accessing this funding, and perhaps concentrate on areas where Wales is, or can be, a world leader. Life sciences is such an example, where innovations emanating from Swansea University have led to commercialization and export. By focusing in this way on our areas of excellence, academics can champion Wales and raise its profile by means of their expertise, can benefit from wider scholarship opportunities, and may forge a clear platform by which future funding can be accessed. Many of these themes were picked out in the Welsh Government's strategy for engagement with the EU, published in May 2012 (Welsh Assembly Government 2012d), which recognized the importance of Europe to Welsh academia, and the importance of Welsh academics in shaping the role of Wales in Europe. Welsh universities are also developing fruitful relationships with countries outside of the EU, as for example, between Cardiff University and China.

Devolution has presented new challenges for academics. Furthermore, the very structures that devolution has introduced have also meant new styles of engagement which will impact on the way academics go about their business.

Inclusion, diversity and engagement

One of the fundamental principles that underpinned the National Assembly for Wales from the outset was for it to be diverse. The body that advised the Welsh Secretary on the internal law of the new Assembly strongly advocated the widest possible principles of inclusivity. The law that created the Assembly boldly stated that it 'shall make appropriate arrangements with a view to securing that its functions are exercised with due regard to the principle that there should be equality of opportunity for all people'. The Welsh Assembly has consistently been one of the most gender-balanced legislatures in the world, and in 2006, achieved the status of having over half its representatives as women.[4] This meant that politics in the Assembly looked different – but more importantly, these numbers have provided the critical mass that brings about substantive change. This includes (after Chaney 2006) the issues that are discussed, the priority they are accorded, and the way in which they are dealt with.

If our society is to be truly inclusive, we must make sure that it reflects these principles, and efforts have been taken nationally to address what can seem like an inbuilt gender *inequality*. For example, the gender balance enjoyed within the Assembly came about largely through political action (not universal!) in ensuring equal ratios of candidates by gender. Still other areas of society remain women-free zones however. Brooks and ap Gareth (2013) calculate that just 26 per cent of Welsh councillors are women; the Equality and Human Rights Commission (2012) has shown that just 4 per cent of the 'Top 50' Welsh companies and 10 per cent of Welsh Government public bodies are led by women chief executives, that whilst 72 per cent of local government employees in Wales are women, just 23 per cent of their chief executives are. This extends into the world of education too, where women make up around 43 per cent of academic staff in Welsh HEIs. However, this ratio has been slowly changing, and Wales now has its first female vice-chancellor and senior female academic managers. At other levels though, women are proportionately more likely to be employed part-time or on fixed-term contracts, with implications for income as well as for career progression and accessing full-time posts.[5]

The challenge for women is therefore all the greater in Wales. We know from academic and policy research (Fawcett Society 2012) that cuts in public sector spending, resulting from the global economic downturn, are disproportionately affecting women. This is partly because the public sector in Wales (as well as across the UK) employs more women than men. The Fawcett Society moreover suggests that twice as many women as men working in the public sector could lose their jobs, and that women's unemployment (at 2012) stands at the highest level for 25 years. Furthermore, alongside having to deal with changes to services and benefits which hit them hardest, women fortunate enough to retain their jobs could be confronted by a widening pay gap, due to pay cuts, with some women fearing the loss of a fifth of their salaries, as reported by Brown in *The Independent* in March 2012. Clearly, this recession must be tackled differently, and the HE sector must play its part.[6] A recent report, *A Woman's Place* (in the workplace in Wales) offers an up-to-date analysis of the current position (see www.chwaraeteg.com).

Another principle of devolution is that politicians and the decision-making process are brought closer to the people. This principle crosses from the abstract to the architectural, and thus underpinned the design of the new Assembly building, the 'Senedd', which opened in 2006. A better sense of closeness to voters has ensured that the Assembly also possesses close working relationships with stakeholders, including business, education, the trade unions and other facets of the Welsh public sector, and that policy-making is vastly different in character and process to the conventions established by the Westminster Parliament (Chaney *et al.* 2001).

HE contribution to Welsh policy-making

Academics have played an important role within the Welsh Assembly and the Welsh Government, through written policy papers, involvement in committees, consultations, providing responses, studies and evaluation data. The Assembly is keen to involve academic and policy experts, both in the scrutinizing of legislation, and in providing detailed research and information. I know that specialist advice has proved crucial to some of my committees' enquiries, and increasingly, academics and researchers have been recruited to provide expert advice to the Welsh Government across every portfolio. Of course, some academics have also made the transition to becoming politicians too, for example in Cardiff West, where the AM also holds a chair in social policy at Cardiff University. But wider opportunities also need to be created to bring politicians and academics together. An example of best practice here is the 'Working Lives' network, based at the University of Glamorgan in partnership with HEI staff at Cardiff and Newport – and much wider. The network aims to record the narratives of change that have affected the lives of academics in the twenty-first century. It also provides opportunities for politicians and academics to come together to discuss some of the issues arising from this research.

Concluding remarks

People are our biggest resource here in Wales, and that is especially true of our academic sector. There is a clear expectation of engagement by all partners, to craft a new style of relationship. The opportunities are exciting as well as challenging, as we must work out how to empower the Welsh people in an increasingly interdependent world. We need a strong, vital, connected HE sector, with academics and researchers playing a full part in all aspects of Welsh life and governance.

Acknowledgement

I would like to thank Robin Lewis for his research support in the writing of this chapter.

Notes

1   Micro or small businesses are those enterprises which employ less than 49 employees.
2   This has been outlined in successive Welsh Government policy documents. For example, see *Putting Wales First: A Partnership for the People of Wales* (2000), *The*

Learning Country (Welsh Assembly Government 2001), *Reaching Higher: Higher Education and the Learning Country* (2002) and *For Our Future: The 21st Century Higher Education Strategy and Plan for Wales* (2009).

3   For example, the EU 'Looking Behind the Metaphors' workshop, Brussels, November 2011 on 'Innovation and Research (Cohesion Policy)' linking science, research, regional development and business: http://www.eua.be/Libraries/Newsletter/Looking_behind_the_metaphors_29-11-2011.sflb.ashx, accessed 9 October 2012.

4   40 per cent of AMs elected in the 1999 election were women, as were 50 per cent in 2003, 46.7 per cent in 2007 and 40 per cent in 2011. The percentages changed to 52 per cent in 2006, as a woman was elected in a By-election to replace a man, and to 42 per cent a few months after the 2011 Assembly election, a woman replaced a disqualified man. See *Women's Representation in Scotland and Wales* (Electoral Reform Society/ Centre for Women and Democracy 2013: 6).

5   In 2009/10, 42 per cent of academic staff were women. See http://wales.gov.uk/topics/ statistics/headlines/post16education2012/120322/?lang=en.

6   It could be argued that the recession has led to greater levels of entrepreneurship, amongst women in particular. See Jonathan Levie and Mark Hart *Global Enterpreneurship Monitor: United Kingdom 2011 Monitoring Report* (2012). See also www.chwaraeteg.com for the *A Woman's Place* report (April 2013).

8

'Human Resource Management' Implications of Working Lives Research

Caryn Cook and Lyn Daunton

Introduction

This chapter sets out to develop and explore some of the implications posed by the Working Lives (WL) findings in the context of wider studies and from the perspective of human resource management (HRM). According to Doherty and Manfredi (2006, 2010), there has been a climate that supports what they call a 'stubborn persistence of a long hours culture' amongst managers and professionals. In the UK, working intensively tends to be translated as the kind of 'commitment' to a job that is thought to be required for career progression. WL members have written about this and the notion of the 'hyperprofessional' in academic life (Gornall and Salisbury 2012; Acker and Webber this volume). The question of whether this leads to academics failing to speak up about the tensions that exist between their 'home' and 'work' lives is part of the exploration in this chapter.

Given the above, we consider the extent to which institutional human resource (HR) departments and managers and the leadership within higher education (HE) have a duty of care towards academic staff. The notion of the 'psychological contract' (Peirce *et al.* 2012; Coyle-Shapiro 2010; Argyris 1960) in the employment relationship is relevant here, in particular, a notion of there being a fair exchange on both sides – 'reciprocity'. In an academic environment, a psychological contract involves a set of expectations by employees in relation to the promises or expectations that are *not* formally written into any letter of offer or contract for official employment. They may be part of occupational or professional cultural norms, which in academic work, can include a collegial environment, informal mentorship, teaching load, support, office and working space, laboratory equipment and time to develop and grow as a researcher (Peirce *et al.* 2012) – as well as expectations of a certain degree of autonomy or self-organized work without supervision.

The 'value' of their side of the contract for lecturers, senior lecturers and professors, may be about recognition received and influence held internationally, peer assessment, and in teaching and research support with students. To the institution and employer, this value may depend very much on an academic's potential to contribute to the achievement of the university or educational establishments in the attainment of *organizational* goals, for example, wider recognition, relative positioning and potential to attract (or receive) funding (Hope-Hailey *et al.* 2005; Guest *et al.* 2003). A good deal of research on human capital and its attributes, its relationship to and impact on organizational results, is available, and this has been linked to what has been termed a 'resource based' view of employed staff (Pennings *et al.* 1998; Pfeffer 1998; Finkelstein and Hambrick 1996; Huselid 1995; Wright *et al.* 1995; Barney 1991). However, for many academics, their tradition has been that they work in HE and represent this discipline and research as much as, and perhaps before, their institution (Kogan and Hanney 2000).

For employers, 'effective' management of the HR generates a capacity to attract and hold employees who are qualified and motivated, with the benefits of having research-active, positive and conscientious academics bringing further organizational goods in a 'virtuous circle'. There are some sceptical commentaries too, however (Guest 2011; Waring this volume). For some, 'modernization' in the HE sector means that 'HRM' within institutions will be both essential and will ensure the well-being of all (Chu and Kuo 2012). But in the process, many academics have become disassociated from this paradigm. That is, they feel little 'ownership' of, and perhaps even resentful towards, the notion of being 'resources' for the institution (Duke 2002), included within a 'resource based view' of the organization (Guest *et al.* 2003; Wright *et al.* 1995). So too, their status may not be fully recognized as being the 'unique selling point' of the institution, and why a student might choose to come to study there (Wright *et al.* 2003; see also Richards on science staff this volume).

Academics, as reported in the HE literature and articulated in the WL research studies, clearly do value the freedom to work from various locations, whether home or campus office, and indeed some individuals in our studies indicated that they have come into the profession in order to have that autonomy (Cook and Gornall 2010; Gornall *et al.* 2008). However, there are organizational implications of these working practices that invite consideration here, including that of responsibility for line management in managing this. There is a fine line between such discussions and 'managerialism' (Deem *et al.* 2007; Deem and Brehony 2005), including concerns about control, disciplinary or negative perspectives, and using relationships around 'audit' to inform everyday practice. With relatively few empirical studies exploring the links between HRM practice, employee well-being and performance relationships within the university (Baptiste 2007), what we find on the ground is that there are contradictions experienced between notions of academic autonomy in particular, and perceptions of organizational control. Moreover, the effects of the pressures (and constraints) on staff to account for themselves, their activity and production on a daily basis – in 'units' or 'bundles' of time, logging whereabouts and being forever 'contactable' (i.e. interruptible and re-prioritized) – makes it worth asking the question of how far this is conducive to good practice within academic or professional life more widely.

Aspects of academic HRM in HE

Increasing policy interventions and targets have altered the ways in which academics work (Musselin 2012; Gornall and Thomas this section). Managers too, now need to constantly justify their actions and decisions, described by Holmes and McElwee (1995) as part of a 'functionalist' approach to human resource management and performance appraisal' (Condrey *et al.* 2011). There has been an element of reflecting back on the time when an academic was free to teach and study their academic subjects without interference from political or external influences, having a share in university decision-making and more amenable terms and conditions of employment (Farnham 1999). Moreover, discussions of 'new professionals' and employment changes in the sector (Mears and Harrison, Part V), indicate that favour has shifted towards what were once considered 'peripheral' groups in HE, and a 'shift' of power within universities themselves (Henkel 2000; Gornall 1999). Such movements, Kogan and Hanney (2000: 54) argue, 'have left academic groups at the base of the system . . . more prone to institutional interventions, because they have implied a weakening of the power of their disciplines, whose expertise provided protection from non-academic influence [in the past]'.

Even the Economic and Social Research Council (ESRC 2006) agrees that universities are increasingly being run like businesses, and as such, must strive to be *financially* successful. This is a major area affecting academic motivation, as well as commitment, job satisfaction and perhaps effectiveness too. It can lead to 'role strain', as new demands are added to 'definition(s)' of academic work and responsibilities. To be a successful business requires not only the business to be in a healthy state, but also its employees (MacDonald 2005), and given what is at stake in the societal and economic role of HE – the numbers of staff employed, qualifications issues, research contracts, and its considerable turnover (Gornall and Thomas this section) – these are arguably essential areas for investigation.

'Strategic' approaches to employee well-being, especially in reconciling personal and work-life 'balance', have attracted increasing interest in the last few years (Paton 2009; Tehrani *et al.* 2007; Waddell and Burton 2006; Kersley *et al.* 2006; MacDonald 2005; Peccei 2004; Warr 2002), and which have promoted various 'family friendly' or 'work-life balance' initiatives looking at employee well-being at work. However, many academics are cynical about these, and of a sustainable 'work-life balance' ever being achieved within HE institutions, with talk of 'hollow laughter in the corridors' when communications are received about university commitment to this. Doherty and Manfredi (2006: 51) report one informant who commented, '. . . the nature of this post is such that you are expected to work such hours as are reasonably necessary in order to fulfil your duties and responsibilities'.

Moreover, one of our findings (Gornall and Salisbury 2012) was that academics tend to overwork when left to self-organize. Another aspect to consider, offered by Nadeem and Hendry (2003), concerns the role that power dynamics play between an employee and employer. In this context, environmental and organizational characteristics influence work-life balance, which is most likely to be achieved where there is a good fit between the intense labour market pull for flexibilization together with the desire of a large proportion of employees for flexible working, and it is clear from our research that the desire is there. Of course, norms of professional autonomy and calls for 'greater flexibility' in employment are not the same thing, and indeed may be in conflict. However, Doherty and Manfredi (2006, 2010) have explored the challenges in finding 'work-life balance' for academics specifically, and they contend that it is the two different *discourses* about the academic role that have underpinned many of these arguments to date. Ylijoki *et al.* (this volume) discuss similar issues in Finland.

In Table 8.1, these two discourses imply paradigmatic differences. They are presented here as a distinction between a 'Plato's Academy' type of working, more associated, it has to be said, with the 'elite' universities, and that of the 'teaching factory', which many will associate with the 'post-1992' university sector. A fundamental difference between the two is of the relationship that academics have to managing their working time. In the Plato's Academy model, an academic has the freedom to organize his or her own time (Himanen 2001) and the boundaries between work and leisure are not always clear. That is, the pursuit of knowledge through research is often also a source of leisure (and enjoyment) for an academic, something we discuss in the Introductory chapter to this volume. However, the 'teaching factory' model illustrates arguably an opposite perspective, that of working in a 'demand-driven', management-led 'teaching as service' economy, where academics are employees before they are professionals. In this mix, of course, are also the elements of choice and preferences exercised by individuals, as well as the more nuanced nature of differing institutions, their traditions and cultures.

Table 8.1   Discourses about the role of academics

Plato's Academy	The teaching factory
Unhappy with rules – values autonomy and flexibility	Prefers formalization: rules about 'quid pro quo', limits to certain kinds of work, clear and transparent workload planning system, formal schemes for compressed hours, home working, etc.
Does not place clear boundaries between 'work' and 'home'. The issue is more about balance within work (i.e. more time to research)	Seeks more protection of 'home' time
Collegiate	Managerial
Conceptualizes the academic as an 'intellectual'	Conceptualizes the academic as an 'employee'
Associated more with being highly research active	Associated more with teaching and scholarship

Source: Doherty and Manfredi (2006).

Official and non-official flexible working practices for academics

Technological advances have made it much easier and perhaps more convenient to work flexibly – from home, or on a train, at a roadside café – and *when*ever as well as *where*ver it is convenient. This is arguably a move towards improving temporal flexibility *depending on the total hours of work*, and it may attract those who do not seek rigid work/life boundaries (Ylijoki 2013 and this volume) (although flexibility can also assist with improving work-life balance (Harris 2003)). With this comes the question raised in 'HR and autonomy' discussions, of trust. There is an importance here of there being an 'implicit' part of the psychological contract that reflects understandings on all sides about 'trust', and this has been well-recognized within the literature (Wellin 2007; Cullinane and Dundon 2006; Watson 1987; Schein 1978; Fox 1974). Some commentators have argued that there has been a '. . . decline in trust and discretion placed in academics [as a group]' (Deem *et al.* 2007), and this resonates with some of the data from the WL informants. Many spoke of higher workloads and longer hours, with financial criteria used as a basis for decision-making (Kelly and Boden this section), remote senior management teams and increasing pressure for 'accountability' in many areas of the role. While these data may imply some inconsistencies when considering the occupational 'norms' associated particularly with 'Plato's Academy' organizations, that is, in the 'old' university sector, where traditions of autonomy have been strong, there is also the matter of the changing focus of the 'teaching factory' type of organization, in their drive to become more research-active, and the issues this poses for these academics and their work. Deem *et al.* (2007: 5) refer to widely-held perceptions that 'collegiality' in HE is being replaced by more overt line-management, where 'audit cultures' are claimed to have encouraged 'deprofessionalization' or 'proletarianization' of the academic professional.

New organizational and 'HR' approaches such as performance review, role analysis/ profiling, appraisal and encouragement of self-monitoring have been put into place to support strategic and cultural change, irrespective of their impact on staff morale. Meanwhile, academic working hours continue to be high. Tight's (2010) research on academic workloads, reported also in the *Times Higher*, showed that academic and research staff still worked around 51 hours a week. In a White Paper on the quality of working life in UK universities (Bradshaw 2008), which was informed by a multiple regression analysis to evaluate which aspects of work were most likely to lead to stress and to threaten staff well-being, the results indicated that some of the 'strongest' predictors of work-related stress were work overload, poor work-life balance, longer hours worked in a typical week, and lack of and dissatisfaction with home/work balance. This was a study of all staff in HE, but academics as a group have been used to managing a complex and demanding workload and working a non-typical daily, weekly and even yearly pattern. Thus, how professional work becomes 'overwork' in this context, and the conditions around it that lead to dysfunction, need to be examined carefully. Moreover, the needs and desires of academics as professionals and employees may differ from those of other groups in the sector or the HE workforce as a whole.

The resource-based view

A resource-based approach, as explored by Wright *et al.* (2003) and Lepak and Snell (1999), could be consistent in a sector where academics, as a 'critical resource', should be able to exert positive pressure on and over their own working conditions. If as argued by Doherty and Manfredi (2006), they are of considerable 'strategic value' to universities in contributing the most in terms of competitive advantage for the individual institution (and sector), they should be able to lever bargaining power. In practice, there seems to be little inclination by academics to exert what Nadeem and Hendry (2003) call the 'ultimate power' of voting with their feet, and therefore there is less labour market pressure to meet the 'needs' of academic staff. Furthermore, whilst drawn from a national or even international labour pool, there tends to be low turnover in academic staffing, by comparison with other professions (Doherty and Manfredi 2006), which may account for there being little evidence to suggest that universities have made efforts to tackle the academic workload issue. Moreover, notions of 'sustainable working' do not yet appear to form part of the 'tablestakes' of academic employment negotiations.

In HE, as WL interviewees stated, there is always more work you could be doing – a lecture to write or a paper to research. However, UCEA, which represents HE employers (reported by Newman 2009), claims that academic staff enjoy a shorter working week, more annual leave and better parental benefits, with better pensions and sickness arrangements, than other workers either in HE or the public and private sectors more widely. However, AUT, which represents lecturers' interests (now part of UCU), contended from its own research some time ago, that there were significant issues for 'work-life balance' (Curtis and Crace 2004) in the sector around academics' work, with around a quarter of academics' working life conducted at home, while at that time, boundaries between home and work in the life of the academic were 'wafer-thin'. This was even more so if, like the 20 per cent of those that were included within this survey, respondents lived with another academic.

Concluding remarks

Ten years ago, the data referred to above (Curtis and Crace 2004) suggested that some academics were checking their emails around five times a day; today this could be so many times an hour. When we consider the increase in technological access, to email, intranet, documents and information, then this clearly suggests that the days are gone when you could leave the office and be uncontactable until the next day. But perhaps academics rarely worked in such routines anyway. Choices and options within the control of the individual academic, of whether to work late at home or work, to be more productive with a day working at a 'home office' as opposed to campus, and so on, have been valued by the profession. This does leave the role of management as an open question, and academics have to accept that there is still a 'your long holidays view' (Cooper 2004) and 'playing with your research' perception by others in 'public' perceptions of their work.

Notwithstanding this, various cases have been tested, and the Court of Appeal and the House of Lords have clarified the legal position of employers. All employers owe a legal duty of care to their employees, but it is not clearly stated that injury to mental health is to be treated in the same way as injury to physical health (Gennard and Judge 2005). It is thus suggested that employers need to take some step towards avoidance of similar claims of injury. This is particularly so when it is considered that a major review for the Health and Safety Executive (HSE) some 10 years ago documented some of the damaging relationships between long working hours and health (White and Beswick 2003).

The way forward may be a better understanding of the drivers and conditions of actual academic working, and of their productivity, and we have tried to uncover and explore this in the introductory chapter. We know that academics may be prone to overwork in some situations, and indeed, that the suppression of the traditional flexibility they have exercised may be leading to further intensification (Gornall *et al.* this volume). The introduction of managerialism and its practices which are more common within parts of the private sector, has allowed management bodies to override academics' professional judgements and skills, in favour of keeping discipline under tight control (Deem 2001). While institutions and employers have been driven by efficiency, external accountability, monitoring and standards-imposition, they may yet need to give greater consideration to the delicate balance between managing flexibly and flexi*bility*, the use of discretion and trust, of supporting academic freedom, in order to retain, nourish and stimulate academic productivity.

Note

Based on a paper first delivered to the third WL conference, University of Newport, November 2010.

9

Narratives of Academics Who Become Department Heads

Alan Floyd

Introduction

In an era of rapid change in the UK higher education (HE) sector, caused by amongst other factors, the effects of globalization, the implementation of the Browne Report recommendations on HE funding and student finance (Browne 2010), and a sustained period of economic uncertainty that has led to severe government funding cuts, it is clear that the role of the academic head of department (HoD) is increasingly important in the leadership and management of universities (Floyd and Dimmock 2011; Bryman 2009). With undergraduate student fees in the UK set to reach a maximum of £9,000 in 2012/13, issues relating to contact hours, teaching standards and tutorial support have all come under greater scrutiny than in previous years. Prospective students and their parents now ask more questions, and it is to the HoD that institutions look, in ensuring the quality of the student experience in their subject areas. While the leadership and management of teaching quality is becoming progressively more important for the HoD, departmental research issues continue to be no less fundamental with the escalating significance assigned to the outcomes of the Research Excellence Framework (REF) and ever-increasing competition for external research grants. Simultaneously, the administrative and people management tasks linked to the HoD role are also becoming more difficult (Deem 2000; Smith 2002, 2005).

Why, then, do academics become HoDs? How do they experience being in the role? And how does being in the role contribute to their future career plans? Previous research by the author in a modern '*post*-1992' UK university, suggests that academics who become HoDs need the capacity to assume a range of identities, and that tensions and conflicts will arise as they try to maintain their teaching and research profile while undertaking an increasing amount of managerial and leadership tasks (Floyd 2012b; Floyd and Dimmock 2011). The research explored here examined whether these identity tensions and conflicts were also experienced in the *pre*-1992 sector. The chapter is organized into four sections. First, the theoretical framework that underpins the research is discussed. Secondly, the data collection methods used are described. Next, three narratives of academic HoDs are offered, under headings that reflect the study's 'life history' approach (Goodson and Sikes 2001), namely, 'Becoming an HoD', 'Being an HoD' and 'Looking to the future'. Finally, in order to connect these localized narratives to broader social and cultural narratives, key issues and questions that arise from this research are discussed taking into account, comparatively, the earlier post-1992 'new university' data.

Theoretical framework

Underlying this inquiry is the sociological perspective that a person has multiple identities, and that these are constantly being formed, re-formed and changed by socialization experiences at home and at work (Burke and Stets 2009; Giddens 1991). Thus, as an individual moves through the life course, they will adopt and experience a range of identities, all of which are influenced by the social situations they find themselves in (Jenkins 2008). Accordingly, I draw on theorists who contend that these identities are formed and developed through a living narrative, constantly being re-told and re-shaped by broader social and cultural narratives. Smith and Sparkes (2008: 17) argue that such researchers,

> ... turn their analytical lens on the socially situated production of identity. In doing so, they further explore the ways a person's past and habits shape self-narration, and the broader and more local cultural narrative resources ... which people draw on, use, resist and have imposed on them in the construction of personal selves, identities and biography.

Adopting this perspective allows new and fine-grained insights into the identity conflicts and socialization experiences that academics may encounter when becoming and being HoDs.

Methods

Based on the research question, *What are the career trajectories of academics who become HoDs in a UK University?* and in line with the theoretical framework described above, I used a life history approach (Goodson and Sikes 2001) and undertook semi-structured life history interviews with 11 academic HoDs from a range of disciplines, all in a research-led ('chartered') pre-1992 university (hereafter called OldU). Critics of the life history approach argue that these data are too subjective, difficult to validate and not generalizable (Bryman 2008). However, the basis of these methodological arguments is antithetical to the underlying assumptions of interpretative research as a whole (Lichtman 2010). In contrast, *proponents* of the approach, while appreciating it has its limitations, assert that it can offer unique and powerful in-depth insights into complex social situations (Floyd 2012a; Punch 2009).

At OldU, the role of HoD is rotated after a period of three or four years. Individuals who take on the role are paid a small annual fee, but the post does not attract a formal promotion. Department heads are normally expected to undertake teaching and research duties alongside their administrative tasks, but they are typically given a reduced teaching timetable to compensate for the increased workload.

Following ethical approval, individuals were identified through OldU's website and then contacted via email. Interviews were undertaken in the participant's office with the conversations being recorded, transcribed and sent back to each interviewee for validation. These data were supplemented with a number of other sources, including the analysis of key strategic documents produced by OldU, and web-based profiles of each of the informants.

In line with a range of authors who argue for the importance of the individual's narrated story in life history research (see, for example, Clandinin and Connelly 2000; Josselson and Lieblich 1993), I analysed these data by crafting profiles of each participant, following sequential guidelines put forward by Seidman (2006). First, all the passages from each participant's transcript that were seen as important in relation to the key research questions were selected and put into one document. A narrative was then created from this, expressed in the words of the participant and in the first person. To allow the profiles to read more freely, hesitation and repetition were eliminated and words were changed, removed or added, to maintain the sense of what was being said. Each profile was then re-read and edited a number of times until one remained that best reflected the respondent's narrative of their career trajectory as told to me at interview.

Voices from the middle

The three narratives presented here have been carefully selected to demonstrate some of the perceived tensions and conflicts that academics experience when they become HoDs at OldU. They include one female and two male HoDs, reflecting the fact that there were more male than female HoDs at the institution. Three key stages of the process have been identified for consideration: 'Becoming an HoD', 'Being a HoD' and 'Looking to the future'. At the start of each narrative, I give a short background of each of the chosen participants, to help locate their stories within the context of their overall career trajectories. For reasons of anonymity, each participant has been given a pseudonym and their specific subject area has not been identified.

Becoming an HoD

Neil is 55 and married. He is a professor and a department head in the arts and humanities field. He went to a grammar school and completed his undergraduate degree and PhD at two different research-led universities. Subsequently, he gained his first lectureship at another research-led university, where he remained for 14 years. He then moved to another institution as a Reader and was subsequently promoted to Professor. He joined OldU as a professor in 2007:

> Actually, I've never been a very ambitious person. Though, on the other hand, I think that as you get older, you tell yourself that you are not a very ambitious person, but

you get a bit hacked off when you see other people doing well and you're not. My willingness to undertake leadership roles has become more prominent later in life. I don't think I've had a spectacularly fast ascent up the ladder, as you can tell by being head of department in my late fifties rather than late thirties. And other people tend to take on this job a bit younger, don't they?

So, I was appointed here in 2007. I was asked at interview whether I would be willing to take on a major administrative responsibility and they said at the time of the interview that nothing would hang on my answer. Though, looking back, I know that wasn't true. I said that I was, and part of the reason I said that I was (it kind of sounds a bit pretentious really) I said at the interview that I thought I'd got through most of my career to date without taking on those big responsibilities and it's probably only fair that I should at that point. So, I was half expecting to be asked to take on the job. The previous HoD retired after I'd been in the post for a year and the head of school asked me if I was willing to do it. There wasn't an interview. It was straightforward . . . because it was a 'head of department' it seemed more like a kind of burden that nobody else wanted to take on; because there aren't many perks apart from having a rather splendid office. So I think they were just basically keen to find someone who was willing to do it, really.

Neil's narrative reflects the sense of duty that he felt to take on the role of department head, born not only from institutional loyalty, but loyalty to the profession as a whole. He also feels that he has taken on the role to shoulder the 'burden that nobody else wanted to do'. The implications of Neil's narrative will be discussed later in this chapter.

Being an HoD

Richard is 59 and married with grown up children. He is a professor and a department head in the social sciences. He attended a grammar school but did not gain the A level qualifications required to go to university and so went to college, gained a HND and began a successful career in the commercial world. At 32, he decided to go back to university to undertake a masters degree, and from there he went back into business for several years. He thus had a very different profile from Neil, and indeed from what might be regarded as a 'typical' HoD. He subsequently took up a teaching Fellowship post at a teaching-led institution and began his PhD, which he completed aged 49. After being promoted to a Senior Lecturer at the same institution, he joined OldU in 2007 as a Professor:

I think that the real issue is budgetary management and we don't have the level of professional support that we need, frankly. I've said for years, 'How can you run a multi-million pound business without having a director of finance?' Any commercial organization would have somebody whose job it is to manage those numbers and we don't . . . So, somehow or other, academic managers have to develop that capability.

Another difficult part of any management role is the people. It's always the people. With the academic world, what one has are 'prima donnas' in some cases. You've got world class experts; you've got genuinely world class experts in their subject area and with that comes a bit of an ego and a point-of-view and of course, academic freedom. And people regularly tell me about their academic freedom. But I sometimes have to remind them about their academic responsibilities too! So managing academics is extremely difficult because you can't tell anybody to do anything. You have to work by engendering their willing cooperation, which in some cases is actively, maliciously withheld.

But it's a very demanding role: a normal day for me is a twelve-hour day. Then there's lots of weekend and evening work as well. And what I have found is that my ability to write and publish has just disappeared. It's very, very difficult to do now. I've had papers published, but they were ones that had been in preparation before I took on the role. I'm still working with a former doctoral student and we're working on a conference paper and we've just submitted an article as well. And I've got a doctoral student who will be finishing this year, so there will be some publications coming from them, but finding the time to publish is impossible. I was speaking to my Dean about this and I said, 'Well, I've accepted that it's just not possible to do that.' So I've accepted that my ability to publish is severely impacted, that I am in fact an academic manager. So that is what I am.

Richard's narrative identifies some of the key difficulties that individuals face when taking on the role of department head. His profile also reflects someone who is going through, or has already gone through, an identity crisis in transforming from an academic to what he calls an 'academic manager'. From the tone of his voice and his body language during the interview, Richard appears to have accepted his 'fate' and begrudgingly assumed his new managerial identity.

Looking to the future

The final interviewee is Serena, who is 46 and married with school-aged children. Not originally from the UK, she moved to Britain with her family in 1981 and attended a state girls' school to complete her A levels. Then she went to a research-led university where she gained her undergraduate degree and her PhD. Following a post-doctoral appointment at the same university, she gained her first Lectureship at another research-led university in the UK. She held the latter post for six years before joining OldU in 1998:

Not being able to research and publish is one of the reasons that I have decided enough is enough and that I am stepping down. I guess I was quite lucky because I had a pipeline of work, so I've had publications come through, but most of them were done way before I became head of department. But I know that I'm now at a point in my research where I need to think ahead, I can no longer rely on work that's already been done. Given the workload, I manage to keep papers going, but not ideas going. And I think that's a massive difference. Within the faculty, we work on a half teaching load for a department head which helps a lot, but it doesn't in reality because the things that a head of department does occupy brain space. It's not that physically you're working all the time, but you get emails from people: there are colleagues who are irritated, there are students who are irritated and you are constantly trying to sort it out. So it's constantly going in your head, and I think that's what takes away the space. So I've managed to keep a trickle. I'm OK for the REF, but I would never be OK for the next if I carried on with this job.

It's not that I would never want to do a job like this again, but certainly I need a few years of research-oriented work to get my research back into gear before I would take on a similar role. In terms of my future, I'm just desperately hoping that my brain will unwind enough for me to think up a new idea. And I'd like to spend the next year opening doors rather than tying up loose ends . . . just spend it thinking broadly and opening my mind to what's happening, and get onto a research path that will take me another ten years, which will be close to retirement.

Serena's profile reflects someone who has become disillusioned with the workload associated with the role and the fact that being a department head does not allow her to maintain her 'true' academic identity through publications and having the space and time to think 'a new thought'.

Discussion

What can be learned from the vignettes presented here? Neil's story of becoming an HoD highlights some of the problems being faced by universities in ensuring that departments are being led by the best people. His journey to the role of department head reflects what Deem (2000) has termed the 'good citizen route' into HE management and refers to individuals who feel that they are repaying a perceived debt to an institution or the academy as a whole, rather than thinking that they are necessarily the best person for the job. It is clear that Neil felt that he wanted to give something back to the academic community by taking on the role of department head, even though he did not think it was a role that he was particularly suited to or that he would benefit from. Indeed, he described the key benefits of the role in materialistic terms – *having a rather splendid office* – rather than in terms of academic or career development. He also believed that no one else wanted to take on the role: *it seemed more like a kind of burden that nobody else wanted to take on.* These experiences were also mirrored in a number of the department heads' narratives in the 'newer' post-1992 university (Floyd 2012b). If Neil's story is indicative of experiences across the university sector, it suggests the need for a more strategic approach to leadership development in HE, particularly as in this uncertain future, nurturing academic leadership is set to become even more crucial for the ongoing success of our institutions (Inman 2009; Bolden *et al.* 2008).

Richard's story identifies some of the key difficulties that department heads may face when in the role – managing budgets, people, and an ever-increasing workload. His narrative also demonstrates some of the key tensions academics can face when they take on managerial roles while continuing their role and identity as an academic. Richard appears to be resigned to this change in his professional status: *So I've accepted that my ability to publish is severely impacted, that I am in fact an academic manager.* As Richard had already experienced a career in business before moving into HE, his trajectory – and thus his professional identity formation and change – has not followed what may be termed a 'traditional' academic path.

Serena's story, by contrast, reflects someone who has followed a more 'traditional' academic route and who is desperately trying to hold on to their core academic identity. If Serena stays in the role of HoD, she feels she will not be able to engage properly with key academic tasks for herself, particularly in a culture of increasing accountability and auditing, and that consequently she will suffer a potential loss of external academic career capital (Floyd and Dimmock 2011). Similar tensions were also found for department heads in the post-1992 'new' university. As Serena says: *I'm OK for the REF, but I would never be OK for the next if I carried on with this job.*

For some writers, an increased atmosphere of 'managerialism' across the HE sector in recent years has exacerbated these conflicts and produced an identity schism between the 'academic managers' and the 'managed academics', with both groups adhering to opposing values (Winter 2009). The assertion is that, in an increasing environment of audit and accountability, academic managers are perceived as 'different' to academics in terms of value frameworks and, thus, their professional identities. Indeed, recent research in the UK suggests that academics look for leadership in relation to shared core values and identities, such as autonomy and self-direction, rather than in relation to managerial processes and behaviours (Bolden *et al.* 2012). To begin to counteract some of these tensions, the researchers suggest the following approach: 'When encouraging and supporting people to take on a more substantial academic leadership role, attempts should be made to appeal to their sense of academic values and citizenship rather than simply transactional managerial roles and responsibilities' (Bolden *et al.* 2012: 72).

The question of whether it is becoming too difficult for academics who take on leadership roles to continue to maintain their academic identity and research profile is a pressing and important one for researchers and policy-makers, both in the pre- and post-1992 sectors. In the face of fundamental changes to the way institutions are funded following the Browne Report (Browne 2010), coupled with the external pressures of the REF, two different career routes appear to be emerging in the HE sector – one in leadership and management and one in research and teaching. If this is the case, could such a model lead to the development of an 'us' and 'them' culture within the profession, potentially dividing institutions which were once perceived as collegial in nature? Furthermore, how does this notion relate to Goodall's (2009) hypothesis that experts make the best leaders and that universities should be led by top scholars rather than by generic managers? Any future research needs to explore these issues across a wider range of institutions and with different HoD postholder profiles – age, gender, background and subject specialism – to see whether emergent factors from this study, and the previous post-1992 study, are indicative of experiences more widely.

Concluding remarks

The three short narratives presented here provide the reader with some fine-grained insights into a number of the tensions and conflicts that academics experience when they become HoDs. They raise a range of issues that need further exploration, for example, whether gender affects the role and experiences of the department head, and what role the professoriate will have in the future leadership and management of our universities (Rayner *et al.* 2010), compared with the role of the HoD *per se*. Two key questions stand out from this study for academic managers, researchers and policy-makers to consider in the future: how are academics best prepared for the role of HoD and further leadership roles in HE; and crucially, how can we ensure that taking on the role is not perceived as detrimental to an academic's own future career?

Note

Based on material presented as part of the *Working Lives* symposium at the CeTL Conference, University of Oxford, April 2011.

10

How Management Accounting Shapes Academic Lives

Rod Kelly and Rebecca Boden

Introduction

Academic working lives have always been constituted in part through the complex social networks in which scholars participate. Historically, these networks enjoyed a significant degree of autonomy from surrounding society, although it is important to recognize that they were frequently inherently hierarchical and sites of the exercise of power (Boden and Epstein 2011). In recent years in the UK, there has been a significant departure from this model in two key dimensions which have engendered a reconstitution of academics' working lives.

The first dimension of change is that, during the past three decades, UK universities have been increasingly 'steered at a distance' by the state, towards greater commercialization and marketization (Tuchman 2009; Wright and Ørberg 2008). The steering mechanisms are provided, *inter alia*, by government regulation and universities' significant dependence on direct and indirect public funding. Consequently, the technology of accounting has been significant in the state's exercise of control over the direction and pace of change in higher education (HE). The result, it has been argued, is an accelerating 'neoliberalization' of the sector (Deem *et al.* 2007; Boden and Epstein 2006).

The impact of these exogenous imperatives on universities as organizations has been well-documented (McGettigan 2011). The second dimension of change, which has been less well explored but which is highly pertinent to the theme of this book, is the translation of these external pressures to the internal hierarchies and power dynamics within universities (Nedeva and Boden 2006). In this chapter, therefore, we focus specifically on how the internal anatomy of the modern university shapes and constitutes the working lives of academics, with particular reference to the role of accounting.

Accounting, like all technologies, is both socially constructed and socially constructing – a product of the social relations and practices which it simultaneously shapes. Accounting is also a favoured technology of managers, government and markets – the same actors who now hold sway inside universities (Boden and Epstein 2006).

In the UK, accounting acts as an important mediator in the relations between universities and external actors; it is the language of accountability, control and competition over and between increasingly marketized and commercialized organizations. And accounting has been deployed *within* universities too, but here the focus is on management accounting: essentially the costing and pricing of production processes and the standardization of products and their quality to facilitate management decision-making.

In universities, the academic processes subjected to management accounting's gaze are knowledge production and dissemination through research and teaching. Authors such as Braverman (1998 [1974]) assert that at the heart of the modern capitalist enterprise (and here we include universities) lies a 'Taylorized' (Taylor 1998 [1911]) management regime designed to organize labour towards profit-maximizing objectives. Taylor's system of 'scientific management' was one based very much on what we would recognize today as management accounting. Such regimes have an inescapable impact on workers' lives, controlling and directing their work (Uddin and Hopper 2001).

This chapter utilizes anonymized[1] data from a real-life example of the particular use of a 'costing and pricing' technology – in this case a university form – to examine the impact it had on a decision whether or not to accept external funds to do some research (Atkinson and Coffey 1997). This fine-grained data, in the spirit of Sparkes (2007), reveals that the senior managers who were producing and using these inscribed (and therefore 'legitimate') accounting figures did not understand them at a technical level. They therefore applied the technology technically incorrectly, and were impervious to corrective representations from the academic worker involved. The form became the site of struggle between the academic and university managers.

The actions of managers in this story are not particularly unusual: anecdotally, we know that such events are frequently played out across UK universities. The level of resistance by the academic in this instance is somewhat more unusual and, as such, offers a documented insight into the lived experiences of academics' working lives that might otherwise be unavailable. This case therefore illustrates how accounting technologies can be used to reconstitute the working lives of academics, commodifying their work and representing the individual as 'loss-making' and, therefore, of limited organizational value within marketized and commercialized universities. Within the academy, the exercise of such power over academics' working lives can have grave consequences for academic identities and freedom and, thereby, the nature of knowledge produced (Boden and Epstein 2011).

Jem's form

Professor Jem Collier was employed at the university to undertake research and teaching/supervisory duties. His post was publicly funded. He is an energetic self-directed individual, passionately pursuing a wide range of research topics, one of which was the increasing levels of managerialism in universities. Collier found a third-party organization which did not usually fund research but which shared his interests. It offered to contribute towards the costs of the research after Collier had sent it a project outline of what he was doing. It was a prestigious project which promised to deliver 'impact' for the 2014 Research Excellence Framework (REF).[2] Jem and his institution were trying hard in this highly competitive environment.

Collier contacted his university's research contracts office (RCO) as soon as he heard the good news and sent them a copy of the project proposal that detailed the work to be done. He understood that, although it was 'his' work, the funder and the university would require a formal legal contract that would enable the transfer of the money in return for an undertaking on the university's part that Collier would do the work. This contractualization of Collier's work had at least two important effects. First, it made the university a formal party to his work, one with a legitimate interest in it as his employer. Second, the centrality of a formal contracting process, and the primacy within that of the notion of the exchange of cash for work done, changed Collier's intellectual endeavours into a commodity.

The budget that Collier prepared for the funder looked something like Table 10.1.

Table 10.1   Jem Collier's simple budget

Item	£
Travel expenses for fieldwork	3,500
Contribution to salary	9,500
Total grant	13,000

The research contracts office was responsible for legal and financial matters connected with research contracts and, for all projects, calculated their 'full economic cost' (fEC). This regime has its origins in 1998, when the UK universities persuaded government that they were receiving insufficient research funds. Government agreed to provide extra funding, but only in return for greater 'transparency' on how the money was actually spent. To do this, the universities immediately established a Joint Costing and Pricing Steering Group (JCPSG) to develop and deploy a scheme called the Transparent Approach to Costing (TRAC). The JCPG was substantially assisted by a private sector consultancy, JM Consulting Ltd, during the project. Universities now have to produce an annual Transparency Review return to the funding councils,[3] disclosing the full economic cost of all publicly and non-publicly funded research and teaching, and all other activities (see JCPSG website). So, the calculation of Jem's project's fEC had to be done to satisfy the external authorities that steer universities, and is meant to demonstrate where the money has been spent.

The RCO calculated the fEC of Collier's project by inscribing the details of his work (which he had provided in his proposal) onto a costing and pricing form. This worked as an Excel spreadsheet, automatically generating calculations. The form was used to record three items described as 'costs'. The first item recorded was the total marginal costs of Collier's project – the costs additionally incurred purely as a result of doing the research, such as air fares and hotels for his fieldwork. The 'costing and pricing' form was then used to record the costs of the time that Collier would spend on the project. Collier thought of this as 'his' time but the university saw it as belonging to the organization, because it paid him for it (even though it was, in effect, passing on money from government, which funded his post). The university included all of the proposed days on the project at Collier's usual salary rate, plus other employment costs such as pension contributions. The marginal costs and the costs of Collier's time were, together, described as 'direct costs'. The third item was called 'contribution to overheads'. This was calculated automatically by the form, which took the figure for direct costs and multiplied it by 25 per cent and then inserted the product in the space designated. The direct cost and the contribution to overheads figures were then summed, again automatically, and the product was described as 'total costs'. Table 10.2 shows a simplified version of this form.

Table 10.2 The costing and pricing form

UNIVERSITY COSTING AND PRICING FORM	
Costs	**£**
Fieldwork expenses	3,500
Salary (pro rata)	22,000
Total direct costs	**25,500**
Contribution to overheads (25%)	6,375
Total Costs	**31,875**
Income from client	13,000
Financial return	**−18,875**
Justification for negative return	

By this automated process, the 'contribution to overheads' came to be considered as a cost. But this is a misnomer, because the 'contribution to overheads' is not an actual cost but merely a designated recovery rate. For example, if a university incurs costs of £40 to process a travel expense claim (the costs of the finance staff, of issuing a payment etc.), then a project involving 20 journeys costing £50 each would incur indirect costs of £800 (20 × £40), but the designated 25 per cent contribution to overheads would be £250 (25 per cent of £1,000). In contrast, a project involving one airfare of £1,000 would incur expense claim processing costs of just £40 but the university would similarly seek a £250 contribution to overheads. The same principle applies with salaries – the cost of an office, library facilities or processing an employee's payroll is the same if they are a junior lecturer as they are if they are a senior professor (as Jem Collier was), yet the contribution to overheads sought from professors will be significantly higher because their salary is higher. The contribution to overheads is therefore not a 'cost' but a form of 'tax', designed to recover the indirect costs of the organization. This is highlighted by the fact that, at the university, the recovery rate for research was 25 per cent, but for commercial consultancy projects it was 40 per cent.

The nomenclature employed by the form, and the fact that the 'contribution' figure was included at all, suggests that the costing and pricing form embodied an implicit assumption that these costs, such as the costs of producing costing and pricing forms themselves, were ones that were part of the cost of Collier doing his work. In a sense, the cost of costing Collier's work was now seen as a cost of him doing his work, yet it added nothing of value to the research itself. A different reading of this situation might therefore suggest that the university was seeking to expropriate income generated by Collier to pay for its own management practices and the people that performed them.

The form was then used to enter the amount that the funder was donating. This was called a 'price'. Again, this was a misnomer as the funds were a gift (which Collier was bound to reciprocate by doing the work), not a price being charged to a customer. The form then compared the 'total costs' with the 'price'. Because the money gifted covered only the marginal costs and some of the salary costs, the form reported Collier's work as having a significant deficit and a large minus number was automatically inscribed at the bottom line. Significantly, the final line of the form, which permitted a qualitative explanation, remained blank because no one bothered to fill it in or even talk to Collier about it.

This completed form can be seen, in the Foucauldian sense, as taking Collier's work, and therefore part of him, and inscribing a particular identity to it – a set of costs against which there was set a (much smaller) 'price' to be paid. So, Collier and his work became, in a very literal sense, commodified and his worth judged monetarily by reference to the profitability (or otherwise) of 'his' work.

If the university were a firm, on the basis of these data, it might seek ways of raising prices or cutting costs (or both) if it did not want to lose money. But a university is not a firm (Pears 2010) and the funder was not a purchaser paying a 'price', but making a gift to the extent it could afford to. So, there was, in reality, no 'price' that could be raised. The marginal costs (i.e. extra costs incurred by the project) were fully covered by the funding. The costs of Collier's salary were sunk costs – expenses that the university could not avoid paying anyway and which were, in any case, fully funded from the public purse. The only cost left uncovered was that of the overheads – part of the overheads being the cost of the form itself. The form, as explained above, did not even attempt to calculate the true overhead costs associated with the project, but merely sought a broad-brush 'contribution' (which it nevertheless called a 'cost').

Common sense suggests that perhaps what should happen in universities at this point is that the negative number should be noted and contextualized within other, broader considerations. In truth, UK funders are not generous and few will pay the fEC of projects. As such, the work of Collier and his colleagues will almost invariably be represented by a negative number on such forms. Neoliberal policy imperatives may, in principle, oblige universities to recover 100 per cent of fEC, but the reality is very different: even the UK government's Research Councils (through which most government money for research flows) will only pay 80 per cent of fEC. Thus, whilst the figures on the form might in theory be used to inform funding councils about how funds flowing into universities are used, they do not represent a robust basis on which to make decisions about accepting or rejecting projects such as Collier's.

These almost inevitable negative numbers, which suggest that academics are failing to pay their way, and are 'losers', might also be thought of as having a disciplinary effect. The individual academic pursuing research will always, in some sense, be in the wrong, because they cost their university scarce cash. This might even push some individuals away from research work, towards more 'customer-focused' consultancy work (where the rate of contribution sought by Collier's university was 40 per cent).

In the meantime, blissfully unaware of the form's journey, Jem's actual working life continued unabated. He was planning the research, discussing it with potential partners whilst juggling liaison with external contacts and his regular teaching load. As usual, he spent a good deal of his 'own' time (Gornall and Salisbury 2012) on preparatory work and had started a box for documents which he kept in his home office (a corner of the family kitchen); a pile of articles to go through for the literature review formed a teetering tower. These hours of work, essentially unpaid overtime, went unrecorded and unrepresented in any of these formal accounting processes.

Collier's line manager was relatively new to academic work and believed that universities should be run as commercial businesses; for him, a 'successful' year in the faculty was one where a 'profit' was returned. This perception of the academy as a business was lent support by the form on the automatically generated Excel spreadsheet. Using the nomenclature of 'cost' and 'price', the form lent authority and prominence to the notion of 'profit'. The form provided management information to Jem's manager, which he could use in a disciplinary sense too; as a non-academic he understood little about the work, and therefore laboured under an information asymmetry. The form offered the capacity to make decisions within a reference frame that was familiar and rational for him.

Jem's manager refused to 'sign off' the form because of the 'substantial loss' that would be incurred; the university could not enter into a contract for the work. Collier was unwilling to accept this, but understood accounting principles and therefore how to be calculating. He opined that all the marginal costs were covered and that the project yielded a not inconsiderable contribution to the sunk costs of his salary. He conceded that the project gave no contribution to the university's central overheads, but explained that he was contractually entitled to pursue his research and that he would do this work anyway (with the funder paying his fieldwork expenses directly), whether or not the university entered into a contract. However, in these circumstances, the university would not get the benefit of the £9,500 to set against his salary costs. Jem also argued that there was no more remunerative work for him to do – there were no opportunity costs at stake here.

Refusing to change his position, the manager repeatedly argued that the project represented a serious financial loss to the organization and that the opportunity costs were too high. As budget-holder, his decision was final. And, whilst he was ultimately accountable to the university governors for projects that he accepted, those rejected never saw the light of day outside of the faculty.

The reconstitution of Jem's working life

The introduction and widespread usage of management accounting techniques into universities has been a significant aspect of their organizational transformation. These technologies were introduced as a result of external imperatives from state organizations seeking to steer universities at a distance. Their impact at the level of academics' working lives are made palpable by Jem Collier's story.

Collier's working life consists of teaching, research and administration. His post is fully funded by the funding councils – that is, by public money. He worked hard, on his own account, to find funding for this project, and was pleased that it contained an element that acted as a contribution to the cost of his salary. Collier genuinely thought that the university would be pleased that he was 'doing his bit' to support the organization, especially as this was not explicitly asked of him. In his proposal and its associated budget (Table 10.1) Collier represented his working life and the relationships (with the university and with the funder) that framed it.

His pre-emptive account of what he was going to do was reconstituted by the costing and pricing technology employed by the university. The university's pre-formatted Excel spreadsheet, embodying predetermined assumptions and calculations, produced a version of Collier's working life from its own perspective. It commodified his work via a process that prioritized the 'costs' and the 'price'. The gift from the funder became a commercial transaction in which the university was the supplier. Collier was recast as a 'loss-maker' who imperilled the profitability of the organization. Thus, the university simultaneously re-framed academic work as a commodity and, in Collier's case, as valueless; by its calculations, it made a loss. As such, it produced a view of Jem that was congruent with the university's image of itself, as a profit-maximizing business.

A number of factors may have prevented the university from taking a more realistic and contextualized view of the costing data it had generated. One is that managers need information to manage and this imperfect and unsuitable management accounting data was all that was to hand: the costing and pricing form was a reality in which Collier's working life was imbued with the characteristics of a 'loser'. The structural power arrangements in the university gave support and authority to Jem's line manager, in *his* decision-making and control over Collier's working life. As the budget-holder, a position of accounting authority, he could not, in effect, be challenged; he was psychically incapable of following the logic of Collier's version of *his* working life.

Concluding remarks

The shaping and framing of academics' working lives through technologies such as this costing and pricing model repay close and nuanced reading. Collier's story yields rich data and thick description (Geertz 1973). Such explorations point to the minute decisions, frequently obscured, that define, control and punish academic work. Most often, we do not see these, and they remain hidden because academics are either not reflexive about their lives and the influences upon them, or lack the technical skills to understand and critique the processes to which they are subject. This case reveals the manner in which accounting technologies are used by management hierarchies and how they impact upon the work of academics. Failure to consider these opportunity costs could be expensive in the long term; such decisions can and do adversely affect morale, careers and individuals' passion for generating new knowledge, with all that that entails for the ability of academics to create really useful knowledge.

Notes

1   All names are entirely fictional.
2   The Research Excellence Framework (REF) (formerly known as the Research Assessment Exercise) is a programme run by the UK university funding councils which seeks to measure the quality and quantity of academic research. The results are used to selectively award government funding for research, rewarding those who perform best in the exercise. The REF now includes a measure of 'impact' – broadly, the extent to which the research has influenced policy or practice beyond the academy.
3   The funding councils are non-departmental government bodies that direct government funds to universities and, as a result, steer and control their actions to a significant extent.

Based on material presented and discussed at the fourth *Working Lives* Seminar, University of Glamorgan, December 2010

11

Human Resources Policies and the Individualization of Academic Labour

Matthew Waring

Introduction

A university is a complex and unique environment staffed by academics with a variety of specialist skills and knowledge. Accordingly, such 'knowledge workers' require freedom, autonomy and high levels of discretion to operate effectively. Human resource management (HRM), it is argued, constrains such academic freedom. The purpose of this chapter is to consider the extent to which HRM has contributed to changes in the working lives of academics.

As background to this, the emergence of a 'mass' system of higher education (HE) provision (Scott 1995), organized on quasi-market principles, has led universities to fundamentally reform their operating systems and management structures (Waring 2009). The importance of 'effective labour management' has also been recognized in this context, and universities have increasingly turned to HRM in order to manage staff. The aim of HRM is to improve organizational performance by stimulating individuals through the use of various 'high commitment' and performance management systems (Guest 1997; Storey 1992).

In this chapter, the trajectory of change in UK HE, leading to the modern, marketized university, is outlined, followed by a brief review and critique of the concept of HRM. The adoption of HRM, following the government and Higher Education Funding Council's Rewarding and Developing Staff initiative (HEFCE 2001), is discussed, as well as its 'individualizing' effects on academics. HRM policy and practice is then considered in the context of a study of UK universities, carried out between 2005 and 2007 (Waring 2010).

Modernization and change

Universities have become increasingly managerial (Deem 2001, 1998) and are now routinely characterized as business corporations competing in an education marketplace to satisfy the demands of the student/consumer. The processes of change that led to this followed a long trajectory informed by the dominant discourse of neoliberalism, central to which is a belief in the virtue of the competitive free market and notions of individual choice (Held 2005). In the UK HE sector, 'a mode of regulation or form of governmentality' (Olssen and Peters 2005: 314) has emerged. Regulatory bodies and agencies have replaced direct governmental control, now operating at a distance, but with the power to ensure conformity by monitoring performance against a range of benchmarks and quality controls (Dean 1999: 165). This complex network of audit and regulatory bodies that extends into academics' working lives (Laffin 1998) enables the government to exercise significant control over the sector and to effectively 'micro-manage' universities (Deem *et al.* 2007).

Accordingly, universities – ostensibly independent bodies – must follow the advice of the Quality Assurance Agency (QAA), which has significant influence over the way that they organize their learning and teaching. Funding councils in England, Scotland and Wales also derive considerable power arising from their role in allocating funds for teaching and research. The highly controlled environment that has emerged has been likened to an audit culture (Strathern 2000), heralding 'a significant break with the principle of academic autonomy' (Shore and Wright 2000: 68).

Governments worldwide have long recognized the strategic role to be played by universities in aiding the development of a more skilled workforce – essential in the global knowledge economy. In the UK, the process of change, leading to an expansion of the university sector and growth in student numbers, began with the 1963 Robbins Report (Committee on Higher Education (CHE) 1963). This accelerated after the 1992 Further and Higher Education Act (DES 1992), which laid the foundations for the subsequent 'massification and marketization' of UK HE (Scott 1995; Fulton *et al.* 1991). The age participation rate (or percentage of all 17–30-year-olds included) currently stands at around 46 per cent (DBIS 2011), in a sector comprising 166 universities (HESA 2012) that are either post-92 (former polytechnics and colleges of HE) or pre-92 (older universities formed before the 1992 Act).

The market principles that were established after 1992 firmly aligned the UK university with the government's developing focus on the economic purposes of HE. It has now become the taken-for-granted logic of the HE sector that the role of the modern university is to prepare graduates for work and to equip them with the necessary practical skills that will help British industry become more competitive, discussed also by Jephcote this volume.

University managers have sought to reform the internal management systems of universities, following conventional business models, since the radical proposals of the Jarratt Report of 1985 (CVCP 1985). The creation of business units, an emphasis on financial management and monitoring of individual performance against corporate objectives, brings the control necessary to ensure more efficient and cost-effective operations. The concern for many academics is that 'modern management' practices, (See Gornall and Thomas, this section) including HRM, do not sit comfortably in an academic environment.

For academics, the ability to work autonomously has long been cherished and recognized as an integral element of the role (Henkel 2005). Further, academics usually perceive themselves as being allied to their particular subject disciplines and are more likely to identify with their associated peer academic communities than corporate institutional objectives. Academic identity is a complex phenomenon (Clegg 2008; Berg *et al.* 2004; Henkel 2000) but certain values and principles have formed into a coherent narrative rooted in traditional collegiate notions, where the recognition of the primacy of academic knowledge and learning as a 'social good' are central.

In the following section, I explain how the current system of university management and the adoption of HRM operates to challenge those principles.

Managing human resources

In 2001 the Rewarding and Developing Staff in Higher Education (RDS) initiative (HEFCE 2001) was launched, leading to a major operationalization of HRM in UK HEIs. By improving standards of 'people management' it was argued that academics could be managed more effectively to achieve their 'objectives' more efficiently. Accordingly, RDS made a percentage of universities' funding contingent upon the production of an HR strategy identifying specific, costed HR objectives.

HRM is a strategic approach to managing people that is 'individualistic rather than collective in its approach to employee relations' (Condrey *et al.* 2011; Armstrong 2006: 11). It seeks to make business organizations more competitive, by employing 'high commitment work practices' (Guest 1997) to deliver higher quality work. A focus on the individual is central to HRM, and line managers play a key role in inspiring and monitoring workers' performance, through the use of regular staff appraisal and target-setting. The logic of HRM contends that improved organizational performance is inextricably linked with *individual* performance. There is an underlying assumption that committed workers should be willing to 'go beyond contract' (Storey 1992) an to demonstrate commitment to organizational goals. HRM also assumes the existence of a unitarist, rather than pluralist, atmosphere, with managers and workers part of a 'team' working towards 'shared' goals (Fox 1966).

The use of HRM in universities is problematic for two reasons. Firstly, significant questions remain concerning the efficacy of HRM itself. Several studies have attempted to establish a link between HRM and enhanced organizational performance (see, for example, Boxall and Macky 2009; Hope-Hailey *et al.*, 2005; Guest *et al.*, 2003; Wright *et al.*, 2003; Gibb 2001), yet the certainty of any link remains elusive (Guest 2011; Keenoy 2007). Consequently, it has been suggested that HRM may be more 'rhetoric than reality' (Legge 2005).

The second problem concerns a more disturbing aspect of HRM. It is contended that whilst HRM is ostensibly about mutuality and the need to develop human assets, it can also be perceived as a technology of management, designed to manage people as 'objects' of the business like any other resource (Grey 2009: 150). Some see HRM as a Foucauldian control mechanism, employing disciplinary techniques such as performance monitoring and appraisal, to turn workers into objects of knowledge (Townley 2002). In such an analysis, workers are 'recast as a depersonalised unit of economic resource, whose productivity and performance must constantly be measured and enhanced' (Shore and Wright 2000: 62) and ultimately discarded.

Such changes have led critics to argue that universities have been transformed into little more than knowledge production factories (Boden and Epstein 2006) employing HRM to direct individuals in the pursuance of enhanced organizational performance in the HE marketplace – which may appear as much a political philosophy or programme as an organizational or business one.

Stories from the frontline

Taking on board the two perspectives on HRM (Legge 2005), of 'people as human assets' or the harder 'technology of control' view, I draw on data collected in three English universities between October 2005 and March 2007. The study was designed in such a way that academics' experience in both old and new universities could be compared, and included two pre- and one post-1992 university accordingly.

At each university, a cross-section of staff from all levels of the organization took part, including the HR director, a member of senior management (pro or deputy Vice-Chancellor), middle managers (heads of department), lecturing staff and a representative of the academic trade unions. Sixty semi-structured interviews were carried out, lasting one and a half to two hours. These generated a set of narratives that provided insights into how people perceived the changes at their own institutions and their varying experiences of and attitudes to HRM in particular.

The three universities outlined below have been anonymized and all respondents given pseudonyms.

- **New-U:** a new university, formerly a college of HE, located on the outskirts of a Midlands county town. A relatively small teaching-led institution with a vocational orientation.
- **Old-U:** a large civic university in a city in the South of England. As a prominent member of the Russell Group, the university is renowned for the quality of its teaching and research.
- **Tech-U:** one of the plate-glass institutions opened in the 1960s, situated just outside a large city in central England. A prominent member of the Russell Group, the university excels in science and technology.

Drawing on the narratives of staff at each university, I now consider the ways in which working lives had changed as a consequence of the institutional adoption of HRM.

Each university had recently undergone very similar restructuring exercises and were clearly taking a more 'corporate' approach. An underlying current of change was evident, creating an element of instability and uncertainty. Examples of such change included a shift from traditional democratic, departmental-led structures to more hierarchical, business-led management structures, following the 'Jarratt' model. The new business units were managed by line managers, supported by a management team and required to operate within tight budgetary frameworks. A range of audit mechanisms were in place to monitor performance and ensure conformity. Senior managers argued that such changes were not only inevitable but had also led to more efficient working practices, to the ultimate benefit of the student.

> We have to be more business-like. We just have to think in that way about managing finance, managing staff . . . it really is essential. And what's more, I do believe that if it's done well it can actually enhance the provision of the academic work and not necessarily impinge on it.
>
> Barbara, senior manager, New-U

Such management discourse was common amongst senior managers, who made frequent use of 'modernization' rhetoric (Ball 2003). Yet academics were less sure about the benefits of restructuring. A degree of resistance may be expected where some change is concerned, but many academics I spoke to were also unclear as to the *rationale* for introducing new structures:

> I think this latest reorganization could prove to be something of a watershed for [New-U]. There are definitely signs of an increasingly managerialist culture developing, and that's quite new.
>
> Ella, academic, New-U

> For me, there has been a lack of communication and as for the way it was done, it has been poor, to be honest. [Restructuring] was going on at the same time as refitting the building and other things, so it was all done in a terrible rush, which has had consequences for teaching – we are still not ready. Staff morale has probably dropped because of the [restructuring] and I don't think it has been handled very well.
>
> James, academic, Old-U

A further reason for the restructuring was to facilitate the introduction of HRM itself. For HRM to operate effectively, it requires a hierarchical structure that empowers line managers, enabling them to appraise performance and set targets for subordinate staff (Storey 1992). The formalization of this relationship is key to the successful operation of HRM, but potentially also creates a tension in a university environment, where a more participatory approach has traditionally been followed.

Each university had an HR strategy in place in line with the RDS strategy. A number of new HR policies and procedures had been developed by each university's HR department and new initiatives introduced, all of which raised the profile of the HR department. Senior managers largely believed RDS had been a positive development. Yet beyond senior managers and union representatives, there was little awareness of HR strategies: 'I don't even know what it looks like – what's it supposed to be about?' (Mark: middle manager, Old-U). This response from Mark, one of the line managers responsible for enacting the policies, is not untypical and is indicative of a clear divide between the 'modernizing discourse' of senior managers and the reality of the experience on the ground. Many of the academics I spoke to felt that the HR department had no discernible impact on their daily working lives. Clark sums up the feelings of many:

'They are very much there to reinforce management strategies . . . I wouldn't go to them if I had a problem, I'd go to my line manager' (Clark: academic, New-U). Such negativity clearly presented a problem. For, despite the increased level of HR activity and the constant rolling out of new policies, the issues that really mattered to staff were not (they believed) being addressed. 'Equal opportunities' was one area where new policies had been developed but many felt that the primary motivation was simply 'legal compliance'.

A lack of tangible evidence to indicate that HR policies were making a difference meant they counted for little amongst many academic staff. Yet despite this apparent failure to make an impact on the ground, it was clear that HRM was in fact having an effect, but in a rather more subtle way. One of the central aims of the RDS policy was to raise the overall standards of HE delivery in universities by improving the performance of academics. Each of the three universities had an appraisal system in place, but the individual experience of it varied across departments, as these two stories illustrate.

> It is not very effective at all, nothing much happens. I have had three with the head of department and one with a line manager. All that happens is the head says something like 'Oh well, we can't solve your problems, you're too good for us, and I expect you'll be leaving us soon anyway.' What use is that to me?
>
> Faith, academic, New-U

> I do believe the whole process of appraisal is inappropriate for academics and what it boils down to is managers keeping an eye on staff. It doesn't make any difference to the way I do things and anyway, as an academic, you shouldn't really need an appraisal to tell you how you are progressing . . . it's such a self-driven career anyway, so what is the point?
>
> Frances, academic, Tech-U

Frances' story is significant and succinctly captures the main concerns of the academics. First, the self-driven nature of academic work and second that any attempt to manage their performance or direct their work was seen as a direct challenge to their autonomy – an essential element of the academic 'paradigm'. The managers who were responsible for conducting the appraisals, including some at a senior level, also expressed concerns about the suitability of performance management in an academic environment. Such doubt concerning core HR policies is revealing, and there can be little hope for policies that are not supported by those who must implement them (Hope-Hailey *et al.* 2005).

Clearly evident was also a growing distance between the modernizing discourse of senior managers and the reality of the academic staff's daily work experience. Many of the latter talked about a growing level of uncertainty arising from a perception of constant change and an increase in the use of audit mechanisms, including appraisal. All of this was associated with a 'top-down' managerial agenda, one that was being imposed on academics with little or no consultation, and was gradually changing their working conditions.

People like me, you know, the academics that I work with, don't really feel part of the wider university strategy. I suppose communication is quite good, but there's a clear divide between academics and senior managers. We are not genuinely involved in that sense.

Janet, academic, Tech-U

Janet's story serves to reinforce the notion of a transference of power from academics to managers. This sense of a 'loss of control' was seen as a challenge to the academics' status in the academy. For despite the variability in implementing appraisals, the majority of staff were required to set targets, or performance criteria that demonstrated how they linked in with corporate plans. Academic freedom was curtailed by this gradual process of individualization, as academics became 'objects of knowledge' through the 'panoptic gaze' of HRM (Townley 2002).

It was apparent that collegiality was still highly valued by academic staff, although they accepted the disputed nature of the term. Nevertheless, such notions as shared ownership, working together supportively, informality and a collective will were still important to them. 'Collegiality' was an appropriate way for academics to characterize those underpinning values and traditions that, it was agreed, were under pressure from growing managerialism. For example, academic departments had traditionally been an important element in the democratic decision-making process of the university, as well as an important source of identity for academics. Their replacement with business units not only diluted the collective power and influence of academics but also intensified the felt process of individualization.

Whilst there was no indication that this would lead to outright conflict, a mounting level of frustration was discernible. Similar to Anderson's (2008) findings, a range of covert resistance strategies, including avoidance and qualified compliance, were employed. Several academics suggested that there was an element of 'playing the game' to satisfy administrative requirements, as these two explain:

. . . I've always found that just ignoring things seems to be a pretty effective strategy. Everything comes via email doesn't it? So you just delete that and carry on as before [laughs].

Troy, academic, New-U

. . . there is a real audit culture now, but most people tend to comply, you know, tick the right boxes, fill out the paperwork and so I don't really get the sense of any serious level of resistance developing over it all – people just do what is necessary.

Mark, middle manager, Old-U

Such strategies are indicative of Miller's (1995) notion of 'bargained autonomy' which implies the freedom academics receive in return for complying with corporate objectives, such as producing research articles, teaching greater student numbers and filling out forms. One can argue that such 'qualified compliance' permits HRM to become increasingly insistent.

Concluding remarks

The profile and staffing of 'human resources' departments has increased as a consequence of HEFCE's (2001) Rewarding and Developing Staff initiative and the introduction of HRM. The production of HR strategies and associated policies has become a major part of each university's remit. It is argued here that the objective of 'HRM' was to increase organizational control over the work that academics do (Willmott 1995), and that despite minor acts of resistance and 'playing the game' in return for a sense of preserved autonomy, overt compliance has increased. As employment conditions and academic contracts have become more tightly and corporately drawn, the 'managerialist' discourse (Deem 2001) has also become more assertive. Almost imperceptibly, the 'HR' agenda had become part of the fabric of every university's operations – 'the way things are done' – assisted by policies such as RDS. But academics have been complicit too (Kolsaker 2008): as managers, opinion leaders, professionalizers and subject experts, through their compliance and lack of an overt critique, strengthening an 'assent' through subtle processes of individuation and subjectification (Dean 2007; Rose 1996). It is possible that the time has come to revisit both formal and 'tacit' (understood) relationships between academics and their employers. In some respects, 'hard' HRM strategies have not necessarily delivered from academics their most 'productive' work (Gornall and Salisbury 2012); indeed, on some of the data here, those practices have led rather to feelings of 'disengagement' (Waring 2009) and lack of creativity in the sector.

Note

This chapter is based on a presentation given to the Working Lives Seminar Series at the University of Wales College, Newport on 8 October 2010. I am grateful to the audience and members of the Working Lives team for their constructive comments and suggestions and to the informants who took part in the original research.

12

Professional Work and Policy Reform Agendas in a Marketized Higher Education System

Lynne Gornall and Brychan Thomas

Introduction

Policies have histories (Skocpol 1992); they circulate (Ainsworth 2002; Flynn 2000), and they also have consequences. Some of these are direct and explicit, others not foreseen or based on political will at all (Lane 1993: 75). While governments may have clear intentions about what they wish to accomplish, it is often the case that the relationship between policy and its impact is problematic. What studies of policy and organizational change do not always tell us, is about the ethos of a sector in relation to the staff experience of everyday working. The Working Lives study sought to document some of the less visible aspects of major further and higher education (FE/HE) policy change for two groups of lecturers in South East Wales. Together with the 'policy narratives' that have informed and facilitated widescale changes in UK HE, we discuss here as context some of the work on occupations, employment and professionality.

Work: a professional's perspective

Work is an important part of our lives, but not all jobs appear to be called 'occupations', still less 'professions'. Indeed, the connotations variously of 'occupation' and 'labour' seem to signify the difference between 'choosing to work/how we use our time' and 'hard work' (or 'labour'). On definitions of terms, an 'occupation' is taken to refer here to a type, as in official categories and classification indexes, often relating to sectors of the economy, while the notion of a job or 'employment' suggests the particular relation and contract with an employer. References to 'work' itself are taken as a description of particular sorts of activity, distinguishing these from other kinds, such as personal/ leisure, where time for example is controlled by the individual. The fairly basic category of 'occupation', as Freidson (2001: 11) has observed, is more often used as an indicator of something else – social class, education, status or income – and has not received much analytic attention to date in educational research.

Professional occupations, like all work, imply forms of knowledge (Kusterer 1978: 138), where the social and economic organization of practice plays a critical role in determining both what knowledge can be employed in work and how that knowledge can be exercised (Freidson 2001: 29, 27; Delanty 2001). The frequent exercise of discretion – or 'fresh judgement' – where individuals derive satisfaction from specialization and high levels of client interaction (Friedmann 1964: 85–88, quoted in Freidson 2001: 23), characterizes arguably the assumptions about professional work that have been held to date by many lecturers in FE and HE. This was an area that was discussed actively in the Working Lives focus groups. Professional discretion and judgement were important in regulatory and other contexts, but individual discretion over academic working was not always similarly respected or accepted by institutions (Boden and Epstein 2011; Trow, 2004). In fact, participants in our group interviews expressed strong views about intrusive supervisory and management arrangements around them, the 'imposed top-down' quality schemes, pressures arising from changing student demographics and funding, and the 'response times' expected by HE management and others today. All of this at the same time as lecturers (in 2007/8) were undergoing role re-appraisals and employment uncertainty.

Where a high degree of autonomy and expertise can be seen to be applied as part of everyday practice, Freidson (2001: 23) terms this *discretionary specialization*, and which we take to be the case in traditions of FE and HE work. Colleges and polytechnics became detached from local authority control in the early 1990s (DES 1992), which established them as institutions with responsibilities of independence and self-regulation (Gleeson 2005), making them directly the employers of staff. Goodrham (2006) identifies this process as central to the transformation of labour conditions for professional practice in the sector. Thus it is argued, lecturers' activities have become concentrated on such things as ensuring that students stayed on courses and obtained qualifications (Hyland and Merrill 2003; Larsen this volume).

Public sector professionals/ism

The public sector has been the area where many professionals in the past have been able to exercise their special role, and to apply expertise and discretion, practices that were often conducted at a distance from the managers of their institutions. Freidson (2001: 12) argues, 'I use the word "professionalism" to refer to the institutional circumstances in which the members of occupations, rather than consumers or managers, control [their] work'. He considers that a profession differs from an 'organized occupation' by being able to control access and entry, and indeed preventing others from performing areas of (specialist) work. This hardly characterizes lecturing in FE or HE today however, but there are tensions around boundaries of work aspirations for professional self-determination on the one side and expectations of control by managers or corporate interests, who wish to 'manage resources' on the other. Thus, the 'freedom of judgement and discretion' in performing the work that is intrinsic to professionalism appears for Freidson (2001: 3) to contradict directly the managerial notion that efficiency is gained by *minimizing* discretion. But is this true in HE? Lecturer and manager roles are often held by the same person, and many managers in HE and FE are, or were, academics. So the relationship is not one that simulates a genuinely 'industrial' model. However, strains between HE managements and academics may be more than just 'a local difficulty'. Fanghanel (2012: 16–18), Ball (2008a), Deem *et al.* (2007: 95), as well as earlier writers (Kogan 1983), have convincingly documented that 'an anti-professional ideology' about 'producer capture' (Ranson 1994: 75) has been operating in education policy dating back to the 1970s. Thus, creating greater competition between providers, Kogan and Hanney (2000: 42) argue, has put managers at the level of the institution firmly in charge. In times of organizational change too, Freidson (2001: 36) notes how power may be withdrawn from one group of professionals, putting others in control, and thus acting as a further threat to the ongoing sustainablility of academic careers or position.

An 'organized occupation' should thus, in Freidson's terms (2001: 12), attempt to create the circumstances under which its members 'are free of control by those who employ them'. This is something arguably that lecturers and their representative bodies aspire to do, but a diminishing and diversifying academic body has other urgent cases and causes to field. Issues of autonomy and discretion may seem abstract compared to concerns over pay or finance issues, job gradings and security, workload and sector expansion or contraction (Musselin 2007). And academic autonomy is rarely discussed or debated *directly* with managers or others in the workplace, our informants said, unless in cases of specific judgements. It was more likely to be raised informally and by proxy, through papers and research, at conferences and in meetings. For staff, it remains a precious if intangible asset, however.

'Reform' agendas and change management

'Change' is not something that has evolved naturally, according to Flynn (2000: 29), but has been part of a *struggle* in which 'reform' was a way of gaining and winning power. Governments aspired to reduce costs without cutting the volume of services by introducing competition, and the adoption by institutions of these 'desired approaches' was often the condition for receiving financial help from the state (Flynn 2000). So staff and even leaders might have felt they had little agency, and were rather bystanding at the process (Ball 2008a: 51). But it has bought compliance, and in this way, reform strands have created a climate in which 'new ways of managing' have been deemed 'necessary', while programmes of organizational and staff restructuring could then follow (Newman 2000: 46).

To understand these shifts, it is necessary to 'unpack the discourse' of modernization, Clarke *et al.* (2000) argue. Part of this involves looking at broader contexts, to explicate and locate what are termed the 'drivers of change', but it also invokes the importance of 'wider stakeholder involvement'. In other words, groups *other* than current 'monopoly providers' or professionals, whose voices (it is argued by policy makers) have dominated the debate thus far (Ball and Junemann 2012: 24; Ball 2008a). 'Modernization' is thus not simply a term, but a *discourse* about processes of change, one which differs from others for Newman (2000: 48), by being fundamentally political, going well beyond immediate internal changes in institutions. But how does it take effect?

Recurring 'narratives' and the circulation of ideas

The 'histories' of policies (Skocpol 1992) that are circulated and narrated are also retold at the organizational, social and interpersonal levels:

> there is no doubt that politicians and managers learn from the trends occurring in the private sector, whether in the use of technology or methods of managing people. Legitimacy may also be enhanced by implementing current ideas about management, or at least by using current managerial language.
>
> Flynn 2000: 35

These ideas, which are passed on in training, presentations, informal networks or contacts, function as compelling narratives about the 'necessity of change'. Policy data and ideas thus circulate outside of the state and within organizations, creating *affirmative cycles* that managers can draw on. These in turn *reduce the need for explanation* and lend authority and legitimacy to new regimes (Flynn 2000: 36). Everyone in HE and FE can recognize these processes, whereby a phrase or term may come to stand for a whole paradigmatic shift in thinking and policy implementation. Below, we bring some of them to explicit attention.

'Innovation and enterprise'

> Colleagues think of the research (as PI of a major funding council project) as my 'own work' and expect me to spend holidays doing it as opposed to [what they call] 'actual' work, such as teaching.
>
> Female, new university, new to HE

The notion of 'innovation' is one that has been used extensively to 'change manage' many types of public organizations and, in particular, teaching and learning in HE and FE (Bissett 2009; Ball 2008a). While *educational innovation* used to be a process initiated, owned and led by academics themselves as practitioners (Hannan and Silver 2000), today new and often different groups are involved. Moreover, the boards and committees of many of the agencies that stimulate 'innovation' are linked to business sectors and government departments, and part of the 'meso' sector where their remit and terms of reference are established. So whilst individual academics may be members of these, it is the external policy drivers that set the agenda. Yet academics' participation in such initiatives leads typically to an increased workload which may not always be recognized by colleagues or managers (see also Cook and Gornall this volume), as in the interviewee remark above.

Choice, markets and competition

The 'revolution' of the 1990s, Clarke *et al.* (2000: 208) argue, was to simulate in the public sector what markets were claimed to have achieved in the private sector. This has led to a focus on organizational and staff performance and linked systems of funding with incentives and targets and has included 'executive' levels of pay for managers and institutional leaders, bringing 'cost accounting' into HE (Kelly and Boden this volume) and wider deregulation of labour markets. Our informants felt that they were not able to give their attention to the most important aspects of the job – student progress, teaching, scholarly updating and subject-area or knowledge development. Many saw 'competition' as unproductive and thought that 'collegial ways of working' were insufficiently recognized or valued. For Ranson (1994: 99), markets have some virtues but they differentiate and can create serious inequity, thereby potentially *exacerbating* existing problems. Brown (2013), Rolfe (2013) and others are scrutinizing and questioning the role and impact that the policies of marketization have had on HE today, but as one interviewee in a dual academic/management role complained, '[Y]ou don't have time to think and reflect, you just have to do, act and produce ... it turns out that academia is not so different from the media industry [where I used to work]' (female, new to HE, new university).

'Customer focus' and client-centred servicing

The debate about 'customer focus' in HE has been closely linked to an increased emphasis on the 'effective teaching' of students or, more properly, their effective 'learning'. This latter was to be facilitated by teaching and support staff in the new era, concomitant with moving from an élite to a more comprehensive system of HE (Burrage 2010; Gornall this volume). After the government-commissioned 'Dearing' and Browne Reports of 1997 and 2010 respectively, the student as fee payer became the 'customer', repositioning academics in their most basic learner/teacher relationships (Jameson 2012). Prior to this, the official and 'policy' narrative suggested that professionals, as monopoly providers, had been pursuing their own purposes, with services arranged more to suit these needs than their consumers, and were resistant to change (Ranson 1994: 75). This approach was divisive, and has led to tensions between staff and managers in HE/FE (see Deem *et al.* 2007) – as one informant (new university, now ex-HE sector) commented, 'We [were] not trusted to do our own work'.

The 'modernizing solution' was to achieve change management by empowering learners as 'clients' or customers. This is not easy to effect: the teaching and learning relationship involves *emotional labour* and an 'ethics of care', which is seen across all areas of education (Salisbury and others this volume). It is also an important aspect of academic service, one too often overlooked (Huyton this volume). Instead, a discourse of 'complaint and dissatisfaction' was opened up according to Flynn (2000: 23), raising issues about the 'standards of services' provided, and in which the wider public might also take up the issues. Such developments, in creating a marketized system of consumers – kitemarked, ranked, accredited, – were also part of the conditions for new sets of systems of audit and accountability that further impacted on core aspects of academics' work and professional judgement (Morley 2003).

Quality measures and performativity

In the conditions described above, HE and FE as newly 'independent' sectors (from 1991; 1993 in Wales) had been subject to a set of regulatory processes with far-reaching repercussions for academic (and institutional) work – 'TQA': for quality assurance in teaching and the 'RAE' exercise for research assessment (Rolfe 2013: 10–15; Filippakou and Tapper 2008). As one informant remarked,

> [A] large chunk of my life – the area I'm operating in – is governed by external bodies who can't make up their minds what they're doing, and so we're reacting and trying to guess what they're doing, where they're going to be going next year . . . so there are all sorts of pressures.
>
> Male, late career, Russell Group university, 2008

More recently, the national Student Satisfaction Surveys (now National Student Surveys) have been developed as further performance measures (Gleeson 2005; Goodrham and Hodkinson 2004). Separately as well as in combination, these new assessments – of teaching, research, learning, quality, student credentialism, satisfaction, dropout rates and other areas – now inform all FE and HE work. This is in addition to the requirements of professional bodies and other traditional influences on curricula and accreditation. Whether such 'quality' and performative policies successfully increase commitment through employee involvement and participation however (Deem *et al.* 2007), or function as control mechanisms that limit autonomy and discretion (Waring; Kelly and Boden this section), is one of the questions that the Working Lives focus groups considered. Many statements suggested the latter, and while some participants were ambivalent because of dual academic/management roles, or also had conflicting loyalties and perspectives, the overall message about outputs and performativity cultures in education was clear.

'Global forces' and national economic competitiveness

'These things are bigger than us', is a common assertion in the narrative about 'wider forces at work which, though intangible, are creating change'. It suggests that neither we nor managers and governors of institutions, even national governments, are fully in charge (Brown and Hesketh 2004: 17–20). Nor are they making the choices that create difficulties on the ground. It is thus an abstract notion – 'change' – that has impact but with no direct author, or interest-based 'agenda', which is to blame. What we do learn is that the public sector (including education) is a 'drain' on national economies, therefore large public sector organizations must be lean, more efficient, flexible, ready for the challenges of World forces. This new global environment includes many and new players, keener, by implication, than we. And it is 'businesses and enterprise', in the private sector of the new resurgent economy, that will be in the front line of the *pressures* of change, not academics. Moreover, our sector will be rescued by the tax-paying receipts of such companies and their new employees. It is a discourse that ignores actual inter-relationships between productive parts of the national economy.

This discourse also neglects the value-adding and complex benefits of individual and societal development that education offers (Nixon 2011; Macfarlane 2007), so that 'less' education may be more costly in both civic and 'social accounting' terms than is recognized (Wilkinson and Pickett 2010). Meanwhile, 'our global contestants for wealth' are countries offering *high skill* and *high value* at *low cost* (Flynn 2000;

Brown *et al.* 2001) it has been argued. Thus, many FE/HE organizations adopted matrix management systems as part of a perceived need for decentralization and modern 'flexibility' to overcome the 'rigidity' of former hierarchical structures of management which, the story went, could inhibit international competitiveness by making them slower to respond to outside forces (Flynn 2000: 38). In some ways, however, aversion to risk and decision-making has increased, and it became easier to 'pass things round'. Moreover, removing educationists' sense of control over the vision and direction of their work, even under the rubric that 'we are all our own managers now', may also reduce intrinsic motivations. In reality, the new managements in fact ran in parallel with old hierarchies, and change did not lead to greater trust, autonomy or professional determination; quite its opposite (Fanghanel 2012; Jameson 2012; Deem *et al.* 2007; Trow 2004). Yet today, given major expansions and changes to the FE and HE sectors, education as a 'business' is lean, productive and very successful despite, not perhaps because of, multiple government interventions (Ball and Junemann 2012; Nixon 2011). We should also note that it is not entirely proper to refer to universities today as if they were public sector; they are not, according to Brown (2013).

Teaching in the service economy

Some of the background to the policy changes and narratives we have been discussing above, implies debates around pedagogy and technological innovation. In a study of 'campus-free' universities, Cornford and Pollock (2003: 60) have raised questions about the effects of change for space, place and professional identities. Gershuny (1978) has also argued that, in a post-industrial society, people move to purchasing more services, in a paradigm of a 'services-led economy'. Following this early work and that of Agre (2002), Cornford and Pollock (2003: 95) claim that what we are seeing here is not just a shift to a 'service' economy, but to a *self-service* economy. What consumers have done in many areas is to invest in goods that enable them to *'produce and consume services for themselves'* (p. 95). The examples of home computing and special services such as printing or online shopping, video or music provide illustrations of this. In such a 'self-service economy', buyers and sellers are encouraged into direct, unmediated relationships unhampered by time, geography or intermediaries, and which are actively facilitated by technologies such as the internet. This was termed 'dis-intermediation' to connote the increasing obsolescence of many of the institutional and organizational processes that had hitherto played a role between buyer and seller, borrower and lender – or student and lecturer. In the new self-service economy then, and underpinned by global ICT, students would be 'expected to do many things for themselves' (Cornford and Pollock 2003: 95).

Staff too, have been encouraged to be more self-sufficient, using PCs and ICT. Where personnel are more self-managing and self-supporting (via ICT), there is less requirement for a 'back office' or administrative support for anyone. It left many of our Working Lives informants feeling less than supported in their expanding employment roles. The modern view in education today is that 'everyone services students', some through teaching or administration, some via support services, and so on. We are thus all service workers and providers. And whilst at one time an academic development unit in any HE would support staff, today these have largely shifted focus to support for learners. In a new HE economy then, learners may be seen as oriented towards resources, delivery systems, flexible learning devices, materials and technologies, and perhaps the institution. But independently of individual teachers, what is the impact of this on academics' occupational conditions?

Implications of 'reform' for academics: HE employment, pay and academic rewards

Government reports and working papers often present HE as an attractive sector to work in. Salary, career, pension, the contribution to society, intrinsic rewards, receive mention. Concerns in the last decade however have suggested that academic pay was left behind with the growth in earnings of other public sector workers (THE 2004). As a result, it was likely that the pay differential between lecturers and professionals in other areas would increase. The widely discussed 'brain drain' of the 2000s was also believed to have been an outcome of comparatively low academic pay in the UK (Collins *et al.* 2007). Government bodies such as the (then) Department for Education and Skills were concerned that poor pay rewards would have an impact on retention and recruitment, in particular, of leading researchers to universities (DfES 2003). Unfilled vacancies in medicine, business, IT and computing were cited in evidence, in relation to science fellows, with a quarter of them working outside the UK, 12 per cent in the United States (Roberts, 2002; discussed also by Richards this volume).

Discussions about academic pay have been relatively absent in the critical literature on HE, although a number of major (funded) comparative surveys of academic occupational labour in different national systems have been reported. These have included Clark in 1987, Altbach (1996), Farnham (1999), Enders and Fulton (2002) and more recently, Enders and de Weert (2009). There are also analyses of academic wage differences according to subject area, age, ethnicity and gender, both contemporary and historical, for example, by Blackaby *et al.* (2005), Ginther and Hayes (1999), Moore *et al.* (1998), Barbezet (1987) and Bayer and Astin (1968). There are *comparisons* of academic pay between countries in the extant literature (Metcalfe *et al.* 2005; Stevens 2004; Ong and Mitchell 2000), but there are very few papers examining the differences between academic pay in HE and other comparable professions (see Collins *et al.* 2007).

So what is it then, in employment terms, to work in FE or HE as an academic today? Around the time of the above commentaries, the UK HE sector was worth some £45 billion, with export earnings in 2006 of around £3.6 billion (UUK website), with 1.1 per cent of GDP going into HE (2.7 per cent in the United States – *Economist* 2004). Today, these figures are an increased 1.3 per cent of GDP spent on UK HE, and a reduced 1.8 per cent of GDP spent on research and development (UUK 2013). The current average figures are higher, at 1.6 per cent and 2.3 per cent respectively, whereas HEI total income is now £27.9 billion annually (2013 data), this includes £3.2 billion from overseas students' course fees. The sector also employs some 378,000 staff, although a professor at a leading UK university will probably still earn less than their

US counterpart (Kitagawa 2012), and higher salaries in the United States have attracted academic staff from the UK in recent years (Finkelstein 2012). But pay will not be the only reason for moving or changing jobs. Fitzgerald *et al.* (2012) and Metcalf *et al.* (2005) have discussed the various reasons for people starting and ending academic employment in English HEIs, and understanding academic mobility, as opposed to employment, is thus an important and ongoing area of interest. Salaries, of course, may seem less remunerative when experiences of workload, performative cultures and long hours of work in the sector are taken into account (Gornall and Salisbury 2012; Ylijoki 2013; Acker and Webber this volume).

Concluding remarks

Over a decade ago, Henkel (2000: 46) pointed out that academics were being encouraged or 'forced' to embrace a range of markets, 'including for new students, for consultancies, for commercial funding and industrial partnerships . . . markets [that are] substantially structured by national policies'. The outcomes of some of the above processes and policies are still being understood, as they have been and continue to be experienced in the lives and careers of lecturers in FE and HE today and also as they operate in and between organizations and sectors. We see indications of some of these in the 'flexibilized' and 'new professional' job contracts in HE (Gornall 2004) that are starting to be regarded as a regular feature of 'postmodern employment' (Cornford and Pollock 2003). But academics have adapted and responded too, both through their practice as collectives of professionals and in their increasing use of newly available technologies. By contrast, with the shift to a discourse about more 'autonomy' for *learners*, however, the 'self-regulation' in daily work practices of professionals – often cited as 'one of the most attractive aspects of the job' for academics (McInnis 2000) – has been eroded by increased external control and accountability. Perhaps it has also been affected by increasing student independence too, the detachment of learners from campus (Cornford and Pollock 2003) and specialist or disciplinary groupings, and from affective relations with tutors.

'Modern management', Newman (2000: 48) argues, was 'sold' to organizations in the public sector because it looked flexible, more adapted to concepts of 'innovation, partnership and decentralization' and was part of a set of ideas that appeared positive and forward-looking. But has it worked? For Rolfe (2013), it has led to the 'ruin' of the university; for one of our informants, the issue was the lack of learning: '[People had] no real idea of what academic work entailed, what it is for, and how it is achieved . . . [it is] a void'. As lecturers, practitioners and researchers, we have yet to succeed in filling this 'gap' in the policy discourse about FE/HE work.

Acknowledgements

Our thanks to Professor Brian Davies and to Professor Alan Felstead, who read and commented on early versions of this paper.

13

Perspectives on Research Management and Capacity Building in Six Countries

Mary Goretti Nakabugo, Paul Conway, Eimear Barrett and Seán Farren

Introduction

This chapter presents findings from a large-scale cross-national stakeholder study on research capacity building for global development research and its interface with the working lives of academics in Ireland (both North and South) and in four sub-Saharan countries (Uganda, Mozambique, Malawi and Tanzania). The stakeholder study encompassed interviews with over 300 academics from 13 universities and 'storylines' with a small group of academics (3 to 6 per institution) from each of the participating universities in the six countries. We locate this study within the contemporary literatures on research capacity building, academics' working lives and leadership of tertiary institutions. In drawing from the extensive dataset, for the purposes of this chapter, we address three findings: (1) the multi-level nature of research capacity building in terms of individuals, institutions and the wider system, (2) global north and south differences, (3) life-cycle matters for individuals and institutions. We discuss the findings in terms of the increasing policy focus on research capacity building and how it is impacting the rhythms of work in and around the academy.

The concept of and initiatives focusing around research capacity building (RCB) have become the focus of extensive activity in third-level institutions. In the context of this drive toward capacity building, involving the channeling of energies both individual and collective, by researchers and policy-makers, the dynamic interrelationship between the individual and collective working lives *vis-à-vis* the organization is an important focus of inquiry. The very use of the term 'building' recognizes that in relation to 'research capacity' there is a gap between current or actual practice and what is or might be possible – both at individual and institutional levels. A number of factors have contributed to the international policy interest in understanding the dynamics of RCB for development (RCB4D) in universities. Among these are the following: (1) knowledge-based aid and an increasing recognition of the role of research in supporting the knowledge economy/society, (2) donor coordination mechanisms and broader ideological convergence of agencies (King and McGrath 2005), (3) the move toward rethinking the relationship between mode 1 and mode 2 (Gibbons *et al.* 1994) engagement, in a new accommodation between university and society, and (4) the far-reaching impact of research assessment exercises (RAEs) in terms of repositioning research within a university's strategic priorities. Of particular relevance to RCB4D is this reframing of the mode 1/mode 2 knowledge generation relationship, that is, where mode 1 is investigator-driven discipline-focused inquiry, and mode 2 is problem-focused and interdisciplinary (Gibbons *et al.* 1994). Within the African developing context, there has been a strong call to embrace mode 2 knowledge generation which is multidisciplinary, and to move away from the dominant individualistic mode 1 as it 'tends to limit the capacity of African researchers to undertake fundamental work with the many-sidedness required to achieve breakthroughs in modern science' (Sawyerr 2004: 226).

Higher education institutions (HEIs) and individual academic staff all over the world are under considerable pressure to increase their research capacity and productivity as a means of contributing to the global knowledge economy (Blackmore and Kandiko 2011; Menzies and Newson 2008). As such, of the three classic roles for academic staff in HEIs, teaching, research and community engagement, research tends to be prioritized. This has far-reaching implications for academics' personal lives as they try to strike a balance between these and other primary roles (e.g. practice supervision in traditionally professional disciplines such as medicine, nursing, teaching and law).

A number of research studies have previously explored academic work lives of staff in selected universities in industrialized contexts such as the USA, UK, Canada and Australia as they try to negotiate time to meet the demands of their multiple roles and home lives (Daunton *et al.* 2008). Others have taken a gender and discipline-specific perspective, arguing that the pursuit of research excellence in professional disciplines such as academic medicine in addition to other academic roles and family responsibilities, produces far more stress on women academics (especially those with young children) than their male counterparts (Levine *et al.* 2011; Currie and Eveline 2011). In a study of gender equity in Commonwealth higher education, Morley (2005) outlines broader gender issues in HE that insert further strain on women academics' research capacity, including the absence of women in senior academic and management positions, the gendered division of labour and gender-based violence.

Research evidence also shows that the competitive nature of HE institutions and the usually 'one-size-fits-all' policies make it more difficult for women academics with families and children to strike a work-life balance (Levine and Mechaber 2006). Such obstacles have in several instances led women academics to drop out of the academic pipeline (Levine *et al.* 2011; see also Chapman this volume). Across gender, there is also an added pressure on academics as they participate and work hard to make breakthroughs, and/or sustain their individual standing in what Blackmore and Kandiko (2011: 404) have labelled the 'prestige economy'.

Overall, there is an 'intensification' of demands on academics' lives as they strive to remain at the cutting edge of research, to secure research grants, publish, be on top of their professions and disciplines, as well as an 'extensification' of work beyond office premises into people's homes and other private spaces (Currie and Eveline 2011). The emergence of e-technology such as laptops, mobile phones, mobile e-mail and internet access has increased the weakening of borders between work and home, allowing 'work for some to be done anywhere, anytime' (Currie and Eveline 2011: 533). While this connectivity and flexibility has meant that individuals are able to accomplish more tasks and at higher speed than ever before, it has also led to an emergence of what Gornall and Salisbury (2012: 135) have referred to as 'hyperprofessional' academics who are rarely able to 'switch off' with possible negative influences on individuals' lives, homes and health (and see also Ylijoki *et al.*, Acker and Webber, this volume).

Most analysis on academic work lives has been undertaken mainly in developed/ industrialized contexts. There seems to be a lack of research into the pursuit of research excellence and the academic work lives of staff in developing contexts, where there ought to be additional stresses resulting from resource constraints and the need for research to contribute to addressing 'development' issues such as eradication of disease, poverty, human rights abuse and illiteracy. What opportunities and constraints there are at institutional and individual level to develop staff capacity to undertake research for development, and how this interfaces with their academic roles and lives, is the main focus of this chapter.

Research context

The underlying aim of the Irish-African Partnership for Research Capacity Building (IAP) was to collaboratively strengthen research capacity in the service of the global development imperative of poverty reduction, in particular in sub-Saharan Africa. In order to achieve this long-term goal, a key activity of the project was a stakeholder consultation, the rationale for which was to establish a baseline understanding of research capacity for international development in the Irish universities and research capacity in general in the four participating African universities. The consultation sought to elicit the views of administrators and researchers within all the nine universities on the island of Ireland (North and South) and four in Africa including Makerere University (Uganda), University of Dar es Salaam (Tanzania), Universidad Eduardo Mondlane (Mozambique) and University of Malawi, on the opportunities and constraints to research capacity building at both institutional and individual levels. It was also intended to document possible ways of overcoming the barriers.

Fieldwork by two of the authors for the stakeholder consultation was conducted over a five-month period in 2008, just prior to the onset of the current economic downturn, with obvious implications for the prospects of implementing certain of its recommendations. Data analysis was generated from individual and group interviews with over 300 research and senior administration staff in the IAP partner institutions. Furthermore, in order to further contextualize the interview and focus group data, a 'storyline' data collection was conducted, with a smaller group of 50-plus academics at project workshop in Entebbe, Uganda involving staff from all participating universities across the six countries. As such, this chapter brings together the findings from the combined interview and storyline data that formed a core Irish-African partnership for an RCB project work package.

In order to understand the RCB4D individual-institutional dynamic, the 'storyline' workshop was held during the second project meeting in Entebbe, Uganda in November

2008. The purpose of the workshop was to provide another lens on the stakeholder component of the study, putting emphasis on the dynamics of individual institutions when a number of people from each participating institution were present and available to provide individual and collective input on focal research questions. During the activity, 40 participants from 12 institutions were asked to graphically depict and then annotate in writing their individual, and institutional experiences/perspectives on RCB4D, respectively utilizing a storyline methodology (Gergen and Gergen 1988; see also Van Driel *et al.* 2009; Conway 2001). It was hoped this activity would complement and possibly extend some of the findings emanating from previous work involving interviews. In presenting findings, we note ways in which the storyline research both complements as well as provides some additional insights on the individual-institution dynamic. In particular, the storylines provide helpful vivid crystallization of RCB dynamics at the institutional level. When both tasks were completed, there was an opportunity for four of the groups (two from Ireland, one from Malawi and one from Mozambique) to share their storyline drawing and written reflection with the full group of 50-plus workshop participants, which included the authors.

Claims

Finding 1: multi-level dynamics of RCB for development

The increasingly strategic focus on building research capacity for development in universities was evident in participating Irish and to a lesser extent African universities. With particular reference to global development-focused research, this capacity building was reflected across individual, institutional and system level dynamics. Overall, the last four or five years have produced positive changes in the research landscape of the Irish institutions. There is a greater value on research and the focusing of research around specific themes or multi-disciplinary research foci (e.g. global development). 'Global development teaching and research' is beginning to find expression in the strategies of some Irish institutions, and a wider recognition that these cross-cut many research strategies.

The most significant opportunities for building institutional capacity for international development research came in the form of commitments to provide finances and/or resources to groups with an interest in this area. There is evidence of multiple mechanisms for the promotion of international development research across the nine Irish institutions. For example, one institution has formed an interdisciplinary group which has conducted an audit of development activity internally, and acts as a platform to facilitate and support individuals engaged in development research. The head of this institution has appointed a standing committee that reports to the university board, to ensure that the strategies of the group fit within the strategies of the university, and to advance international development within the university.

A second institution has employed a member of staff to build the capacity for international development research at the institutional level. This position was established by the head of the university with the aim of focusing international development initiatives and providing a single point of contact.

International development activities are also supported at the highest levels in the Irish institutions. Furthermore, there is a recognition that development research cross-cuts virtually all academic disciplines. All of the nine Irish institutions have established linkages with institutions in developing countries. In fact, many of these collaborations involve at least one of the four Irish-Africa partner institutions with memoranda of understanding already in place.

Efforts are being made to mainstream and incorporate development or development-related studies into the curriculum. This is being achieved through the introduction of specific development modules or 'streams' into pre-existing courses and by the establishment of dedicated courses at the postgraduate level. There are numerous examples of the range of postgraduate courses in the sciences and humanities with a focus on international development, available through Irish institutions, including anthropology and development, development education, global health, human rights, intercultural studies, to mention a few.

The opportunity to engage in low-cost/low-key research was seen by some Irish stakeholders as a basis for building individual research capacity. For example, they noted that 'research in the humanities does not involve a lot of money as compared to research in the natural sciences' (informant SH038E). As such, researchers in the humanities and some areas of the social sciences aware that not all research requires large amounts of funding to engage in research, irrespective of availability of big grants. For instance, in education, there is the opportunity of working with teachers in schools as research partners, as noted by one of the staff interviewed: 'Teachers are willing to accept us in their classrooms – we have credibility in the community and are warmly welcome' (informant SH066E). Research opportunities may therefore arise in the course of normal teaching and supervisory work.

Finding 2: global north-south differences in RCB

Within the African institutions, the culture of mentorship and peer support is quite scarce. This has, in many instances, created a big 'generation gap' with many upcoming researchers struggling on their own in largely competitive research fields. In addition, while postgraduate training at masters and PhD level was considered a basic starting point to individual RCB, African stakeholders noted the difficulties in accessing postgraduate training opportunities locally and abroad. Fees for postgraduate training are extremely high, and it is quite difficult to undertake and complete studies without any external form of funding.

Staff in African institutions also mentioned the lack of basic infrastructure such as high speed internet, reliable power supplies and office space as a hindrance to their individual RCB. Many staff lacked personal computers and depended on labs and internet cafés. The problem of low salaries was also a major barrier to research capacity development. Many staff engaged in part-time teaching in private universities and consultancy work to supplement their meagre salaries. Others strived to take on as many extra evening teaching classes as possible to earn some extra income, at the expense of dedicating time to engage in research.

While the research funding environment in African partner institutions has improved over the years with ongoing funding streams from institutions such as Sida/SAREC and NORAD, there was still dissatisfaction – as noted by one academic in the health sciences: 'There's no support for research, we do it because we like it. It's hard to get a team if the research doesn't provide money – it takes time away from private practice where you can earn money' (informant SH105H).

Limited research funding prompted a number of staff members to take on any funded research assignment that came up or what some termed 'engagement in opportunity-based research', even when they didn't have the specialist knowledge of the discipline. This in the longer term meant that people lacked the opportunity to build research capacity within their own disciplines; publishing became difficult, and many had resorted to becoming generalists.

Staff in African institutions also mentioned the lack of research skills, such as grant proposal writing and research management, as a barrier to their individual RCB. One academic noted:

> There are lots of cases of people offering money but this is bad for capacity because African partners don't need to write proposals when other people are bringing the money in. But this leads to problems when the money finishes . . . we need to develop the skills to attract funding on our own.
>
> Informant SH096H

Others who had trained abroad felt the training they had received was sometimes detached from the African realities, especially in science disciplines. Those who had been exposed to new methodologies or high-tech facilities and equipment could not easily apply their skills on return to their countries, as the context and available infrastructure differed considerably:

> Sometimes students get trained to use high tech equipment and then come home to an empty lab. They should be given starter packs. In Swedish collaborations, after the scholarship people are equipped, they train PhD students then give equipment for the lab, there is also mentoring of young researchers, this helps with staff retention.
>
> Informant SH221H

Finding 3: life-cycles matter: Individual and institutional

The individual and institutional storyline workshop both endorsed the three above claims but also gave an important person- and institution-specific dimension to how we can understand RCB for development. For example, a number of key findings emerged with respect to low, high and 'turning points'. Furthermore, one of the advantages of having both individual and collective storylines created by the same participants for their own university settings, was that it facilitated some insights into the relationship between individual and institutional RCB4D, as perceived and represented by workshop participants. For example, questions such as:

- To what extent did individual and institutional storylines mirror/reflect each other or not?
- What are the issues and implications for understanding RCB if these storylines are very different?
- What is the role of wider system level dynamics *vis-à-vis* RCB4D at both individual and collective levels?

Low points: Individual

Individual participants identified a range of 'low points' including:

- administrative load for senior academics (mentioned by many);
- new degree programmes/new work;
- career change; moving institution;
- contract with university (e.g. part-time status);
- difficulty defining research focus with view to long term impact;
- drying up of resources in 1980s;
- shift of focus from research to consultancy;
- teaching took priority – a hazard in a professionally-oriented area such as education;
- high teaching loads.

What is particularly salient in relation to the factors identified above as *low points* by individuals is the significance of workloads (for both those new to academia re. teaching and those at senior levels re. admin), institutional culture (e.g. limited/no focus on development) and wider cultural-economic context (e.g. Celtic Tiger in Ireland; lack of funding in 1980s). In highlighting the stress resulting from heavy workloads, one female academic noted:

> Research calls for a lot of time from us. Large classes and attending to students is time-consuming. Trying to fit research within the time is challenging ... we have a night degree program, and you're at campus until 10:00 pm. I don't know if the administration sees the work that goes into preparing lectures; it is far more than the contact hours. Work with students never ends. On holidays you're marking. There is huge pressure.
> Informant SH075G

Low points: Institutional

Participants in their institutional groups identified a range of low points including:

- fragmentation (two of the Irish partner universities);
- pre-Belfast Agreement; Research Assessment Exercise (RAE) (Queens University Belfast) – link to understanding of knowledge in universities, i.e. RAE and fragmentation;
- 1990–2007: lack of funding and development not a priority;
- poor internal networking;
- 'inward-looking' orientation in Ireland during Celtic Tiger growth, over focus on science funding with agenda of 'national competitiveness'.

Similar to the low points identified at individual level, wider cultural, economic and political factors were seen as influential (e.g. national focus on competitiveness at expense of development-oriented research; dividend flowing from 1998 Belfast Agreement in Northern Ireland). Two issues emerged as particularly significant at institutional level, namely the need for (or lack of, in these instances) institutional coherence and internal networking within universities *vis-à-vis* RCB4D. Whereas support for individual researchers was expressed more by individuals with regard to their own research, the importance of coherence and networks was viewed as vital at internal institutional level, possibly because individual researchers may have their own networks and own focus in terms of specifics of their chosen research, whereas building an institutional focus on RCB4D demands, it appears, some institutional prioritization focused on a coherent RCB4D agenda, supported by internal networks.

Turning points: Individual

Individual participants identified a range of 'turning points' including:

• external networks leading to partnerships;
• changing institutions (dramatic change in opportunity for research for development); change in life-worlds (back from Africa);
• seeing previous investment pay off;
• confidence in own research strengths;
• undertaking and completing PhD and then access to major researchers via well-funded research project;
• time allocated in workload to research;
• social development back on agenda and a personal move back into this research area;
• teaching development, role of colleagues in different disciplines.

Perhaps what is most noteworthy here in relation to turning points, is the sheer diversity of factors that individuals perceive as positive turning points. Some of the turning points reflect positive research opportunities in early career, initial motivation provided by building toward grant proposals, securing funding and seeing the impact of initial work/investment. Common across many of these is that some positive experience, be it direct or vicarious in terms of development, appears to provide impetus for further engagement in development research/projects (e.g. this can range from seeing others' work on the ground in Uganda to securing funding collaboratively).

Turning points: Institutional

Participants in their institutional groups identified a range of turning points, including:

• 'progressive embedding' of development (e.g. one university in Northern Ireland); development going university-wide (one university in Northern Ireland);
• Irish Aid funding: critical mass of interest in developing countries (one African university);
• new development-related postgraduate degree programmes;
• loss of staff to new university;

- critical mass of interest;
- a strategic plan;
- appointment of two 'development' professorial Chairs;
- Irish Aid/Higher Education Authority project/universitas 21/new staff.

Of note in relation to the 'turning points' identified was that many of these lead to high points or were related, with other factors, in the 'high points'. For example, in National University of Ireland Galway, the funding of a development network provided opportunities to focus on possible linkages with system-wide research funding such as the Programme for Research in Third Level Institutions (PRTLI). As such, small-scale seed funding for networking provided opportunities to link development research to wider research bids.

Arising from the storyline activity, how are we to understand and represent research capacity-building for development? First, as an activity designed to aid understanding of RCB4D within institutional settings, it provided an important reminder of the particular dynamics at play in given institutions in terms of the past, the present and future possibilities. For example, comparing the 'roller-coaster' storyline created by one institutions' staff, provides quite different explanations and insights into development-oriented research now, compared to the 1970s and 1990s, as well as now and in the future. Second, while recognizing the interwoven nature of individuals and institutions, perceptions of participants, in terms of 'low', 'high' and 'turning points', suggest that different factors and experiences may be both salient and critical at these levels. For example, in relation to low points, individuals viewed *workload* and *support* as important, but institution groups' emphasis was on *coherence* and *networking*, in terms of RCB4D, at the level of the organization.

Concluding remarks

We discuss the findings under the key headings: the multi-dimensional nature of RCB4D and the emergence of increasing international or global development as a significant trans-disciplinary endeavour in universities. First, RCB, as complex and multi-dimensional, confirms what is in the literature – that it is important to confirm and understand and conceptualize it well, vis-à-vis *development-oriented* research. We argue that development as a research focus has its own history and dynamics that are worthy of considered attention from the perspective of academics' working lives.

'Development' is an increasingly important issue for society, nationally and globally. In terms of universities' research emphases, this is reflected in, for example, the increased funding for development-related research in Ireland and the UK (e.g. Irish Aid/Higher Education Authority initiative; Department for International Development – DfID – initiatives recognizing the unique role universities and academics can play in contributing to global development challenges; see also Chapman on civic society). In this context, it is important to have a thorough understanding of the constraints and support underpinning development research in varying university contexts, nationally and cross-nationally.

Planning needs to take account of and be addressed at both individual and institutional levels. As Ncinda (2002: 1699) observes (emphasis added):

Training [*individuals*] and institutional development should be closely inter-related, in order to get away from building empty research structures with no trained scientists who can use them or, on the contrary, to have trained scientists with no facilities to work in. Both should be trained incrementally.

While clearly linked, there may be strategically-important *differences* in emphasis, to address the individual and institutional optimally, notwithstanding their interlinked nature and potential for synergies across levels.

Paying attention to past experiences is vital, but a sense of future possibilities and constraints also needs to be addressed. As such, strategies for addressing RCB4D will, of necessity, have to take into account specific institutional dynamics and wider influencing contexts, in order to tailor RCB4D to meet local institutional, national and trans-national needs and priorities.

Finally, while all academics the world over experience more or less similar stresses on their lives as they try to strike a balance between research, teaching and community engagements, those working in less industrialized contexts in Africa have even larger burdens. Challenges such as poor research infrastructure, lack of funding, and research training that is detached from the reality on the ground, have been highlighted. In one of the partner institutions, for example, the head of the Information and Communications Directorate stated that her university had a total download speed of 9MB/s (megabytes per second) for all staff and students compared to a speed of 4MB/s in the average European home (informant SH115G). This has consequences for access to online resources as well as online communication, which is central to research capacity development. Universities in such constrained contexts would be better off desisting from rushing to embrace practices such as 'RAEs', which are inserting more pressure on academics' working lives even in the most industrialized contexts.

Acknowledgements

The research upon which this chapter is based was funded by an Irish Aid grant to Irish African Partnership for Research Capacity Building (IAPRCB) under the Programme for Strategic Co-operation between higher education institutions. We would also like to thank IAPRCB Executive Steering Committee and research offices in the 13 participating institutions that facilitated the data collection. For further information on IAPRCB see: http://www.irishafricanpartne rship.ie.

Note

Our links with the *Working Lives* team began with a mutual attendance at conference presentations at the Society for Research in HE event in Liverpool, December 2008.

14

Sustaining Academic Professional Careers

Andrew Rothwell and Frances Rothwell

Introduction

This chapter explores academic professional life in the UK from the perspective of individual faculty staff. The early part of the twenty-first century marked a critical time for the university sector and its employees, with significant changes resulting in an end to security of tenure for many academics. They may find themselves at risk today not only in terms of a current post, but of their careers and professional stature itself. To support this, we present below a brief review of the broad changes that have affected work and (typically, managerial) careers at the end of the twentieth century. Two concepts are given specific focus: employability, and continuing professional development (CPD). The challenges for academic careers presented by changes in the wider labour market and the implications for career sustainability are also discussed. As a positive perspective on the academic career future, we offer a model of academic employability (see Figure 14.1) developed from previous studies with professional workers, and consider what sorts of CPD activities academics are likely to undertake, and their attitudes to this. The chapter concludes by suggesting that failure to engage in CPD can jeopardize the employability of individual academics, and indeed the sustainability of the higher education (HE) institutions which employ them. Finally, we propose a research agenda.

Work and careers in a new millennium

In the UK context of the wider changes of the last century, some of the consequences include the decline of traditional industries, jobs and skills, and the advancement of the idea of a 'knowledge based economy' (Drucker 1969). Rapidly advancing technology, allied to the automation of business process, in both manufacturing and administration, has produced a requirement for individuals with technical skills and a capacity for change. But it has also brought the loss of many transactional operator-type posts (Birdwell *et al.* 2011). At the same time, an increasingly globalized economy is oriented eastwards to the Pacific Rim and China. Organizations in the West it is said, went on 'crash diets' to reduce costs, but did not necessarily become healthier (Doherty 1996: 471), and downsizing and delayering processes effectively eradicated many of the structures that had supported former long-term salaried careers. This reduced the availability of low-skilled work, saw a raising of the educational 'bar' for entry to the workforce, the decline in many occupations traditionally associated with male employment, and a propensity for discontinuity in careers and career progression (Clarke 2009; Brown and Hesketh 2004).

The notion that the 'knowledge-based economy' might prove to be a sustainable model for employment proved to be incorrect due to 'offshoring', whereby higher-level work could be done (cheaply) anywhere in the world which had a technically literate, English-speaking workforce (Rothwell *et al.* 2011). Career survival became a matter of flexibility, adaptation and transferable skills that transcended organizational boundaries. For the employee, this has meant retraining to change the shape of one's career (Hall 2009; Beard and Edwards 2005).

Academic work

While these changes affected many aspects of work and careers for numerous mainstream occupations, the academic faculty in the UK was characterized, on the whole, as enjoying stability and security unknown across other western professionals – until now. Altbach and Musselin (2008) describe how fewer than half of academic appointments in the USA are now on the 'tenure stream' which formerly created a long period of apprenticeship, as in Germany, in the '*mittelbau*' system of working as post-doctoral researchers or research assistants. This is not to say that redundancy was unknown for the UK faculty: more than 10 years ago *Times Higher Education* (THE 2001) reported the likelihood of massive academic job losses in London institutions. Even prior to the current round of funding changes (DBIS 2011), a range of factors threatened the sector's stability. These included a changing demographic, competition from private sector (often overseas) providers, and challenging reports of poor international student experiences that threatened the UK university 'brand' overseas (Bekhradnia and Bailey 2009). Even in the recent past, it had been relatively rare for 'tenured' and permanent staff to face redundancy (UCU 2009). However, that situation is changing, as 'open-ended' contracts are introduced, where employers may treat postholders *as automatically at risk of dismissal* if a particular funding stream comes to an end (UCU 2009: 1).

Such concerns are not confined to lower-ranked HE institutions (HEIs). Trainor (2011) reports a voluntary severance scheme at Cambridge University, while Gappa and Austin (2010: 1) comment on the difficulties some US universities also face: 'They must create environments that attract highly diverse students, find new sources of revenue as traditional sources decline, maintain and enhance their technological infrastructure within budgetary constraints, and respond to numerous demands for accountability'. Meanwhile, '[academic] faculty members must have a wide array of skills to support the breadth of their students' learning needs. Knowledge continues to expand exponentially, challenging faculty members to stay current in their own area of expertise' (Gappa and Austin 2010: 5).

Although these authors focused on work-life balance, in perspectives on the changing nature of academic work in a US context, where non-tenured positions are common, they do identify technical updating, workloads and interdisciplinarity arising from 'research at the intersections of disciplines' (2010: 6) as CPD issues expressed by academics; Gale's (2011) account of academic identities among early career academics in the UK, however, reminds us that concerns may relate not just to the HE sector or country but to career positioning too.

Employability

In spite of these concerns, things are not entirely bleak for the academic faculty in the UK. Baruch and Hall (2004: 247) have suggested that academic work has more in common with what they call 'new career models' – the now contested concept of boundary-less careers – because of academics' ability to transfer their work into another institution requiring the same disciplines (Inkson *et al.* 2012). Other features that are common to contemporary career forms include relative autonomy, a focus on outputs over process, and the importance of networking for promotion and progression opportunities. Enders and Kaulisch (2006: 91) rather see the traditional importance of individual reputation, achievement against 'academic' criteria – publications, research funds secured and so on – as the basis for promotion. Such career patterns, they suggest, are increasingly challenged by managerially-driven agendas, declining tenure for non-professorial staff, the 'professionalization' of academic management and a global labour market for talented individuals (p. 93).

While 'employability' – identified as the ability to keep the job one has or to get the job one wants (Rothwell and Arnold 2007) – has been a recent preoccupation of academics in respect of their students, the new climate for UK universities means that in future, faculty will have to pay far greater attention to employability for *themselves* and to evaluate their individual career options. Previous research with UK professionals (Rothwell and Arnold 2007), adapted here to the context of academic work, is represented in Figure 14.1. It suggests that 'employability' at an individual level may be associated with a complex interaction of factors. Our definition of 'employability', therefore, is not just a matter of 'getting on' in the sense of moving up in the institutional hierarchy, but may underpin the ability to change role (possibly sideways) to sustain employment at all, or to be able to move out to a related or different role in another organization or sector altogether.

According to Hillage and Pollard (1998), 'employability' could be regarded as either a unitary construct or as one with two related components – 'internal' and 'external'. We have extended this to encompass four dimensions (represented in Figure 14.1), including *internal* 'self-belief' factors, the organization's internal labour market, alongside *external* labour market factors, the demand for the specific occupation, and the influence of the general state of the wider labour market.

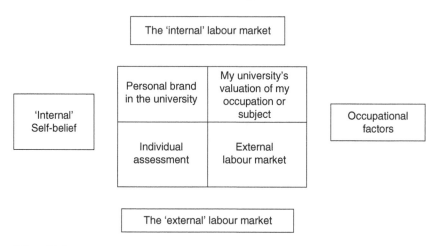

External influences

Figure 14.1   Academic employability model
Source: adapted from Rothwell and Arnold (2007).

Taking these broad distinctions and starting with internal 'self-belief/valuation of me': in the case of academics, 'internal employability' means one's personal 'brand', social capital and reputation, internal personal networks and awareness of internal job opportunities, whether promotions or for redeployment. It may also suggest one's level of qualifications, the relevance of skills held, and the extent to which ongoing CPD is evidenced. Dacre *et al.* (2012) describe an approach to enhancing employability for undergraduates which is based on developing emotional intelligence: we suggest that this should also be a dimension of the individual element of *academic* employability. Further 'internal' dimensions of employability include a changing demand for one's occupation or subject area. In some institutions in the UK, demand for subjects such as those related to business has declined, while demand for traditional subjects, such as the sciences and economics, has increased or revived (Dacre *et al.* 2012).

This subject-based perspective links to the domain of *external* aspects of employability. 'Demand' factors affecting subject areas are likely to be strongly based around dominant market priorities, although the employer 'brand' of the institution is likely to have some influence too (Ambler and Barrow 1996; Minchington 2010). This may be in a positive way, such as where a notionally 'lower-ranked' HEI has some highly-rated individual subjects, or in a negative way, where a very poor employer brand might overwhelm the positive reputation of an individual department. The general state of the labour market will also influence individual employability, such as whether alternative employment options are still available, or if there is positional conflict for jobs from new- or late-career entrants to teaching. Today, this includes those coming to HE from other sectors and into teaching- and learning-related posts, such as the category of 'new professionals' discussed by Gornall and Thomas (2001), Beetham *et al.* (2001). Finally, an individual's networking skill, reputation and personal profile (qualifications, experience) are likely to be highly significant in making career progression moves. The authors have personally experienced calibrating two HE careers across types of employment, disciplines and sectors (see also Hudson's personal perspective (this volume), discussing Bourdieu's notions of 'capital' applied to her own HE employment).

In the UK, current concerns regarding graduate employment and the difficult state of the graduate jobs market (AGCAS 2012) could also impact negatively on academics. And in subject disciplines where student employment outcomes are less positive, this may itself affect course (and staff) demand. Thus, we note how policy changes can have indirect implications for lecturers' employability too.

Continuing Professional Development

As academics ourselves then, we are advocating the potential of 'CPD' as a means of sustaining an academic career. The implications for institutions if lecturers fail to develop their knowledge-base through research, consultancy and scholarship are considerable. In terms of knowledge and skills development, academics face two competing sets of challenges. Firstly, 'knowledge obsolescence' (Rothman and Perrucci 1971), sometimes referred to as the 'half-life of knowledge' (Machlup 1962). Secondly, there is the expectation that staff will incorporate new and rapidly-advancing pedagogical practices in facing the challenge of motivating and teaching a new generation of 'digital native' students (Prensky 2001). We call this need for keeping up with specialist knowledge at the same time as responding to student or pedagogic drivers the *'dual professional'* aspect of the academic role. It places individuals under considerable pressure to maintain CPD in both areas. Thirdly, there is the expected wider requirement of 'scholarship', interpreted as academic updating, and traditionally instigated either by the individual (Elton 2009) or driven by a critical learning community (Laycock 2009a), not institutionally directed or through a programme of events (Hall 2009).

There is a dearth of research on the CPD that academics undertake and their motivations for so doing. However, Bradley *et al.* (2008) have reported a three-stage programme of research carried out within a community of practice across four Midlands universities in the UK. They investigated the CPD academics undertook and their motivations, while noting the challenges faced. An 'action' group was formed following identification of common issues across the four institutions, and this included an acknowledged *variable engagement* with institutionally-sponsored development programming by academics. Subject professions (health or business) have their own CPD requirements it is accepted, and at the institutional level, a strategic imperative to develop the 'staff resource' to keep pace with change, was initiated. The first stage of the study involved key informant interviews with individuals across the subject areas, followed by a cross-faculty survey (N = 118) in one institution. The second stage involved qualitative data collection from key informant interviews and focus groups across all four institutions. A final stage sought external insights on the data gathered, through four workshop/seminar presentations aimed at educational development practitioners. Note that quotes included here are anonymized.

The findings included some striking similarities across subject disciplines in respect of academics' CPD preferences – reading, attending conferences, network groups, browsing websites and spontaneous learning arising from everyday activity – and there was a clear *non*-preference for managerially- or institutionally-driven staff development activity. There were also some disciplinary differences: professions allied to health had no issue with portfolios and reflective processes for CPD, which contrasted strongly with most other subject areas. Art and Design respondents rated working as a practitioner in the field highly, while other subject groups did not. There were a number of relatively common priorities for future development, however, including support for applied research, preparation for management roles, and for pedagogic development. The
results reinforced the perception of a considerable diversity in practices, needs and requirements, alongside the challenge of accommodating these within overarching university frameworks. While many staff regarded CPD as part of their professional responsibilities, they frequently articulated the view that organizational support could be better:

> As a profession we have a strong ethos of CPD, but funding is an issue and support from management is also a problem. Time frame and the organisation of the teaching we deliver needs to change to enable us to engage in CPD and develop our skills.
>
> Respondent from health field

These results from the initial stage of the Bradley research were broadly supported by the second-stage data. While there was undoubtedly an enthusiastic core of CPD advocates and ambassadors amongst the academics, there were also a significant number of lecturers who had little engagement with CPD. These had diverse and often highly individual needs, were staff for whom CPD was either very difficult or a low priority, were struggling with heavy workloads, and felt unsupported by their managers. Such individuals may be some way distant from their initial professional formation, in either part of their own 'dual professional' role. Generally amongst the respondents, subject updating was identified as an individual academic responsibility, with professional (subject) groups an under-used resource to deliver this, something important for HEIs to consider. The third stage brought in expert external reviewers, which confirmed that within the sector, the job title 'lecturer' could cover a wide spectrum of work (Gale 2011) – including contractual position, pedagogic practices and the balance (or lack of it) between teaching and research.

If one theme could be picked out from the whole of the 'Midlands' research, it would relate to the 'ownership' of CPD. A starting point for the group's activity had been a perception of poor engagement with 'staff development'. Academics, perceiving themselves as professionals, were often very well disposed towards keeping up to date, but resented being directed to do so. They preferred to do this in their own way, through scholarship or research. As one person commented:

> I feel the emphasis needs to be less on encouraging people to simply attend training courses (and thereby tick boxes . . .) and more on encouraging and facilitating the ability for people to participate in collaborative forums for the exchange of ideas (. . . within or outside the University). Many people don't particularly like attending training courses but somehow feel obliged to do so to demonstrate they are fulfilling their learning objectives.

The trends observed by Bradley *et al.* (2008) are supported in part by subsequent research. Remmik *et al.* (2011), for example, found that early career academics in particular valued the support gained from their scholarly 'communities of practice' across the sector, and that this was an important part of their occupational socialization process. Shortland (2010) noted the importance of effective peer relationships for giving feedback, and that this could be a positive driver for academic development. Field (2011) has commented that the consensus on what made CPD effective within a range of educational contexts included mentoring and coaching, and that mentoring in particular worked best where the culture of the organization facilitated reflective enquiry, and where emotional well-being, emotional intelligence and collegiality were valued institutionally (p. 172). Taylor and Wilson (2011), distinctively, have emphasized the importance in CPD of individually-directed professional learning and critical enquiry, consonant with academics' traditional sense of autonomy.

Discussion and recommendations: sustaining individual employability through CPD

While it may be tempting to identify CPD as an assured way to help sustain academic careers in challenging times, this has to be tempered by recognition of the difficulty many individuals have in engaging with development. This may often be attributable to factors not of their own making, such as workload, management style, organizational context and culture, or else subject-related issues. As emphasized by Altbach and Musselin (2008):

> Successful universities and academic systems require career structures for the academic profession that permit a stable academic career, encourage the 'best and brightest' to join the profession, reward the most productive for their work, and weed out those who are unsuited for academic work. Without a career structure that attracts quality, rewards productivity, and permits stability, universities will fail in their mission of high-quality teaching, innovative research, and building a 'world-class' reputation.

We suggest that university employers need to engage much more in providing a range of flexible opportunities. It is in the universities' own interests to have academic faculty who are professionally competent, pedagogically skilled, adaptive and possess the career resilience to help sustain their institutions in challenging times. The accelerating pace of change presents two challenges however: a steep learning curve for early career academics who are struggling with the preparation of new teaching materials, establishing research, understanding pedagogic practices and coping with organizational restructuring (Gale 2011). On the other hand, established faculty face the challenge of managerial exhortations to 'step up' in an increasingly performative environment. Little wonder that many profess a desire for exit, whether via early retirement or a different post, even though this may result in a talent drain in the sector. Such 'human capital' challenges were exacerbated by changes to university funding which placed some UK institutions at financial risk (UUK 2013; UCU 2010), and whose effects could exacerbate 'binary divides' between academics and academically-related groups (Gornall 1999) in the sector.

We thus offer the following recommendations. First, HEIs have a duty of care to academic staff to support them in maintaining their professional development, by allowing some flexibility in work allocation, while also setting clear indications of what the role expectations are within the organization. This is essential at a number of levels including the maintenance of subject status, the enhancement of organizational flexibility, the ability to cope with changing circumstances, new sorts of students, research, and 'engagement' partnerships. Second, HEIs as communities of learning and scholarship, which is generated and sustained by the academic faculty, are distinct from other educational sectors and the increasing number of 'for-profit' providers. They are in a key position to attract students from across the world to study, to create the basis for HEI reputation and global standing. Yet at the institutional level, some academic employees struggle to maintain their scholarship, even though this clearly serves a 'greater good' in the corporate sense. But individual academics as 'dual professionals' have a responsibility to maintain scholarly development to sustain their own careers and employability, *independently of the institution*. They should do so by having regard to both the external as well as the internal labour market. We acknowledge too, that CPD is especially challenging for those academics and related staff who are in self-employment or providing 'bought-in services' as freelance workers (an increasing group as we write), who may thus lack access to formal organizational support systems and strategic CPD resources. Recent experience as a freelancer by one of the authors has informed the view that professional associations (in this case, the Chartered Institute of Personnel and Development) can provide valuable CPD opportunities in such situations. The Higher Education Academy in the past had excellent subject-based networks, but currently lacks the same local structures.

Concluding remarks

Relatively little is known about how academics in the UK navigate their careers. There has been no large-scale systematic study of how the academic faculty (in the UK or elsewhere) select, commence or develop professionally, or undertake career decision-making and achieve career success. There is also potential to extend research on academic CPD, presently focused in teaching-orientated universities, across the 'binary divide' to research-intensive institutions, and to include colleagues in academic-related roles and 'flexibilized' employment. Nor have the factors related to professional learning, scholarship or innovative aspects of employability research, (such as emotional intelligence) been fully explored for HE (Dacre *et al.* 2012). Another question is how far greater engagement with academic professional development actually enhances individual employability. Finally there is a need for the sector to investigate the extent of 'performative' links between the talents of individual academics, their use of CPD and organizational success. A deeper understanding of these important factors would seem to be timely.

Note

Paper based on collaboration with the *Working Lives* team (2008) in Wales, and presentations at the IPeD conference, University of Coventry, 2009–10.

Part Three

The Academic Role, Professionalities and Prospects

Introduction

Lynne Gornall

Part 3 brings together new work, new writers and the work of leading thinkers. We begin with the sharp but ironic eye of **Strathern**, who turns her forensic intelligence to a thoughtful new set of reflections on *the role of the examiner* in academic life. Typically, the approach is comparative, and we are treated to a journey of insights from a conceptual artist of the written word, where the efforts of Aboriginal health workers to do their best seems to outclass the more exotic work of US professors' 'strategizing' on research council panels. That most important but concealed of academic roles, the examiner, is followed by an 'insider' account of an equally significant role, the neglected and invisible work of the *academic as personal tutor*. An established academic, **Huyton** in the UK, draws our attention to the private places and solitary work of teachers as they support and mentor their students 'behind closed doors'. It is a subject rarely discussed in the mainstream of research literature or indeed 'managed' life, and whose value is hard (perhaps) to calculate in these most accountable of times. The work of **Cheng** comprises a study of *how teaching may be celebrated and rewarded* in higher education (HE) work. From the vantage of the teaching and learning unit, her study showcases this most valued of academic roles, its satisfactions and pleasures. She highlights UK teaching 'recognition' schemes and views about these innovations from an expert 'new community' of practitioners, discussing how a sense of academic identity is affected by formal as well as informal rewards.

Sato is also based in a central unit for the professional development of staff. The awkward positioning of *young faculty development academics* is set out for us here. This is Japan, and a 'baby boom' generation trying to make its way in a world full of uncertainties and employment ambiguities, Now they have to decide whether to bide time or to specialize in 'educational development'; and what to do about research – give it up or hybridize? Sato reveals the logic of how these staff navigate the structures and divides of HE occupational life, in trying to define a 'future' path. Crossing boundaries and evoking cultural stereotypes is an area examined by **Bertani Tress**, reporting on *Latin American academics* working as lecturers in the UK. Here, through their own words, we are inducted into their world, complex, differentiated – not so different – and, much like Strathern's health workers, struggling to remain resilient and adapt. We follow the efforts to do 'a good job', the British colleague as 'other' and somewhat unwelcoming at that, in their everyday UK working lives. The story **Richards** tells, of the *UK research scientist*, is also a salutary one, this time of gender, generation and the end of careers in academic work, as she recounts the status and issues around a 'researcher life' in fixed-term contract university employment. Career options narrow, planning is hazardous as science and research council-funded posts come to an end. Some recommendations are proposed, in trying to make the future different from the past. Issues of *work, overload, emotion and identity* are again foregrounded in a contribution from North America. **Acker** and **Webber**, based in Ontario, Canada, present the words of three *women academics at three different career stages*, on the experience of being evaluated, of self-evaluation. The chapter and its title concern the othering of women in academe. An interviewee, the most experienced, points to a new absence of language for analyzing gender and work impact in higher education today. It is a study that highlights the still unsettled locus in the land of HE work that women occupy. Is it a promised land or a compromised one, the authors ask? **Ylijoki, Henriksson, Hokka** and **Kallioniemi-Chambers** from Finland also focus on time and temporality, and the contradictions embedded in the use of email and administrative work practices, something the Working Lives team has also written about with 'established' academics. Here, the focus is on *younger and 'early career' staff in Finland*, and a wonderful irony suffuses the recounting of tasks, of a 'working life' at the keyboard. So why not take a holiday, when you can be at work at the same time! The 'dilemmas' of practice, workload, collaboration and fragmentation are expounded by these authors, in ways that will be recognizable in many national contexts. The chapter provides a useful framing for the report at the beginning of Part 4, of the Working Lives' study on UK academics' use of email at home.

15

The Academic as Examiner

Marilyn Strathern

Introduction

This chapter considers an area that is one of great personal responsibility and significance in formal education, but also perhaps the most concealed by the system and its procedures. The duty to examine is often regarded as too routine to mention, although it is a highly important dimension of academics' business. In this chapter, I go outside the UK and outside the higher education (HE) sector, to raise some issues about the place 'evaluation' has in working lives.

When, in the 1990s in the UK, I was at the beginning of trying to deal with the requirements of the audit systems of the Higher Education Funding Council for England, notably the old Research Assessment and Teaching Quality Assurance exercises, turning this into a topic for research as well as for administration, I recall being brought up sharp by one evident fact. A voice spoke up from those listening to a paper I was giving. My tone had been critical, ironic, distanced. The voice came from a student; she pointed out that academics carry out audits themselves all the time. Of course they do! Every time they set and mark examinations.

Examinations, a background

Despite readily agreeing that we are all part of 'the system', it took me a little while to recover from a sense of foolishness, to appreciate the gift that this student had given me. I looked into examinations a bit, and was fascinated to find a paper by a theorist (Hoskin 1996) from management accounting. In it, he traced current auditing practices as they have been introduced into HE (and elsewhere) via commerce, to the introduction in the mid-eighteenth century (the 1760s) of written examinations within European universities. My own university (Cambridge) and its college system contributed to changes that were also being felt, for example, in Paris and Heidelberg. When examinations ceased to be oral and began taking the form of written answers to questions, they lent themselves to other forms of enduring accreditation too. Ranking was always a possibility, but open to dispute: in the 1790s, it was mooted that all answers be marked numerically. It was now clear who was first and 'best'. Colleges encouraged this, because of competition among them to show who had the best students. The students' results were regarded as a mark of institutional as well as personal success. Thus, the idea of an examination as the formal testing of human activity joined with quantification, that is, a numerical summary of attainment, and with writing, which meant that the results were permanently available.

Alongside measurement came a new morality of attainment: if human performance could be measured, then targets could be set and aimed for. This in turn gave rise to mechanisms by which other kinds of performance could be measured too. Around the turn of the eighteenth century, the concept of 'accountability' was making its way into the commercial world, creating those modern forms of accounting from which our present impetus to audit in part comes. That financial and human performance could be combined, led to the development of accountancy techniques, which laid open just how businesses and firms were operating. And the notion of 'performance' became such a ubiquitous concept that it is salutary now to think how it came into being as a tool for judgement. The universities meanwhile went on developing their examination system. It had its human costs. It was not until the changes in examining came about that there was anything like a 'fear of failure' hanging over the heads of students. But then it took hold. As early as the 1770s, one who went on to become a professor of mathematics and university vice-chancellor found himself '[fearing] till the result was known, that he had completely failed' and 'in a very desponding mood' (quoted by Hoskin 1996: 274).

We might put this 'cost' alongside some very distinct advantages, ones that could also accrue to the students being examined. The opportunity – or the 'right' (as we might say today) – to be examined was one of the platforms on which a century later, in the 1860s, pioneers of women's participation in HE took a stance. In order to demonstrate that girls were quite as suited to enter university as boys, they spent much effort in cajoling the authorities to set tests for women pupils. In Cambridge, for example, the great step was to persuade the Local Examinations syndicate (which had recently introduced written examinations as a key means to raise standards in secondary schools) to admit girls to their public examinations (e.g. Sutherland 1994). The examinations were valued as an 'external agency', in the words of the time, that would at once test and attest to the soundness of the girls' work. The second step was to insist that women students be given the same university examinations as men. And the demand was explicitly for the examination and its results. It was a long time, however, before women were granted any *degrees* on the basis of these results.

Now I do not propose to praise or defend university examination systems with their various forms of appraisal. But all this suggests the interesting question, for HE, of how students would *like* to be audited? I use 'like' not to evoke the rhetoric of choice, but rather to suggest that we think about desire. Of course it is not something we often think about, especially in the context of university examinations. We know of other fields, notably sport, which are built upon the desire to be tested, or indeed on a desire to receive criticism of one's performance as a mark of its interest to others.

And examination is also not just a matter of getting grades – people might actually *want* to be tested. What then would be the best means? Here, I take just one component of the process: in relation to the 'right' to be examined, what about the 'duty' another must then take up? What about the responsibility to examine – and do examiners ever *want* (desire) to examine? My two historical vignettes simply assume the figure of the examiner, but it might be worth looking at this figure more closely here.

The 'examiner'

There is an interesting observation to be made, anthropologically and sociologically. One feature of UK HE by contrast with the US, for example, and with certain exceptions such as for coursework, is the norm of examinee anonymity. Traditional practices of anonymity meant that as far as examinees were concerned, an examiner's identity was not revealed (even if it could be discovered). In this, the examiner's anonymous persona contributed to the 'impersonal' ethos of the whole examination process. Ideally speaking, examinees would be judged against standards that would apply to anyone, procedures being administered by persons who knew what the standards should be, and who had no direct interest in the outcome of any one case. The observation is this, that the persona of the 'impersonal examiner' is essential for the system. Yet the requirement to examine falls on individuals as a *personal* responsibility.

Setting and marking exams, reading coursework material, assessing theses, these are all taken-for-granted duties of any academic teaching post in an HE institution. So much so that one hardly talks about it. Nonetheless, in the department I have recently left, the outstanding mandatory requirement – it outranked all other imperatives – was attendance by academic staff at the annual examiners' meeting. Final decisions had to be openly seen to be collectively taken by all, yet when it came to making an assessment, giving a mark to a piece of work, what is laid upon the examiner is a personal responsibility. The responsibility should be discharged with care and diligence, and cannot be delegated. No one else can do it.

This also means being prepared to work under considerable pressure. Examinations thus embody the very concept of a deadline. Like taking exams, or getting work in on time in continuous assessment, marking papers probably *has* to be done under a degree of pressure. Examining requires a specific orientation of time and energy on the part of the examiner, who must submit to a regimen that requires personal concentration and some dedication. It is a form of practice that is not unique to examiners, of course, and rising to the occasion is what most people do most of the time. Relatively rare then, the horror stories such as colleagues having to break into someone's office to retrieve chaotic piles of unmarked scripts.

Academic examiners in some respects may be compared to bureaucrats in the old style (pre-entrepreneurial) civil service in the UK, as described by du Gay (2009, 2000); I say 'old' because much of this has now been swept away in managerial reforms over the last 30 years, changes that have affected organizations of all kinds in the UK. Then, the relationship of the person to the role was clear. They were servants of the state, indifferent to party or partisan creed. The ethos of office meant that any private, political or moral commitments had to be set aside. What was required of the person was a mode of conduct that appeared 'impersonal'. Like the examiner, this responsibility could not be delegated.

The old and the new (now getting old!) can perhaps be summarized as the contrast between such impersonal, procedural, hierarchical bureaucracy, and the (newer) flexible, de-centred entrepreneurial body. The 'newer' is much more like a corporation, particularly in the way it facilitates the development of individuals, who become accountable *as* individuals for their functions and outcomes. This latter model of organizations is one whose management structures are horizontal rather than vertical and where individual responsibility and self-management are elicited through peer review and appraisal schemes (du Gay 2000). 'Responsibilization' thus becomes a path to *self*-fulfilment. The new public administrators are required to develop feelings of 'ownership', deploying enthusiasm for their work. They should be 'committed champions of policies whose primary function and responsibility has been in effect, as du Gay comments, 'to deliver the government's [party political] agenda' (2009: 374). Indifference in these circumstances is read as attachment to an alternative party programme (with consequences). We might want to keep a wary eye on such change.

But if it is the case that the impartiality of examiners continues to be desirable – and would we want examiners with a more entrepreneurial spirit? – the question remains of how we would reproduce that system, the persona, that kind of person.

Wider fields

Putting the figure of the examiner into a wider field could lead us out of the immediate situation, to consider what is happening to assumptions about audit at large. Are there models or warnings (or promises) for how the examiner's role might evolve? To give food for thought, I briefly introduce two situations, one within HE and one outside. They will lead us outside the UK too, to North America and to Australia. What is unusual about these two accounts is that they take for study figures not so often the focus of sociological research (in the case of the American) or anthropological research (in the case of the Australian).

Michele Lamont, a professor of sociology at Harvard University, has a monograph, *How Professors Think* (2009), on 'the curious world of academic judgment'. Based on US materials, it is about the responsibilities of peer review. The Australian anthropologist Tess Lea, by contrast, is worlds away. Called *Bureaucrats and Bleeding Hearts* (2008), her study of health provision in Aboriginal North Australia is a narrative about the persona of the 'new' bureaucrats, who struggle to discharge what they perceive as 'responsibility' for introducing 'change' without deforming local culture. Let me take the account that comes from furthest away first, where we will encounter auditing and evaluation in, to the academic, an unusual guise, and where we find 'teachers' but not of the university or school sort. It offers an example of the nitty gritty of a work programme that uses examination skills of a kind.

The personal and impersonal

Bureaucrats and Bleeding Hearts is all about learning, teaching and evaluation, even though it is set far beyond any academic milieu. It is about the delivery of health care to the Aboriginal population of North Australia, and in particular, about the staff of health care services, who are in a state of permanent uncertainty about whether their actions will have any effect. The gross indicators of effectiveness are obvious: statistics tell of premature death and depressing rates of suicide that refuse to decline. The overall judgement is that the health of Aboriginal people has failed to improve, and might even be getting worse (2008: 150), something the staff have to live and strive with.

Aside from bare statistical registers of the overall impact of the health services in the Northern Territory, is the evaluation of the performance of the health officials themselves. Not in terms of the outcome of their activities or anything like a formal examination, but in terms of the kind of service they deliver: their effectiveness as service providers. Implementation plans are rolled out with performance indicators (2008: 178–9), and targets are given numerical thresholds (2008: 158–9). Direct evaluation of their work is one among many co-existing instruments for monitoring impact – annual reports, data summaries, programme reviews, workshop recommendations and project status reports. The modes of evaluation and assessment that are brought into play involve constant reporting on what the health officials have or have not done. An inordinate amount of time, as it appears to many of them, is taken up with this associated paperwork. The officials are thus always open to the criticism that their work has not led to outcomes, or that it repeats what has been tried before, in the stop-start, white-dominated activities of their predecessors (2008: 225). By the same token, they can be bitterly disappointed when external consultants, brought in to appraise some part of the service, fail to do a proper job. In other words, they fail to introduce procedures for evaluation that will help fix perceived problems, and only come up with platitudes about what the people on the spot already know.

Now I have turned to this case less as an example of examination and evaluation procedures as such, than as an example of people carrying out responsibilities of a highly personal kind. These health workers are bureaucrats who ascribe to an impersonal ethos of public service; but as personnel, they also have to be personally enrolled in the task. The reason for this is that the occupation puts demands on them as working persons. It is a difficult job; turnover is high and self-fulfilment is left to take care of itself. The whole approach to Aboriginal welfare is governed by the need to communicate and the attempt to teach. 'If only the Aboriginals knew how unwell they are', it is said over and again, 'they would surely prevent their own disorders and live differently'. And they would be open to the workshops, fact-finding missions and health instruction programmes that the health officers try to bring them: 'better quality and more accurate information' will eventually become 'better self-understanding for the Aborigines', is their belief (Lea 2008: 121).

But intervention is not the only axis of accomplishment, for these officials also live in a post-colonial world that insists on respect for local cultures. Therefore the teaching cannot be done in any manner that smacks of being patronizing, and the health workers' greatest fear is of the collateral damage that might be done to Aboriginal lifestyle in attempts made to transform their health (2008: 146). Indeed, the bureaucrats fall over backwards to take sensitivities of all kinds into account. They are in a constant learning situation, desperate to be liked, yet vulnerable as to how they are judged by the local population.

So a major requirement is that they must always navigate with great care, using personal skills of communication, their own judgement and stamina – not just in facing unaccustomed living conditions, but in battling for funds, supplies, equipment and transport against other government services – as well as in terms of policy against a distant central office. A strenuous introduction to community working is given to every recruit, and 'the last thing' is always the evaluation sheets (2008: 87), which must be filled in every day. Constantly working to improve the programme, the organizers beg for 'feedback' from the recruits on the way they have carried out their job. For with care goes the sense of responsibility that the health worker bureaucrats feel for their subjects: regarding themselves as to some extent to blame for the chronic ill health that continues to dog the local population, it is also what compels them to continue their efforts. What they feel is, so to speak, felt on behalf of the health service in general; they *personally* act as part of this impersonal machine. This is far from the stereotype of the bureaucrat as indifferent and with no feelings (after Herzfeld 1992), or an official 'who works by a fixed routine without exercising intelligent judgment' (Lea 2008: 224).

Towards the end of her book, Lea lets us know that she worked as a bureaucrat too. And she admonishes the reader: we should not discount 'the tremendous work of imagination invested in academic and bureaucratic rationalities alike' (2008: 228). So too, her subject of study has not been so much the artifice of bureaucratic constructions as their social life, and how they are brought to life by social beings. For there is another side to these officials, whose job demands that the worker has 'sensory experiences, in every single moment of every single day', yet that needs 'to be reframed within the interpretive grid of interest-free, depersonalized, betterment-oriented service delivery' (2008: 262).

Now examining as a relatively short-lived experience is very different from the daily commitments and struggles of the Australian community health bureaucrats. And I can think of situations where the last thing one would want is for one's examiner to be experiencing the full sense of his or her lived environment. It can be preferable to have a slightly distanced attention to the 'script' or 'text' in hand. Both situations however, involve an inculcated and practiced kind of attention. If we go back to the position of examiners in the university system, Lea's ethnography offers an invitation to think *where else in our lives might we encounter examiners again*. The thought might encourage us to look anew at the work of the university examiner, and to ponder a bit on how academics do it. But just supposing one could directly observe the social life of examiners, what would that turn out to be like? We have a surrogate to hand in Lamont's volume.

The social life of examiners

How Professors Think is a very different book. It concerns a rather particular form of examination, the peer review of research grant and studentship or fellowship proposals in the US. As the author says at the end, the study might offer useful insights into other forms of academic evaluation such as with peer review journals, university presses and tenure review (promotion) committees (Lamont 2009: 248).

Peer review is an evaluative exercise undertaken as a professional service on the part of academics for the community, in other words, their own community. The academics are thus drawn from the ranks of those who also serve as examiners of undergraduate and graduate work. Given the multidisciplinary nature of funding bodies, the review process invariably throws them into the company of colleagues from a small handful of other disciplines. Five organizations were the subject of Lamont's study, including the US Social Science Research Council. The principal part of the study consisted of interviews with panellists, and programme officers across history, English literature, sociology, political science, musicology, economics, classics, philosophy and anthropology. Lamont had access to sample proposals and attended meetings of three panels.

This was a completely different kind of enterprise, in both the research and the object of research, from Lea's account of bureaucrats in Australia. However, what stands out most is Lamont's emphasis on the role that emotions play in the peer review process. She is referring to several things when she uses this term – the quality of relationships among the panellists and their interactions; the vehemence or enthusiasm with which panellists support or reject proposals; the passion they show for their disciplines. Above all, she refers to their conviction that 'the system' *works*, and that, when all is said and done, it is as fair as it could be. That can be an emotional thing too.

The US system is organized so that the final judgements are made in concert with others, even though much of the work of the reviewers (mainly reading their assignment of proposals, from 18 to 80 at a go in these cases) is done by panellists in isolation. Then there are the occasions when all meet up, to go through a shortlist with assessors from the disciplines associated with their particular grant body. So people are reading across disciplines too. Meetings are governed by explicit expectations and a general protocol. But the panels also develop informal rules of their own, ones that make the job possible. These include collegial conduct, deference to expertise, respect for disciplinary sovereignty and being open to other people's arguments. They also include a desire to get the job finished in time. Like regular university examiners, panellists work under pressure, both in meeting the deadlines for reading (often taking time out of other work at weekends) and in the intensive one- or two-day gatherings where the shortlisted applications are discussed. It is here that they come under scrutiny themselves.

The research council bodies want panellists who will do the job well. There is no question about getting their applications marked and scored; the question is how well it is done. This seems to turn largely on the conduct of the meetings themselves, that is, how people conduct themselves there. And panellists are looking at other panellists; in making their evaluations, the reviewers themselves are being evaluated. In the eyes of both the organization and fellow reviewers, what is being evaluated is how good a committee person and panel member they are. This includes reading the papers carefully, having a wide range of knowledge on which to draw, and a recognition of the persuasiveness of the arguments that reviewers put forward. There are explicit ideas about how a panel should behave, so panellists learn that being a good committee person also means respecting the consensual nature of decision-making, holding back as well as coming forward, accommodating different views and approaches, correcting for bias, giving clear reasons for opinions, ensuring consistency of standards across disciplines, bracketing off one's own interests, and above all, not holding up the flow of business. However, while being a 'good committee person' can to some extent be measured – in the way that being a judge of intellectual promise cannot – I doubt that this is the prime reason for the emphasis being put there. Rather, for the participants, as with the health officers, this kind of work has a life of its own.

Now it should be evident that although much adjudication by these reviewers is done long distance, when it comes to the final panel meetings there is no anonymity for the panellists, who indeed meet one another face to face. Nor is there at this level any anonymity for the applicants either, since part of the application consists of their curriculum vitae details. We might then ask what if anything would count as 'impersonal' in this context. Lamont, herself, both insider and outsider, makes it clear that in the majority of instances, panelists *desire* to make the process work, and work fairly. This is not just in order to dispatch the task in hand, for the panellists show a surprising degree of dedication to the overall project of academic attainment. They wish to see excellence advanced and standards upheld, wanting the 'best' candidates to win. She suggests that reviewers adopt a pragmatic conception of 'truth' (or at least of what constitutes a 'fair evaluation') as something inevitably provisional and defined by the best standards of the community at the time (2009: 240). Proposals may thus demand different standards, because they shine under different lights (p. 241). Reviewers may favour their own type of research while *at the same time* being committed to rewarding the strongest proposal overall.

Defending excellence is central to the concept many academics have of themselves, and Lamont concurs that reviewers' self-identity is tied to their self-concept as 'experts who can stand above their own interests'. That does not mean that they are disinterested in the process however: '[e]valuation', Lamont writes at the outset of her study (2009: 8), 'is a process that is *deeply* emotional and interactional'. By the same token, defending 'excellence' can lead to dispute, acrimony even, to partisanship. Panellists 'invest themselves in decisions and share excitement with others' (2009: 239), dismiss what they do not like as 'boring', declare 'idiosyncratic preferences':

[a] geographer expresses her frustration with a political scientist who refused to use [what she considered] the most appropriate tools for evaluating a proposal that focused on meaning . . . 'he was not willing to hear that or entertain that, and it made me mad' [US English for angry].

2009: 134–5

an historian criticizes another historian for her lack of disciplinary flexibility ... 'I mean she always had this one little test that she seems to be applying to everything'.

2009: 134–5

a political scientist, supports a proposal inspired by rational choice, although he is very critical of the paradigm: ... 'It just seemed to me crazy, unethical virtually, not to support this [outstanding] proposal, even though you don't agree with it methodologically'

2009: 134–5

a sociologist ... says 'If there [are] some really fine projects that come along looking for funding you would just get extremely excited about it at the level of intrinsic interests. But I might just say, 'Well you know, here's another culture project', whatever. But why should I stand in the way of a really excellent project because it doesn't get my blood boiling?'

2009: 194

So what about the question of what might count as impersonal in these situations? Let me suggest it has already been answered in the very act of being a 'good committee person', which can also encompass a 'personal' desire to see an impersonal system function properly. This is personal and emotional work, in a system that demands 'fair' and accountable outcomes. As for Lea's health workers, attachment to abstract goals elicits emotions. If the system works, this may well be necessary to its working. The professors' panel behaviour involves strategizing, parading knowledge, horsetrading, saving face, achieving compromise and 'good enough' solutions – whatever it takes in getting the job done. In the Australian case, Lea comments how the 'impersonality' of bullet-point diagnoses of problems and solutions 'triumphantly displaces the din of everyday affect' (Lea 2008: 262). But it can also be liberating 'to gain some sense of the lived-in, externally driven and consensual limits on our own agency' (2008: 237):

[w]ording yourself out of the picture, 'disimpersonating', takes considerable, practiced personal ... investiture (2008: 262).

Concluding remarks

Between these two books, we see sketched something of the contrast that can face students in HE once they have taken their final exams. On the verge of graduation, the question may go through their minds of whether to continue in academia or not. Whichever way their decision goes, freshly examined students (so to speak) may well encounter regimes of assessment beyond those they have left behind. Even if not in a teaching or examining situation like the one they have just come from, there is no finality to examination as such. Moreover, they could well find that they themselves become examiners of a kind too.

In my two examples, the case of peer review is closer to that of the conventional examiner, showing how evaluation continues throughout life in education, as a constant part of general academic process. In the case of the health workers with a mandate to 'teach', evaluation is evident as part of the monitoring of performance, and intended as much to give reassurance over the attainment of targets, as judgement of individual work. It reminds us of two sides to such life: teaching and assessment, the point being that when one rises with a sigh of relief from one's last exam, one has by no means met one's last examiner. Perhaps the two accounts make university examiners and their responsibilities, and some of the duties and roles of academic life itself, seem a little less isolated from 'the life of work' in general than their impersonal character might otherwise suggest.

Acknowledgements

This is the text of a lecture given in the Working Lives Seminar Series, Welsh Education Research Network, Cardiff, in May 2010. My warmest thanks for the opportunity, and for the scrutiny it received. Its theme comes from an earlier invitation to speak at the 2009 C-SAP (Centre for Sociology, Anthropology and Politics in teaching and learning) conference in Birmingham on 'Roles, Rights and Responsibilities', under the title 'Responsibility, life and the examiner'.

16

Personal Tutoring in Academic Work

Jan Huyton

Introduction

Individual tutorials in private offices are among the most invisible encounters in universities. Baker *et al.* (2006) have noted ways in which researchers have sought to articulate the student voice in these encounters. Researchers have also commented on the affective relations involved in individual tutorial work with students (for example, Owen 2002; Easton and Van Laar 1995; Earwaker 1992). So too, a study of academics on their experiences of workload intensification (Ogbonna and Harris 2004) noted that the individualization of work, 'emotional labour' and lack of collegial discursive space were factors that both created and exacerbated challenging aspects of academic lives. Another perspective, the notion of 'the academic citizen' (Macfarlane 2007), theorizes a motivation to engage in a 'service role' in education beyond researching and teaching, to include counselling students and mentoring colleagues. Still the voice of the tutor has remained relatively unexplored.

Following the editors' Introduction to this volume on some of the significant but 'invisible' aspects of academics' work (and see Daunton *et al.* 2008), this chapter offers an insight into otherwise hidden work in higher education (HE). It takes data produced using participative methods that were designed to capture the voice of the tutor. Ten subjects, drawn from a range of British universities, participated in the study. Each articulated the micro-context of tutor-student interaction, using reflective written journals. There followed exploratory critical reflection undertaken face-to-face with the researcher, underpinned methodologically by an exploration of the importance of collaborative discussion amongst peers. This moves away from the perspective of 'workplace individualization models' which focus on competitiveness, and may ignore more 'collegial' working styles (Trowler 2008; Macfarlane 2007; Ogbonna and Harris 2004). The method proved effective and transformative, revelatory even, for most participants, while producing rich qualitative data for the study. This chapter concentrates on observations by participants of the context and essence of 'personal tutoring' as they saw it. It should be noted however, that while the term 'personal tutor' is commonly used in the policy and discourse of HE, there is no universally understood definition of the role or professional pedagogical practice for this.

Practice models

Three models based on Earwaker's studies (1992) are used in the literature for discussing personal tutor practice. The 'pastoral model', whereby students are allocated to a specific tutor deemed responsible for pastoral and academic support, may be problematic in practice. Some tutors are less available than others, and some students fail to engage with their tutors for a range of reasons (Crozier *et al.*, 2008; Macfarlane 2007). 'Professional referral models', by contrast, rely on provision of support from staff employed centrally in student services departments (Thomas 2006). Earwaker's 'integrated curriculum' model (1992) involved timetabled group tutorials that were designed to encourage and facilitate supportive relationships between students and between students and staff. Owen (2002) and Yorke and Thomas (2003) found this to be proactive and developmental, and a move away from more 'problem-based', remedial approaches (Laycock 2009a) to framing the personal tutor-student relationship and its topics.

The tutors

Taking part in the study were 'Mark', 'Phil' and 'Erica' (Russell Group institutions); 'Danielle', 'Angela' and 'Anne-Marie' (post-1992 institutions); 'Dylan', Alexander ('Alex') and 'Will' (1960s civic universities) and 'Martin' (HE in a further eduction (FE) college). These are all pseudonyms. In the following discussion, the types of institution are referred to as Russell Group (RG), post-92, Civic, and HE/FE.

For Phil (RG), 30 years of experience working at his research-intensive university led him to conclude that today's students were more willing to approach personal tutors. His view was that, historically, students 'just got on and managed'; this was shared by seven other participants. Each mentioned that when *they* were students, they would not have approached academic staff about personal or pastoral matters at all. Some would not have sought help even for academic difficulties.

Martin's 15 years of HE tutoring experience had been spent in three universities and he was now in an FE college. He remembered a more collegial system for staff and students, more opportunity for student peer support, and a range of staff who would be supportive to students at a college 'community' level. He described 'a strong welfare system' based around the personal tutor, with students living in halls of residence supported by wardens. Most of his students now travelled to university daily, eliminating the collegial support mechanisms offered by a residential community. Many of Martin's current students were working long hours to fund their university experience and to support their families, often taking night shifts in local supermarkets. Martin felt that the loss of the residential community had been a causal factor in students seeking help from him as a tutor. This accorded with research by Wilcox *et al.* (2005), Holdsworth (2006) and Crozier *et al.* (2008), who demonstrated the supportive value of social friendships between students, and the fact that those who live at/commute from home may miss out on these forms of peer and social support.

Phil (RG) was clear that today's students were dealing with problems rather more serious than the normal pressures of university life. He particularly mentioned students with 'caring' responsibilities for family members. Other tutors mentioned students with a range of quite complex family scenarios or financial difficulties, and students who were dealing with their own health issues. Phil was adamant that responding to this was not an indicator of 'therapy culture' (Ecclestone and Hayes 2009), but part of a discourse about a 'duty of care' by the institution:

> [O]rdinary services should be able to pick this up, but they won't, because students aren't in the ordinary world, they are in a university world. If they go and see their GP then they might get referred through there, but I think the personal tutoring service can provide something better.

Most students at Phil's university were residential, living within an academic community that was external to the local community. Unlike Martin (HE/FE), Phil seemed to favour an individualized rather than peer support system for students, yet his description of *practice* indicated a team approach, amongst both personal tutors, and between them and other professionals acting in 'referral mode'.

Some tutors articulated their tutoring 'ethos' by distancing themselves from the positions of others. Anne-Marie and Danielle, both from post-92 universities, and 'Erica' from the Russell Group sector, were quite clear that their engagement with research had been affected by colleagues who avoided individual contact with students. Such colleagues had neglected their broader 'citizenship duties', they argued, to concentrate on research output. 'Practice' in these contexts seemed to be determined by individual discretion rather than a shared or wider sense of collegial working.

Most participants felt that practice in personal tutoring related to the culture of their academic discipline. That being so, it was possible to detect a sense in which informants from more vocational areas felt that some colleagues had not moved on from vocationalism, and treated students in the same way as they would treat community-based clients. Two such participants distanced themselves from what they felt was an inappropriate 'nurturing culture', describing colleagues who approached working in an academic setting as though still a community worker. As Dylan (civic) comments: '[A] couple of them are like that and treat the students as 'young people' in that sense. I don't, I treat them as students'.

Service, boundaries and signposting

Tutors in the study generally worked to an amalgam of the 'pastoral' and 'referral' models, whereby they would signpost students to other professionals as necessary. This was largely determined by individual judgement, and there was a marked lack of knowledge of any wider or theoretical debates around personal tutoring models or the political and policy context of this aspect of educational practice. This resulted in a tendency to draw on personal reference points rather than a shared understanding of the boundaries of appropriate ethical practice. Humphrys (2005) has stressed the importance of regular dialogue and debate between academic staff and student services' personnel, but the responsibility for productive working relationships here seemed to be located with individual tutors, and did not emanate from institutional imperatives. Managers had a role in allocating lists of students to tutors, but were largely not involved in any supervision or development of personal tutoring practice. Erica (RG) and Dylan (civic) comment:

> I wouldn't hesitate to refer students on. I think it's really good. What's there is excellent and I would hope that if we can't necessarily do it ourselves, we can always refer students on.
>
> Erica, RG

> I think part of that role, that central service role, is to make the services widely known [to tutors and students] and for the personalities to be widely known as well. But it doesn't seem to be that way.
>
> Dylan, civic

Communication with other professionals was not necessarily related to the positioning of role boundaries. 'Erica' and 'Phil' (both RG) and 'Alex' (civic) each described well-developed avenues of referral to centrally-located student services, which they felt reflected strong boundaries to their personal tutoring role. Yet each also described some quite complex and sustained interactions that they had with students, acknowledging that they also spent time after work worrying about these:

> I got an email from the student last year in March or April saying that he was looking out at [the cliffs] thinking how beautiful it was. I didn't go and visit the student but I made sure that he was okay the next morning. Because students do throw themselves off [the cliffs].
>
> Phil, RG

> Even with training and experience, there are still some students who you go home thinking about. 'Number 3' that I wrote about, because obviously that wasn't my first and not my last interaction with him, and I think about him an awful lot because his situation is really difficult and he's extremely isolated.
>
> Alex, civic

In some cases, the student services' professional was seen as complementary rather than an alternative to the intervention of the academic member of staff. This seems unsurprising given that academic staff are in a unique position of trust to build integrated social and academic relationships with students, as Macfarlane has noted (2007: 137). 'Therapeutocracy' theories (Habermas 1987; Chriss 1999) see the proliferation of professionals for helping with personal problems as an indication of the move towards association with unfamiliar others, in preference to more meaningful engagement with helpers from one's own community. Tutors participating in the study did note the tendency for students to seek out the 'ear' of a familiar member of academic staff, in preference to less familiar student services' professionals.

> I do find that students do go to particular people within the school. They don't go to everybody; we have got a personal tutor system so theoretically they are evenly spread out for personal issues. But it doesn't happen like that, they choose the person that they feel comfortable with . . . I am one of those people, and that is because I've obviously given the impression that I want to help, that I am there for you etc. Which I think is great because that is how I feel, but then sometimes I get angry with myself for being that giving, if that makes sense.
>
> Angela, post-92

Accessibility of tutors

The issue of time is also relevant, particularly in relation to the notion of 'instant living' (Bauman 2000). Academic staff were often more easily accessible, compared with student services professionals, who were usually available on an appointments basis. Tutors described situations where they had been approached at the end of a lecture, or where students had arrived unannounced at their office door. Only two tutors had clearly defined boundaries in terms of not operating an 'open door' policy, others felt that no matter how busy or tired they were, there was a personal, moral and ethical duty to respond 'in the moment'. Many were uncomfortable even with asking a student to return later at a more convenient time.

Though many felt impelled to respond instantaneously, a number of tutors also commented that they were picking up extra personal tutoring by being physically present in their offices. In fact, implications went beyond simple workload inequities, to the very heart of career progression and how this work was valued. There was general agreement that 'research is what counts' in HE employment today. This overshadowed 'personal tutoring' in terms of recognition and reward systems: Will (civic) felt it was important to be 'good enough' as a tutor, but that it would be foolish to spend too much time on performance in this area, whereas Erica (RG) felt uncomfortable that the research agenda had often been sufficiently strong to displace her student-centred ethos.

All participants used 'nurturing' imagery which they either identified with or distanced themselves from in terms of personal tutoring practices. 'Gendered' distinctions between 'research activity' and 'student support' work, with research valued for its masculine rationality and student support being undervalued as feminine nurturing (Leathwood and Hey 2009; Bellas 1999; Morley 1998) undoubtedly informed some of the data in this study. Indeed, Hochschild (2003) suggests that more 'emotion work' is undertaken by females, who are performing the nurturing role of protomother. However, within the sample of lecturers here, the gendered nurturing role was performed by *both* male and female tutors. Moreover, the four participants who were parents consciously drew on their parenting experience to describe their roles with students.

Specific issues

Eight tutors described being approached for help by students with mental health problems. This is not a new phenomenon, given the findings of previous studies (see Owen 2002; Easton and Van Laar 1995; Earwaker 1992). Most tutors were untrained in mental health awareness, and all were unsupported and unsupervised in this aspect of their work. This supports Stanley and Manthorpe (2001) findings, that a significant number of personal tutors were not confident in dealing with mental health problems, and that universities were reluctant as organizations to take on this role. Tutors did not appear to have considered that they might effectively be ameliorating some of the detrimental effects of wider education and social policy on student mental health, by supporting individual students in the private space of the personal tutorial. This critique aligns with Bauman's (2000) view, in arguing that the individualization and depoliticization of modern society allows issues to remain with the individual and not become problems for the state. There was no sense that tutors recognized their part in this.

There was simply no institutional forum for tutors to discuss issues such as these, and, in many cases, they had taken on students' problems because they were worried and concerned about them, even if they lacked the information and experience needed to make effective referrals. Rana (2000) suggests a great deal of emphasis is placed on the visible and tragic stories of students who develop serious mental health problems, yet with little recognition given to the support offered by tutors that prevents minor problems from escalating. Dylan (civic) had a simple yet effective ability to notice and intervene when a student was not dealing well with the death of her mother. Other examples from amongst the sample included intervention with a student's landlord, and assistance with feelings associated with marriage breakdown, child abuse and serious long-term illness. Such interventions ranged from guidance on procedures (e.g. extending assignment submission dates) to more fundamental direct assistance. We shall never be able to discover what the outcomes would have been had these interventions not taken place, or whether they prevented more serious health consequences for the student. The consequences for tutors are clearly apparent however.

Tutoring as unseen and unsupervised

The solitary nature of the tutor experience was striking. In many cases, taking part in the reflective study had been the first opportunity for participants to discuss situations where a student had presented with challenging personal or emotional difficulties. Literature on counselling supervision indicates the importance of facilitated reflective practice for competent and ethical working (for example, Feltham 2000). 'Alex' (civic) had found one of his managers to be sceptical about supervision, thinking it was a forum for staff complaints rather than a professional development function. Three tutors reported having discussed their work with their respective spouses, who acted as unofficial support mechanisms for these difficult scenarios. Others had turned to friends or particularly trusted colleagues. The implications for confidentiality are self-evident, but the tutors in question did not see this as particularly problematic.

Morley (1998) has cautioned against the propensity for institutions (and tutors themselves) to overlook the support needs of tutors engaged in 'emotion work'. Consequences for the welfare of the tutor are quite clear when one considers the literature on burnout, and the fact that giving support to another can leave a practitioner feeling their own needs have been overlooked (Hawkins and Shohet 2007; Bakker *et al.* 2004; Ogbonna and Harris 2004; Wilkins 1997). Most tutors agreed that they did not request support for themselves for fear of appearing vulnerable or inadequate. This is an example of Fineman's theory of the stress trap of professionalism (2003), whereby practitioners feign invincibility. For some, the need to appear invincible was related to a perceived academic (and wider) culture of stoicism. Others described occasions when they had approached line managers for support or supervision, only to be told they were being inappropriately 'needy' (discussed also by Dixey and Harbottle, this volume).

These experiences challenge Ecclestone and Hayes (2009), who caricatured the 'therapeutic university', where tutors persistently and inappropriately seek support for the emotional demands of the role. These authors also characterize 'reflection' as a 'purely therapeutic model of practice' (p. 101). This contrasts with the idea that reflecting in or on action is a fundamental means of transforming and developing practice (Schön 1987). Habermas (1987) argues that without dialogue, practitioners will be unable to achieve the detachment needed to avoid self-deception. A facilitator, whether this is a peer or a professional supervisor, can raise awareness of tacit routines and rituals that may obscure a tutor's own ability to notice and critique the basis on which they have conducted their practice. All tutors in the study produced well-considered reflective journals about their personal tutorial interactions. These indicated however, that the culture of the HE workplace did not generally allow space for 'reflective practice'.

A more 'collegial' model (Macfarlane 2007) by contrast, offers opportunities to develop a shared, collective personal tutoring ethos. Where collegial activity was described in this study as 'discussions and mutual support about personal tutoring issues', it had developed largely around friendship groups rather than any HE programme or disciplinary team's initiative. 'Offloading' to colleagues or sharing experiences was infrequent and informal however, tutors often relating this to the lack of shared time and space at work. Phil (RG) described a more solid, reciprocal process of discussion and disclosure between long-standing colleagues. He expressed concern about colleagues at the start of their careers, for whom 'demands of research and bureaucracy' were now much greater, resulting in fewer opportunities for collegial discussions and sharing of practice. Martin (HE/FE) also had a historical perspective of space and time for formal and informal collegial dialogue. He felt this was no longer present in the workplace culture in HE. Participants who were newer to the job had fewer reference points for notions of 'collegiality', and thus appeared to view a lack of collegial space as the norm.

A questionnaire conducted with informants several months after their participation in the reflective study revealed an increased critical awareness of practice and context, and stories of transformative discoveries from individual and collegial reflection. This leads us to conclude that reflective practice and academic citizenship are not simply 'nostalgic notions from a bygone age' but fundamental professional development mechanisms for consistent, equitable, ethical practice, and ones that need to be supported through regular opportunities for facilitated reflection. These are management, institutional, human resources and leadership matters, as well as individual, professional and sector.

Concluding remarks

Whilst emotional labour theories (Hochschild 2003; Salisbury this volume) and 'therapeutocracy' (Chriss 1999; Habermas 1987) present relevant analytical frameworks, Macfarlane's notion of 'the academic citizen' and its associated 'service role' adds an additional dimension which is helpful in contextualizing academic workplace and culture. These theories together raise awareness of the unacknowledged consequences of the service role, opaque role boundaries, and the sense of decline of academic citizenship in HEIs. The reflective data may lead us to conclude that working in isolation with individual students has become normal, perhaps precipitated by a decline in perceived 'collegiality' reported by those participants with more extensive experience, and considered in more detail elsewhere in this volume.

Now we must thank our 10 participants for sharing their experiences, and consider whether the opportunity to reflect on their practice using reflective journals and critical reflective discourse was helpful. All 10 commented on the transformative and awareness-raising qualities of reflecting on their personal tutoring practice. For most, this had meant a clearer understanding of roles and boundaries, sometimes resulting in discussions with colleagues about collective understandings of practice. For Will and Dylan (both civic), reflecting on contextual issues had brought new awareness of the institutional and policy constraints of practice, and both had become more sensitive to issues of 'individualism' and 'competitiveness' amongst colleagues. Angela and Anne-Marie (both post-'92) had complained of being unable to undertake PhDs because of their demanding workloads. Both, after taking part in the study, now had clearer boundaries and had managed to find space to begin their research. One tutor who had been struggling with stress-related illness described how the reflective study had helped make links between boundary-setting and tutor well-being. Martin's HE/FE experience was an exception, in that he had been spending even more 'welfare-type time' with students, perhaps because of worsening staff-student ratios and extra workload pressures that had affected his ability to engage with research and embark on a doctoral study.

This should not be the end of these stories. Further reflective discussion is needed to deal with the discoveries constructively. Whilst some participants had continued to be more reflective, most noted that reflection had stopped in the absence of external facilitation. The effects of the policy climate on workloads had caused most to be pessimistic about the prospects for reflective or collegial space, some commenting that they had an increased sense of individualism and territorial competitiveness now, in a context where funding was increasingly at risk. The academic community must remain alert to the welfare of its citizens and of means to address this effectively, sensitively and intelligently. A future research project could explore with academic managers, human resources and student services' staff, this in relation to 'the student experience' in HE. It is perhaps time for the potential of Earwaker's 'integrated curriculum' model (1992) to be fully realized.

17

Professionalizing Teaching Identity and Teaching 'Excellence' Schemes

Ming Cheng

Introduction

Understanding 'academic identity' is important in helping to explain academics' belief systems and actions (Fanghanel 2012). Some writers see academic identity as related to different academic roles and disciplinary areas (Becher and Trowler 2001). For others, it is something undergoing a massive transformation, as new divisions of labour in higher education (HE) lead to re-defined notions of academic professionalism (Fanghanel 2012; Barry *et al.* 2006; Nixon 2003; Nixon *et al.* 2001). Specific factors may also influence perceptions of identity. These include the type of university involved, academics' professional role and status, employment type, level of seniority and career specialization (Clegg 2008; Blackmore and Blackwell 2006; Sikes 2006; Enders 2005; Henkel 2005).

Teaching identity

In order to take forward some of these considerations, this chapter explores academics' identity in and through their teaching. Teaching constitutes a fundamental part of academic work (Clegg 2008: 330), where notions of individual autonomy and control are most valued: a deep sense of engagement with teaching, Clegg argues, creates space for the exercise of personal autonomy. There is also an increasing emphasis on university teaching in the UK, which is lately indicated by the Browne Report (2010) and awards of national teaching fellowships by the Higher Education Academy (HEA). These developments suggest a trend for notions of 'good practice' in HE teaching to be encouraged and rewarded (Turner and Gosling 2012), more 'embedded' in mainstream academic employment and institutional policy perhaps, than hitherto.

This chapter seeks to provide an insight into how individual academics understand their identity as academics when there is an increased importance given to teaching at the national level. It will explore whether winning a university teaching award reinforces and disseminates 'good practice' within an institution, and the reasons for this. Understanding perceptions is important, because there is limited research into whether the growth of teaching award schemes is really linked to academics' own values about the importance of teaching (Kreber 2000; Macdonald 1998). For example, Fanghanel and Trowler (2008) have argued that award schemes misrepresent the nature of academic work. Critically, they suggest that these have *not* created cohesion between teaching and research activities at all. Similarly, Turner and Gosling (2012: 415) observe that many staff have expressed detachment from teaching recognition schemes in HE.

Professionalizing teaching identity

Of the different interpretations of academic identity, one view is that academics are loyal primarily to their subject areas (Becher and Trowler 2001; Healey 2000). This view is closely linked to an image of academics as the 'products' of traditional disciplines, in a quest for scholarly knowledge, and detached from the world of everyday life (Beck 2002). For some writers, academics formerly gained autonomy and status from their membership of such a professional community – their subject grouping – which protected them from the external influences of the government (Beck and Young 2005; Kogan and Hanney 2000). However, the marketization, expansion and diversification of HE (David 2011), together with quality and audit processes, and the development of new ways of teaching and assessment, have arguably led to the emergence of some *new* forms of academic 'professionalism', discussed also in Section IV of this volume. These are particularly in relation to 'pedagogy' or consideration of the nature and practice of teaching (Nixon 2003, 1996). Nixon describes them as involving a new form of agreement-making between professionals and their publics, where academics sense their identity as something derived from a capacity to learn from, listen to and move forward with the communities they serve.

Related to this, institutional and policy mechanisms, including the setting up and funding of Teaching and Learning 'practice' centres in the UK (CETLs), have thus become established in order to encourage, stimulate and resource such practitioner learning and development (Sikes 2006; Skelton 2005). The Higher Education Funding Council for England (HEFCE) has assumed the management of the Teaching Quality Enhancement Fund (TQEF) (1999–2009), the 'Centres of Excellence in Teaching and Learning' (CETL) network, and the Higher Education Academy (HEA) in order to underpin and develop institutions' own and the sector's Learning and Teaching strategies (HEA 2008a). The HEA itself provides a national focus for institutional teaching and learning excellence through the National Teaching Fellowship Scheme (NTFS), to reward academics in teaching in England and Northern Ireland (HEA 2008b). As a result, all HE institutions today are encouraged to recognize and reward 'outstanding individual teaching achievement' corresponding with these national schemes.

There has been a gap in qualitative research however, and evaluation of Teaching Awards recognition, while those studies available have been mainly confined to the national schemes (Gibbs 2000). There is a view, that in order to encourage involvement in 'teaching excellence', by both academics and their subject groupings within the discipline areas (Trowler *et al.* 2005; Skelton 2004; Warren and Plumb 1999), and to build wider credibility, that 'evaluation' needs to be set within institutional contexts. There is thus an opportunity to contribute data from case studies of individual institutions.

Research methods

This chapter will explore how the 'winners' of Teaching Excellence Awards in a 'post-1992' modern UK university viewed the impact of winning the award on their own teaching identity as HE professionals. The aim is to explore understandings of how academics' teaching is valued personally and extrinsically, and to consider how this relates to notions of 'good teaching practice' in HE. The winners (my informants) were nominated for *outstanding contributions to student learning* by their colleagues and students. From this, two research questions were developed, to consider:

1   the effect of winning a Teaching Excellence Award on the winners' own self-perception as 'teachers in HE'.
2   The extent of the impact of winning the award on the encouragement of good pedagogic practice more widely within the institution.

Seventeen interviews were conducted, comprising university Teaching Excellence Award winners (n = 15), together with two panel members (n = 2) of the award scheme's board. The semi-structured, interpersonal nature of each interview enabled attention to be paid to individual differences. The interviewees were from six different schools/departments, and were selected to provide a representative group of academics based on gender, subject area, experience and seniority. The informants included professors, principal lecturers and senior lecturers. Three had also received National Teaching Fellowship Awards. Each interview began with a short briefing about the project, and care was taken not to 'cue' participants to formulate responses in line (or otherwise) with the study. It was also important to ensure that the identity of interviewees was sufficiently anonymized and could not be deduced through the use of 'quoted' material.

Findings: perceived identity as teachers

There was considerable common ground in how the award winner interviewees considered their teaching identity. Unanimously, they related this to the disciplines they worked in. This corresponds with the argument that 'disciplinary differences' influence how academics understand their core professional identity (Becher and Trowler 2001; Healey 2000; Becher 1994). For example, a male lecturer in occupational health described his identity as both a teacher and as an occupational therapist: 'It's true that you normally say your profession first. I might say that I was an occupational therapist, but I would see myself as, um, as now of course after so many years, first as a teacher' (TEA3).

'Teacher' and 'lecturer' were the most frequently used words to describe interviewees' identity as teachers. Eleven of the interviewees called themselves lecturers or teachers, and six preferred the title of 'teachers' to that of 'lecturers', which is interesting in an HE setting. One reason was that they thought people outside the academy might perceive a university lecturer as a 'pompous person' who 'knows it all', and as someone who was unapproachable. The other reason given was that the term 'teacher' was also easier to understand for outsiders. A female interviewee from the School of Business further explained her feeling that the term 'lecturer' was connected not only with teaching, but also with individual personality factors together with the development of teaching *skills in a specific discipline*:

> I think if you are a really good teacher [then] you can teach, not almost anything [but] some things. My communication skills and my ability to explain something fundamentally well ... [is over and above what] I do within the sphere of the legal environment.
>
> TEA1

One male participant in the study expressed doubts about whether 'teacher' or 'lecturer' would be the best terms to describe his teaching identity. He referred to this as principally being 'in the classroom with the students'; in other words, as something *relational and interactive*:

> I love what I do but the main thing is the teaching, and I know 'teacher' doesn't really describe what I do in terms of [labelling me as] the 'wise one' and you need to learn from me. I do see it as a group activity. 'Lecturer' just sounds – but I don't give lectures – so I'm not quite sure what the word is. But that's the biggest buzz, the actual being in the classroom with the students.
>
> TEA11

The above comments illustrate what most interviewees said, that they related their teaching identity attributes to values and activities around helping students. Teaching skills, subject specialism and the 'understanding of teaching' were thought of as the key elements that informed this sense of occupational identity and also personal self-worth. This can be understood as aspects of the 'knowledge base' for teaching, as well as dimensions of *pedagogical professional knowledge* in HE (Berthiaume 2007). They also connect to notions of the 'emotional' content and context of teaching/academic work referred to in Part I of this volume, and by Huyton in her work on personal tutoring in HE.

Valuing teaching

There have been a number of studies on the understandings of teaching (Pratt *et al.* 1998) and of how academics experience their work in this area (Malcolm and Zukas 2009; Prosser and Trigwell 1999; Trigwell 1995, 2000; Trigwell and Prosser 1997). From them, we see that individual conceptions of teaching often illustrate one of two views: teachers who see their primary role as conveying special or general knowledge, and those who see their 'teacherly' role as to develop students' own conceptions of learning. The former is a fairly 'traditional' perspective, and while it has its place, would not today be regarded by many lecturers or others as very progressive in pedagogical terms. Unsurprisingly then, and in this 'new university' context, most of the interviewees in this study identified with the latter view. But beyond this, they also saw their *teaching* as a process of stimulating the desire of students to learn, and to become independent learners themselves. This approach, of teaching for 'learner autonomy', is also discussed in Part IV of this book (Ecclesfield and Garnett; Rogers).

All the award winners I interviewed saw university teaching as a 'rewarding job': their teaching would enable students to see that there were opportunities beyond the life they currently had, as well as giving different ways of thinking, that went beyond normal or 'typical' modes. Again, teaching would give students confidence in *learning*, and thus develop independent skills, enabling them to 'keep on learning', something Nixon (2011) discusses in the context of the 'public' role of HE. As a result, they could flourish creatively, developing their own 'enquiring' and cognitive ability through out life. A third view was that teaching could help relate students' learning to work practices, and help them to feel 'empowered' in the labour market. These perceptions suggest that the award winners understood their pedagogic role as a complex one, where they not only presented ideas and concepts through teaching and professional engagement, but also led students to think how to act on these now and in the future. The conceptualizations suggested that 'teaching' was considered as something far more than an 'occupational activity', but as a 'professional calling' and 'vocation', with moral responsibility for the students' beneficial learning experience and ongoing development (Carr 2006).

The informants in my study affirmed that they were proactive in motivating and inspiring student learning. Positive changes in students then reciprocally affirmed and stimulated teachers' own valuing of and passion for teaching, increasing their own confidence and enthusiasm. A male interviewee from the School of Law was impressed by students' motivation in attending his course, even though they did not receive any credits: 'One of the things that struck me the most about the law student participation [is that] whereas the police students *have* to do it and they are being assessed, the law students volunteer' (TEAW7). Another interviewee from a Health Professions school described students' increased confidence after undertaking her course:

> Students say they're coming back with a greater confidence in themselves and in their knowledge [base]. They're coming back with a sense that they've done some good, which has made them feel that they've actually made a difference to people's lives.
>
> TEAW6

This 'virtuous circle' helped to create active and independent learning among students, and consequently was perceived by academics in the study to have made them feel as 'equal participants' in the learning process. A female interviewee from a business studies background emphasized how treating her students as 'equals' could bring the benefit of different information and experience to the class:

In my practice, I don't ever see myself as passing on 'knowledge'. It's about stimulating knowledge [development] . . . because they've all been exposed to media of some kind, film, TV, [whereas] obviously I can't see everything that's available to see.

TEAW12

The 'teaching excellence' interviewees affirmed the role identified in the literature (Biggs and Tang 2011) of 'committed teaching' as contributing to student learning. They related students' intellectual achievements to the notion of teaching as a 'rewarding profession'. However, it has to be stated that few distinguished academic careers appear to have emerged to date solely through the 'teaching' route – as a number of observers have commented (Sikes 2006; Young 2006) – or at least ones that have been widely celebrated and valorized in the sector.

Perceived value of the award

Apart from two academic interviewees who commented that winning the award had little impact on their identity and practice, the remaining 13 acknowledged its value. They found that it had strengthened and professionalized their sense of 'academic identity' *as* teachers, and further increased their commitment to teaching itself. This does support the view (promoted by agencies like the HEA) that teaching awards could work as a strong incentive to improve academic practice. Indeed, they are becoming a standard way for institutions to give recognition for this role (Carusetta 2001; Seldin 1999; Wright 1995). When good teaching is rewarded and sustains academics' commitment to the improvement of the pedagogical role, it creates positive feedback cycles – and a strong practical argument for institutions to explicitly honour the scholarly work of teaching. The two interviewees who attached 'limited importance' to winning the award included one who was from a modern languages background, who did not want to be perceived by students as a 'special' teacher simply because of the award. This is also identified and discussed by Turner and Gosling (2012). This lecturer's goal was to help students think in a way that they would not do otherwise: 'I want students to feel that I'm an excellent teacher or an interesting teacher because I showed them something which otherwise life might not have shown them . . . [and not because of winning an award]' (TEA10).

The study also revealed that though the participants spanned the age and career ranges of academic professionals, the value of the award was better appreciated by early-career academics than by their more established colleagues. A professor explained:

My profile had already been established before I got the teaching award. If I was a new, a relatively new lecturer . . . I'm sure that it would probably have motivated me to do things that perhaps I wouldn't have thought of doing before.

TEA4

This participant accepted that an award was more likely to motivate a relatively new lecturer to innovate, take risks and experiment. Another interviewee saw the role of the award as an explicit institutional affirmation that teaching and learning were important:

> It shows [that] the university values teaching and the learning of students of course, that's the most important. It shows that [the university] values learning – student learning – more than just valuing research.
>
> TEA3

Thirteen of the interviewees appreciated the value of the award as beneficial to teaching at both institutional and individual level. However, they were also aware that, although the award would encourage wider interest in 'good teaching' in the institution, it had not necessarily increased the *status* of teaching *per se* within the university. *Research* was still being prioritized in 'status' terms (Ginns *et al.* 2010). There was a feeling that the institution wanted to use the award scheme to improve its profile for teaching quality (as attractive for students). This was seen to be (driven) by external competitiveness factors rather than professional/pedagogical values, as the university in fact became more research-intensive. It is paradoxical: the award scheme, despite its 'success', had not effectively improved feelings about the status of teaching in the institution, or redressed the perceived 'imbalance' between teaching and research there (NCIHE 1997: para. 8.9; see also Walker 2006). Nevertheless, the teaching award at the case study institution was perceived by two-thirds of the interviewees as a morale-boosting way to acknowledge those academics who had developed good teaching and learning practice with students and courses. Terms used included: [it is] 'an accolade', 'a nice gesture', 'a launch platform' from which to try new ways of teaching:

> The award is [a] kind of 'backing' to me to sort of say 'Well, you're an award winner', there's almost an expectation that you're going to push the envelope and try new things, because what you've done up to now works, has been recognized, i.e. 'don't stop there, keep going'. So it's, yeah, it's a kind of launch platform.
>
> TEA2

Another interviewee from the Media School also described the 'accolade' as a motivation to further develop and improve, putting more ideas into practice:

> To be recognized for what you do is obviously very flattering . . . and gives you the motivation and the sense to carry on . . . taking your best practice forward for what you've been recognized for doing.
>
> TEA12

Thirteen of the study participants had a sense that, although their teaching practice as a whole would not necessarily shift dramatically as a result of winning the award, it was a tangible, personal and public recognition of teaching competence and professional success in a key area. They planned to include it on their CVs. A lecturer from the School of Law commented on the 'boost' to his own confidence:

I have always seen myself . . . as a competent teacher as well as a lecturer, as a facilitator of learning, and that award sort of consolidates that feeling that I had about that aspect of my role.

TEAW7

This increased confidence expressed by many of the interviewees suggests that winning the award worked as more than 'tokenism' for the academics involved. While many recent HE changes might have reduced the confidence and self-esteem of some academic staff, the award reinforced their sense of agency as pedagogically-engaged professionals. Interviewees valued this sense of greater self-esteem brought to them by the 'external' recognition and wanted to improve further. It showed that the institution agreed with them in valuing and perhaps prioritizing teaching, and the importance of developing more 'teaching knowledge' strategies. Perhaps the greatest reward, however, was that the recognition arose from the assessments of their students and colleagues.

Concluding remarks

This chapter has explored how winners of an excellence award in a post-1992 university in the UK interpreted the impact of this on their understanding of themselves as academics and teachers. It revealed that most felt that 'research' in the institution was still prioritized, yet that winning the award did reinforce their own sense of professional engagement, and that the scheme had given public recognition to what they most valued in their work – teaching. On a broader note, the scheme had not significantly increased the status of teaching or work with students within the institution, they thought, even though it was within the 'modern' university sector.

Not all academics are convinced of the value of teaching awards schemes (Turner and Gosling 2012; see also Waring this volume). However, there is now a growing community of *teaching-rewarded academics* in HE, and their comments on the importance of teaching, student interaction, engagement and learning, are arguably values that are common across the academic profession and institutional types (Fanghanel 2012). Perhaps it is the case that these now constitute a growing and increasingly important 'advocacy' group for academics' teaching role in HE.

18

Younger Faculty, Identity and Careers in Japan

Machi Sato

Introduction

Universities in Japan have experienced significant changes in the past few decades, and researchers have shown how changing conditions of work and new types of appointments have impacted on occupational identities in the sector (Barnett and Di Napoli 2008; Whitchurch 2008; Land 2004; Henkel 2000; Gornall 1999 discuss the UK context). There is a need too for new research, to investigate how academic staff in various roles make sense of the changes in their working life and contributing to a broader understanding of the (re)formations of professional identity that are taking place.

An emergent group of staff in Japan working as faculty or educational development staff – 'FD staff' – yet on academic contracts, offers a case to investigate. In this chapter, I ask how these FD staff make sense of their lived experience and professional identity, with a particular focus on newer academics acting as FD staff in Japan. Elsewhere, including the UK, 'faculty development' has been actively practised and developed in various forms in higher education (HE) for many years, and these staff can give an account of skills, careers, values and a knowledge-base as practitioners (Dawson *et al.* 2010; Carew *et al.*, 2008; Eggins and Macdonald 2003; Baume 2002). In the current study, the newer academics shared similar life experiences and faced similar difficulties in promoting institutional FD, they understood the dilemmas between practice and research, but these hindered their making commitments and decisions about their professional identity.

Based on ethnographic fieldwork, I argue that the term '*tantōsha*' allows FD staff in Japan to create a semantic space for negotiations between different types of identities, either practised or idealized. '*Tantōsha*' can be used as a label to address anyone responsible for something and literally means 'a person in charge'. In the context of a university, it also indicates that the person's main professional identity could be something else. Therefore, using this term allows Japanese FD staff to consciously or unconsciously avoid finalizing their professional identity – and the communities to which they belong. There are a number of similar terms in use internationally for faculty and educational development 'FD' type activities. In the chapter, I use the term 'faculty development', when referring to endeavours in English-speaking countries, and '*FD*' for Japanese, practices because '*FD*' is the term used in Japan.

The study

The impact of the 'lived experience' on the understanding of job and professional identity is an important area. From a review of literature written in English, it is apparent that what underlies the field of faculty development, and is now shaping it, in countries with advanced practices, such as Australia, the USA and the UK, are the experiences and values of the faculty development staff themselves (Sato 2010). The research reported here, is of an ethnographic study of an *FD* unit at a single university, over a period of 12 months, which is used to understand how *FD* staff make sense of and develop their professional identity. The method included participatory and observation attending the various seminars and workshops related to *FD* staff outside of the university. In addition, 20 in-depth interviews with staff and researchers were conducted at this and other institutions in Japan.

Background to *FD* in Japan

The term 'faculty development' refers to the concept and practices in place to support and improve the work and performance of academic faculty members. Outside Japan, it developed in the 1960s, where faculty or educational development roles expanded in this area (Land 2004). Such educational development terms and activities were introduced to Japan from the UK and US in the 1980s, by a group of HE researchers who were spreading the idea and taking on board previous calls for 'educational reform' in Japan, and also in response to challenges from students to traditional teaching practices (Sato 2010).

Despite the energy of the pioneers, this 'grassroots' approach did not embed *FD* in universities in Japan, and interest declined during the ensuing rapid growth of the economy in the 1980s. A decade later however, MEXT, the Japanese Ministry of Education, Culture, Sports, Science and Technology (2009, 2008) adopted the term *FD* as a strategy for improving HE. It explained *FD* as: '[I]nstitutional research and training about the mission or purpose of the university, education, and teaching methods' (MEXT University Council, 1998). Terasaki (2006) criticizes this definition because it presumes that *FD* is basically about 'improving lectures!'. Similarly, other researchers have expressed concern, arguing for broader ways of understanding the concept of *FD* (see Hata 2009; Inoshita 2008; Arimoto 2005). In fact, this definition soon became a source of confusion within the *FD* community itself, as we will discuss below.

The Ministry also introduced a series of HE policies and funding opportunities to promote *FD* practices, and this led to a rapid increase in the numbers of posts related to the *FD* sector (MEXT 2009, 2008). Beetham *et al.* (2001) and Hudson (2009) have reported on similar developments in the UK during the 1990s (and see also Part IV this volume); in Japan, these posts included appointees taking up roles on *FD* committees, offices, or within an independent centre in the institution. A growing number of people, especially newer academics, thus became involved in offering institutional *FD*. Interviewees described this sudden increase of *FD* posts as the '*FD* bubble' in the academic job market, implying that they predicted it would collapse sooner or later. It was nonetheless a welcome phenomenon for those who were looking for an academic job. Most of those hired were junior academics who specialized in educational studies – educational psychology, sociology of education, HE studies, early child education and so forth. Universities considered that an individual with educational studies as their background should be able to organize and practise *FD*, because *FD* was concerned with 'improving university education'.

To further promote the practice, the Japanese Ministry made it *mandatory* (in 2008) for universities to practise institutional *FD*, noting the critical role that *FD* staff could play a key role in ensuring the 'success' of the policy. The regulation stated: 'The university should offer institutional training and carry out research to improve [the] contents of lectures and educational methods' (Clause 25-3, The Standards for Establishment of Universities, in MEXT 2008).

Following this Act, some 40 per cent of HE institutions set up centres, committees, and other forms of units to be in charge of *FD*, while 90 per cent also organized some form of *FD* activity (MEXT University Council, 2008). Yet the effectiveness of institutional *FD* in improving university education was also being questioned. Confusions over the definition of *FD* were partly led by the fact that it was an introduced, 'foreign' concept. Academics had been dealing with issues in 'education' in their disciplinary communities and faculties for decades it was felt, which now would be treated as 'faculty development' in the new regime. Because the term was non-existent in Japanese vocabulary in the past, it became *FD* staff's responsibility to persuade other academics that what they had been doing in fact was '*FD*'! In short, *FD* staff who did not necessarily have expertise in *FD*, were caught in a complex situation of promoting institutional *FD* – even as its definition was being contested.

Difficulties in implementing institutional *FD* and usefulness of the term '*tantōsha*'

Despite the central mandate in 2008 for implementing institutional *FD*, it has not been an easy task. Many of the universities studied still lacked an institutional strategy, and sometimes, under the name of '*FD*', brought everything related to university education to it – and to the *FD* staff too. Thus their remit could include evaluation of lectures, student consultations, curriculum development, institutional orientation for newly-appointed lecturers, and organization of seminars and workshops on teaching skills. A national survey of *FD* units (Arimoto 2004) confirmed the general absence of institutional strategy-making in relation to *FD* and some of its effects. It had caused hardship particularly to newer faculty, who, due to a lack of working experiences at university level, were uncertain about institutional *FD*. It became clear that they tended to focus on what they could do, instead of what the university or faculty members needed, when carrying out their '*FD* staff' roles. Inexperience in the role as an academic also put *FD* staff in a difficult position. They inevitably needed (in their role) to work with established professors and university members at management level; as one *FD* staff member in his twenties said,

> I think it is very exciting to be able to work with all those senior faculty [academic] members, but I need to fight with the strong pressure all the time. They may be thinking 'Who are you young boy to tell me what to do about the university education? What do you know about?'

Several other interviewees shared a similar view. They needed strong diplomatic and communication skills, as well as academic credibility to conduct their role effectively, as Beetham *et al.* (2001) and Hudson (2009) have also noted in UK studies of new teaching and learning professionals. The resistance that some academic faculty members expressed *against* the notion of *FD* was another cause of difficulties. These saw *FD* as yet another government policy to interfere with academic autonomy and freedom, and regarded *FD* staff as their 'agents of change'. Being cautious about how to 'come across' in the institution (see Bertani Tress, this volume) is one of the challenges *FD* staff face in Japan, as elsewhere (Hudson 2009; Lee and McWilliam 2008; Carew *et al.* 2008; Manathunga 2007). Being on the 'wrong side' of the academic-administrative divide (Gornall 1999; Beetham *et al.* 2001) – in academic-related work that is based in a 'support' centre for example – can create barriers to establishing good working relationships with academics in certain 'development' situations (Harland and Staniforth 2003: 28).

Under these circumstances, the term '*tantōsha*' ('the person responsible' for something) is a useful label that offers a 'multivocal' possibility. The way that *FD tantōsha* introduce themselves offers a good example. They would often say 'I am an *FD tantōsha* at my university but my major field is educational psychology'. In this case, '*FD tantōsha*' for the individual is the label of the position. As a consequence, many academics will see *FD tantōsha* as 'one of them' who just happened to have been given some added responsibility, and therefore they sympathize with the *FD tantōsha*. Because the *FD* staff are often on a short-term contract, however, the temporariness of their position also allows *FD* staff to avoid making a commitment or taking on a commitment to their responsibilities. One manager responsible for supervising *FD* activities said, 'We get new *FD tantōsha* from different faculties every two years. By the time they get used to the work, they have to leave … so, it's hard to expect those *FD tantōsha* to make a full commitment [to *FD*].

In order to solve this problem, some *FD* staff argue for the importance of establishing the *FD* role as a specialized profession, rather than the 'generalized' and ambiguous category it is has been to date. In the next section, I introduce some *FD* staffs' attempt to view the role as a 'new profession' by introducing the label '*FDer*'.

FDer: creating a new career path

The concept of 'faculty developer – '*FDer*' – introduces a new way of understanding the *FD* role, with possible career advancement for *FD* staff. Some *FD* staff have been actively promoting the idea of '*FDer*' in Japan. This arose out of dilemmas and experiences in facing demands to act as a practitioner as well as an academic, and also in promoting *FD*. Over the years, they have developed a better understanding of the role. Thus they began to create a boundary around the work. Then they had begun to realize that in order to be a responsible *FD* staff post-holder today, they needed to gain specialized knowledge. They also recognized that this was not the kind of work one could do while working as a regular academic, which required one to research and teach. Thus, they began to search for a role model and naturally investigated the situation in the USA and the UK – because the term 'faculty development' was imported from these countries originally. Here, they found a new profession, of 'faculty developer'. Some began to use the term '*FDer*' to promote the idea of *professional*, that is, dedicated, *FD* staff. As these *FD* staff began to gain reputation, both inside and outside the university, the term '*FDer*' also attracted attention. The confidence of the 'new professionals' in these roles was supported by interactions with faculty developers in other countries, being invited to speak at other universities in Japan, in meetings with other *FD* staff, and encouragement to promote the idea of professionalization of *FD* staff as a whole. In other words, the institutional community and the community of faculty developers overseas supported this formation of professional identity as *FDer* in Japan. But it has also stirred up reactions.

Mixed reactions

Once the term '*FDer*' began to gain currency, *FD* staff and researchers in HE studies all over Japan started to ask among themselves and each other, 'Would you call yourself a *FDer*?'

The reaction to this question of newer academics, acting as *FD* staff, was mixed. The sense of responsibility and wanting to be 'useful' was shared by most of the interviewees. However, they said that doing well with *FD* did not necessarily have anything to do with one's identity or profession, it was about job responsibility (and perhaps just employment). The biggest concern about the idea of an *FDer* was its career path. An *FD* staff member in their early thirties argued that there was no such job as *FDer*:

> I don't know if it is possible to create *FDer* as a new career [in Japan] . . . I have seen faculty members working together to improve their education in the collegial manner. So having *FDer* [roles] might not promote *FD*. Also, I am not sure about the career path of *FDer*.

Another *FD* staff member in their mid-thirties described the discussion about *FDer* as '*FD* staffs' act of searching for identity'. By having the boundary around the position, *FD* staff were wishing to feel more relaxed in their position in HE. But this interviewee expressed concern that such a boundary might also restrict flexibilities in pursuing a career, for those who were still at the early career stage, and might impose a fixed model of *FD* too. She said,

> For someone like myself who is still in the junior and fixed-term position, it feels . . .
> as if someone is trying to attract our attention by using the word '*FDer*'. It gives the
> message that 'If you become *FDer* then your career would be guaranteed . . .'

An informant in their late-thirties worried that the 'first generation' of *FDer*s, who had other expertise, might be able to survive in roles in the sector, because they do have these other disciplinary specialties and would be able to pursue them if the *FDer* role ended up not working out. However, the problem for the more recent generation of *FD* staff was that if they trained as *FDer* only, they would not be able to survive should the universities stop hiring for these roles: 'It would be irresponsible for our generation to create a new career when we don't even know if the position might be sustainable'.

As such, the label of '*FDer*' to most of my informants meant a restriction of their professional identity and career path. Without having a similar kind of support from the institutional community and other communities, therefore, it would be too risky for individual *FD* staff to make the decision to pursue *FDer* as a profession. By contrast, the label of '*FD tantōsha*' is a useful term, as it does not suggest any restriction; but to understand the hesitance of newer academics acting as *FD* staff in seeing their role as part of a 'new profession', it is relevant to include some background on this generation of early career academics.

Historical, cultural and demographic background to the experiences of newer academics acting as *FD* staff in Japan

Japan experienced its second 'baby boom' between 1971 and 1974, peaking in 1973. These are called '*dankai no sedai junia*' or 'baby-boom generation junior' and many *FD* staff in their thirties fall into this category. They often describe their own generation as an 'unlucky generation'. As one describes: 'We had to survive examination hell but when we were in the third year of undergraduate study, the economy crashed so we then had to survive '*shūshoku hyōgaki*' [the ice age of the job market]'. By the time they had completed their undergraduate studies, the government was pushing to enhance postgraduate education. Former Imperial universities increased their numbers of postgraduate students, and this led to an increase in the number of graduates with PhD qualifications. There was an excess of doctorates, and in 1997 the number of PhD-holders exceeded the number of academic posts available (MEXT 2009). But the birth rate in Japan had also declined, and less children meant fewer students, with decreas-ing income for universities. Facing tight budgets, universities increased the numbers of academics on fixed-term contracts, instead of hiring new full-time faculty staff. Understanding this tough academic job market, the new generation of academics were thus motivated to build their research and teaching profiles by trying to get involved in research projects. They aimed to publish as many articles as possible and to carry out other activities, such as working outside of the university, and more importantly, networking.

Current 'early career' academics are thus affected by these factors right from the beginning of their career, and it led them to think they needed to leave as many career options open as possible. It is understandable that they have avoided electing to establish a professional identity only as *FD* staff.

Tensions over research vs practice

Another element affecting matters of professional identity is the university sector's strong emphasis on the 'practice' of *FD*. They want *FD* staff to engage in *FD* practice, instead of 'research' on or into it. A a professor in HE said, 'The university see *FD* staff as *sokusenryoku* [to be able to complete tasks immediately] so they are expected to do a good job straightaway. They don't even have time to stop and think what their specialties might be'.

As a result, *FD* staff tend to feel that they are expected to act solely as a practitioner. Sometimes they are explicitly warned off research, as an *FD* postholder on her first appointment, after completing a PhD, reported:

> During the job interview, the interviewer told me not to carry out any research between 9:00 and 5:00 because the post was created to carry out practices. So I told him that I am trained to research and it is impossible for me not to [do] research.

In getting involved with *FD*, staff therefore have to decide whether to practise *FD* as '*gyōmu*' or to practise *FD* and carry out research based on its practice. '*Gyōmu*' literally means 'business affairs' and 'duties'. In the context of Japanese universities, academics use '*gyōmu*' to refer to anything that has nothing to do with what is considered as the core of academic work, or research and teaching. For example, some academics call the centre responsible for *FD* '*gyōmu sentā* (center)' because *FD* is neither research nor teaching. Some interviewees reported their decision to treat *FD* as '*gyōmu*', and thus carried out their own specialist research *outside* of their practices. Many explained (in interviews) the difficulties of keeping a research profile up to date while working only on *FD* practice, recognizing the significance of having good publications to pursue an academic career path. They often faced the stress of balancing two conflicting types of role.

Those *FD* staff who decided to continue with their research activities tended to carry out practice-based research, what in the UK/US would be studies related to educational development or teaching and learning. This did not necessarily reflect their original academic base, however, and the purpose of any research undertaken was to improve the effectiveness of *FD* practices – and give credibility to this practice. Some senior faculty academics showed that they did not approve of it, and one professor said many of these writings were just '*jissen hōkoku*', 'practice reportage'. A comment also made was that there were too many '*sentā kyōin*' around, or academics affiliated with a centre and not a faculty, and too little research without a sound disciplinary foundation. *FD* staff were (and are) thus left in a dilemma of wanting to continue their research to sustain an academic identity, but not knowing a way of carrying out academically-sound, yet practice-based research.

Concluding remarks

So what is '*FD tantōsha*'? As a term for *FD* staff, 'persons responsible for something', it puts the question of the concept and practices of *FD*, and the more dedicated 'professional identity of the '*FDer*', on hold. It thus takes a load off the shoulders of the individual. Ironically, this also prevents continuity, and a maturity of discussions about *FD* in Japan. More importantly, it postpones the development of an emergent new type of academic or professional form of work in the sector. It means that Japanese '*FD* staff' do not need to choose between the academic profession and of being *FD* staff as part of a new profession. They thus try to keep their options open, and 'not making decisions' was the decision they made in order to survive. This 'multivocal', vague and ambiguous label, of *FD tantōsha* allows both *FD* staff and the university to remain 'unfixed' about a professional identity. By maintaining their academic identity, the staff have been able to sustain more 'collegial' relationships with other faculty members.

The temporariness of the position '*FD tantōsha*' implies that the individual does not need to commit to the role for good. It then depends on them to decide if and to what extent he/she does so. '*FD tantōsha*' is a term that allows *FD* staff not to take 'too much' responsibility, and helps navigate complex working lives – employed as academics yet practising 'development' in new professional areas of HE in Japan.

Acknowledgement

I am grateful to all the institutions and individuals who allowed me access to their workplaces and spent time sharing their stories with me. I would also like to thank David Mills, Takehiko Kariya and Roger Goodman who helped me find my way to complete this DPhil research. I was going to present this story at a conference in March 2011 and also hear the Working Lives paper, but I had to cancel because of the Great East Japan Earthquake that hit where I live. I was not able to see the point of continuing my research when so many people were struggling to sustain their daily life. It was then Lynne Gornall, attending the conference, found my abstract, emailed me and invited me to submit a proposal for this collection on HE working lives. Naturally it became the turning point for me. I thank Lynne and her colleagues for giving me this opportunity and making me part of the Working Lives network.

Appendix: list of interviewees

Table 18.1 List of interviewees 2008–2009

No.	Affiliation (pseudonym)	Position	Date of interview
1	Ayame University, national, multi-disciplines, top 20, located in the major city	Associate professor, social science	October, 2008
2	Hagi University, private, multi-disciplines, top 20, located in the major city	Professor, social science	June, 2009
3	Fuji University, private, multi-disciplines, top 20, located in the major city	Associate professor, social science	June, 2009
4	Ayame University, national, multi-disciplines, top 20, located in the major city in the east	Associate professor, educational technology	September, 2009
5	Sugi University, national, multi-disciplines, top 20, located in the major city in the west	Assistant professor, higher education, *FD tantōsha*	September, 2009
6	Take University, national, multi-disciplines, top 20, located in the major city in the west	Associate professor, educational technology, *FD tantōsha*	September, 2009
7	Take University, national, multi-disciplines, top 20, located in the major city in the west	Postgraduate student, higher education	September, 2009
8	Nazuna University, private, multi-disciplines, top 50, located in the major city in the central	Administrator, *FD tantōsha*	July, 2009
9	Hasu University, private, specialized field, top 50, located outside the major city in the east	Lecturer, educational sociology, *FD tantōsha*	September, 2009
10	Beni University, private, limited disciplines, top 200, located outside the major city in the east	Administrator, *FD tantōsha*	September, 2009
11	Mizuna University, national, multi-disciplines, top 20, located in the major city in the north	Postgraduate student, educational technology	September, 2009
12	Mizuna University, national, multi-disciplines, top 20, located in the major city in the north	Professor, higher education, *FD tantōsha*	September, 2009

13	Murasaki University, national, multi-disciplines, top 50, located in the small city in the south	Associate professor, educational psychology, *FD tantōsha*	September, 2009
14	Research institute		September, 2009
15	Yanagi University, private, limited disciplines, top 200, located in the major city in the north	Professor, law, *FD tantōsha*	August, 2009
16	Yuzu University, national, multi-disciplines, top 20, located in the small city in the north	Associate professor, higher education, *FD tantōsha*	August, 2009
17	Yomogi University, private, specialized field, top 200, located in the major city in the west	Associate professor, educational technology, *FD tantōsha*	July, 2009
18	Kaede University, private, limited disciplines, top 200, located in the major city in the west	Professor, higher education	September, 2009
19	Hinoki University, national, multi-disciplines, top 50, located in the small city in the west	Associate professor, educational management, *FD tantōsha*	November, 2009
20	Momo University, national, multi-disciplines, top 20, located in the major city	Lecturer, higher education	December, 2008

Note: all names and locations have been anonymized by the author.

19

Latin American Academics Coping with Work in UK Higher Education

Maria Bertani Tress

Background

While there is increasing interest in the USA, in studies focusing on Latin Americans in educational contexts, and represented in publications such as the *Journal of Hispanic Higher Education*, there is a paucity of European literature on this population. Moreover, most of the American studies focus on students, few examine staff. The US-based research also employs largely quantitative data collection methods, and while this may illustrate what is going on with Latin Americans, it fails to reveal the underlying explanations for factors such as 'persistence', academic 'identity' and 'acculturation' in how they experience their higher education (HE) work. The study reported here is qualitative and part of ongoing doctoral research. It examines the perceptions of academics of Latin American origin who are working at different universities in the UK. The research questions focused on how they saw working in Britain, the cultural challenges faced, and modes of coping with problems that they encountered.

Brief theoretical context

The terminology and notion of 'resilience' emerged primarily from the health sciences and investigation of psychopathology in Europe and in the USA. A handful of pioneering psychologists – Garmezy (1971), Rutter (1979), Werner and Smith (1982) – primarily interested in child development, bridged the study of 'risk' and 'resilience' as two concepts, bringing them into the mainstream of social scientific studies of human development. Typically, 'resilience' has been considered as the act of surviving despite stressful circumstances (Bonanno 2004). Indices of positive adaptation at the individual level, such as 'bouncing back quickly after hard times', for example, are being developed (Smith *et al.* 2008) and mostly confirmed by self-report measures. In other studies, 'resilient' outcomes have been identified within descriptions such as the 'preservation of health and well-being' in the face of adversity.

'Resilience' has also been applied to the experiences of coping constructively with change, with professional groups such as nurses (Jackson *et al.* 2008), and also to teaching professionals (Winter and Sarros 2002), the subject of this chapter.

The study

Participants for the study were selected through 'snowball' sampling, which is mainly used when the research population is part of a minority or 'difficult to find' group (Liamputtong and Ezzy, 2005). Such is the case with academics in the UK who had migrated from any of the 20 countries of the geographical/political region known as Latin America.[1] Subjectively, interviewees who accepted the invitation to participate were those who already considered themselves to be 'Latin Americans'. In formal census groupings in the UK, many Latin Americans would be categorized as 'other', that is, not covered by existing groups ('Mixed White', 'Asian', Afro-Caribbean' and so on).[2] Hence each participant 'passed on' the contact details of a fellow academic who would be willing to take part in the research. Because of this 'referral sampling', the universities where informants worked are similar, that is, they tend to be research-intensive institutes across the UK. But the subject backgrounds of participants were diverse, and ranged from disciplines in management, electrical engineering, earth and environment sciences, to humanities and Latin American studies. All have pseudonyms in this chapter.

The research sample eventually comprised 20 academics (both male and female). In-depth, semi-structured narrative interviews were used to collect the data, which produced rich, illuminative and 'grounded' texts. These were in the form of 'personal stories' where subjects expressed their opinions as well as the ways in which they coped with the situations described. The following discussion is grouped around a small number of themes: experiences of stereotyping, life as an employee in the UK, communication issues, teaching and identity as lecturers. Finally, there is a discussion and conclusion.

Cultural stereotyping

It may be argued that the challenges faced by Latin Americans are not too different from those experienced by other UK academics. So what then is different? To begin with, particular types of cultural stereotyping. One of the informants described how, at least initially, she was associated by colleagues and authorities with stereotypes from the Latin culture. These included notions such as a 'very relaxed attitude toward work requirements' and associated with the word *mañana*. This is the idea that things get put off for another day. As 'Mariela' recalls:

> I once said to another colleague, who could understand a little bit of Spanish, the word *mañana*. My boss overheard this and said: 'Oh *mañana*, *mañana*, you always come up with your *mañanas*', as if saying that we always leave things for tomorrow.

I've heard jokes with the word '*siesta*' and the word '*mañana*'. These things are not common for big cities in Mexico. Maybe if you go to little towns yes, and many years ago . . . but at least in big cities you never take the siesta . . . Just judge me by what I do!

Mariela shows that she feels challenged by this, but also asserts her self-worth. Stereotyping can go both ways of course. 'Enrique' comments on his feelings about UK colleagues:

[In the UK] there is also this unhealthy curiosity for others, to enjoy gossipy situations, which for foreigners, is hypocrisy. I don't think that it is hypocrisy, it is more complex than that . . . but those circumstances – in an essentially English society and institution – for someone who doesn't understand that society . . . is very unpleasant . . . not as much unpleasant, it is actually hard. That was the hardest part in my [28 years] being here.

That the meaning and emotions attached to each situation could be personal as well as cultural becomes evident in another experience recounted by Mariela: 'My boss sometimes ask[s] me if we have planes [at home] or ride horses. I told him 'I do know how to ride – that I didn't bring my horse. But I did have my gun with me!' She makes the point that because of the hierarchy (this is her manager), and as an 'incomer' she is not equally able to trade explicit cultural prejudices – Enrique refers to this too. As Mariela told the interviewer,

'You can answer [people] with a joke but you don't reply with a British stereotype – like saying 'British people have a stone heart' – although they may have a stone face . . .'

In her language, she 'plays' with the notions of stereotyping, both UK and Latin. She adds, 'I know that I should not be offended by stereotypes. For them [it] is like talking about a glass, if the glass if empty or full. But for me this is MY glass, so you are talking about *me*!' Perceptions that stem from the cultural background of each academic thus transfer to the workplace, impacting on professional situations, understandings and relationships.

Life as an employee in the UK

Views of informants on activities that involve life as an employee in UK HE, such as teaching-related or administrative tasks, varied from one academic to another. For Enrique, grading students and attending to their requests outside of the classroom was regarded as 'just part of the job'. But for another, 'Edgar', these involved a cultural adjustment from what he was used to. This informant stated that an 'excess' of his time was occupied with 'administrative' work, not only regarding such things as assessment procedures, but also in what he regarded as time in handling students themselves. Edgar thought that British academics viewed undergraduates especially as needing to be treated as if they were children. To illustrate this, he used a Mexican idiom, *tratarlos con pincitas*, which would be equivalent to the phrase and meaning '[we have to be] tiptoeing around them'.

It might be argued that administrative affairs are a burden for all academics, but several informants were trying to do everything expected in a very high quality way, to avoid attracting criticism. 'Raúl' comments:

> I think I work more than the time I spend [at] home. I would like to be more balanced but I don't see how. Being efficient would be having an assignment and telling myself: 'I will work and finish it in two hours, and if I finish in that time, good and if not, still good'. This is one of my problems: I am more of a perfectionist, so nothing is ever done completely: there is always something that can be better, and I am always trying to do it better; and that is not efficient. As I have been told many times, 'perfect is enemy of the good'.

The interviewees said that notwithstanding issues such as those quoted above, they felt grateful to be in their current situation, and so chose to remain 'humble'. Often, they used the term *aguantarse*, which literally means to carry oneself over, meaning 'taking everything in' without complaining. Enrique speaks about having to deal with aspects of the British personality. He was one of few foreigners in a 'not very diverse' HE institution (HEI). In his opinion, staff were well travelled but also 'too English'. What did he mean by this?

> [British] people have a certain type of reserve, an inability of breaking a certain personal space, to shorten that personal space [between themselves and the others] ... In this society, it is important to [appear indifferent] in certain circumstances. Otherwise, you are looked [at] suspiciously.

He had worked in the HEI for more than five years, in a predominantly (white) British institution. Showing some of the qualities of 'resilience', Enrique adds:

> Maybe I would like to go back [to that HEI] the way I am now. I already have the strength and understanding to adapt, but [now with] comprehension to understand and handle it. Precisely for me it was very hard to handle it well ... let's say, productively. [At] that time, it was a relief leaving that institution.

In retrospect, academics worked out what resources they needed to handle these challenging situations, reviewing, and trying to learn from experiences what it was that made interaction at times difficult.

Communication and relationships

The way those from abroad – including Latin Americans – interact and communicate within a 'British' cultural context goes beyond the exchange of the correct phrases in the English language. It is necessary to understand the meaning underlying the spoken or written expressions. Or should we say the *intended* meaning, because this may vary both from what is actually said, and from the meaning understood by informants. What is spoken and what is received may be very different, provoking resultant behaviours that could further compound a situation. This can be illustrated in Table 19.1, a humorous chart that circulates amongst non-native speakers.

Table 19.1   Beyond language: meaning and understanding

What the British *say*	What the British *mean*	What others *understand*
That's not bad	That's good	That's poor
I was a bit disappointed that	I am annoyed that	It really doesn't matter
Very interesting	Clearly nonsense	They are impressed
Correct me if I'm wrong	I'm right, don't contradict me	I may be wrong, please let me know
I would suggest . . .	Do it or be prepared to justify yourself	Think about the idea, but do what you like

Source: extract from Anglo-EU translation (quoted by Liberman 2011 and others). Full list accessible by web search 'Anglo-EU translation'.

Another informant, 'Nadia', in a dispute with a colleague who she felt had discredited her, spoke of academia 'as a very incestuous place'. She also brought to this an understanding of a more 'collectivist' culture and an image of herself as 'part of a community', in this case, an academic one. Hence when misunderstandings arose, she tried to resolve what she knows of both contexts, and to 'control' her feelings. Colleagues' comments could be emotionally 'disruptive' however, and she admitted to feeling 'very bothered' sometimes, if 'it [the situation] tastes bad to me . . . this competitiveness and jealousy'.

Mariela, who we met earlier, also had a colleague that she described as 'very mean', someone who:

> . . . wanted that every email I was going to send was sent to her first, then she would read it and then I would send it . . . This left me a little bit shocked and I thought that it was because my English was not good enough. I was also afraid of talking on the phone for the same reasons . . .

A challenge like this could arise when both academics lacked confidence in English – her colleague was also from overseas. Perhaps administrative policies about email have led to over-cautious supervision, strengthened in this case by being second-language speakers of English. However, it was also perceived as unfair treatment by Mariela, and shows how a fear of prejudice and sometimes sensitivity over written language can increase difficulties and tensions in the workplace.

Teaching and identity as lecturers

Most of the academics in the study did not report lecturing itself as problematic. However, some of the academics, Edgar and Raúl, said that when teaching, the challenge was the number of students, up to 200 in a classroom. In these conditions, two issues arose for them, closely related:

- – The ability to gain control in class.
- – Getting a sense of respect from the students when teaching.

Edgar:

I come from an environment where the lecturer knows the students by their name, and can even know the parent of the students. There is a closer relationship between the student and the teacher, and much more respect.

Raúl:

There are times in class that the students ask me about something and I don't know [the answer]. Previously that would cause me anguish. Now I see it as very normal that one does not know things, the worst thing you could do is try to fool the students. It is also not the end of the world isn't it?

Edgar gives an example of what he considers a disrespectful activity:

Students know that they shouldn't be using their mobile [phones] in the classroom, and one of the students was using his in my class. I took it off the student and put it on my desk telling him 'you shouldn't be using the mobile'. [Interviewer: As you would do in your own country]. The student replied 'that mobile is worth £300'; for a moment I doubted on how to react to that answer, I felt that the student was trying to provoke me, saying that the mobile is expensive and I would have to pay if I break it.

This struggle with respect might be part of differences in national teaching systems, whereby in some countries the teacher is regarded as the highest authority. This is in contrast to 'westernized' systems, in which lecturers are still experts but are also 'facilitators' of students' intellectual development, who encourage critique. This would have cultural implications that are rarely discussed or considered. The attitudes towards work, and its personal relevance for Latin American academics in UK, is also something that seems to change when working in the UK HE context. 'Juan' takes a practical approach, showing his insights into British culture and acting upon this:

I often find that for students to take you seriously, you have to be more serious than you really are. Not being 'serious enough' would be very contra-productive, in the sense that people will not take you seriously. You learn very early those things.

'Being serious' and 'hard-working' is the way that Juan counters potentially negative cultural stereotyping, such as that described earlier by Mariela, of Latin culture as easy-going and putting things off. 'Jaime' understands that it is also important to work hard as part of the lifestyle and working life in UK HE: 'I sometimes work really hard, without breaks. So I set short goals, so I don't feel the week so long'. In these and other comments, it is possible to see not only how the Latin American academics see themselves but also, through their eyes, how their descriptions and perceptions contain insights for members of the British culture and academy too.

Discussion

The 'working life' experiences sampled above from Latin American academics in UK HE give a sense of different sorts of challenges on top of the pressures that emanate from being a UK lecturer today (Fanghanel 2012). These workplace situations and the notions underpinning them can be summarized in Richardson's (2002) usage of the term 'disruptions'. Disruptions mean that if an individual's paradigm is changed, this may result in negative or positive outcomes. It means that a new piece of life's puzzle is there to (potentially) add to the individual's view of the world: but adding to this puzzle also means that pieces affected by the new item may themselves fall apart. Being offered a new job or suddenly being courted are 'disruptive' because they represent future change – even though they are not completely unanticipated changes to one's current situation.

Developing this idea, the challenges for Latin American academics represented a change that disrupted their balance temporarily, and required a process (or application of skills) to regain a sense of proportion and normalcy. In this sense, the challenges experienced could be grouped as (1) the way the academics related to others (peers, colleagues, authorities, students), (2) adaptation to the culture, language and workplace, (3) relationships outside the academic domain, and (4) their own personal, social and academic identity.

Findings here show that Latin American staff, in common with many British academics, struggle to manage their time and to maintain working relationships, but they also described an extra sense of hopelessness and incompleteness: 'I could have done more', 'I wish my day was 36 hours long'. These comments were related to their capacity to manage processes that ranged from adapting to new ways of working, to understanding more specific tasks like marking examination papers and assignments, answering emails, drafting and signing letters. But these staff *did* get things done, and were proud of their achievements and work produced, accommodating to the UK 'work ethic'.

For some of the academics (especially men) the challenges appeared to be about keeping motivated to cope with the requirements of the job, acting responsibly, mostly when doing research, and also when things became more of a routine. For others (especially female academics) the challenge was often related to presenting a good image of oneself, appearing upbeat and enthusiastic when teaching: 'Like playing a part in a play', one Peruvian academic said. This is consonant with the concept of 'academic labour' developed by Hochschild (1979), who highlighted the consequences of roles that are attributed to each gender in the classroom. So even when the individual is not feeling like it, there may be expectations of being warm and open, this particularly so in relation to expectations of those from Latin American cultures. Other challenges identified by the sample were more distinctly related to issues of overseas nationals working in an environment outside of their own countries, in other words, away from their extended family.

The staff reported coping with challenges by positive thinking and focusing on the advantages of having a life in the UK. Especially for female academics, they reported a greater sense of gender-related emancipation than they would expect in their native countries. Raúl (earlier) showed that using themes from UK culture helped adaptation and 'on the job' survival. Mariela expressed her ideas about coping as 'you must be able to have passion for what you do; if you have a project or a class you cannot just say "it's only a class, I don't care if I'm not prepared for it". And, as she also points out in relation to more difficult times, 'If you don't dissociate [i.e. 'switch off'] . . . you live everything like receiving a stab, thinking "I am going to die", you have to switch off feelings'.

'Dissociating' for Mariela was a way of cutting out hurtful issues or information. But it also provided the opportunity of 'seeing herself' from another place and helping to 'get back on track'. By contrast, Nadia struggled to control and hide her emotions, even if she well understood the feelings or motives that she suspected lay behind others' behaviour. The way in which these and any academic develops 'resilience' in their working environment needs much more examination. The informants in the study were living several lives, speaking and thinking in two languages, practising a profession in a culture with different norms, yet having a vantage point of being able to move back and forth culturally, that could give them momentum forward. Mariela shuts off painful areas for a time, and Enrique knows 'to himself' what the British 'face' is and means, and he knows he cannot express this or respond back, but locates himself through this. Nadia wants to be a collegial peer but sees the dangers of others' sense of rivalry in the marketized workplace, while Juan realizes the importance of appearing 'serious' in order to be taken seriously. Work, for Jaime, has to be 'seen to be important *to you*' by others; Mariela uses counter stereotypes and her private humour to bolster morale.

Concluding remarks

The HE workforce has been experiencing multiple challenges – in professional autonomy, organizational change, conflicting demands, and reconciling work-life balance (Le Cornu 2009; Deem 2001; Taylor 1999; Evans and Abbott 1998; Slaughter and Leslie 1997). These have emerged in a context where institutions do not always appear to be very rewarding for those labouring in them. Some of the reasons for this stress are given as role ambiguity, work/tasks overload, unreasonable pressure from managerial groups, a sense of powerlessness, and tensions in peer relations. Individually and together, these may have a significant impact on academic occupational experiences, most notably in senses of physical and psychological well-being, but also in judgements about perceived effectiveness, competence and adaptation (Gu and Day 2007).

The response and situation of Latin American academics' undergoing disruption and change – some of it positive, some negative, but which they try to constructively work through – is also complex. It involves the use of personal resources entwined with experiences and perceptions from others. We can learn something from the strategies for coping and resilience of these colleagues, as well as from the sometimes unique challenges they must overcome in their UK work.

Notes

1   Twenty countries of the Latin American geographical/cultural region. This excludes the Caribbean Islands, not considered as part of Latin America.
2   Many studies describing the working lives of Latin American groups are situated in the USA of the late 1980s and 1990s. Census instruments tend to cover only certain ethnic identities, thus, 'White', 'Afro-Caribbean', 'Mixed White', 'Asian', and so on, but exclude others. One cannot tick a box called 'Latin', although the term 'Hispanic' would be available in American questionnaires. In most other studies, Latin-origin people are largely grouped with other ethnic groups as 'people of colour', or are assigned (without irony) within the category *other*. So specific dimensions of analysis in the contextual field are under-developed for these informants.

20

Research Careers and Fixed-Term Contracts: A Science Case Study

Sarah-Jane Richards

Introduction

Max Perutz, Nobel Laureate for his work on the structure of haemoglobin (1962), considered this discovery to have been a 'grand enterprise' of solving a problem and taking risks; it had also taken him more than 16 years to achieve (public lecture 2000). Sydney Brenner, Nobel Laureate for discoveries concerning genetic regulation of organ development and programmed cell death, openly acknowledged that his seminal work of mapping the nematode genome would probably not have secured support under the current scheme of UK research funding. Scientific discovery on the identification of the double helix or gene transfer in embryonic stem cells would have been impossible within the short-termism of today's UK research grant system, yet major health treatments emerged from them.

This chapter charts the experience, the institutional and policy contexts, of an academic career in medical research on fixed-term employment contracts. The period for which the author was in academic science was 1980–2000; this experience as well as wider contexts and evidence is drawn on for the chapter as a whole.

Scientific research, grants and employment

Throughout the 1980s and 1990s, scientific research in the UK was primarily undertaken either within universities or in specialized research council institutes, units or centres. 'Cutting edge' science was typically viewed as a 'vocation' rather than a career with a lifestyle of long hours and self-sacrifice, dedicated to the understanding of a disease, structure or mechanism. This was not 'for commercial gain' but to 'unravel the mystery' of a scientific conundrum. High profile publications, international recognition and job security should follow. This was the *esprit de corps* of many research teams.

Irrespective of the sources of research funding, a post-doctoral scientific career invariably was defined as either (1) a research-focused, full-time, fixed contract, and

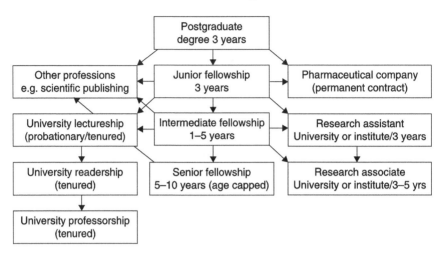

Figure 20.1   Career structures flowchart

with the salary paid from grant support either as a primary grant holder or whilst recruited to a project of a grant holder; or (2) salary paid by the university for teaching, while conducting research part-time alongside this; or (3) the pharmaceutical/biotechnology industries, where the salary was paid by the company to pursue the company's research strategy (see Figure 20.1).

Within the area of biological and medical research, the research grant framework was developed in 1913 to distribute research funds through the Medical Research Council (MRC) and later the Biotechnology and Biological Sciences Research Council (BBSRC). These operate alongside the charity sectors, such as the Wellcome Trust and British Heart Foundation, and together have become the major employers of UK research scientists.

For PhD students, securing post-doctoral funding was invariably through one of the above bodies (see Figure 20.1). For junior post-doctoral scientists, salary support came from a grant in one of two kinds. The first was through securing 'Fellowships' that paid salary and research project costs. This had the advantage that a fellowship was transferable with the investigator and thus was the favoured route for graduates with a PhD in science, and future career mobility in mind. The second alternative was to be employed at an institution as a post-doctoral scientist, on the grant of a senior investigator. In this scenario, the younger scientist was in a subordinate position, with little or no influence on the direction of the research. So, to establish an independent research career, the 'fellowship' option was the crucial one, but such 'middle to senior' posts are more costly, and there are fewer of them.

In my own case, leading a medical research team investigating brain injury and Down's syndrome was not sustainable after 15 years as an MRC external grant-holder, because of age bars on tiers of funding. Thus, researcher redundancy or a lack of career progression are effectively 'built into the system' from the outset, as issues of personnel and capacity.

Science employment opportunities and career options

Individuals contemplating a career in the pharmaceutical industry, or else a lectureship, would have to choose their post-doctoral field of specialism with care. Cancer research, heart disease and HIV/AIDS all receive generous support from proactive large charities such as Cancer Research UK, the Terrence Higgins Trust and others. These fields offer greater employment security compared to 'less popular' disease research areas, such as Alzheimer's, hearing loss or tinnitus, for example. So too, researchers working in fields that do not benefit from the large funding endowments of the charity sector also suffer potential career and job description problems. Moreover, PhD students undertaking research within a university setting are likely to have had opportunities for some teaching or tutorial work; this would give an advantage over older or external post-doctoral applicants once competing in the jobs market. Even those university institutions that put a premium upon research still give an important role to teaching profiles within science departments.

Many university-based post-doctoral scientists who were frustrated by the hours spent seeking competitive research grants, turned in the late 1990s to the developing pharmaceutical, biotechnology and science 'spinout' sectors (Barton 2008). These posts offered attractive salary packages, cars, company share schemes, private medical care and support for the all-important attendance at international conferences and meetings. The drawback was the commercially-oriented environment of the research, which, as underwritten by company strategy rather than scientific discovery, could be abruptly curtailed for business reasons. For the 'career' scientist then, a failure to renew or gain successive short fixed-term grants in their area of specialism has led to uncertainty, possible career/job jeopardy and unemployment (Oliver and Hooley 2010). Apart from consultancy and related 'freelance' options (including, say, science journalism), a final option for the later post-doctoral research scientist would be to retrain and enter another profession. In my own case, I funded a legal training, and entered a new employment sector entirely. For those on the open market, they are competing for jobs with internal candidates, people experienced in the industry sector, and newly qualified, 'cheaper' applicants.

Employment in higher education

The Dearing Report of 1997 noted, not with approval, that there existed a high rate of 'casual' (non-permanent) staff contracts in the higher education (HE) sector. The survey revealed that approximately 25 per cent of all teaching staff and nearly 100 per cent of HE research staff were then employed on fixed-term contracts. More than half of all academics surveyed had been employed on a fixed-term contract at some stage in their careers, having already spent at least two-thirds of this time as 'casual' staff (Dearing 1997, *Report 3*). Moreover, 'teaching only' fixed-term contracts, at 36 per cent in 1995/6, had risen to 61 per cent by 2004/5 (UCU 2007). While *research staff* in all subject areas in universities had traditionally been appointed on fixed-term contracts, this change in employment practice was new to *lecturing* staff.

Just prior to the publication of the Dearing Report, the Concordat and Research Careers Initiative (1996) was launched by CVCP, the Committee of Vice-Chancellors and Principals. This identified the need for more effective career management of contract research staff within UK HE. The research councils were charged with a remit for this, and the move towards permanent contracts for senior research fellows began. By 2002, however, the Roberts Review of postgraduate education revealed that 42 per cent of UK research scientists were *still* being employed on short, fixed-term contracts, and without any defined career path. Roberts recommended an urgent introduction of 1,000 academic fellowships directed towards permanent assistant lectureships, akin to the US system (Roberts 2003, 2002). But this did not happen, probably due to HE budgetary constraints (RCUK and UUK 2008).

Whilst not every university with a strong research portfolio is able to accommodate lectureships for research fellows on expiry of their stipends, some have moved forward in positive ways. Birmingham University, for example, created 50 post-doctoral positions in 2011, leading to tenure (Gill 2011). The wider picture however remains bleak: competition for posts is high, and UK science jobs attract applications from the international community. Indeed, in 2007/8, 27 per cent of full-time academic staff appointed within HE came from outside the UK, with the most common group for recruitment being from the EU (Locke and Bennion 2010; HESA, 2009). Thus, candidates are competing in a truly international market – which of course leaves open the option to seek posts abroad. This can also be more difficult for late-career staff. Data has yet to be collated concerning the extent to which EU academics appointed to full-time positions within the UK HE system progress on to permanent contracts or remain on serial fixed-term contracts (Ackers and Oliver 2007). There is moreover a gender dimension to this distribution of posts. The Higher Education Statistics Agency's (HESA) annual audits reveal that the number of females on fixed-term contracts has always exceeded male counterparts (HESA 2012, 2011a, 2010a; Oliver 2009; UCU 1995–2006).

Research assessment and HE science/research posts

In 1986, the UK government and HE funding councils introduced the Research Assessment Exercise (RAE) as a way of monitoring, assessing and quantifying university research output. RAE audits were conducted in 1996, 2001 and 2008. These offered unparalleled scrutiny of research activity and publications, underpinning future public research investment strategies – and also having major repercussions for research career sustainability. The RAE was regarded by many academics as over-competitive and divisive (UCU 2008, and see Kelly and Boden this volume). It was felt that it downplayed developmental, capacity-building or simply 'hard to quantify' subject areas. It was controversial in the scientific community too, where critics declared the assessments misleading because the publications of approximately 30,000 full-time research staff on fixed-term contracts were not included in the assessment (Madden 2008). The complexity of evaluating and comparing the performance of academic departments was also evident. Judgements were based on measures such as the quality and quantity of publications and fulfilment of non-exacting short-term projects, whereas 'success' and 'achievement' in science might be regarded as aspiring towards the major discovery, such as those of Max Perutz, Sydney Brenner and other Nobel Laureates (Agasisti *et al.* 2012).

The Roberts Report (2003), commissioned to review the RAE, recommended abandonment in favour of a 'Research Effectiveness Framework', or 'REF', with benchmarks that could be applied to any university discipline or department nationwide. 'Centres of Excellence' in research should be identified and funding awarded to them, it recommended. Like its predecessor, the REF was to distinguish university teaching functions from research activities within a more 'transparent', financially distinct and self-sustaining system (but see Kelly and Boden this volume). In science, this would be based on the hoped-for translation of scientific discovery into commercialization, assisted by academic-industry 'fusion partnerships'. The first assessment is scheduled to be completed in 2014.

Such research assessment processes have ramifications that affect investment in teaching and research, as well as in applied developments. The outcomes have wide-ranging consequences for staff, students, as well as for potential employers and business partners. Thus, university websites hold out names of 'top scientists' to potential course applicants with the suggestion of 'frontier scientific research and discovery' as part of the teaching curriculum. But this takes place at the same time as the links between teaching and research in university science appear to be growing more tenuous. There is an increasing use of 'professional tutors' and teaching-only posts, with staff employed in short fixed-term contracts with few or no links to research. Concerns over such 'teaching-only' appointments have been raised with government by the academic unions for some years (Oancea 2009; NATFHE 2006).

From research awards and 'rewarding careers' to insecurity

Despite the above issues, the expectation today is that science and scientists will play a pivotal role in the national economy. This 'science revolution' and the extent to which it impacts upon the career structure and employment of research scientists is considered below.

As can be seen from Figure 20.2, the pyramidal structure of jobs and funding positions for grant-funded science posts means that success with securing the next award becomes harder with each successive round. Fewer stipends are available as each stage proceeds, and research funding today is offered to greater numbers of PhD students and junior post-doctoral staff than to senior scientific personnel. Thus, in 2011, the MRC funded 1,900 PhD studentships compared to 400 fellowships across all levels (MRC 2011a). This is in order to train a 'next generation' of scientists. But it further disadvantages staff as they progress in experience, age and seniority. The structure continues to impose a highly competitive environment within HE research employment, in which high attrition rates are the norm. Senior staff thus become increasingly *in*secure as their grant-funded career develops, and their salary costs to employers rise. Thus, *unless at the top of his or her game, the fixed short-term contract*

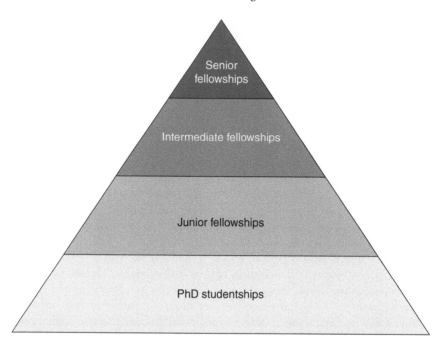

Figure 20.2   The pyramidal structure of fixed-term research awards

scientist will be continually counting down to employment uncertainty. This distinguishes the research scientist from a university lecturer in general, or clinician in particular, who have undertaken grant-funded research in parallel and in secondary mode to a primary salaried employment.

The restructuring of research careers

For a scientist with a track record, failure to achieve essential funding may be outside of their control, but a harsh outcome in career and personal terms. It may be that their area of scientific investigation is no longer the remit of 'priority areas'. Thus, for instance, the MRC under government direction in the 1980s and 1990s, targeted the areas of HIV/AIDS and tropical disease, whereas diseases of the elderly were not at the forefront for funding. Later, prion disease and Creutzfeld Jacob disease became the focus, and now stem cells and translational research claim the primary attention. While such imperatives change from time to time, the dominant categories will have a major impact on whether or not an applicant's work is selected for funding. With ever greater proportions of funds set aside for 'priority areas' less funding remains for even the best original basic research or even the brightest of investigators.

The processes by which such key national priorities have been determined has been questioned by academics, professional bodies and unions (Stronach 2009). In their submission to the House of Commons Science and Technology Committee in 2011, the Universities and Colleges Union (UCU) called upon research councils to remain independent of government when determining strategic research areas (UCU 2011a). Figure 20.3 gives an illustrative biomedical career trajectory.

- The absence of a scientific research career structure for those who were employed on fixed-term contracts led to high attrition rates at every level of post-doctoral and senior fellowship.

- More male scientists than women sought university lectureships during their first or second post-doctoral positions. Thereafter research was undertaken as a secondary activity. This may have introduced a gender bias with more males progressing up the lectureship ladder while leaving female scientists to withstand the attrition rates of the fixed, short-term contract (Metcalf *et al.* 2005).

- The impact upon career development was more severe and more likely to occur the higher a scientist climbed up the fellowship award system.

- The older an individual was at the time of securing the last research stipend, the more likely he or she was to be age barred and less likely to succeed in securing alternative sources of research funding, a university lectureship or employment in a related field of endeavour.

- Women who sought maternity leave or who had the responsibility of child care could not sustain the 'long hours culture' for the performance intrinsic to a competitive scientific research stipend and were therefore disadvantaged in that market.

- Careers and financial planning advisory services were not availed to senior scientists who faced redundancy in the face of fixed-term contract expiry.

Figure 20.3   Example: careers of biomedical research scientists 1980–2000

Age remains a major occupational issue in the research sector. Each level of funding within the pyramid imposes upper age limits. In 2000, scientists over 45 years old were barred from applying for MRC senior research fellowships. Unlike the age capping applied to other post-doctoral grants, there were no personal stipends to follow on from the senior research fellowships either: Perutz, we recall, took 16 years of work to reach his prize-winning development. Moreover, while 'lateral' career moves into lectureships or related industries may be options at more junior levels (see Figure 20.1), it has become increasing difficult for scientists in their forties to convince a university interview panel that they possess the knowledge to deliver a modern course syllabus. The reality of working within such a specialist environment is that there are few related scientific careers available to the research scientist, even after 15 years of senior post-doctoral academic employment or research leadership.

There is also a lack of formalized 'good practice' at a system level (Freedman 2009). Experienced staff leaving science or research work need assistance to move into productive new career pathways. This is in fact a missed opportunity for the sector, to facilitate new entrepreneurships, supported spinouts and future partnerships with former staff, in order to develop new and innovative research *collaborations* (Roberts 2003).

Scientific research and careers in science in the twenty-first century

UK governments have taken greater ownership of 'science' than hitherto, with visions firmly focused on generating wealth through the optimization of scientific discovery and its commercialization – as well as promoting 'public engagement' in ways formerly unheard of. The emergence of university satellite institutes within which academic research and commercial enterprises work cooperatively in 'fusion partnerships' is testimony to productive HE-industry, commercial, science and research collaborations. However, the underlying occupational structures of employment for scientists have remained largely unchanged. More positively, and in line with accepted good organizational practice, the MRC now spends 12 per cent of its grant-in-aid on research training and career development (MRC 2006). This supports around 5,700 research scientists in universities and other organizations at any one time. Yet here too, we see mostly fixed-term contract employment without permanency, and where every three years or so, staff face redundancy. Unless they become university lecturers, and few will have that option, there is no career structure for these scientists at all. The importance of the researcher's personal and career development is recognized as a key principle within the Concordat to Support the Career Development of Researchers, however (RCUK and UUK 2008).

Career development grants remain the MRC's frontline form of investigator support (MRC 2009). These stipends, while still reflecting the 'pyramidal structure' (Figure 20.2), provide funding across different levels of career requirements, from junior fellowships through to intermediate awards and senior fellowships. Each stipend runs contiguously, although a career break is possible. Such funding is intended to support 'bright scientists' at the beginning of their careers and for a maximum of 15 years, after which – and at around 40 years old – the scientist is expected to apply for other sources of stipend. Few, if any, will be available. There is thus little to distinguish this MRC career programme from that of earlier decades, and other than some tenured positions that remain within the Council's institutes, the MRC continues to provide mainly fixed-term contracts of relatively short duration. Employers however now are urged to deliver training in 'transferable skills' to assist fixed-term contract research staff to become competitive in both internal and external job markets, and to be able to access independent advice on professional career management (MRC, 2009; RCUK and UUK 2008). I am not a *social* science researcher, but there are clearly issues here around employment structures, age and gender, and the mobilization of what Brown *et al.* (2001) call 'talent', and aspects of professional or knowledge 'capital' (Hargreaves and Fullan 2012).

Enshrined in the government's latest policy for HE, *Higher Ambitions: Research Innovation and Knowledge Exchange* (DBIS 2009) is the commitment to support centres of research excellence (see Figure 20.4). It also includes the pursuit of

- European directives and research funding frameworks which established ring-fenced areas of research grant investment.

- European directives and frameworks for the harmonization of HE objectives for research including mobility between member states (RCUK 2004; UCU 2011b).

- Supplying £100 million to universities for long-term research projects (BIS 2013).

- Government funding for the commercialization and translation of scientific discovery.

- University Research Excellence Framework (REF) accredited centres attracting research investment and facilitating partnerships with technology, business and industry.

- MRC and BBSRC research council funding providing scientific training, career development and 'priority areas' of research funding. MRC technology to develop and commercialize 'blue sky' technology;

- Extending the right to request flexible working and develop a new system of shared parental leave (BIS 2013).

- Development of the MB PhD programme for clinical research careers.

- The charitable sector—which remains the largest single investor in biomedical research, to provide scientific training, career development and 'priority areas' of research funding including technology development.

Figure 20.4   The vision for scientific research in 2010–2013

specialized research that will translate into 'outcomes with economic benefit across a broad range of disciplines'. Complementing this, the MRC's 'e-Val' system has been developed for monitoring research progress, productivity and quality across the Council's entire portfolio (MRC 2009). This regards publications, products, interventions, intellectual property, spin-off companies and income generated from such enterprises as defining the collective accomplishment. However, its 'Next Destination' programme, which is designed to monitor retention of scientists within the profession, fails to report any data on research staff retention upon expiry of their fellowships (MRC 2009). It does take note that in 2010, eleven per cent of researchers had moved out and into the private sector (MRC 2011b). Disappointingly, such absence of information does not permit a determination of attrition rates and the point at which this is occurring in MRC-supported scientists' careers.

Concluding remarks

Since the 1980s, the MRC has employed *five times* the number of doctoral students than its total numbers of fellowships for senior staff who are 15 years or more into a post-doctoral career (MRC 2011a). This chapter has highlighted attrition rate and mobility issues as well as the lack of longer-term opportunities for academic research staff who, as they become more experienced and specialized, face increasing employment insecurity and precarious futures. There are implications for *science* here, as well as research, knowledge and careers; as Max Perutz (2000), quoted in the introduction, noted over a decade ago:

> [Younger scientists today] are under great pressure to produce publications, to produce results so they are really pushed to take on only problems which are safe and which you can answer within the time of a grant of 3 years, and I think that is a sad thing. You shouldn't worry too much how long it might take and whether it will be possible to solve the problem. Just as in other walks of life, in science, if you want to win you must take risks.

In this context, a move towards a common trend of a system of 'disposable' (fixed-term) employees is hardly desirable (*Prevention of Less Favorable Treatment Regulations*, see EU 2002). Initiatives that have supported newly qualified researchers and early careers lecturers have been welcome. However, the UK needs complementary measures for science careers at *later* stages of the cycle. That this situation affects women in greater proportion than men has been frequently noted in reports to date (TRSE 2012). Furthermore, it is a matter of national as well as institutional self-interest for the student science curriculum not to be lost within a system of 'professional tutors' (see also Acker and Webber this volume).

Analyses of career pathways in today's biomedical research sector reflects a similar picture to those of the 1980s, in which research teams failed to build on the acquired knowledge of mid to late career science academics, and teams themselves disbanded. It is a shortcoming within the UK's scientific programme which, if not addressed, will lead to the loss of international competitiveness. Many Asiatic countries train and retain their scientists irrespective of age and gender, while British scientists are forced, often reluctantly, into alternative career pathways.

21

Academia as the (Com)promised Land for Women?

Sandra Acker and Michelle Webber

Background: Competing trends

It is not difficult to find commentaries concluding that women academics in Canada have considerably improved their position in higher education (HE) compared to the past. We should quibble with this picture however: women are still under-represented in the top ranks; they experience a salary gap; and they are over-represented in the least secure sector of academe (CAUT 2011). On the other hand, much of the overt discrimination is now in the past, and women's presence in HE is much more visible than it was decades ago. For example, the proportion of women among full-time academic staff has increased from 12.7 per cent of staff in 1972–73, to 36.6 per cent of the total full-time academic workforce (of 44,934) in 2010–11 (Statistics Canada 2012; Ornstein *et al.* 1998: 11). As well, some of the policy improvements and intellectual transformations are impressive. However, advances for women occurred at the same time that universities experienced rapid transformation, through corporatization, managerialism, entrepreneurial activity, audit cultures and resource restrictions (Newson 2012). Newson even suggests that women's efforts to be 'good girl' academics may be furthering the corporate agenda; a number of writers have thus considered that the wider changes may in fact be having a deleterious impact upon women academics' situation (e.g. Menzies and Newson 2008; Smith 2008; Morley 2005).

Our data offer a chance to see what some contemporary Canadian women academics think about their work lives and to make some comparisons with earlier work from the mid-1990s and early 2000s, studies with which we were associated (Acker and Webber 2006; Acker and Armenti 2004; Acker and Feuerverger 1996).

The HE policy environment in Ontario

Canada has an unusual policy environment for education. There is no national department of education, and almost all educational functions are the responsibility of the provinces. As a consequence, it is sometimes thought to be a 'partial exception' to forces such as 'academic capitalism' (Slaughter and Leslie 1997), though others have argued that this kind of exceptionalism is largely illusory (Metcalfe 2010). Nevertheless, there is no direct equivalence to the kind of performance-based research funding exercises that national governments have imposed on countries like the UK (RAE, REF), Australia (ERA) and New Zealand (PBRF).

The interviews we use in this chapter took place between September 2011 and March 2013 in the Canadian province of Ontario. They occurred as Ontario HE policy was in a turbulent space, with the introduction of various agreements and initiatives required of institutions and new bodies to put them into practice. One writer called it the 'year of living dangerously' for Ontario's HE system (Jones 2012). A new government minister responsible for colleges and universities initiated a flurry of activity along neoliberal lines, most of which came to at least a temporary halt when the Ontario Premier suddenly resigned, and then the Minister resigned to make a bid for the premiership (unsuccessfully). Nevertheless, a recent report from the Higher Education Quality Council of Ontario (HEQCO) states that 'government must play a more active, assertive and purposeful role to drive system-level planning and change' in HE (2013: 18).

The study

Our research explored ways in which academics in Ontario understood developments around accountability and related trends in contemporary universities, and how their academic subjectivities reflected these understandings. With Ontario's turbulent policy context developing around us, and in a larger study, we selected academics for interview from across the social sciences. Universities were included from each of the three groupings, which are known in Canada as 'Maclean's magazine' categories: medical-doctoral, comprehensive and primarily undergraduate 'types'. Like other provinces in Canada, Ontario has mostly public universities, including all those in our study. For this chapter, transcripts of interviews with the 10 women in the main dataset formed the basis underpinning the 'emergent themes' noted below. However, and using pseudonyms throughout, we focus specifically on the narratives of three women academics, to illustrate the policy and institutional contexts of their working lives. The informants were drawn from three different universities, three disciplines, three ranks (assistant professor, associate professor and full professor), and three age groups.

Lillian Porter is a full professor in her 60s; *Teresa Lincoln* is an associate professor in her 50s; and *Katie Ray* is an assistant professor in her 40s. We trace in this chapter two of the themes that arose in the research, and which touch upon a number of related issues in this volume, namely 'evaluation' and 'overwork'.

Evaluation

What is being evaluated?

Performance evaluation was a major theme in earlier studies by Acker and colleagues and we have continued to study the 'disciplinary' function of reviews for tenure, which are a stressful and important part of academe in North America (Acker *et al.* 2012). In the current interviews, what stands out is the equating of 'performance' with the submission of an annual report which is then judged; all institutions seemed to have a version of this process. Our participants variously called these 'annual' or 'activity reports', 'reviews', 'performance evaluations' or 'merit'. Procedures for these reviews vary, and can be complex and cumbersome, sometimes including monetary rewards either rolled into one's base salary or paid as a 'bonus', and sometimes not. Participants objected to the 'overemphasis' in evaluation reports on publications and grants and complained about the amount of documentation required and the time involved. They also mentioned the convoluted ways in which work was scored, the divisive impact of comparisons among colleagues, the 'steering' effect on what kind of work was valued and where it should be published, and the inadequacy of the measures used, especially student course evaluations. As Teresa remarks about the latter,

> It is multiple choice . . . a very superficial evaluation of one's . . . performance . . . and it goes directly to the administration. They may see it even before you do . . . it is an unnecessary measure of . . . popularity, instead of one's actual performance as a teacher/professor.

'Performance' was too often equated by managers, interviewees thought, with publishing: '[I]t's not about quality, it's about numbers' (Lillian); 'Publish, publish, publish' (Katie). Katie is an assistant professor on the so-called 'tenure track', which means that she will undergo a rigorous evaluation at around the fifth year of her appointment. This review will determine whether or not she receives a permanent position – something also discussed by Richards (this volume) in the UK. Being turned down for tenure, although it rarely happens, would mean the end of her appointment. Katie expands on the significance of this feeling of insecurity and instability:

> Everything [pre-tenure faculty] do and every evaluation that occurs affects our likelihood of success of tenure, so I think that has to be understood within that context . . . my entire career is at stake right now. All of the years of post-graduate education are at stake right now.

Teresa too is very aware of her status: 'I'm still not a full professor and I may potentially think about the application for full professorship'. She reflects on the way in which pressures to apply for *larger* external grants have increased over the years and the requirements to 'pre-specify' too many things in a grant application: '[These are] killing [the] things that are exciting about academic research. I want the research out . . . to circulate it, people reading it and responding to it . . . public discussion and debate around these issues'.

Research is not the only area of concern. The women comment on the problem of student course evaluations being used by university administrators despite their acknowledged defects:

Teaching I think is the biggest problem because it's basically solely determined on course evaluations and there's a lot of problems with course evaluations. I mean if a kid gets a bad grade, they give you a bad evaluation, no matter how good a teacher you are.

Katie

Often, [female faculty of colour] find that there is not much respect for their authority in the classroom. The students treat them quite differently than they would treat a white male faculty member, and it just becomes sometimes difficult to manage the classroom, altogether.

Teresa

Evaluation as discipline

The interviews went beyond listing specific drawbacks of the procedures and touched on a level perhaps best identified as academic 'subjectivity'. These processes of evaluation are arguably more than a nuisance, they are a form of *discipline* in a Foucauldian (1977) sense; for Lillian the evaluation process is subjective and political:

It's totally subjective and [for] some people, especially those working from critical frameworks, like feminists and so on, you could do cartwheels off the CN Tower [a very tall Toronto landmark], you would not get any more than [an] average [grade].

While the tenure evaluation process is clearly high-stakes, the 'annual report' does not on the surface seem so problematic. By contrast with other countries (Elizabeth and Grant 2013), there are no consequences for departmental funding or reputation that rest on these reports. Even where there are salary additions, they are relatively minor amounts. The participants also expressed concerns about the lack of transparency in judgements of merit, the paucity of feedback and an absence of consultation or wider inclusion in decision-making in the actual process of assessment. Echoing a comment widely expressed by academics elsewhere (see Jephcote; Waring this volume), Teresa describes 'a new environment of competitiveness as opposed to collegial[ity]' in Canadian HE. Asked where the pressure was coming from, Teresa said that one could see it all over but 'at the university level I think it is very much coming from the Dean's Office and it is just creeping up over the years'. The annual review, however, 'feels real': '[it is] one time in the year when you yourself are reviewing your overall performance and looking at whether you could have done more or differently. So it does actually feel quite real' (Teresa).

For Lillian, however, the new regimes of 'entrepreneurialism' define you: 'We're supposed to bring in money . . . If you don't bring fame and fortune to the university . . . you're not contributing in the way that the university values'. What comes across in these quotations is a sense of the loss of something previously valued (Taylor 1999) and a concern that competitiveness and performativity are dominating the work that academics do, whether or not they perceive a more fundamental transformation of what the university is about (Polster 2012). Moreover, while critical of what the various evaluations represent, the women were also making strenuous efforts to 'do well' on them, perhaps reflecting the internalization of a 'drive to achieve' that accompanies many academics throughout their careers (Gornall and Salisbury 2012). While the consequences for individuals and departments of annual reports are fairly minimal, the idea of being evaluated – and possibly being considered inadequate – has a strong impact. The external surveillance, then, triggers a powerful *self*-surveillance.

Overwork

Working hard

As in the earlier studies, the women talk about how hard they worked:

> I hear many colleagues say things like, I can't wait for the weekend so I can do my work; I can't wait for my vacation so I can get to my research; right, so it's like, you do it in the crevices of your time, the times when you're supposed to be rejuvenating, when other people go to cottages and put their feet up. I go nowhere without papers to read.
>
> Lillian

> I put in anywhere from 50 to 80 hours a week, if not more, sometimes 100 [hours].
>
> Katie

> We are overloaded in terms of teaching, research [and] service.
>
> Teresa

> You know if I have 15 PhD students . . . it is a full morning or a full afternoon [each] . . . there's no way of reporting that on my annual report.
>
> Lillian

One of the issues for these academics was that the 'real work' did not always seem to be recognized, but that they were, as Lillian put it, increasingly overwhelmed with 'what I call busy work'.

Time, technology and fragmented work

Lillian reflects on how much time is spent doing *uncredited* administrative work and brings up the impact of technology:

> I contact them, and they'll say oh, it's all on-line, just go there and you'll find it there. Well that takes time for me to go to the [site and] then the links aren't always exactly self-evident . . . and by the time you find the form you're looking for, 15–20 minutes

might have gone by. If they had just given it to you, you could just sign your name [laughs].

'Finding the form' is an example of what Gornall and Salisbury (2012: 139) call the 'meta-logistics of the modern academic workload' – work you need to do in order to do the work; Butterwick and Dawson (2005) refer to 'shadow work', while Ylijoki (2013) and her informants speak of 'wasted time' as opposed to 'real work'. The concepts allude to the 'backstage' efforts, such as fixing the photocopier or organizing papers to take home, that one has to make in order to do the 'productive' work. Polster writes of the 'daily announcements, memos and workshops introducing and explaining university rules and their continual changes', many of which also circumscribe academic autonomy (2012: 125). Illustrating this point, Ylijoki's (2013: 250) participants lamented at length that they were being kept from meaningful work by 'a mass of different kinds of separate tasks without a clear connecting plot, with frequent interruptions and under heavy time pressure'. Teresa refers to something similar in terms of submitting her performance reports: 'To be honest, I don't know what happens. [laughs] . . . At [University], everything is submitted electronically, so there's a sense of everything disappearing in a black hole . . . [For post-tenure faculty] there [is] no feedback'. So information goes in, but nothing comes back.

Emotions of overwork

> I don't have a weekend off, ever . . . I'm already burnt out. I have a [child] in crisis, so do I adapt? Yes. Do I work harder than my body will allow? Yes. Do I cry? Yes. Do I have anxiety? Yes.
>
> Katie

But asked about the satisfactions of academe, she says: 'you know when we talk about flex time, what other job has that extent of it, none that I know of, so I think it's one of the best careers out there'. Gornall and Salisbury (2012: 149) indicate something that Katie also seems to be saying, that the advantage of academe is it *allows* one to overwork, or perhaps that there is no overwork, just work. Lillian, more than 20 years older, still struggles with similar issues. Responding to a question about whether she feels accountable to anyone, Lillian responds forcibly:

> I absolutely do and . . . I just feel constant pressure to work all the time, and that's not just hyperbole. I truly feel constantly, constantly under pressure to do work. My family will tell you that I'm constantly in my study on the weekends and at nights and this part makes me weep because I'm tired of not getting more than four hours a night, you know that kind of stuff? . . . And yet there is no recognition of the actual work.

Emotions suffuse this context of internalized surveillance: Katie is working around the clock and still worries that her entire career is at stake as she moves toward tenure; Lillian describes how hard she works and how little she sleeps, how underappreciated she feels. Teresa says, 'I only have so much time and so much energy to fight' so she seeks 'more friendly colleagues' to share concerns with and tries not to 'pay too much attention to the issues that are especially disturbing'.

Accounting for individual(ized) performance is not new in North America. Tenure, promotion and merit systems have a history that pre-dates recent accountability initiatives, and interestingly, our participants made few explicit connections between their working lives and provincial accountability or quality initiatives. We believe that the penalties and rewards associated with these policies are (so far) operating mostly at the institutional and departmental level, and have not yet had a (recognized) major impact at the individual level. The emotions seem to be focused on the idea of managers or colleagues, not external bodies, judging their work, and by extension, judging their right to be 'real' academics. Some writers believe that emotions are the particular target of surveillance and self-policing (see Salisbury this volume), and our study provides an example of the way in which emotions are harnessed in the process of creating the 'new academic subject' (Zembylas 2013: 166).

Emotions are also evoked when participants use gendered or familial analogies, reminiscent of Acker and Feuerverger's (1996) finding that women academics feel ambivalent about others' (and their own) expectations that they will care for and nurture students while their male colleagues appear free from such responsibilities. Katie says, 'students come to me when they're in crisis, I walk them to counselling services'. Despite her junior position, she is doing a lot of supervision of theses and projects. Similarly, Lillian remarks, 'we [women] do spend more time, students do come to us with more issues because they feel more comfortable, we're a bit more like their moms'. Huyton, also writing here (Part 3) argues that her (male and female) informants' analogies were 'parental' rather than specifically gendered, a difference of emphasis that could be explored further in future research.

Concluding remarks

In this chapter we used the words of three representative women from our research study in order to offer a sense of what aspects of academic work concern them. The specifics sometimes differ from those of the past. 'Finding the form', for example, points to a new level of dependence on technology, while increasing levels of regulation intensify the work process. On the other hand, students' desire for interpersonal support and mentoring, mentioned above, is an old story in HE.

The three informants are at different career stages, yet there are many similarities between them. Overwork, especially for women, and unhappiness about evaluation were issues in the earlier studies – women were and are 'doing good and feeling bad' (Acker and Feuerverger 1996), still 'sleepless in academia' (Acker and Armenti 2004). These themes go hand in hand: overwork is the 'means' to the 'end' of performing well. The women's academic subjectivities conveyed a strong sense of 'being judged', as well as a fear of being 'found wanting'. This response reaches well beyond issues of tenure and includes other 'performance' assessments such as the annual review that continues throughout their careers. These academics make regular and conscientious efforts to prove their worth, but are mystified when the reports seem to go nowhere, or when their accomplishments are unrecognized.

Despite the reported gains for women noted in our introduction to this chapter, 'gender' continues its work behind the scenes, so that many female academics felt 'not-quite-the-norm'. Lillian, the most senior and experienced of our participants, suggested that 'feminist language' was being lost as a means to address and discuss some of these issues. It continues a finding from our earlier work (Acker and Webber 2006) and also in many other and older studies (Acker and Feuerverger 1996; Aisenberg and Harrington 1988), that new times may simply have taken old norms and updated them.

22

Balancing Working Time and Academic Work in Finland

Oili-Helena Ylijoki, Lea Henriksson, Virve Kallioniemi-Chambers and Johanna Hokka

Introduction

The academic profession has undergone profound changes over the last decades. Academics are said to have become 'managed professionals' (Rhoades 1998), who are increasingly subordinated to external policy and market steering, following the trends of the 'neoliberalism' agenda of performativity and 'academic capitalism' (Slaughter and Leslie 1997). Combined with the changes in the university-society contract, technological development has also contributed significantly to this transformation. In particular, new information technology has drastically shaped the daily practices in university teaching, research and administrative tasks, involving new tools for control and governance, as well as for autonomy and self-regulation in work (see also Introduction this volume).

In this chapter, we explore the impacts of information technology on academic work from a temporal perspective. We draw upon the thesis of social acceleration, which claims that modern subjects are regulated and dominated by an invisible and unarticulated time regime, speeding up living and working in the era of late capitalism (e.g. Leccardi 2007; Eriksen 2001; Adam 1995). Rosa (2010) distinguishes three forms of social acceleration: 'technological acceleration' (speeding up of transportation, communication and production), 'acceleration of social change' (rapid change in organizational forms, values and lifestyles), and 'acceleration of the pace of life' (increasing tempo and rhythm of living). These aspects of social acceleration turn organizational life, including academia, into space that is experienced as more hectic, instantaneous and intense than before.

Our starting point is that technological acceleration, closely intertwined with other forms of social acceleration, has profound effects on the work experiences of academics. Information technology and email (which are also explored here in Thomas and Gornall this volume) are paradigmatic examples of technological acceleration which have altered the tempo and rhythm of academic work. The general rule of the information revolution introduced by Eriksen (2001: 70) applies well to academic work: whenever there is competition between a slow and a fast version, the fast version wins. As a norm, emails have overruled slower modes of communication and become 'domesticated' (Berker 2006) into a natural and integral part of work practices.

Relying on this kind of temporal approach, we investigate how email has shaped academic work and the lived experiences of academics in the Finnish higher education (HE) system. In addition, we will mirror our results against the findings of the Working Lives (WL) team in the UK which has looked at autonomy, email use and self-managed work in the spaces and places of mobile working for academics – and its problems. The empirical basis of our chapter is comprised of three focus group sessions involving 12 Finnish junior academics (nine women, three men) working in two research-intensive universities. All interviewees had recently gained doctoral qualifications and were currently working as university lecturers and post-doctoral researchers. Their disciplinary backgrounds were all in social sciences. Interviews were conducted by two research group members together, and a focus group lasted about one and a half hours. The topics covered were 'daily work practices and experiences'. Email use was not raised by the interviewers, instead it was spontaneously taken up by the academics in a variety of ways during the interview discussion.

Dilemmas in email practices

We present *three 'dilemmas'* that were discerned in our analysis of these data. They shed light on the tensions between the opportunities and constraints involved in email use in different aspects of the academic role. In connection with each dilemma, we offer quotes, translated from Finnish, to illustrate the core features.

Dilemma 1: flexible crossing between work and non-work zones vs. email trap

This dilemma comprises the choices and pleasures of temporal and spatial autonomy that email enables, but then again the dilemma also points out how this elasticity may sometimes end up colonizing one's personal life. Academics may even find themselves in an email trap.

Email allows the crossing and stretching of temporal and spatial boundaries. Emails can be read whenever and wherever the recipient wishes, allowing a personal tempo. One need not be a 'technological whiz' (Skelton 2005) to achieve this. Instead, email is a daily routine domesticated into all aspects of academic work: research, teaching, administrative responsibilities and the 'third mission' of external links. Hence, in the experiences of the junior academics, email is a taken-for-granted part of daily work practices and communication: 'I forgot to mention it. It is so common that you are continuously so tied to email that you don't pay attention to it any more' (Focus group I).

Flexible boundary-stretching between work and non-work zones enhances opportunities for effective working and communication. There is hardly any place that email checking is not possible. In addition to reading the emails in the office, one can email in an inspiring cafeteria, when commuting to work or all through one's hobbies. In this way email is lowering the boundaries between working hours and leisure time.

As has been shown for UK academics (Cook *et al.* 2009), it is not uncommon among our interviewees to use email while at home early in the morning or late at night:

> Then I totally forgot email, my day started in the morning at six o'clock when I opened email and sorted it out.
>
> Focus group I

> The last thing I did was – I mean that at home I did do some work in the evening, checking my emails and managing to arrange a Skype meeting for the next day. So that was my evening task then.
>
> Focus group III

Moreover, email enables combining work and non-work commitments. The interviewees emphasized that email was a handy tool to deal with one's business and private affairs smoothly. While emailing at home, one may at the same time do the household chores. Interlinking work and non-work roles may even entail 'empowering' elements, as one is able to simultaneously attend to work duties and private responsibilities. This creates experiences of being a productive worker and a devoted care-giver at the same time:

> I have that kind of situation that I have a puppy and that's why I often work from home if I can, so that it won't have to stay alone too long. Yesterday I didn't have any particular reason to come here [at the university] at a certain time, so I worked at home until 12 o'clock. I have noticed that it's often quite efficient. When I can stay at home, sit at my morning coffee table with the computer, that's the time I can really get down to business. And I also took care of some administrative duties. I answered a large number of emails and so on.
>
> Focus group III

However, email also brings pressures to be constantly available and plugged in. Like the results with the UK academics (Gornall and Salisbury 2012: 151), the Finnish interviewees seem to be 'always on' and not to 'switch off', which may stretch the boundaries between work and non-work too extensively, and jeopardize privacy. In these moments, self-discipline and willpower are necessary to defend and protect the non-work zone: 'I have learned not to open the email in the evening' (Focus group II).

Academics mention experiences of being caught in an all-embracing online checking that generates stress and exhaustion. Being 'always on' (Gornall and Salisbury 2012) may therefore lead to an *email trap* from which it is difficult to break away. In these cases, the interviewees rely on an illness analogy and speak about addiction and dependency: 'After I got home, I did check my emails, I am totally dependent on it. I would like to get rid of my mobile phone where I have my emails because I read them all the time' (Focus group III).

Balancing one's temporal and spatial coordinates requires boundary awareness and an ability to protect privacy in a technologically-overloaded academic work environment. Email practices often conform to the personal preferences of time, space and willingness to be in contact, but this routine may also become an over-commitment, a nuisance or even an addiction that keeps junior academics on a tight leash. From this perspective, email can be seen as a form of governance, offering a convenient technological tool to intensify efficiency, productivity and accountability in academic work – all strongly called for in recent Finnish HE policy documents (Nieminen 2005).

Dilemma 2: efficient student contacts vs. uncontrolled email load

This dilemma covers the advantages and disadvantages of email in the teaching context. On the one hand, email saves time and enables the academics to work effectively. On the other hand, email creates challenges and impossibilities of managing the message load.

At the university, where the numbers of students at one lecture can be 1 to 200, it is a relief to the academics to circulate information via email. Email use decreases the amount of face-to-face contacts and phone calls with individual students. With a small time input and less staff involvement, a teacher may thus take care of various odds and ends related to teaching. Moreover, up-to-date pedagogy relies on virtual communication. Email is an integral part of the virtual learning environments that expand the spatial and temporal flexibility of teaching and student counselling. One interviewee said: 'I'm now delivering a lecture that is ready-made and very popular among students, and they are sending plenty of questions about optional ways to take the exam. So I dealt with that examination stuff [in that way]' (Focus group III).

Despite the benefits, however, the interviewees also expressed some negative experiences, discussing the downsides of email. They spoke especially about the difficulties and burdens of coping with email *overload*, as well as students' unrealistically high expectations:

> As a lecturer I get lots of inquiries about everything related to the studies. The students ask different types of questions and it takes – it has been a surprise – a huge amount of time. The students themselves probably think that it's just one little thing that they are asking. But the thing is that before I have sorted them all out and answered to a student, it has been very time consuming.
>
> Focus group II

The interviewees agreed that the threshold for contacting teachers via email was low, and generated excessive work. Furthermore, they reported that students appeared increasingly insensitive to their teachers' workload and expected an online *service*. For example, they might ignore a deadline, but contact the teacher at a later time, expecting immediate guidance. Hence, the interviewees said that it would not be such a big mistake if they occasionally refused to deliver a 'non-stop online service'. They may, for example, 'forget' to answer a student's email, convinced that the student will contact them again!

Work experiences of the intensified service role in teaching were so common that the interviewees started sharing their coping methods, as reported also in the UK

'Working Lives' study. They underline that it is important to distinguish what type of tasks and issues can be handled via fast and impersonal email and what require a more 'restful culture' (Kallioniemi-Chambers 2010) involving face-to-face encounter. Likewise, email breaks were recommended to gain control over the use of time: the interviewees can stop email contacts with students for a while and take time for other duties. However, this strategy may end up with an extremely overloaded mailbox too, which then binds them to responsive behaviours even more intensively. An extreme suggestion was to wholly cut out emailing of students and to replace email with more traditional modes of communication – weekly consultation hours and phone calls. Paradoxically then, although email is a key tool for productive communication in teaching, it may also turn out to be an unproductive device to be ignored and avoided:

> I have some good tips on how you can manage if you have lots of students at the same time. You shouldn't agree to answer the emails. Instruct them [students] to call you by phone during office hours instead. Everything happens much faster on the phone. I no longer answer them by email.

> Yeah but on the other hand, in that case, you are even more at their mercy in one sense; you'll be answering the phone anyway!
>
> Focus group II

Thus, consideration of 'the email dilemma' by these university teachers focused on how to find a balance between email overload and what the WL team have looked at as 'self-managed' time (Introduction this volume; Gornall and Salisbury 2012). Email is agreed as a flexible and efficient tool, facilitating fast communication and counselling with a large number of students. In this sense, its use contributes to the aims of Finnish HE policy, aiming at cost-effectiveness in academic work, speeding up of study times and intensifying the degree production. However, the role of 'non-stop service provider', called for both by students and university management, tends to colonize academics' time, leaving few options for other duties. This is a severe problem especially with regard to research work, which was the most rewarding part of work for our interviewees. As a consequence, time for teaching and time for research tend to be in tension in young academics' experiences – something Cook *et al.* (2009) found for established British academics too.

Dilemma 3: collaborative research practices vs. work fragmentation

This dilemma concerns the tension between increasing collaborative possibilities created by email on the one hand, and the growth of work fragmentation and time pressure related to it on the other hand.

While talking about their work, the interviewees spoke of a diversity of collaborative practices, especially in research work, that are facilitated or made possible by email. They co-author articles and applications, negotiate research consortia, edit scientific journals, organize conferences and so on. Irrespective of spatial location, colleagues can be reached rapidly and easily via email, which enables smooth and efficient cooperation, not only nationally but also worldwide:

> I did take care of some email matters. We are possibly applying for an international consortium project so I sent some emails related to this. And then I belong to this research network in the USA, and we are arranging a workshop. So I sent emails related to this workshop and suggested a speaker because they haven't been able to find one there.
>
>   Focus group II

Co-operation with colleagues is highly appreciated by junior academics, since they feel that it improves the quality of their work. In addition, collaboration with good partners is said to be personally very motivating, also rewarding and empowering. Intense email exchanges create shared experiences and a sense of being connected to one's colleagues, irrespective of their spatial location. Academics' accounts of email communication may even closely resemble face-to-face interaction:

> I have written ... a number of articles with colleagues with whom the collaboration goes really well and you can really think together. It is absolutely fabulous. Yesterday, for example, when I read the article, I got the feeling: this is extremely good. And then you realize that it is circulated around the world among different colleagues for comment, so that the article has really been edited properly. You grasp that I would never have done this all by myself and those others wouldn't have done that all by themselves either.
>
>   Focus group II

In this way email promotes the establishment of larger research projects as well as the internationalization of research work. Traditionally, research in social sciences has mainly been organized individually, each academic pursuing her or his own research interests. However, recently, HE and science policy in Finland (and in most other western countries), has pushed research practices into a more international and collective direction, emphasizing the virtues of big science and large international networks. Email has provided an important technological tool to carry out these policy targets at the grassroots level of academia.

The other side of the coin is that large and intense networks require a lot of work and time. Even though the email etiquette allows time autonomy in responding, the interviewees emphasize the need to take good care of research partners and to be ready to respond as soon as possible. Although students' emails can be put on hold, this seems not to be the case with the partners. In practice, this means that academics have to reconcile between different schedules and to adapt to the temporal orders of their collaboration partners. It follows that working days and weeks tend to become fragmented, as academics have to be ready to interrupt their other duties and to be available to their 'connected' partners when needed. Contrary to the results by Gornall and Salisbury (2012: 145) who reported that a small number of informants saw email interruptions in a positive way as 'breaks' and 'preventing excess', our interviewees saw only disturbances to their concentration on work:

> The downside of collaborative writing together is perhaps in some way the deadlines. I have four articles with four different writing groups that consist of two to seven people. And then the paper is circulated among seven people and each edits it one after another. Sometimes we discuss it and then it moves to another direction.
>
> Focus group II

Likewise, in large, often international projects, decisions and actions require a lot of discussion, creating long email chains, usually accompanied by Skype meetings. This takes much time and energy. The use of a foreign language – English – seemed to be no issue for the interviewees, whereas cultural competence and sensitivity *was* raised as an extra requirement and strain. Clearly, academics working in different national and cultural contexts have been socialized into distinctive communication codes that have to be taken into account. The interviewees even mentioned a 'burden of small talk', where international collaboration often requires long versions of informal and polite communication not typical of the more straightforward Finnish culture:

> I have noticed that it takes a lot of time to manage the social relationships. Especially if there is an international project going on, you are expected to be writing emails like very nice, yeah, right, this is going really well. And you are constantly expected to deal with stuff like how to get through some opinion in some forum and so on. So after all it takes a huge amount of time.
>
> Focus group II

Thus, the spatial independence and temporal rapidity offered by email facilitates collaboration worldwide. This opens up new possibilities and empowering practices especially in research work, but email can also simultaneously produce work fragmentation and time scarcity, which decreases the temporal autonomy of academics. As a result, academics need to balance between the allure of large and intense collaboration networks, which are not only personally gratifying but also strongly advocated by external policy steering, and guarding one's own personal working space and time.

Discussion: the email paradox

Email has become 'domesticated' (Berker 2006) as a comfortable, useful and reliable device within academic work. While it may increase spatial and temporal autonomy, email is not only a rapid and flexible tool to handle impersonal, day-to-day routines, but also a means to sustain social relationships and create shared, personally meaning-ful experiences. In this sense, email enables new kinds of communality and 'politics of we' (Seddon *et al.* 2010). It is noteworthy that this 'togetherness' seems to apply to research networks, but not to students and administrative staff. Furthermore, while email communication between colleagues is interactive, with both parties involved in sending and receiving messages, communication with students and administrative staff tends to be seen as a 'one-way' relation, with academics as the receiving and reacting party. Hence, the same technological tool is assigned different meanings, depending on which aspect of the academic role one is speaking about.

While being 'a blessing', email is thus also experienced as 'a curse' (Currie and Eveline 2011). From this angle, email is one of the key elements of technological acceleration, creating 'fast time' (Eriksen 2001) and 'scheduled time' (Ylijoki and Mäntylä 2003) with decreasing autonomy and self-direction in work. Based on our results, email use is inherently intertwined with overload and fragmentation of work, as well as experiences of time pressure, exhaustion and feelings of powerlessness (e.g. Ylijoki 2013; Gornall and Salisbury 2012; Currie and Eveline 2011; Menzies and Newson 2008; Sabelis 2007). Since emails can be sent and read almost anywhere at any time, it is difficult not to be available for communication. Although email use has its own daily and weekly rhythm, being busiest late mornings and early afternoons during workdays (Flaherty and Seipp-Williams 2005), academics tend to feel a pressure to stay constantly plugged in. Moreover, email communication also entails alluring and captivating features, sometimes connected with obsessive and addictive aspects. This dilemmatic combination of pleasure and stress was also found by Gornall and Salisbury (2012), whose concept of 'hyperprofessionality' avoids an 'addiction' metaphor, to locate its use in the arena of 'professional work'. In this, our results with junior Finnish academics resemble closely their findings with senior academics in the UK. This suggests that technological development and related policy shifts are associated with similar kinds of changes in academic work practices in different countries.

Due to the paradoxical role email has in academic work, different kinds of profiles in email use can be constructed, each presenting an 'ideal typical' picture. There are academic profiles with a strong positive undertone: *conscientious organizer, efficient teacher* and *devoted research collaborator*. These types entail an empowering potential to use email in ways that increase autonomy and scope for personal space and time in work. By contrast, *email 'addict', overloaded teacher* and *hyperactive networker* represent the 'darker' side of academic profiles, with increasing subordination to externally-induced time regimes.

The key question for academics is how to find a balance between these types and to construct a personally fitting way to relate to these profiles (Daunton *et al.* 2008). The email paradox, which is epitomized by *both* an increase and a decrease of autonomy, illustrates an inherent contradiction of technological acceleration which takes place in the current societal context (e.g. Rosa 2010; Eriksen 2001). Technological development – email technology in this case – enables fast communication and saves time. However, this does not mean that people gain extra time. Namely, email also *accelerates the pace of work* by increasing the total amount of information and communication, also often imposing an informal obligation to be always available and ready to respond (Gornall and Salisbury 2012; Menzies and Newson 2008; Sabelis 2007; Ylijoki and Mäntylä 2003).

Thus, paradoxically, there is less time because of this 'time-saving' technology.

Part Four

Technology, New Pedagogy and Teaching and Learning Roles

Introduction

Brychan Thomas

In recent years, an increasing volume of literature has discussed the 'effects' of technology on teaching and learning in higher education (HE) institutions. This includes aspects such as technology, pedagogy, the virtual classroom and new learners. According to Mitwa (2007) this growing area has been inconsistent and incoherent. There have also been contrasting viewpoints on the importance and adoption of technology for academic activities. This body of work can be considered to predominantly encompass two dimensions – the effect on teaching (the first dimension) and the effect on learning (the second dimension). As a result there appears to be a 'gap' which concerns the effect of technology on academic working life itself and this can be termed the 'third dimension'. Through consideration of this *dimension*, it is possible to provide light on the impact of technology on academic working lives, professional identity and change, and the new pedagogy and changing roles in teaching and learning.

The first chapter of **Part 4** by **Thomas** and **Gornall** investigates information technology (IT) in higher education working lives. The chapter explores the *impact of uses of technology and information by academics*, a discussion set in the context of *a 'sociology of work'* literature alongside perspectives on the role of technology in workplace productivity and displacement. A second chapter by **Rogers** examines teaching in the virtual classroom where *teaching and learning (T&L) online is explored in terms of 'leadership' attributes* that contribute to perceptions of effective e-learning in virtual classrooms. It is argued that pedagogical leadership qualities are as significant in virtual classrooms as in conventional teaching roles, and that attention to T&L attributes online can highlight sometimes understated and tacit aspects of teaching professionalism.

A third chapter by **Ecclesfield** and **Garnett** explores *new learners, new pedagogy and an emerging craft professionalism*. These authors consider how new technologies influence relations between teachers and learners in the context of two major UK policy areas: 'widening access and participation' and 'lifelong learning'. A fourth chapter by **Hudson** reveals *what it means to be a 'new professional' working in educational development with learning technologies* in UK HE. This chapter is a reflexive exploration of the notion of 'habitus', 'capital' and 'positioning', applied within HE, thus providing insights into 'one's own group' rather than just the case study of an individual or organization. Finally, the last chapter, by **Gornall,** considers teaching and learning staff ten years on from her original research in 1999, to ask whether the 'new professionals' are 'becoming indigenous' in HE today. The account is less a report on studies done, than *a reflection on narrative, 'otherness' and research on professionals in education and change.*

23

Higher Education, Information Technology and Academic Work

Brychan Thomas and Lynne Gornall

Introduction

Working life shows a complex picture regarding the use of information technology (IT) and related changes in organizations (Felstead, *et al.* 2005; Handel 2003). The culture of the workplace and its professional groups is a factor (Chase 2008), as well as the ways in which IT applications are used (Shaw 2001). A number of studies in human relations and knowledge have problematized employees' flexibility and personal involvement in IT-use and the general employment dynamics of the workplace (Pyoria 2005; Tolsby 2000; Martin 1999). So too, the Working Lives (WL) team has been investigating aspects of the nature of occupational change viewed through the lens of academics as HE workers (Cook *et al.* 2009). In this environment, technology has impacted significantly on administrative and core 'academic' teaching work, as well as research activities and processes. In this chapter, we present some illustrative findings on academics' everyday information and communication technology (ICT) use.

This small-scale study began by asking academics about how they used their computers. Surprise was registered by informants, who said that they had never actually articulated this, except as a passing 'moan' about systems or workload problems (discussed in the introductory chapter). It was also quite clear that they had little or no idea of how their colleagues worked; so too, colleagues would have few clues to their methods, strategies and operations, especially out of sight, at home. But this is a large part of everyday working life in employment today, so following Spradley (1979) and others, we set about uncovering some of the more 'hidden' aspects of this most familiar if 'mundane' of areas.

The context: technology and work

IT permeation in the workplace of industrialized nations over the last 30 years may be described as saturated. This has been evidenced in a number of places and reported in journal articles and books (Chase 2008; Cornford and Pollock 2003).

The same has been the case for the educational working environment (Handel 2003) and in many ways, HE and further education (FE) have been ahead of other organizations in adapting ICT for professional work (NCIHE/Dearing 1997). Like any other sector, education is in a competitive environment, and while technology has the ability to change how institutions operate (Tolsby 2000), influencing the nature of work processes and relationships between individuals and groups, it is also affected by the ways in which we use it too (Turkle 2007). In education, the 'Dearing' Report (NCIHE) of 1997, arguably set the agenda for the importance of ICT in learning modes for the future, as well as some of its repercussions for teaching and support work. More recent studies (Elliott and Urry 2010; Felstead 2008) have highlighted the cultural, temporal, spatial and relational repercussions of mobile technologies for employment and everyday life, and below, we consider some of the 'Working Lives' ICT findings on academics' desktop work today.

WL short study on academics' use of ICT

The WL study was a small-scale preliminary investigation, prior to and part of a larger one on employment change in UK HE. A qualitative methodology was used to examine the perceptions of professionals, based upon classical sociological and anthropological approaches to the study of work and cultures of technology use (Fischer 2003; Auster 1996; Van Maanen and Barley 1984). The study comprised a series of focused interviews with academics on the role of ICT in their professional tasks, and included questions on where their IT systems were located and how they used them. This covered use of email at home, proportions of emails received, what the emails were about, use of more than one email address, and the 'pros and cons' of electronic working. We asked about the management of the computer desktop, and whether there was a counterpart to having a 'tidy' or 'untidy' desk, and how this was organized, filed and managed. There were 16 interviewees, located in universities in the UK South Wales area, and these included a mix of 'pre-1992'/research-based and new/teaching universities. Six of the interviewees were male and 10 were female; within this, 14 were involved principally in teaching, and two mainly in research; 11 said that they had a combined teaching and research role, while 11 had management responsibilities too. The length of service and time spent working in HE spanned from 1 to 20 years; one participant had worked less than five years in HE, six from 6 to 10 years, three 11 to 15 years, and 6 for 16 to 20 years.

IT use home and work: some findings

Home workspace

The 'normal workspace' that interviewees reported included the classroom, laboratory, office and home. Seven described the classroom as their normal workspace, and all 16 quoted the 'work office'; 11 said that the 'home office' was a regular 'everyday' workplace too. All participants but one spent time answering emails from home. For some, there was no difference in being 'at home' or 'in work' for this; emails were received from students, managers and colleagues alike. At the time of collecting these data, many informants used laptops, often in conjunction with desktop computers. Half of the interviewees said that they shared a PC at home with others, four had their own PC, two shared a laptop computer, while 10 said they had a laptop for sole use, which they used for work at home. With regard to the main location of the computer, the categorizations of home spaces were themselves interesting, from 'An office up in the eaves. It's well-organized – desk, shelves, bookcases, in-tray, out trays and a pinboard! Oh and I have a computer with broadband connection'; to 'Box[room] open shelves . . . and it looks dire'. Six people said that their 'office' was 'wherever they were at the time', that is, on the sofa, in the kitchen, in the bedroom – or 'mobile within the house'. As one commented, 'A laptop usually – laptop-based, whenever I can get 10 minutes'. Another: 'I work on trains, planes when travelling to conferences. Different sorts of work of course in different places and spaces'.

Staying organized

A key area of inquiry concerned the *organization* of electronic information for work at home, and how the 'work' of organizing this activity was organized (Gornall and Salisbury 2012):

> My PC desktop? Uncluttered. Nothing 'whizzy' – a lot opened and minimized in the bottom of the screen.

Two interviewees used a digital memory stick for storage and transfer, five had email inbox folders to save and file information, one specifically used the Outlook Express application folders for file storage, seven had hard drive folders on their PC, while one had hard drive folders on their laptop for saving data. There were therefore numerous ways of organizing material. Some informants also had remote access to university main systems and their backup and archiving routines, so for them there was 'no difference' between campus working and being at home – so long as their systems were dependable! But for others, home working meant copying files in advance or emailing documents to themselves for later 'home' use. An interesting phenomenon in a form of backup and information organization was the practice of *self-emailing*: electronic 'to do' lists, re-sending (to self) documents for backup and keeping current information to hand. These techniques were used so that important information was not 'lost' in the daily incoming email blizzard, described by several informants.

Another fascinating area was the discussion about email attachments. Half of the interviewees described how they usually separated documents that arrived as email files. These were detached from the covering message and conscientiously filed or stored; three informants left attachments attached, putting them together in a mail folder. Three others left emails within the inbox and two used a mixed approach, detaching only 'important' ones. There were different views about the efficacy of 'attachment separation' or leaving covering email and document 'appended together', and whether 'filing in folders' or alternatively using 'search' and 'find' functions to retrieve were more effective. Since personal-use technologies are managed by the individual and have made us all 'our own secretaries now' (Gornall 2004), these aspects of academic work illustrate the abundance of operations to be performed and the extra tasks involved in the 'new' ways of working (Neumann 2009).

Crossed platforms

In the four years since the study, the multi-functionality of mobile phones has impacted significantly on work routines, and many staff now use more than one phone or device, with multiple digital contact lists and address books. They may also be using a variety of different ICT and telecoms systems, providers and networks, not all mutually compatible, integrated or inter-operable. This introduces time-consuming micro-work for users. Many people now also have more than one computer open on the office desktop, and flip between email and texts on a mobile phone at the same time as a replicated system on a large screen or laptop, all simultaneously active. Thus, as well as facilitating work, technology is also a *complicating* factor in employees' lives (Gornall and Salisbury 2012: 140). Many academics reported a mix of self-funded devices (laptops, phones) and systems, which they supported themselves, whose use crossed 'home' and 'work' functions and activities. Clearly in this context, individuals also have different 'affordances' in their approach to and use of such technologies, as others have considered (Prensky 2001).

The majority of interviewees (15 out of 16) thus used more than one email address to separate and organize their lives, with the aim of keeping personal and work use and activities separate. Four said:

> [I use a] different email address for [my] personal emails.
>
> Informant, new/teaching university

> I have a separate address for friends and try to keep my occupational and social networks clearly separate. Of course some friends are colleagues [too] but it's healthy to keep things separate, it's a strategy to keep me sane.
>
> Informant, traditional/research-based university

> I have a personal email address but I don't use it ... [however] it means that I am constantly looking at work stuff even when I have personal emails!
>
> Informant, new/teaching university

> Colleagues know that I won't access email from home.
>
> Interviewee, traditional/research-based university

Who are the emails from?

The areas of work that emails related to depended on the academics' role and the time of year in the educational calendar. In our questions about the proportions of emails and sources, there was inevitably some 'guestimating'. Two commented:

[I get] mostly emails dealing with staff and information things. If dissertations or assignments are due then student emails go through the roof.

Informant, new/teaching university

Roughly – ten percent students, sixty percent internal colleagues, twenty percent managers and ten percent external colleagues.

Informant, new/teaching university

Giving consideration to these comments, it was estimated that about a third of main general (work) emails were from students, with the largest numbers from internal colleagues. Smaller numbers were received from internal managers and external colleagues. There were other emails from various senders depending on the informant: 'Who are my emails from? Voluntary work, personal ... stuff, family ... but mainly work – doctoral students and their supervisors' (Informant, traditional/research-based university). Another response suggested that emails arose:

From *colleagues* about committees or research writing, bidding or co-taught courses, marking. From *students* about supervision appointments, pastoral matters, feedback on their drafts. All sorts of matters come down the line! You have to keep an eye on it every day, even if off site ...

Informant, traditional/research-based university, emphasis added.

The areas of work that emails were typically about are shown in Figure 23.1.

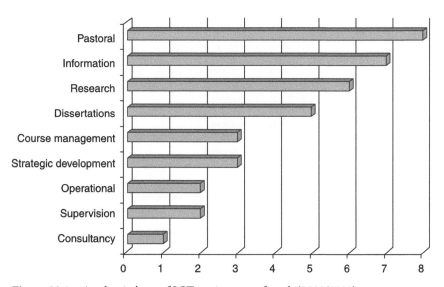

Figure 23.1   Academics' use of ICT: main areas of work (2008/2009)

The work of the work: views about e-working

Narratives and comments about the benefits and advantages of e-working were accessibility, ease of use, personal effectiveness for work ('productivity'), flexibility, providing good communication, ability to maintain contact, saving time and paper, and speed.

> The pros include: track changes, useful for students, enjoy batting emails back and forth with [colleagues:] . . . [but] expectations from other people – who expect quick responses 'just have a peek at this' try to regulate myself looking at emails.
>
> Informant, traditional/research-based university

> The pros of electronic working are that it is effective but human contact and support [are] needed as we all have similar roles.
>
> Informant, new/teaching university

> [A]ny time anywhere . . . accessibility, immediacy and feeling connected to colleagues and students. Being able to upload material for my students into VLE BlackBoard! Communication with researchers across the globe!
>
> Informant, traditional/research-based university

> Speed, clearing up urgent matters. Passing stuff that matters 'on and up' quickly.
>
> Informant, new/teaching university

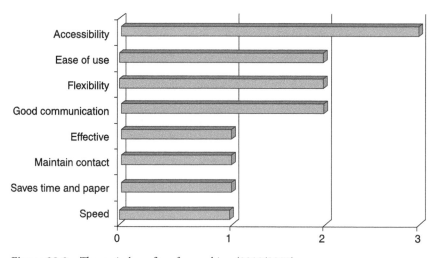

Figure 23.2   The main benefits of e-working (2008/2009)

Views about the main disadvantages and drawbacks of e-working were 'information overload', 'too quick a response expected', 'restricting face-to-face communication', being 'time-consuming' and also 'too easy to access' (causing distraction). There

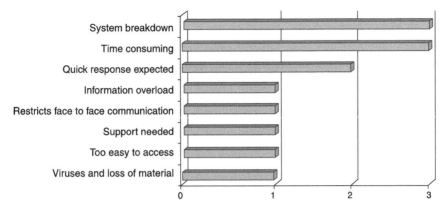

Figure 23.3 The main disadvantages/drawbacks of e-working (2008/2009)

were also comments about 'systems breakdown' and 'support' needs, that 'bad things happen', such as when viruses or faults could cause a loss of material.

Working alone with technology, some issues

With the increasing pressures of work and the important need for working both in the campus office space and at other external sites and at home (Gornall and Salisbury 2012), the role of flexible work and a flexible work schedule becomes important (Mottl, 2000; Felstead *et al.* 2005). The participants in our pilot study said that their 'working from home' time was mainly *computer work* using standard software applications, such as word processing, spreadsheets, presentational media, email, internet and occasionally research software.

The 'ubiquitous' and 'pervasive' aspects of IT and ICT use means that, as with other technologies in the home, little technical understanding of the way in which they operate is required. However, we have scant information on how academics and other employees learn how to use, develop practices in, problem-solve or manage their systems, especially when working independently, mobile or off-site, and there is scope for further research work here. Moreover, IT use, technology and information, its organization, storage, retrieval and archiving, are discussed by HEIs largely only in technical, strategic or regulatory contexts, whereas 'keeping up' and managing ICT systems and use is an issue for *all* staff every day. So too, on-campus IT upgrades may not make it to the home desktop, and therefore use of systems in different versions undoubtedly continues, compounding home/work complexities of our contemporary occupational and social lives (Elliott and Urry 2010: 30–31).

Given that so much of this effort and productivity is unseen – discussed in our introductory chapter – we asked informants what 'intersubjective' knowledge staff had for understanding how colleagues worked. Information was sketchy.

How do colleagues work?

- Probably like me.
- Not sure.
- Can't speak for others . . . same as me, I guess.
- [I know] whether they work from home but not how [they work].
- [They] know I work from home, but probably not *how* much.
- [You're] expected to be available [wherever you are].
- Never discussed [it].
- Assume similar – am I typical?

In the study as a whole, the interviewees gave thoughtful, often individually-specified responses, sometimes quite hard to co-categorize. Thus, the 'home workspace' was described variously as 'a family room', 'a box-bedroom', 'a dining table area for private study', 'attic office' and so on. Moreover, and as an intriguing marker, it was clear that despite efforts previously invested by households in the setting up of a 'home office' this was increasingly obsolete, as mobile technologies meant the equipment could stay with the user: 'I have a dedicated study. Prefer to be in the kitchen though [with my laptop]'; 'I have an office but it is used for storage, [I] work on a laptop on the sofa, with TV on in the background'.

The modes of working discussed above rarely seem to be picked up in discussions of work, let alone workload allocations and audits. Yet as ICT, technology and internet-based work grow – together with changing models of course delivery and study in education (Cannon 2004; Rogers this volume) – there are broad implications for changing work patterns by both tutors and students. Thus, a better understanding of ICT use by both groups – and staff as employees – may be critical for UK HEIs to address.

Concluding remarks

This chapter has reviewed a small-scale study that explored aspects of occupational change through the use of IT for work. It asked academics to discuss, somewhat uniquely, their personal routines and procedures for home-working via computer, something that is not seen or directly observed by colleagues or institutional managers. Current studies of home working and teleworking (Tietze and Musson 2005; Gundry and Salter 2005; Felstead 2005; Morelli 2001; Huws 1999) may assist in bringing this 'unseen' employment world to further attention. Given developments in both flexible working and e-learning, as areas that impact on both the wider workforce and all learners (Selwyn 2012), such insights can potentially be applied to far larger populations of people. We argue for 'ethnographic' approaches (Hendry 1999) to such studies, ones that frame 'organizational' worlds as including the home and the mobile 'systems' environment (Elliot and Urry 2010). There are challenges here for professional bodies and staff groups too, as well as employers. We also need critiques rather than just 'celebrations' of technology and its achievements, approaches that go beyond 'pro' or 'anti' attitudes, latest 'features' and technical details (Woolgar 2002). Further research attention to the *affective* and *contextual* aspects of human engagement with technology use would be repaid. This could include ambivalence around our 'tethering' relationships with the gadgets in our lives (Turkle 2011: 155), and a framing around the dimensions of what Elliott and Urry (2010: 15) call the 'mobilities paradigm'. Perhaps these may lead to a more connected, holistic conceptualization of technology use within education and HE work, and 'grounded' studies. This would also set IT use within new discourses about work roles, culture, gender and the blurred boundaries of everyday working for everyone.

Note

Based on a paper presented to the fourth Working Lives seminar, Trefforest, December 2010.

24

Teaching in the Virtual Classroom

Susy Rogers

Introduction

Hiltz coined the term for a classroom in an electronic space – the 'virtual classroom' – in 1986, and we have seen how new learning technologies create opportunities as well as challenges for teaching professionals (Carswell 1998). Whilst traditional face-to-face classroom teaching involves verbal and nonverbal communication, with the eye and the voice arguably at the centre of the craft of successful teaching, it is sometimes assumed that any teacher can transfer these 'face-to-face' skills to online pedagogy. However, aspects of what are described as teachers' conventional 'leadership qualities' (Avolio *et al.* 1999), it is argued here, can also play a significant part in 'virtual' classroom teaching practices, with other skills that have to be acquired and nurtured in training too. Following Armellini and Jones (2008), Rogers (2011) investigated the role of teachers in electronic learning environments ('e-learning'), and the teaching role in online education. This was applied in particular to 'asynchronous' networks, where teaching and learning are not in real time. Asynchronous e-learning includes 'on-demand delivery' which aims to give learners more control over the pace, process and content of study. However, e-tutors may be put under pressure, as e-learners and other peers who have time to think and prepare, may then anticipate immediate responses. In a synchronous learning environment, this 'time delay' does not occur.

The research looked at teachers' 'e-moderation' behaviour in e-learning, with participants who were higher education institution (HEI) lecturers. At that time, this sort of professional updating was seen by institutions as part of their continuing professional development (CPD) for staff, in the new modes of learning following the 'Dearing' Report (NCIHE 1997). The lecturer's role as 'e-moderator' includes tasks and activities associated with mediating and facilitating learners' online interaction and study. Salmon (2011) describes the role of an e-moderator with a number of metaphorical descriptors – as an online tutor, facilitator, coach and 'guide on the side'. The role as 'scaffolder' (of knowledge) and expert is also observed by other researchers (Squire and Johnson 2000; Wozniak *et al.* 2007). Skilful 'scaffolding' supports the progressive acquisition of knowledge for e-learners to construct new knowledge; teacher as 'expert' is, of course, a traditional knowledge-giving role. After nearly a decade of experience in computer-mediated education at Monash University and elsewhere, many observers recognize that effective e-moderation underpins high *quality* experiences and delivery of online learning (Berge 1997; Palloff and Pratt 2007; Armellini and Aiyegbayo 2010). Monash was one of the first to promote not just 'distance learning', but it trained academic staff to become online teachers. Thus, for successful teaching and learning online, lecturers need to develop this capability. The assumption underlying the framing for the present research was that teachers' classroom leadership attributes could be as important in 'virtual' classroom environments as they are in conventional ones (Rogers 2011). The aim of the university training studied was that lecturers would be able to become recognized e-moderators, in meeting the growing development for e-learning and online modules across the institution in its strategic development.

The traditional and the virtual classroom

Some 'modernists' say that teachers are unnecessary when e-learners can learn online, collaboratively in peer-group self-led teams (Salmon and Lawless 2006). Conrad (2004, 2007) challenged this, but few studies or courses have embraced 'leadership qualities' as an essential ingredient in developing professional practice in e-learning contexts; Kahai *et al.* (2004, see also Sosik *et al.* 1997) are among the few researchers who have done so. Qualities in the classroom such as charisma, presentation style, enthusiasm and conveying a vision to the learner, as well as bringing groups together, empowering learners to achieve specific goals, could be noted as part of this leadership skillset (Rogers 2011). For learners, Wenger (1998) argues that the role of the tutor should be to help develop collaborative communities of practice (CoP), especially in virtual classrooms (Wozniak 2007). In fact, a critical issue that has concerned educationalists and institutions about 'new' learning media is that learners may withdraw from courses and drop out because of poor engagement. The teacher/e-moderator role is thus seen as crucial in helping to create and sustain positive environments and interactions for learning (Berge 1997; Thorpe 2009).

Models for e-moderating 'as teaching' are scant (Salmon 2002; Laurillard 2002; Garrison and Anderson 2003; Moule 2007; Rogers 2011). In an initial case study, Rogers (2004) explored the potential of selected 'leadership qualities' for application in online teaching, using a research sample of 30 practising e-moderators from a single post-1992 HEI. Some illustrations of pedagogical leadership qualities can be cited as someone who is not just a task-giver, but empowers others and encourages them into new areas of learning safely, providing stimulation, motivation and a forward vision; they recognize individuality in learning, and are usually recognized by others as providers of pedagogical leadership.

A self-administered Multifactor Leadership Questionnaire for e-moderators (MLQ-E) was designed (Rogers 2004) with 39 customized items from the Bass and Avolio (1997) paradigm of transformational/transactional leadership. Responses were analysed for principal components, producing a scree plot that highlighted four factors which were important to those individuals: (1) an 'idealized' leadership role, i.e. e-moderator is admired, respected and trusted, and online learners aspire to emulate their online tutor behaviour; (2) intellectual stimulation, where e-learners are challenged to think creatively, being provoked by e-moderators to review 'old' assumptions; (3) inspirational motivation, where an e-moderator energizes e-learners with ambitious goals, instilling the vision that these are achievable; and (4) individual considerations, where e-moderators support individual needs by giving e-learners increased self-confidence and encouraging self-actualization. Rogers (2004) found how academics in 'e-moderator' roles recognized their own leadership qualities embedded in their online roles and relationships. These qualities were seen to underpin what are known as 'transformational' behaviour types – i.e. where online learners are helped to achieve ambitious goals.

Following this research, a second exploratory study adapted Kelly's ([1955] 1991) 'personal construct' theory methodology to identify further the attributes that might be operating. The sample this time consisted of a different set of e-moderation practitioners (N = 17) but from the same HEI. The elicitation process employed triads of selected elements from a set of six online teaching competences (namely, weaving, archiving, summarizing, scaffolding, knowledge construction and socializing). It then linked the outcomes from this with perceived e-moderator *leadership* attributes (task-giving and motivation) and their perceived *e-learner* attributes (collaborative capability and knowledge construction ability). It was found that varying degrees of leadership attributes were perceived to match varying degrees of e-learner attributes, corroborating Roger's (2011) *pedagogical variation* model for online teaching and learning.

Pedagogical leadership

The qualities of *leadership* of a teacher underpin and shape his/her pedagogical role in online teaching and learning (Rogers 2011). Authentic leaders, according to Hughes (2005) strive for *relational transparency*, i.e. by being open with information, encouraging sharing of ideas, allowing appropriate self-disclosure, and being more trustworthy in anticipation of greater trustworthiness. Such 'authentic' qualities would arguably be advantageous and beneficial (to learners) when transposed to online teaching roles. Four expressions of appropriate self-disclosure, illustrated below, between authentic leaders and followers – learners here – were described by Avolio *et al.* (1999) as related to: (1) goals/motives; (2) identity; (3) values; and (4) emotions. As Hughes (2005: 89) says, followers' motivation *increased* when they knew,

> *why* they were doing what they were doing (goals/motives), *trusted* who they were dealing with (identity), *understood* and shared in the values underlying the decision-making (values), and *felt secure* in sharing and trusting in the expressed emotions of themselves and those with whom they worked. [emphasis added]

Leaders who self-disclosed with others were more likely to establish relational transparency. Our argument here is that this could be applied to online teaching, to increase commitment and motivation, and help deter e-learner drop-out. Using technologies for learning can create barriers, and a rise in students' anxiety and/or lack of confidence (Boyle and Wambach 2001; Curtis *et al.* 2002; Hong *et al.* 2003). If these negative feelings can be overcome, and teacher qualities are posited as having importance in this outcome, then learners can take advantage of the identified benefits of e-learning. Carswell (1998) discusses these benefits as the self-paced, self-directed and 'just-for-me' qualities. Grow's (1991) staged self-directed learning model suggests that different methods are relevant for teaching students at various specific stages of development – although not all concur with the 'stages', evolutionary model – in education. It is suggested that many different teaching styles may be effective, and it is unlikely that there is a single specific teaching style or orthodox constructivist, 'one-size fits all' approach effective in learning online (Jones 2004). For Grow (1991), pedagogical difficulties can be frequently explained as 'mismatches' between teaching style and learner stage, so problems actually emerge as such mismatches, for example in 'directive' or non-directive teacher presentation and support styles.

What e-learning can do is enable more *collaborative* study. Links between local as well as physically separated learners and experts, together with wide access to materials, generates online learning communities of inquiry (Garrison and Anderson 2003/2007). The role of the teacher as a pedagogical leader is most valued here (Rogers 2011) because in an e-learning system within an online discussion forum, for example, learners (1) are encouraged to ask questions, including ones they might not want to ask publicly in conventional face-to-face classrooms, (2) they can elicit personal opinions and self-disclosure in learning and self-development mode, and (3) are able to share and encounter ideas *between peers* in a wider than normal environment (Hiltz and Wellman 1997; McCloskey *et al.* 1998). E-learners are free from fixed timetables and able to select learning activities and materials from well-maintained, high-quality archives to meet their needs – authentic resources that suit their interests and which are accessible at any time. It approaches the ideal goal of 'learner self-development', supported by skilled teacher-facilitator *leadership* (Rogers 2011). This is by contrast with 'instructivist' modes of teaching and learning, whereby information is from the 'teacher as expert' and uni-directional, putting learners in more 'passive' mode (Ramsden 1991).

Reprofessionalization of a community of practitioners and its research

Just as there are advantages for learners in acquiring new skills, knowledge and expertise via online learning, so too, accessibility of the same resources for the CPD of teachers and lecturers themselves is equally important. The 'e-moderators' course studied was an example of this. For some, the re-skilling of lecturers and teachers for online work amounts to a process of 'reprofessionalization' of staff (Armellini and Jones 2008). Professions, their groups, and institutions need to be at the forefront of designing and providing such courses (as well as those for student learners), because the pedagogical context of updating is important. So too is the manner and process of independent evaluation and pedagogical research by educational professionals (Ellaway *et al.* 2004). In this context, Hudson (2009) argues that 'communities of practice' can be an important catalyst for the development of shared knowledge and expertise using distributed networks, and which is arguably applicable to both CPD and '*ab initio*' education. As Zhang (2003: 204) comments, 'it is a daunting task to maintain a well-educated and high-performance workforce in the global economy of today'. This is important for teachers' ongoing employability (see also Rothwell and Rothwell this volume) but also for the future career prospects of their learners. It is having an effect too in the emergence of newer educational professionals (after Gornall 1999; Hudson 2009 and others), in that new genres of professionals are entering education as teachers, 'e-coaches' and 'virtual trainers' for online learning (see also Ecclesfield and Garnett on craft professionalism, this volume). Conventional lecturers and teachers need constant updating too.

The scope for online education and training is growing, with its advantages of convenience, being able to decide on when and where the virtual classroom is encountered and entered, all as much-celebrated attributes. This gives great and radical flexibility compared to traditional teaching and learning spaces, which moreover, run in parallel with an inflexible employment, institutional and contractual environment in further and higher education (FE/HE). The portability of laptops and handheld devices means that employers may no longer wish to give employees time or 'time-in-lieu' for CPD, but rather depend on them to take 'time out' themselves for qualifications and upgrading (see also Laugharne *et al.* this volume). Andrusyszyn *et al.* (1999) have shown that as the population of e-learners increases, so too does the need for developing guidance. But this includes not just pedagogical support but also the need for help in the use of learning systems, given their obsolescence, as one 'enabling' technology is superseded by another. This is an area that conventional teaching staff, in their own upskilling, have been struggling with for some time. Thus, there are issues associated with the new flexibilized learning systems, that can suggest considerable areas needing strategic or organizational problem-solving (Haskel and Slaughter 2002).

Flexible learning and working

Flexible round-the-clock access to learning and teaching systems in online pedagogy has created individual, employment and work-time issues. Networked computer-based platforms and the achievements of cross-national telecommunication technologies, with internet, search tools and smart applications, suggests that the potential for less didactic, more flexible modes of teaching and learning will grow. Fewer limitations on access or retrieval mean that 'peer' learning is also increasingly enabled. However, this access, availability and enlargement may pose a serious problem for e-tutors, with ever-increasing postings online, for example, with expectations of responsiveness. Berge and Collins (2000: 89) consider that the volume of online 'traffic' (the number and frequency of posts) is always a concern: there is just so much time in a day and space in the inbox. The range of posts to these lists could range from 1 to 600 per day.

Working Lives research suggests that academics in HE spend numerous overtime hours on some of their most 'productive' work, although often with little official recognition of their efforts (Gornall and Salisbury 2012). It is acknowledged by government that UK organizations have contributed to this, by encouraging a 'long hours' culture, 'to the extent that more than 20 per cent of the total workforce and a considerably higher proportion of managers and professionals, work in excess of 48 hours a week' (DTI 2002: 15). At the fourth 'Working Lives' conference (October 2010), and with a background in sciences as well as education and pedagogy, the author explored the notion of 'personal rhythms of working', in the context of 'virtual teaching' and online learning developments. I asked whether, by extension, we are moving towards an assumption about some form of infinite professional working spaces, and the dangers and risks in this.

Biological time affects, in no small degree, the productivity and health of people and employees. Working 'out of phase' with one's 'biological clock' may bring a cost in health and well-being, and also in terms of other relationships at work as well as at home. Employers and individuals, working online and 'attached' to their electronic gadgets, including mobile phones and iPods, need to be aware of how their performance and alertness decreases with night-time or 'round the clock' activity (Dijk and von Schantz 2005). Yet managing and counteracting these trends could become a pressing professional and workplace concern. Early experiments (Sharma 2003), where non-humans were constantly forced to shift their biological clock, resulted in substantially lowered life expectancy. So, whether by choice or necessity, 'workaholic' virtual space workers may well be putting their health at risk. Schein (1996) noted some time ago how graduates, as new employees moving into large organizations where computerized workloads were being taken home for later completion and often in the early hours of the morning, were beginning what could become a 'career lifestyle'.

Concluding remarks

In the 1970s, the writer Illich (1971) foresaw the notion of a 'learning web' that would bring global access to learning with free communication between learners and teachers. Today, as people retire earlier and live longer, 'life-wide' learning (Barnett 2010) is becoming more prevalent in many parts of the World. Teaching and learning are no longer restricted to classrooms (Lawton and Katsomitros 2012). People, therefore, with different cultures, beliefs and backgrounds, may register at any one time as e-learners for a variety of online courses. Education and attainment have long been associated with aspiration and hard, intensive work, sometimes for extensive periods of time. Teachers' conventional leadership, professional learning and management qualities will therefore be ever more important in newer pedagogical environments, and extended research in this important new area is therefore pressing. As Turoff (1995: 3) observes, 'once we free ourselves from the mental limits of viewing this technology [virtual classroom] as a weak sister to face-to-face synchronous education, the potentials for revolutionizeing education and learning become readily apparent'.

Note

Based on a paper presented and discussed at the Working Lives seminar of December 2010.

25

New Learners, New Pedagogy and an Emerging Craft Professionalism

Nigel Ecclesfield and Fred Garnett

Introduction

The broad concept of 'widening access' and the evolving term 'lifelong learning' are two key themes by which we can characterize government policy across the UK since 1997 (discussed also in Part I of this volume). Both have been used to underpin policies seeking to engage a greater proportion of the adult population in education. A critical agent impacting on educational work practices and professional accountability has been the introduction of new technologies into all aspects of teachers' working lives.

As well as being used for learning and teaching, these technologies are used also for managerial functions, audit procedures, room occupancy, student attendance, for example, and the production of data for quality assurance. This has created pressure on educational professionals to use technology in all aspects of their work, leading to a blurring of the boundaries of time, place and role in occupational life (Gornall and Thomas 2001). Since 2010, these 'blurring' tendencies have been reinforced by the large-scale adoption of wireless, mobile and tablet technologies in the personal lives of learners and as well as staff.

We argue that not only do teachers' own conceptions of their activity influence how they work, but also that technological changes have affected relationships, especially between learners and teachers (Haythornthwaite 2010). Teaching in post-compulsory education utilizes techniques and interventions – often described as 'pedagogies' – that range in approach from teacher-centric to learner-centric. Whilst technologies, including those labelled as 'Web 2.0', offer the potential to support different approaches to learning and teaching, they are most often utilized to support *teacher-centric* modes of delivery. They are less often used for engaging in the negotiation of content and the sequence of delivery with *learners* – still less in engaging them in co-creation and assessment of learning activities and outcomes, which are also amongst the affordances of such technologies.

In this chapter, we draw on experiences and material from the UK and elsewhere, to explore how learning might develop these affordances in education. Throughout

2011, the authors were involved in surveying the views of further education (FE) teachers about their practice and attitudes towards the use of educational technology in professional work (Ecclesfield *et al.* 2011). We draw on a sample of 1,000 practitioners in England, along with 400,000 words of reflective responses on the contexts of use. We argue that the creative possibilities in learning and teaching have mostly been neglected during technology-driven changes in working practices. This work on practitioner attitudes to technology sheds new light on the skills and qualities needed by educationalists today, and the consequent professional development areas that arise. We have also identified concepts and developments areas that might be useful in enabling teachers to review and re-conceptualize their practice, in beginning to re-affirm a new 'craft' professionalism in post-compulsory education.

New learners

Firstly, we note that learners and practitioners are rarely engaged in the formulation of policies and the setting of targets or objectives, whilst the needs of employers are frequently privileged there. Secondly, participation in post-compulsory education has increased throughout the last decade (DfE 2011) especially in higher education (HE), where graduate numbers have doubled in the past 10 years. (Office for National Statistics 2012). The recent emphasis on work-based learning in HE signals the intention of UK governments to encourage those in work and holding vocational qualifications to develop their learning through working, to gain accreditation at graduate level and beyond. The Nixon Report (Nixon *et al.* 2006) suggests however that this is not unproblematic, citing pedagogy, staff support and employer awareness as issues that need to be addressed, with concern too about the consequent pressures on educational professionals. Our findings support a need for learner-centric practice, collaborative continuing professional development (CPD) and greater institutional awareness of changing practices, as new technology use increases (see also Rothwell and Rothwell this volume).

New curriculum

There has been a trend in post-compulsory education for the curriculum to focus on the needs of employers as well as the skills needed for current employment. This has been accompanied, however, by reductions in both the learning 'offer' of non-vocational adult education, to just those courses that are self-financing, and in the subject provision of HE. Closures are highest in areas such as humanities, modern languages and arts subjects (UCU 2012). FE, because of its historic focus on skills training and vocationalism, has been required to act most 'responsively' to such policies and policy changes (Foster 2005; Leitch 2006 discussed also in Jephcote, this volume). Yet limitations in the learning offer, and reductions in curricula, arguably make such responsiveness more difficult to achieve. The Wolf Report (2011) in England demonstrated how difficult it has been to date to achieve 'greater control' of vocational content and accreditation. Meanwhile, Radin (2006) has employed the term 'demeaning professionals' to discuss the ways in which those working in post-compulsory education across the UK have been subject to new management disciplines and inspection practices, as discussed by Waring, and Kelly and Boden, in this volume. Radin (2006: 82–84) uses the UK Research Assessment Exercise (RAE) as an example of these processes, which have increasingly narrowed the scope and purposes of educational work in parallel with the narrowing of the curriculum (UCU 2012: 3).

However, the wider access to information, that Wikipedia and the increasing availability of learning resources such as open education resources (OERs), the Open University, Open Learn and MIT's Open CourseWare bring (as internet and web-based resources), contrasts with the 'narrowing' curriculum trend outlined earlier. This wider access to resources offers the potential for bringing individuals and groups together for learning in different ways, as explored in Wenger's notion of 'digital habitats' (Wenger *et al.* 2009). Haythornthwaite and Andrews (2011: 35) refer to a 'dialogical exploration of learning', emphasizing the relational and networked qualities of learning, that can arise both within and outside of organizations. Such developments indicate that new curricula can emerge from a wide range of circumstances and interests, as well as being capable of use in the context of traditional subjects and disciplines, bringing individuals together from across organizational and other boundaries.

Seen from our perspective, the new curricula now being developed using the Web and other new communication technologies (such as Open Learning and Massive Online Open Courses (MOOCs)) are moving from being the work of expert groups to becoming open for co-creation and participative learning. Potentially this allows for both the provision of more real-time information, and new forms of knowledge development, to promote and support learning in the future. This is somewhat similar to Castells' (2010: 135) concept of 'the creative audience', whereby communicative subjects 'integrate various modes and channels of communication in their practice and in their interaction with each other'.

New pedagogies

In the 'Open context model of learning and the craft of teaching', and in our paper to the Working Lives seminar series, we argue for a view of teaching as a 'craft'.

Table 25.1 A schematic of the PAH Continuum

	Pedagogy	**Andragogy**	**Heutagogy**
Locus of control	Teacher	Teacher/learner	Learner
Education sector	Schools	Adult & further education	Research
Cognition level	Cognitive	Meta-cognitive	Epistemic cognition

The open context model uses the PAH Continuum (Ecclesfield and Garnett 2010) to present a continuum of learning strategies for teachers. The PAH Continuum (see Table 25.1) makes appropriate mixed use of *pedagogy* i.e. understanding the subject-based nature of learning activities in a way that enables the production of learning resources by the teacher; *andragogy*, supporting the collaborative processes of the learning group, negotiating content and sequencing of learning, and *heutagogy*. This last enables the development of original responses to the learning being engaged in by learners, including co-creation, as well as original ways of presenting work for summative assessment These definitions were developed through the work of the Learner Generated Contexts Group (Luckin *et al.* 2010) and have been used as an organizing principle to help design learner's technology use by Thomas Cochrane (2010a, 2010b) in the product design degree at Unitec Auckland. The notion of 'andragogy' in particular allows for communications around shared work that is intended to amplify participant understanding of the subject and also leads to group work for formative assessment. We return to the theme later.

Another development showing an increasing appreciation of learner needs and input into their own learning has been the work of Sugata Mitra and his collaborators on self-organized learning environments (SOLE) or self-organized mediating environments (SOME). Mitra and Dangwal (2010) show that learners' own interests and motivations, when allied with an accessible technology, can lead to significant learning with minimal input from 'teachers'. They found that mediation by an appropriate person did improve learning and retention, but this did not, in itself, require any subject knowledge (pp. 686–688). The engagement of students in the process of shaping their learning with teaching staff on London's University of the Arts MA in Photojournalism, through the use of the Drupal software platform, which allows them to work with professional photographers around the World, resulted in learners redefining both their personal practice and their view of the contexts in which they will operate as putative professionals in their chosen field (e.g. documentary photography and photojournalism). Finally, Ian Cunningham, working with younger learners usually excluded from school or with personal problems, has shown how the 'self-managed learning' context of South Downs College enabled appropriate learning activities to be identified for participants, including negotiating learning programmes and attendance in conventional schools to work towards GCSEs. In these examples, the teachers/facilitators move between roles; presenting, negotiating and facilitating. They use their professional skills combined with an ability to contextualize knowledge and information to support learner engagement, learning and reflection and to demonstrate 'the desire to do a job well for its own sake', as Sennett (2008) defines craft.

New professionalism

Today, professional knowledge and practice is sometimes 'demeaned' by political agencies and funding bodies. The RAE in HE in the UK created results, according to Radin (2006: 84), 'that over-measured research to the detriment of teaching', adding that while some academic professionals did well, others were 'penalized for their investment in particular subject areas and inability to meet defined outcome measures' (p. 84). Professionals were 'often faced with conflict between quality standards and efficiency standards' (p. 86). In the UK, funding is linked to efficiency measures whilst learners' views are only given weight as consumers of services (e.g. in the National Student Survey), rather than as active participants in learning.

Meanwhile, new technologies and devices are continually being adopted and configured for use in the home as well as they are leisure, workplace and educational settings, increasingly for personal use and to support interpersonal exchanges via the internet. This constantly changing and evolving context is characterized by O'Reilly (2005) as being in *'perpetual beta'*. We see the emerging craft of teaching, in part, as using communications media for developing learners' abilities to create and manage their own learning, by enabling learners to develop new collaborative and personal literacies (including their ability to create conditions for learning itself), scanning for developments in their subject areas and professional life, and communicating and collaborating with peers for personal, professional and community purposes, including for mentoring and reflection

In *The Craftsman* (2008), Richard Sennett argues that practitioners, such as those in the earlier examples, need some 10,000 hours to acquire mastery of their profession (at least three years of full-time work). This 'craft professionalism' means moving from the safe and mechanical uses of skills to being able to deepen and extend their technique into more creative activities of innovation, whilst maintaining professional and ethical standards. Our argument for a new craft professionalism suggests that professional skills in teaching throughout post-compulsory education imply the ability to use the framing device of subject delivery in order to:

- encourage participative group communications;
- offer the possibility of using new ways of presenting the resultant learning for assessment.

Where this is happening, the implications for learners of deploying such skills would be a better 'learning to learn' process. In the context of digital technologies, this also requires appropriate literacies for present-day 'digital habitats' as characterized by Wenger *et al.* (2009), in order to facilitate 'lifelong learning in a digital age' (LLiDA). The concept of 'digital literacies' as referenced by JISC (2010b), comprises the practical skills necessary to function in the increasingly digital worlds of learning and work.

With the wider range of options for learning and assessment available through Web 2.0 technologies, a teacher's ability to 'broker' learning opportunities may emerge as the key role in enabling learners to make best use of the available options. This will require a critical engagement with these technologies by all participants in learning-related activities. Cochrane (2010a) and his colleagues in New Zealand engage teaching staff, students and technicians by calling on 'technology stewards' within course teams, whose expertise can help users adapt technology for specific learning purposes, and whose focus is not on technology but on supporting learning and teaching. What LLiDA and Cochrane's work shows is that greater trust in both the learners' skills and knowledge of technology can be harnessed to support both personal and interpersonal learning. Haythornthwaite (2010), informed by work from the USA, re-conceptualises this view, and describes learning developing:

as an **outcome** of relations–

A community holds a knowledge of its history, and information resources for dealing with new situations

in **spaces**

Such as affinity spaces, third places, geo-community spaces (libraries, community centres, churches), online learning communities, public and community spaces, online and face-to-face spaces; each space offering the possibility for different learning relationships

as a **relation** that connects people

A student learns from a teacher; students learn together from a teacher; novices learn from each other

as **production** as well as consumption

An individual contributes content to a discussion, wiki, collaborative artwork

Teachers can encourage and co-create learning in these ways, using both formal and informal methods, face-to-face and virtual spaces as well as fostering collaboration and mutual support outside structured settings. Mitra's (Mitra and Dangwal 2010) curiosity in using unsupported technology for learning takes our consideration of how much input is required by learners into a different arena. He shows that self-organized and 'minimally mediated learning', and based on simple framing questions to shape activities, combined with internet access, can be a powerful means of stimulating learning and assessing its outcomes.

Building a 'craft professionalism'

In the UK, some practitioners are transforming their engagement with learners by beginning to 'appropriate' many technologies for learning and teaching. They are incorporating typical learning technologies, such as virtual learning environments, into their work, along with many other social tools, such as 'apps' (software applications) and handheld devices, using creative and dynamic approaches and with a focus on the students' learning experience. In particular in FE, we have tried to demonstrate that the exercise of an 'ethic of care' (see Salisbury this volume) is consistent with and related to notions of a new 'craft professionalism'. By this, we mean the principled uses of technology for student-centred learning and in the context of pedagogically-nimble teaching.

By its nature, this new craft professionalism is both challenging and potentially disruptive, as it may draw upon networks outside of the boundaries of current institutions, using 'open' technologies, and also engaging the emerging ideas of 'open scholarship' proposed by Gideon Burton (2008; see also Garnett and Ecclesfield 2011).

We now see it as critical that institutions foster the emergence of such a new craft professionalism in the following ways:

- openness to negotiation with learners, to meet their needs and accessibility requirements, as well as opportunities for staff to develop craft skills in teaching;
- collaborations to promote the widest opportunities for learning;
- institutional networking to both engage with wider developments beyond organizational boundaries as they happen and, potentially, to influence policy and policy-making;
- technological diversity to meet a wide range of needs;
- agility to respond and adapt appropriately to changing circumstances.

Concluding remarks

We contend that the landscape of professionalism is being constantly redrawn by the twin demands of policy and changing technologies. Consequently, developing a craft professionalism that incorporates a use of technology to create artfully-produced student-centred learning experiences and based on an 'ethic of care', will be critical in coping with the future demands placed on educational professionals and learners alike. As the key 'new professionals' (Hudson, Gornall this volume; Beetham *et al.* 2001) of the sector, the responsibility for this is in part with the educationalists involved. Whilst the notion of craft has a number of meanings we want to appropriate it here to help educational professionals understand the new digital habitats in which they now operate. We believe that the notion of *craft* – the development of skills, knowledge and learning, enhanced by reflective engagement in communities of practitioners – is an important emergence in discussions of professionalism and learning, in todays narratives of 'working lives in post-compulsory UK education'. The PAH Continuum, with its recognition of subject-content, shared work and reciprocity in adult learning, is our contribution to applying this to dilemmas of learning and teaching in the technology-informed environments of modern current practice.

Note

A version of this chapter was presented and discussed at the Working Lives Seminar in December 2010, Trefforest, Wales.

26

'Habitus' and Meanings of a Career in Learning Technologies and Educational Development

Alison Hudson

Habitus

My very early experience of education was shaped by my ability in sport and forms of positioning and control, which I later understood to be acts of socially constructed symbolic violence. Pierre Bourdieu uses the concept of 'symbolic violence' to identify a 'soft' form of psychological violence activated by a holder of capital, as a means of controlling the agency of individuals with less capital. Individuals comply and accept the World as it is and thus find the dominant order 'natural' (Bourdieu and Wacquant 1992: 168). For example, as a 10-year-old primary school pupil, I was seated in the classroom according to gender and according to my ability, assessed through end-of-term tests. I can clearly visualize the divided and stratified classroom with the 'top boy' seated at the front on the right and the 'top girl' seated at the front on the left. I recall that the status afforded by the seating positions was not discussed in the playground, although we all 'knew' who was in front of us and who was behind us.

My secondary education experience was formed by my transition from a working-class environment to that of a middle-class academic environment of a girls' high school, which highlighted issues of both class and gender. Motivated by my interest in art and mathematics and my ability and passion for team sport, I had an ambition to be a teacher from an early age. At the time, I was unaware that it was viewed as 'a good job for a girl'; it was simply what I wanted to do. I attended a college of teacher education and went on to teach in secondary education for a number of years. I reached a point in my career, eventually becoming a departmental head, which placed me in a strong position to take on a management role. However, I decided to leave secondary education to spend time with my young family. During this period, I extended and strengthened my formal qualifications in mathematics teaching and, in the late 1980s, moved into higher education (HE) to work in a polytechnic. This was a fixed-term, part-time contract as a teacher educator of mathematics. Significantly, it was also a time when desktop computers were being introduced into the classroom and were most often seen as the 'domain of mathematicians'.

'New' technologies

At the time I entered HE, much excitement and rhetoric was generated by the arrival of computer-based 'interactive' media, in the form of microcomputer-controlled analogue interactive videodisc systems. To begin with, most development activity centred on the private sector, with major companies such as British Telecom using multimedia technologies to support the training of their staff, in what were called Flexible Learning Centres. Towards the end of the 1980s, the UK government allocated relatively large amounts of funding to public sector agencies to pursue public/private sector technological collaboration (Boyers 1988).

As a teacher educator in a mathematical science department, and with interests in art, mathematics education and the use of computers, I was in a prime position to become involved in such initiatives. The new technologies of the period seemed physically daunting, mysterious and incomprehensible. Nevertheless, the potential benefits of using computers and other media creatively in education made the projects seem particularly exciting and appealing for me. I was invited to join a small team of teacher educators from other HE institutions and became involved in a variety of national projects, all of which explored the use of computers and multimedia in educational settings. This involved working on school- and college-based research and development projects funded through agencies such as the Department of Trade and Industry and the Department for Employment. While gaining knowledge and experience as valuable social and cultural capital, I was also unintentionally becoming drawn towards a highly political agenda, one that sought to 'harness technology' for educational reform and national prosperity. Such national debates were highly stimulating at a personal level, focusing as they did on teaching methods. And while the perceived potential of the 'new technologies' was balanced by difficulties of organizing and managing access to limited resources, it seemed that they were also likely to have far-reaching effects on emerging educational agendas.

A 'new' professional

The start of the 1990s was a critical career point for me. The initial emphasis of funded development projects was aimed at schools and further education (FE) colleges, with little funding available for research and development in the HE sector. This prompted me to take a proposal to the departmental head to establish a centre aimed at supporting research and development on the educational use of interactive technologies and multimedia. While the response was positive, economic capital – i.e. funding for salaries and resources – had to be sought externally. And so it was that in the early 1990s, I established a Centre with a focus on the use of interactive multimedia and associated educational research, and my career in HE, as a 'new professional', began in earnest.

When the term 'new professional' was used in the late 1990s alongside changing work boundaries in UK HE (Gornall 1999; Beck 1999), attention was drawn to the proliferation of job titles that were beginning to be applied to various forms of work associated with support for teaching and learning in this sector. Perceptions of what it meant to be a new professional varied substantially; for example, Gornall (1999: 45) described new professionals as an 'emergent new group' having hybrid roles for the support of teaching and learning, while Beck (1999: 227) saw the new professional as 'servicing the needs of re-formed institutions' which had become dominated by economic imperatives, market forces and new forms of management. Both were parts of the story! Indeed, as the imperatives of globalization began to drive wider change in HE, similar centres and variations of the 'new professional', in particular of the educational developer and the learning technologist, could be found throughout Europe and more widely in international settings (Roxå and Mårtensson 2005; Grant *et al.* 2009). The initiation of such units was indicative of the increasing impact of desktop computing on teaching and learning, as well as the onset of an emerging entrepreneurial and more business-oriented culture in HE.

Nevertheless, the Educational Technology Centre was unconventional for that time in the sense that success was dependent on interdisciplinary teamwork and it relied entirely on funding raised externally. This thus anticipated, by a number of years, the interprofessional work, 'development periphery' and enterprise cultures of universities highlighted by Clark (1998) and the 'top-sliced' funding for academic development. Perhaps for that reason, I had a great deal of autonomy in deciding the direction of the Centre, its work and its networks.

The 'new' university

In 1992, when the polytechnic made the transition to university status, a comprehensive restructuring began that involved drawing faculties into large 'schools' and bringing central departments together. This type of restructuring could be seen in policy documents such as the Follett Report in 1993 on library services, which called for more joint and collaborative 'cross-service' working in HE. It also led to a series of initiatives backed by substantial amounts of funding, including the establishment of the Joint Information Systems Committee (JISC) and funding for the creation of new and extended library buildings. Academic libraries were clearly expected to respond to the increased student numbers, the challenges of 'student-centred' learning and opportunities afforded by 'new technologies' in education. In anticipation of an institutional restructuring process at my 'new university', a move of the Educational Technology Centre to the library seemed to be a good idea and, shortly after moving into the library, my position as the academic leader of the Centre was made permanent (i.e. tenured).

The move marked the start of valued work relationships with colleagues who were committed to providing the highest level of support to students and staff. However, this was also a time of increasing pressure on institutional budgets, demands for efficiency gains and greater 'client' orientation. Thus I moved away from my subject discipline, mathematics education, towards what was to become a highly political and centralized position within Academic Development.

'New professionals' in the 'new university'

The central position of the Educational Technology Centre in the mid-1990s can be seen as part of a much bigger picture, especially with regard to supporting 'widening participation' in HE policies (DES 1992). Following the restructuring of the institution, the Educational Technology Centre, along with other units, which most notably included a newly formed Educational Development Unit and a Unit for Research into Teaching and Learning, all moved into a new central super-department which had the library at its heart. The strength of the super-department meant that its outreach was immense. A new building was purpose-built with the aim of creating a learning space in which ICT and multimedia could be integrated with traditional resources, and where new practices of support for learning could be developed.

This was also a period of extensive change for many university libraries, not only in the UK. While there was some scepticism among HE staff generally about the financial imperatives driving new models (Kogan *et al.* 2000), for me, the approach to change in my department was marked by openness, and a shared vision to provide quality support to both staff and students. Accordingly, the work of the Educational Technology Centre began to find a balance between externally-funded work and activities that provided support for staff across the university. Throughout this period, I began to carry out small-scale studies and to write papers with colleagues. I was eventually asked to take on the role of Educational Research Coordinator for the larger department, in addition to my other responsibilities.

As the need for support grew, the Centre expanded and so a need emerged to foster the careers of staff appointed to the new posts. It became necessary to create generic job descriptions that emphasized expertise in the production of multimedia and web-based material and in educational design. At that time, in the mid-1990s, there were few examples (if any) of similar jobs in the university or elsewhere, nor were there routes to formal certification in such areas, indicating perhaps that this 'type' of new professional had not yet been established widely. Thus new job titles were created which could fit into the somewhat disparate constraints of existing university career structures. The nature of the Centre's work in the mid-1990s matched many of the characteristics and definitions of practice found in the later literature on new professionals and learning technologists (Gornall 1999, 2004; Beetham *et al.* 2001; Oliver 2002; Land 2004; Gosling 2008). While more recent attempts have been made to formally acknowledge the 'learning technologist' role, job titles, practice and professional career routes remain diverse (Hudson 2009; Browne and Beetham 2009).

Symbolic, social and economic capital

The repositioning of the Educational Technology Centre within the new super-department meant that the work was more closely aligned with the university's two related units for Educational Development and Research into Teaching and Learning. However, each grouping represented a different sub-field of 'new professionals' within the new Centre; that is, each group was positioned at the same level in the structure and, following Bourdieu's view of positioning within a field, maintained its own 'logic, rules and regularities' (Bourdieu and Wacquant 1992: 104).

While the Centre had grown and developed on the basis of external funding, an aim was for it to be accepted as a mainstream academic unit. Thus a further move for closer integration of the work within 'educational development' was proposed. This was significant as it meant a change in line management, and moreover, that the status of the Centre had shifted. It moved from a sub-field in its own right to incorporation into another sub-field of power. Another significant factor was that the Centre relinquished responsibility for its own finances (which included external income). The perceived gain in symbolic capital was one of academic recognition within the established social order. But it was also accompanied by a shift in social capital (in this case, line management) and a loss in the control of economic capital. It is interesting to note that Bourdieu (1986) sets economic capital at the base of all other types of capital.

Over the next few years, during the late 1990s, digital technologies, the internet and the world wide web laid the foundations for changes that were to dramatically affect education, popular culture and society. Invitations to support faculty-based projects and to participate in national and European-wide initiatives increased; indeed, the discourse around ICT was no longer just the concern of specialist units.

Increased monitoring, bureaucracy and diversification

Towards the end of the 1990s, UK policy trends were set in motion which were to profoundly influence the purpose, shape, size, management and funding of HE. The main impetus for change came from the National Committee of Inquiry into Higher Education (NCIHE 1997, known as the 'Dearing Report'). The Report approved of universities working more closely with business and aligned with economic policy, but also called for HE institutions to widen participation and focus on the needs of students. Echoing Dearing, a 'landmark' speech made in 2000 by David Blunkett (2000: section 8–12), then Secretary of State for Education and Employment, asserted that universities were to be 'the powerhouses of the new global economy'. The 'Greenwich speech' provided a comprehensive view of what HE in the process of change might be like.

A managerial shift was also discernible, initially signalled by a faster pace of change and increased bureaucracy, particularly in relation to funding. This was accompanied by an expansion of peripheral units to support business imperatives similar to the models discussed by Clark (1998). At first, this was understood as a necessary response to a recognized need for better financial monitoring and the increasing pressure universities were facing to generate 'third stream' (i.e. external) income. To some extent, this constituted a paradox. On the one hand, a shifting emphasis in HE towards enterprise and innovation was in train; on the other, there were heightened levels of accountability, administration and bureaucracy (Barnett 2000; Ball 2000; discussed also in Gornall and Thomas, this volume). Hence, the nature of the work may have provided new opportunities, but the environment became increasingly competitive and business-orientated. Feelings of success were then often offset by inner conflict, uncertainty about professional identity, and questions about purpose in HE.

From 'learning and teaching' to e-learning

At the start of the year 2000, learning, teaching and assessment strategies became a significant feature of academic practice. It was a time when the central management of many institutions sought to extend its power over a dispersed workforce, introducing more complex intermediary structures (Henkel 2002). For academic members of staff working in educational development, our work became more strategically managed.

At this time, the Educational Development Unit became responsible for the 'rolling out' of the university's recently licensed virtual learning environment (VLE). Parallel to this, the unit was also responsible for developing and supporting the implementation of university learning, teaching and assessment strategies. The scale of the two projects was immense: the 'rolling out' of the university's VLE meant the provision of additional resources and new 'e-learning' posts. The introduction of the VLE was a major project for the university, and staff in the Educational Technology Centre provided the necessary additional support. Eventually, in 2002, the struggle to secure permanent posts for staff in the Centre was finally achieved; this had been a personal and professional aim for nearly a decade. However, it also meant that, once again, new job descriptions needed to be created. The new job descriptions were multi-dimensional and aimed to strengthen and balance pedagogical and technological dimensions of the work, while opening up career routes leading either towards academic posts, or to work of a more technological nature. This step-change for new professional staff, towards a more stable and improved position, is identified in Gornall's updated study of new professionals '10 years on' (Gornall 2009).

At the same time, 'widening participation', opening up HE to a more diverse student body, became a policy imperative for all UK universities. The drive to widen access was often set against a backdrop of financial constraint. Thus, while VLEs were being pursued as learning environments aimed at creating more open and flexible conditions for teaching and learning, utilization of VLEs also became linked to costings, targets and statistics about user access. Indeed, it seemed there was a danger that complex social processes could be reduced to figures and seemingly arbitrary categories of judgment (Ball 2003). This could be seen as a critical point in my thinking, at that time, as I struggled with issues that were challenging my own values about technology and educational change.

Career crossroads

When the university initiated a further restructuring, in 2005, many colleagues from the Centre for Educational Technology took the opportunity presented of moving to higher-status academic scales and into a new area that focused on innovation and e-learning. However, as is often the case, while restructuring may serve to strengthen internal social capital for some, it weakens it for others. As Schön (1967) warns in his seminal text on *Technology and Change*, the processes of reform may often erode concepts of role and function without offering something clear to replace them.

When I reflected on my own professional profile in HE, I could see that I had worked across different communities of practice and had therefore developed a multi-professional identity, a characteristic of new professionals in HE (Gornall and Thomas 2001). I thus had a wide range of cultural and social 'capital', in terms of networks, knowledge, skills, and formal accreditation. At the point of the second restructuring, I found myself at a significant career crossroads, and took the decision to pursue my interests in educational research. I had wanted to complete a doctorate for some time and was delighted to be able to take up a tenured position in a Swedish university. This offered a focus on teaching and research in a department well-known for its educational work with new technologies. Here, I spent five fascinating and valuable years, during which time I completed my doctoral thesis. I returned to the UK in 2010 to take up an educational research post and later moved into a senior post to work predominantly in the area of continued professional learning, with masters level and doctoral level students. My longstanding interest in the use of new technologies in the field of education and professional learning continues.

Theoretical underpinning and concluding remarks

In writing this narrative, the theories of Pierre Bourdieu and other key authors were drawn on to reflect on an experience of working in a changing HE as a 'new professional' over a period of 20 years. While Bourdieu's (2003) argument is that the writer should take her own position and habitus into account and be self-critical, it is nevertheless also the case that a narrative constitutes a personal testimony and therefore can be neither neutral, objective nor distanced. However, the approach that Bourdieu (1986) offers to understanding the practices and trends of professional fields, includes a helpful and productive set of concepts, such as habitus, field, position, agency and capital. 'Habitus' was seen by him as a set of deeply-founded dispositions and beliefs rooted in the daily practices of individuals and groups, which thus contribute to the accumulation of 'capital' and to the values and practices that constitute a 'field'. 'Habitus' has been a determining factor in the development of my professional identity and career advancement. It was a factor in my earliest educational experiences and in my decision to teach. It was also a factor in the professional investments that I made and the eventual outcome of the various university restructurings with which I was faced. Indeed, both Land (2004) and Hudson (2009) identify personal values as being influential in terms of 'orientation', work and career route for new professionals working in educational development and with learning technologies.

My professional route through HE, like many new professionals, took me into uncharted territory, unstructured roles and an unforeseen micro-political/

organizational environment, where practice became increasingly influenced not by fundamental values and ethics, but by technologies of control aimed at changing the characteristics of the field. As Bourdieu points out, within any field or space there are forces, struggles, risks and investments. There is competition between players and sometimes ferocious opposition. All of this indicates a belief that the 'game' is worth participating in. This personal story, considered alongside other data on new professionals working in similar settings (Hudson 2009; Gornall 2009), suggests that the values one holds and how one's social, cultural and economic capital is accrued – one's personal disposition, shaped by social and cultural characteristics and location in an intellectual field – all play a part in career pathways and routes through work, which are continually re-formed by new nexuses of power, as do the strategies adopted by other players in the game. This chapter should therefore be understood as a reflexive exploration of these, providing insights into disposition and 'one's own group', rather than as a case study *per se* of an individual, educational centre or organization.

27

Becoming 'Indigenous' as 'New Teaching and Learning Staff' – and a Reflexive Review

Lynne Gornall

A personal background and positioning

Cohen's (1986) *Symbolising Boundaries* is a collection by anthropologists 'at home', one that always repays a return visit. Within this, Phillips' (1986) notion of 'degrees of belonging' (and separation) is one I have drawn upon and cited in thinking about groups and occupational identities in the academic workplace:

> It is in the symbolic that we now look for people's sense of difference, and in symbolism . . . that we seek the boundaries of their world of identity and diversity.
>
> (Phillips 1986: 2)

This chapter represents a re-visiting too, of earlier work (in 1999), of *New professionals: change and occupational roles in higher education*, an exploration of the status and boundaries of new entrants into higher education employment in the early 1990s:

> This emergent group is employed in roles clustered around changing forms of support for teaching and learning. These staff often have non-traditional job titles, cross-role posts and non-traditional contracts and conditions of service.
>
> (Gornall 1999: 45)

The role, rise, and funding of these new posts was closely allied, it was argued, to new policy formations, and while the appointees operated in areas close to academic work, they were not on academic posts *per se*. They were not obviously 'support' staff either, and those categorizations, together with the questions raised about boundaries, the nature of spaces between groups, identity and relative positionings, were part of the issue. So too, ideas informing wider changes and micro-organizational politics suggested explanations based on 'cultural' as well as 'structural' perspectives.

Looking back: 'anthropology at home'

The field and discipline of anthropology provided the resources and the conceptualizations for the study, but also the reflexive practice (Clifford and Marcus

[1986] 2009). It includes this 'looking again' review. The new teaching and learning (T&L) groups were structurally marginal in occupational and contract terms, but also a pivotal part of the sector's vision for a new era of 'flexible' student-centred learning in HE. As one HE informant commented: '[They are] equivalent to lecturers – not the same – but equivalent . . . people who are helping the institution's learning and teaching' (Manager A, modern university, fieldnote 2001). Another said, 'Effectiveness in this role means a fair degree of confidence – and being good out in the institution, but without making waves . . .' (Manager C, traditional university, fieldnote 2001).

The 'new' staff were a collection of scattered individuals on unusual and limited contracts, part of an early movement, but barely identifiable as a group (Oliver *et al.* 2004). If one existed, they were not on the 'organizational wall chart' as Grint (1991: 146) would say, nor were they in the official statistics (Gornall 1999, 2004). It raised the question not only of boundaries, but also of visibility itself:

> The teaching and learning new professionals are inhabitants of new territory . . . They are 'threshold people' who fall on or between boundaries, a 'liminal' status, which social anthropologists argue, carries implications of both marginalization and power.
> (Gornall 1999: 48 after Leach 1976; Turner 1969; Douglas 1966)

The research question suggested was, during the expansion of HE, who and where are the extra staff, and how are these posts funded?' It was 1994, and the newly-unified HE sector (DES 1992) had only just begun to gather data, through a recently-formed state organization, the Higher Education Statistics Agency (HESA). I began collecting and tracing these statistics as they were published, year on year, while pursuing doctoral research at Cardiff. By day, I was appointing 'new professional' staff at the University of Glamorgan and working closely with academic departments, services, and 'new' professionals, in fostering educational innovation.

It was clear from the published evidence that academic staffing and HE funding of personnel had remained relatively stable over a couple of decades (Gornall 2004: 10). But this was also in a period when the graph of student intake, from 13 per cent HE participation in 1980, to 43 per cent by 2003, in what Court (2004) described as a 'century of expansion' and resembled a picture of a rocket launch. Questions about the 'new' groups could not be answered in the same way. The sector statistics covered only academics and, of these, only *full-time* posts (Gornall 1999, 2004). So, alongside a demographic mapping of academics using HESA, I undertook structured survey work on 'new professional' staff across the sector.

In my own career, it was only when as an academic moving into a teaching and learning development role and based in a university IT centre, that the strength of staff feeling about status and 'difference' in the academy impressed itself on me. Staff in 'support services' felt that their voices in the sector were largely unheard and their contribution under-recognized. They too had been affected by technology and 'human resources' changes, and the student expansion of over a decade or more. My new role gave access to these 'voices' and the experiences of 'hard to reach' groups in researching HE policy change and employment. Services and support staff saw *academics* as part of a powerful body, able to define things, having a strong voice internally, and with influential connections. Other evidence however suggested that academics at that time were feeling far from powerful: quite the reverse (Taylor 1999). They saw developments in the sector as 'an attack' on the profession (see Waring this volume), the removal of tenure, and undermining of employment contracts without consultation, a broadening of the educational agenda – student capability, course modularization, quality monitoring, flexible learning ('learning without lecturers') – were all cited (Nixon 2011; Morley 2010; Ball 2003). In fact, as Taylor (1999: 145) saw, academics' experience at that time was more akin to a sense of 'grief' from 'loss and change' than of being 'in control', where 'former strengths' had come to look like 'inflexibility'. Now 'on the other side' too, I came to understand and appreciate the work of colleagues in support roles, modes of knowledge-sharing, cooperation, professionalism and service management. Theirs was a strong ethos of creating accessible learning resources, which had to be achieved despite constant criticism, unhelpful attitudes and even boundary problems with other groups who were promoting IT literacies and learning in the institution at the time.

Research(er) and 'otherness'

In academic writing and research, there is another tricky area. That is, that in 'making visible' and becoming perhaps (people may think) an advocate for a group, this may suggest the 'my village syndrome' at work, as people in anthropology say. That is, for informants, a view that 'here at last is someone who can tell our story and make us famous' – or at least show the 'best' side of things and perhaps air some grievances (Clifford and Marcus [1986] 2005). I was mindful of this when reflecting on thought-provoking discussions at postgraduate seminars in Manchester, where distinguished authors recounted the unofficial stories of their inter-relationships in the field and 'of interpretations' later committed to print and published (Clifford and Marcus [1986] 2005; Geertz 1988), wondering 'did *they* [the informants] read these?' It was true too, for the new T&L professionals. I had made a shift, from descriptions of 'otherness' and 'para', or 'neo'-academics (Farnham 1999; Bocock 1994) in representing them as all but invisible structurally, to a 'coming out' label of *new professionalism*: 'groups defined by "what they are *not*" as opposed to what they are, constitute a kind of "other" in cultural systems . . .' (Gornall 1999: 44, quoting Leach 1976: 63).

These staff had not been written about as a group, and were struggling as incomers in the competitive HE labour market. Given the version of HE staffing where academics were '*the people*', leaving everyone else was in a binary limbo as something *not*, the problem for an analysis (as well as a lived experience) was that the new T&L people were not support staff either. Between boundaries then, but having raised the profile, would they like what had been said about them? In the case of the new professionals, I wondered whether a group wishing to join the mainstream and advance their careers in HE would value being identified as 'other' or 'marginal' – even though this was a description of *structural* positioning, and of a *role* not a *personal identity*. Being 'liminal' and 'in-between' may not be morale boosters in difficult times, compared to more upmarket descriptions, such as of 'their consultative, empowering, communicative, critical thinking [role]' (Hilsdon 2011: 5–6). On the other hand, anthropologically, inbetweenness can be a powerful positioning, not bound by the conventions of other categories; it may thus be 'appropriated' and used opportunistically.

In a connected world, what informants think of us and what we say, especially for an 'anthropology at home', makes the 'far away' study, remote monograph text or obscure journal article a thing of the past. Today, informants can re-tweet our comments and publicly question what might be regarded as homilies, pieties and partial representations – rendering the *author* (cf. informant) somewhat as 'other' too. Presenting the findings back to the constituent communities face-to-face then, here at a conference presentation, thus carried some risks. At least I could see where interest and attention were directed. In one session, a slide on payscales led to an impassioned discussion amongst the audience itself about divisions and hierarchies in HE roles. The emotional force of this was very clear, in relation to perceptions of occupational distinctions and status across the sector (Gornall 2004: 108).

Telling stories: new professionals as 'not' and hybrid

To describe the 'positioning' of new T&L professionals is therefore to signify, via a written text, an intentional effect. In other words, to make visible the roles, values, meanings and perspectives of the 'others', and in this specific research, to locate and problematize new types of work. Telling the story of the 'stories' of new professionals – of how boundaries and structures provide both affordance and constraints in conducting their tasks – is also to engage in a 'narrativizing' process (Rees and Monrouxe 2011). This is in a different 'voice' from first-order informant data (Gough, this volume) but we need to be vigilant about its boundaries too. So what are 'new professionals', and where are some of the boundaries with groups they are 'not'? This is important in delineating their culture and community (see Strathern 1981; also Sebalj *et al.*, for 'Elmdon', an English village), and to distinguish them from other, near-relative, communities.

Broadly speaking, the new professionals in T&L differed from academics on the one hand and other support professionals on the other, because in general they did *not*:

- teach students (or staff) (though they sometimes ran workshops or short courses);
- assess students (despite possible involvement with exam or essay tools);
- engage directly with the institution's student population (their links were with learning rather than learners);
- offer services or comprehensive support (more involved in localized projects with potential for scale);
- undertake autonomous academic research (cf. evaluations and reporting on findings, or action research related to role).

(Gornall 2004: 120)

To state this is rather hurtful to the new professionals, as they are trying to become 'indigenous' and part of the 'mainstream' (Gornall and Thomas 2001). They value and generally aspire to academic and scholarly work, including to the roles and status of these. However, here are also precisely the lines – boundaries – they would have to cross in order to fulfil such aspirations (Gornall 1999, 2004). But they are not 'technologists' either. The caveats above are important: T&L new staff *may* be undertaking research and do publish, they *do* engage with students, offer advice and services, but this may not be the specific remit or contract of the post. There are also many examples of what Beetham *et al.* (2001: 1.3) call 'established professionals' moving across into 'new professional' roles, and these often *do* bring aspects of role with them. Thus, former academics feel empowered to identify research areas – my own case is in this category – and former support professionals know how to set up and manage a service. The situation is fluid, and many of the issues are in change (Hudson 2009).

'Core' new specialist staff were still also relatively small in number (less than 2,000 staff, according to Beetham *et al.* 2001: S1.3.4), compared with say academics (at that time, some 116,450 staff (HESA 2002)), but hardly insignificant. Part of a movement in both pedagogy and employment (Gornall and Thomas 2001), they were part of a 'paradigm shift' that was also 'a catching fire' in the sector (Land 2004: 10).

But paradigm shifting is hard work, and the new T&L professionals have looked for sources of advocacy and support (Shurville *et al.* 2009; Oliver *et al.* 2004; Oliver 2002). While 'otherness' might not help directly, I sensed they did not have a problem with the description of 'hybridity', '"new professionals" as agents of T&L change are thus potentially valuable assets ... [will HEIs] reap the benefits of change management and investment in the T&L "new hybrid" staff? ... [For] where else but in people is the competitive advantage?' (in Donkin 1995, quoting Pffeffer, see Gornall 1999: 48). So what does the differential employment, occupational and organizational positioning of the new T&L professionals tell us about how they see the sector and working life?

Stories of liminality and power

Although at the centre of things – including changes – on the ground, the new professionals in teaching and learning did not feel so secure or valued (Hudson 2009). Their status as transitional was one of 'becoming'. But things could be worse. They could have been academics: 'disciplined', 'remodelled' 'flexibilized', 'demeaned' (Ball 2008a: 3; Nixon 2011: 9), or perceived as conventional support staff: 'they tidied the books and cleaned the mice ... looked after the hardware ... things like [that]' (Manager D, 2001).

If notions of 'otherness' can be difficult for those to whom we as authors apply them, then ambivalence about relationships of *power* may be even more complex. Having described the new roles as between important boundaries, included in neither group of the two main 'divides' in the sector (academic/support), there was another part of the analysis to include. This was about the opportunities that being 'between' could offer. But this analysis was also to locate structural ambiguity as part of an occupational change (restructuring) that had an agenda. Following Johnson's (1972) early examination of relationships of sponsorship and patronage, it was clear to me that the threshold cross-border work of the 'new professionals' in T&L was underwritten by powerful policy interests:

['marginality'] can be a *powerful* position ... associated with change desired by executive groups, who may circumvent normal reporting lines, and afford postholders elements of discretion and range of work, which traditional roles may lack.

(Gornall 1999: 47)

The new learning paradigms discussed by Land (2004) and others, and the new forms of employment that were shaped and resourced through agencies and bodies of a reforming 'meso' state (Clarke *et al.* 2000:10; Sharpe 1993), were policies 'designed to displace traditional employment groups at the core of the organization' (Gornall 1999: 8, quoting Hendry 1995: 18). And while new T&L *professionalism* might instantiate values such as 'self-help', a belief in the positive role of technologies and a sense of 'working at the frontier' of innovation, these are also features related to forms of individualism expounded in detail by Macpherson (1962). 'Neoliberal' values and norms (see Quinn 2010; Elliott and Urry 2010) had defined the era (Ball 2008a; Gornall and Thomas this volume). The new professionals largely do not share these underpinning ideologies, ones that promoted their role, (Hudson 2009), and indeed their culture is a strongly *collaborative* one, with a commitment to developing knowledge-rich pedagogies and 'inclusive' learner development. As Hilsdon (2011: 4) says, they are generally opposed to 'a student skills "deficit" approach in education', arguing rather that it is the '*environment* of learning that provides the key'.

A decade on, in a new survey (Gornall 2009) the T&L professionals continued to 'enjoy their work in HE' and to appreciate its flexibility and scope. They were 'proud' of their occupation and being part of a growing professional group that was gaining increasing internal and external recognition, and felt valued for this contribution (Gornall 2009). We can see this as a positioning of new professionalism within a discourse of 'modernity', 'progress', 'adaptability'. Informed by Castells (1997), we might say that their 'landscape' is a relational one, that downplays the role of 'technology' or received structures. They 'bring into HE ... management and contextual skills ... working with people to implement change – influence – quite difficult to do' (Manager B, fieldwork note, 2001).

'True folk': narrating the T&L professional stories of HE

Academics in the sector no doubt have what Phillips (1986: 124) would call a 'long association', but what would the 'stories' and narration of 'HE change' by new professional staff be like – and can we (after Geertz 1988) adequately tell their story?

The ethos of the new professional T&L staff, I argue, is positive, aspirational, with a sense of moving outwards across the institution and sector, and upwards too, with their high ranking links (Gornall 2004). New T&L staff want to 'set the learner' free. They see learners as constrained by technological barriers, spatial environments, limitations of timetables, lectures – lecturers too. They want to see students with flexible access to resources, high degrees of autonomy and scope to pursue learning, lifelong and life-wide (Barnett 2010). Learners 'are also our peers', 'co-producers' too, in what Oliver (2002: 250) calls a 'collaborative curriculum', involving 'reciprocal learning' and within a whole variety of formal and informal settings (Ecclesfield and Garnett this volume). The environments and contexts of these may be multiple and mixed, the communities often online, networked.

> ' "New specialists' were perceived by all the groups involved in the study as the 'true' learning technologists: multi-skilled and peripatetic but with learning technology work at the core of their professional identity . . .' (Beetham *et al.* 2001: section 1.3).

New professionals are not just part of a new culture however but have also *brought a new culture* into HE. This is their wider contribution, and an organizational opportunity. The 'stories' the new T&L professionals tell are of egalitarianism, in what is perceived as a 'hierarchical' sector. They bring a 'networked' culture (Elliott and Urry 2010:46) of *lateral links* (Gornall 2004) supporting 'access' to HE and its goods, which they see as intrinsically beneficial, and for all kinds of learners. It is thus an inclusive vision, emphasizing the importance of underpinning structures and support (Hilsdon 2011: 4). Communication and interpersonal ways of working are key assets of new and 'postmodern' groups (Beetham *et al.* 2001). But career, and status, the *contracts* of 'belonging' are important too (cf. Cook and Daunton this volume). As Goodson (2003: 5) points out, there is always a danger that 'the world of "stories", "narratives" and "lives" [may] lead us away from context and theorizing, away from the conceptualizing of power'.

Concluding remarks

The 'new professionals' represent, and in themselves signify for others, I argue, a (valued) notion of 'modernity' in HE. This is by contrast with both academics and 'support' staff or other established groups. In their mix of 'soft skills' of discourse, educational empathy, persuasive style and willingness to engage, network and interact, alongside the 'magical' expertise around software, technologies and 'new media', they have strong 'capital', (Hudson, this volume), and offer 'extended value' to the organization. They are also recognized by institutions and managers as practical and knowledgeable, able to apply and problem-solve without technological fixes or withholding knowledge from others. Their lack of a sense of any 'entitlement' over resources and territories or 'power bases and empires', as one manager remarked, is important too, as something that other support groups were suspected of. Referring to this, one HE manager praised new professionals in particular as having a 'lack of baggage' in the job (Gornall 2004).

The 'new hybridity' described by Elliott and Urry (2010: x) thus locates something dynamic, occupationally and symbolically. But 'mobile life' can be mixed, with 'novelty and peril, possibility, experimentation and risk, never far away':

> [new specialists in learning and teaching] are torn between the academic culture of research and publication, the professional culture of service provision, a commitment to student learning, and the "political" culture of promoting organizational change (reporting interviewees, Beetham *et al.* 2001: 10.3.3).

For the new professionals in T&L, a hybrid and cross-border, inclusive, modality which 'othered' them in the institutional landscape also conferred distinct advantages. It gave a multi-dimensional perspective, an extensive as well as a broad and inclusive reckoning. 'New professionals' may be becoming closer to integration and 'indigenous' status (Gornall 2009), but they remain 'different' too, and in 'difference' they retain an important identity (Kristeva 1991). This makes the narratives and data of 'new professional' perspectives of wider value, not just for institutional stakeholders, but from the 'academic' standpoint too. Perhaps through scholarship and autonomous research and in (new) collaborative exchanges of 'capital', each group can help to tell the *new* (as well as the 'old') stories of HE change. As one informant in a T&L new professional role remarked: 'I think everyone's got a bit of teacher in them' (interviewee, Beetham *et al.* 2001: 8.2.9).

Acknowledgements

Thanks to 'new professionals' in teaching and learning who took part in the studies, colleagues in IT services at the University of Glamorgan, Dr Debbie Meakin and the Hull College FE/HE research group. A number of people have supported or encouraged this area of study: Alison Hudson, Helen Beetham, Steve Jones, Paul Bailey, Martin Oliver, Graine Conole and Carolyn Siccama. Roger Cannon, Stephen K. Jones, Jarmila Davies, Sheila Lehman, Brian Davies, Marilyn Strathern and Ron Cobley. Based on a paper to Centre for Sociology, Anthropology and Politics (C-SAP) conference, Birmingham and with thanks to Dr Jeff Fairweather. Acknowledgments to participants at ALT Manchester, IPED Coventry and CETL Oxford for feedback and discussions about 'new professionalism' in HE (2009–2011), and to David Lewis (research support).

Part Five

Research and Professional Learning

Introduction

Caryn Cook

This volume overall has brought together experienced as well as newer researchers and writers, with perspectives on work in higher and further education (HE/FE) from 'within' the academic role as well as from 'without'. To be engaged in research is also to be involved in the processes of professional learning, and this **Part 5** seeks to explore some such processes in ongoing studies. First is the work of **Laugharne, Carter** and **Jones**, and their research into the experiences of staff participating in a professional doctorate programme within a 'teaching intensive' post-92 institution. *Using appreciative inquiry, the authors ask about the role of learning at work.* This is the first phase of ongoing and evaluative research and seeks to inform the staff doctoral programme development itself.

Next, the very nature of the research that perhaps began the journey towards this collective work, referred to in various chapters throughout the book, is discussed by **Cook** and **Gornall**. They describe using *'reflexivity'* as a research methodology for examining 'teamworking' processes within the Working Lives group, and discuss some of the conditions underlying the formation of *collaborative groups, and their learning*. Their notion of a new *'inter-collegiality'* in relationships may suggest perhaps some lessons, given the current 'trend' of encouraging and even demanding collaborative practices.

Continuing this investigation of the changes and innovations happening within HE, **Mears** and **Harrison** explore the changing roles and responsibilities of academic working lives in what they describe as the *'growing complexity of the division of labour'*. Some of the tensions and ambiguities around the purposes of the modern university are considered, and how this is reflected in the type and nature of advertised posts in the sector. They focus specifically on *'third space' jobs*, in a bid to assess the extent of some of the changes, and also to suggest further research questions in relation to possible future work.

Gough provides a *'curated' review of work*, that reflects the range of interests and topics for ongoing and future inquiry in the sector. Following from the previous chapter, and consonant with the theme of this section – learning, research and professional development – *the chapter gives 'voice' to some of the research that is not* *yet completed, written up or indeed in progress.* In seeking to give a representative view of some themes of inquiry around education, Gough ranges into FE as well as posts and roles outside of 'academic' jobs, the question of what it is to leave the academy (and 'find yourself') and much more. This is an innovative chapter model – a form of 'living literature review' – in which the contributors actively co-operated in the account. It is an approach that underpins a principal ethos of this book – 'inclusion' – incorporating openness to multidiscipliniarity and plurality.

Following the work of the authors in Part 5, **Barnett** provides a thought-provoking set of ideas in his concluding chapter of the book. In *observations and discussion on 'academia as workplace'*, some reflective resources not just 'for the journey' but also for the future are explored, to assist those whose habitation in the sector and profession continues.

28

Promoting Change in Higher Education and the Professional Doctorate

Janet Laugharne, Mary Carter and Eleri Jones

Introduction

UK post-92 universities have undergone exceptional change over the last 25 years, in response to policy directives imposed by successive governments (Barnett 2011a). Coping with increased student numbers on a lower unit of resource, universities have had to demonstrate enhanced accountability (McCaffery 2004) and deliver both research and 'enterprise' activities with 'real-world' impact. A more outward-looking higher education (HE) sector has emerged, with greater emphasis on the role of leadership and management roles (Deem and Johnson 2003). Indeed, all HE institutions (HEIs) now operate in a more competitive environment, so adaptability is essential.

Staff in HE work within a culture of a broad commitment to notions of 'collegiality', varied lines of accountability with few intrinsic rewards, well-developed subject sub-cultures, and a tradition of rotating management and leadership responsibilities (Pennington 2003). The implications for those engaging in 'change' projects are that the ability to 'influence' is arguably as important as the authority to 'control'. For middle managers, there are particular challenges: securing agreement can be problematic and resistance to change may be exacerbated by trends for new initiatives to be 'top down'. As Berlach (2011: 1) observed, 'a change stimulus in education usually comes in the form of an edict from a superordinate (leader), through the conduit of a subordinate (manager) [and] on to a field worker (implementer)'. Frequently, individual and collective responses to such initiatives are: 'Why?'

Another challenge for senior academic staff in post-92 universities is that many were recruited when vocational experience was considered more important than research experience. In the league table environment of UK HE today, universities have worked to build research capacity and outputs for successive 'assessment' exercises. This has resulted in a shift in staff recruitment towards doctoral qualifications, leaving those without such qualifications feeling vulnerable, as Young (2010: 54) remarked: 'During my employment in HE, I have been required to be a generalist, turning my hand to whatever needed covering, thus, recent emphases on research and specialization, coupled with job insecurity and redundancies [have] left me feeling vulnerable'.

This chapter focuses on the experiences of staff participating in a professional doctorate (ProfDoc) programme in a post-92 teaching-intensive university. The programme has seven named pathways: business administration, education, information systems, tourism, health, sport and ecological building practices. The ProfDoc model focuses on *change agency* to develop 'new applied knowledge appropriate to the workplace'. This is undertaken mainly through 'action research' in investigating and implementing 'change' projects which aim to contribute products/ processes at the cutting edge of professional practice. The doctorate's overall aims were to:

> provide evidence of high level subject expertise and relevant professional knowledge and experience . . . at the forefront of the discipline/profession and . . . likely to enable graduates to make a significant contribution to their chosen field . . . as professional educators, applied researchers/developers or leaders in public/private-sector organisations.
>
> University of Wales Institute, Cardiff 2010: 3

The approach adopted in our study of the ProfDoc programme was that of 'appreciative inquiry' (AI).

Appreciative inquiry

A collaborative approach like AI is one way of addressing rapid, unsettling organizational change, since AI emphasizes integration of personal relationships and tasks to promote team-building and focus on what has worked well previously. There has been a shift in evaluation studies from merely observing events, to a more 'transformational social science', facilitating change (Reason and Torbert 2001 cited in Reed 2007: 65). Increasingly, this type of research is undertaken by individuals in organizations, often as part of accredited professional development schemes. Bartunek *et al.*'s (2000) work identified common themes in what may be termed 'manager-led action research projects' typically catalysed by the manager's superiors and forming part of their job description, with other participants as sub-ordinates and needing to 'buy in' to the project. Data-gathering can be formal and informal and the manager has a personal stake in the project outcome. Many will recognize these features of the new HE organizational landscape.

AI is based on David Cooperrider's (1986) PhD research on organizational development. Cooperrider interviewed doctors on what they really valued about their work and found that highlighting 'positive' aspects encouraged respondents to talk freely. Analysis of the conversations showed how informants believed working practices could be improved (Cooperrider *et al.* 2008). This approach differed from previous research with health care professionals, that tended to be

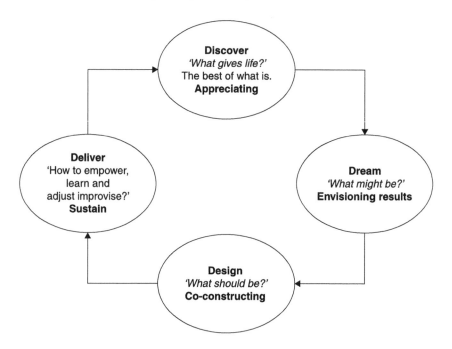

Figure 28.1   The AI cycle
Source: adapted from Cooperrider *et al.* (2008: 5).
Reprinted with permission of the publisher, Crown Custom Publishing, Inc.

problem-oriented and focused on the stresses and strains professionals experienced (Reed 2007).

AI has been used successfully in varied settings, including HE (Chapman and Bowen-Jones 2008; Chapman 2011; May and Bridger 2010). The University of Worcester, for example, in partnership with the Institute of Sport and Exercise Science (ISES) used AI to improve the learning experiences of disabled students. It modelled Cooperrider *et al.*'s (2008) four principal AI stages (discover, dream, design and deliver) – see Figure 28.1. Concluding, the researchers commented:

> [AI] succeeded in its aim of encouraging ISES staff to review and further improve their inclusive academic practice . . . the project had indeed supported the University to move closer towards its vision of 'being a high quality University with an international reputation for excellent, inclusive education'.
>
> Chapman 2011: para. 18

It was hoped that applying AI in this study would help develop organizational good practice, enabling staff to collaborate in 'co-creating' the future (Reijerse and van Domburg 2010).

The study

This study focuses on the experiences of HE staff engaged in change agency within their professional lives and participating in the ProfDoc programme. Although not designed specifically as a vehicle for staff development, the ProfDoc has proved attractive with 14 staff enrolled (four having recently completed) since its inception in 2006. We aimed in the study to explore the experiences of staff on the ProfDoc and ways to improve the programme itself. AI was used to identify positive features of the process (Cooperrider 1986), and this is the first phase of an ongoing, evaluative project informing ProfDoc programme development which sought to identify broader issues of change agency, as perceived by staff engaged in the ProfDoc process.

Methodology

A single post-92 university operating the ProfDoc scheme across four campuses was used. A questionnaire based on the 'discover' phase of the AI cycle was developed, to explore the views of academic staff in two key areas: first, the ProfDoc in the context of their own learning; second, participants' understanding of change in the university and the impact of their change project on university practice. Six questions focused on staff experiences of the ProfDoc and four sought to elicit perceptions of the change project each was undertaking, together with their experiences of the change process itself in the institution. The questions were sequenced following an in-depth, reflexive 'piloting' interview with one of the authors of this chapter (Carter), herself undertaking an EdD. The questions were uploaded into an electronic survey tool and an invitation to participate with project information was issued to staff on the programme, via email. Of the 14 members of staff (13 academic and one administrative) studying for the ProfDoc (or having recently completed it), 8 completed the questionnaire: 5 on the education pathway, and 1 from each on the sport, health and management pathways. One further interview was conducted with a member of staff who had recently completed an EdD externally. Thus, survey data from eight staff and two interviews provide the empirical data upon which our analysis is based. All respondents were given pseudonyms and, as far as possible, are not identifiable by their discipline. Although this is a self-selected group and relatively small in number, it represents three-quarters of those studying for the ProfDoc at the time of writing. These views are of value in considering 'change agency' in HE during an exceptionally volatile period.

Outcomes

The participants' responses are presented in two sections. The first relates to staff experiences of the ProfDoc. The second discusses the link between the change project and the institution. The study was undertaken between 2005 and 2011, at a time of great change, which some staff found quite overwhelming:

> ... the changes are so radical and widespread that it's very unsettling and difficult for people; they don't know where they are; in a 'sort of limbo'; it's been going on over a

very long time as I realized through my research . . . people are waiting for something to happen; there are financial restraints, course closures and job losses; we are all trying to work through the cycles.

Margaret

Staff experiences of the ProfDoc programme

Staff valued the ProfDoc's opportunity to focus on research as part of their role in HE: '[it helped] broaden my work experience and gain some space to do some research around my teaching' (Mark). Staff liked the way the change project related to their day-to-day working lives, and especially their teaching and professional roles: 'To gain sound grounding in research methods [was valuable] in order to be better at teaching research methods on undergraduate degrees' (Hannah). It was notable that only two replies actually mentioned career development as an explicit motivation for undertaking the ProfDoc.

Asked about what they had brought from their working lives to the ProfDoc programme and what they found most enjoyable, there was much positive comment. Six referred to their professional experience in the field, four commented on their teaching experience or their scholarly activity, while three commented on their reflective practice. One respondent (Margaret) reported that doing the ProfDoc had actually helped her define her new role in the university.

Other responses highlighted, in particular, the enjoyment and interest in working as part of an 'academic community' of researchers. There was a sense of personal and professional satisfaction in achieving the various milestones and gaining new subject knowledge:

[I liked] being involved with other members of staff who are also researching their practice. (Keeping each other motivated) [and] getting to know members of staff from other schools.

Gina

[There was] a feeling of academic and professional validation. [I gained] an improved understanding of research methods and this has had a significant impact on my work. I feel that my colleagues (and hopefully my managers) respect me more for having undertaken studies at this level.

Jane

When asked what staff had learned about themselves during their doctoral study, informants identified motivation, determination and organization as key qualities. Doctoral study alongside routine duties revealed different qualities:

. . . I have a very strong capacity for managing a very heavy workload and that my powers of concentration and levels of motivation are very high. I can work on my own initiative and take responsibility for very complex tasks. I can be relied upon to complete very demanding tasks in trying professional circumstances.

Jane

The difficulties of undertaking the project were also evident:

[I] underestimated the time I would be able to spend on it. [I] overestimated [my] confidence level. Committing the appropriate time is stressful [there is] never a good time.

Brian

I work to facilitate/support others – downside being that my research tends to be pushed down the line.

Gina

Here the issue of time and of being enabled to prioritize the doctoral study were clear barriers to progress. An indication of the areas undertaken for the doctoral projects is given in Table 28.1.

When asked if staff anticipated their working lives would change following the programme, there was a noticeable difference in tone. Here the responses were uncertain, tentative or negative, with the equivocal word 'hopefully' used by several respondents. As one explained: 'that seems to be the next mountain after I have scrambled up this one!' A perceived lack of opportunity post-doctorate was echoed by the staff member who had studied externally at a pre-92 institution. She wanted to continue her research but reported: 'There is nowhere for me to go with it' (Jean). This is an area of concern for the university and reveals a perceived strong dislocation between the career aspirations of its academic staff and its mission to develop research alongside teaching and innovation.

When asked if they thought their own change project would make a contribution to knowledge, individuals were both hopeful and specific, as can be seen in the responses presented in Table 28.1.

It is perhaps not surprising that many responses were outcome-orientated and related mainly to professional practice. This reflects the overall aims of the ProfDoc identified earlier in this chapter. Only two replies specifically referred to 'pure' or 'traditional' research – Jane, who had recently completed her doctorate, and Jean, who had undertaken her ProfDoc elsewhere. The issue here is the tension between focusing on 'contribution to professional knowledge', demonstrated strongly by the respondents as members of staff, and other types of 'contribution'. A better balance between the 'internal contribution' and participation in the wider research community needs to be struck between academics, the ProfDoc programme, institutional development and personal aspirations. This point is revisited in later sections of this chapter. However, with respect to the ProfDoc, the examples in Table 28.1 pinpoint a contribution to applied knowledge at the cutting edge of professional practice and these staff can rightly be seen as 'change agents'.

Table 28.1 Anticipated contributions of the ProfDoc change projects to knowledge

Respondent	Anticipated contribution
Brian	Action research which involves members of the department. Sharing findings with colleagues.
Mark	Support for a new group of students.
Sarah	Bringing new applied knowledge into my subject area.
Gina	Closer integration between research and enterprise activities undertaken by academic staff in university.
Hannah	Delivering on the objectives of the university and the professional body.
Jane	Impact on the wider world of research, influencing other researchers, increasing knowledge in the area.
Patrick	Contributing to pedagogic practice in HE, particularly the role of the teaching team.
Margaret	Raising awareness of the role of heads of department in HE including training and creating a forum across the university.
Harry	Adding to definitions of key terms in the professional community through undertaking the research project. Developing an interdisciplinary product for end users.
Jean	Publications in research and professional journals. Participation in special interest research groups.

The link between the change project and the institution

The remaining questions in the study explored the link between the change project and the institution. Staff were asked if they believed their project would positively impact the institution. Most responses (N = 8/10) agreed with this statement. Several staff were at the beginning of their ProfDocs, so their answers were in the tone of 'not yet': 'I believe it will have, when it is finished' (Gina); 'I feel it will in the future' (Harry). Some were positive in a more qualified way: 'Yes, in a peripheral way – heads of department are now receiving training' (Margaret); 'Yes, although much of what I did is becoming less relevant as so many other events are overtaking it' (Patrick).

In relation to how the institution had improved since individuals had begun their studies, the responses were fairly positive, particularly with regard to capacity-building and attitude to research: 'There is certainly encouragement from my department to research' (Mark). Here academic staff noted the positive effects of undertaking their ProfDoc on their individual profiles; for example, with funding for conference attendance and learning new research skills. Staff commented often on the time needed to undertake the change project and the challenge of integrating it into their overall workload:

> They [senior management, SM] should give staff dedicated time to undertake such projects – there has been none for me.
>
> Sarah

> Although grateful that they [SM] are paying my fees I would welcome a sabbatical or teaching relief to get on with the research.
>
> Mark

These comments illustrate the issue of limited resources and time for research development in a post-92, teaching-intensive university. Juggling competing demands was also raised by the staff member who had undertaken the doctorate externally to the institution:

> ... students among the post-92 universities have similar challenges of not enough space to do the doctorate; it's the issue of capacity-building, of novice researchers and limited resource; an institution 'finding its identity' and the balance between teaching and research.
>
> Jean

Discussion

Cooperrider's AI research was influenced by an earlier study (Gergen 1982) which suggested that existing research traditions failed to acknowledge interactions between research and practice. This argued that insufficient attention was being paid to developing ideas, as people got together to 'co-construct' interpretations which could significantly influence how they acted:

> ... as different people interpret the world, there are different stories of what is happening, existing alongside each other, and attempts to establish the 'truth' by checking the factual accuracy of accounts ignore these possibilities of interpretation
>
> (Reed 2007: 26).

Gergen's work complemented AI and provided a theoretical foundation for Cooperrider's ideas which evolved into 'a philosophy and orientation to change that can fundamentally reshape the practice of organizational learning, design and development' (Watkins and Mohr 2001: 21).

Coughlan (2001: 49), writing about 'insider' action research projects and the challenges facing manager-researchers, describes how they 'need to combine their action research role with their regular organizational roles and this role duality can create the potential for role ambiguity and conflict'. This particular challenge is echoed in the current study, though it was not necessarily seen as problematic: 'The ability to overlap many of my professional duties with what I needed to do in order to develop my study and gather data . . . helped enormously' (Jane).

Criticisms of interpretivism (e.g. Saunders *et al.* 2007) emphasize its focus on individuals, which makes making generalizability problematic. However, as Saunders *et al.* (2007: 107) point out, 'the interpretivist could argue that generalizability is not of crucial importance' as organizations are ever-changing and cannot actually be 'captured' in time. If they can, things have changed again soon enough. So what is deemed important is the 'present state', where individual experience is valuable precisely for the insights it provides.

Concluding remarks

Generally, the close, positive link between the change project and professional practice came through clearly in responses. Despite a diversity of individual responses (as expected), some common themes emerged. In particular, considerable pride in achieving a doctorate (to an extent against the odds) and a relish in the fresh challenges associated with the individual change projects.

> Induction was fantastic, a brilliant opportunity to think for the first time since I've been at the university. I'm really pleased with my Director of Studies and find it very beneficial to speak with her about how to embark on the research.
>
> Hannah

> The course has made me review and to an extent it has reinforced my personal values/ philosophy, which I see as a positive thing.
>
> Harry

The experience of the staff member who had studied externally highlighted, by contrast, some positives about the university's ProfDoc. For example, this participant alone referred to the Wales' policy dimension, and gave a different interpretation of 'contribution to knowledge' from the staff who had studied internally, and were less orientated towards 'research' than 'professional practice'. But she also referred to the lack of integration of her ProfDoc into the 'day job' which had exacerbated competing demands on time and focus, unlike the university's ProfDoc model. The latter 'generated what I would consider day-to-day data that is relevant to the research itself' (Jean).

The AI approach adopted for this small-scale study was deliberately positive and may, of course, have promoted rather more positive responses. However, the overall tone of responses to some questions remained negative, despite their upbeat tenor. The negative areas warrant further investigation, and future research will explore how the effectiveness of change projects is limited by issues of workload, time management and staff's lack of confidence about how they will progress their careers after the programme. One of the expected outcomes of AI, however, as conceptualized by

Cooperrider *et al.* (2008), is the creation of 'provocative propositions' or ideal goals, based on key themes for change.

Six such provocative propositions have emerged so far from this modest AI study, as follows:

- staff engage in ongoing dialogue about their research during the course of their study and form interdisciplinary communities of practice;
- staff 'change projects' flow from and inform institutional planning;
- change projects help build research capacity and integrate research and teaching;
- institutions foster change champions through effective staff development;
- research and innovation, linked to teaching, is a strong feature of staff change projects and is demonstrated by contribution to knowledge through high-quality research outputs;
- staff, as change agents, deliver innovative outcomes in products and services that enhance the value and reputation of the university.

It is intended that the next phase of the AI study will feed back the six provocative propositions into the ProfDoc committee, so that it can work to strengthen the synergy between professional practice and research. It will explore in its 'dream' and 'design' phases (Cooperrider *et al.* 2008) how the programme can develop and empower individual staff, enabling them to deliver effective change projects for the institution and leading to the 'delivery' phase of the AI cycle.

The question of addressing the balance between teaching and research in HE lies at the heart of this process, as the views reported here of staff on this ProfDoc programme demonstrate.

29

A New Collegiality in Collaborative Work and Practice

Caryn Cook and Lynne Gornall

Working together

The Working Lives (WL) team comprised a cross-HEI (higher education institution) group of five people who were invited to come together for a new piece of research, initially in Wales. The work was successful in many of the criteria laid down by the Welsh Education Research Network (WERN) and the Economic Social Research Council (ESRC). This included in partner-making, research capacity-building, data collection, general productivity and dissemination. It was less successful in immediate 'published' outputs, however; reflecting on this, the present chapter seeks to explore some of the practical as well as theoretical issues underpinning what were regarded as 'achievements', or otherwise, in partnership working in the WL academic research. As Goodson (2003: 25) asserts, 'Stories should not only be narrated but also located . . . moving beyond the self-referential individual narration to a wider contextualised, collaborative mode'.

In sickness and in health

Our story is of how a group of people from different backgrounds and institutions with differentiated 'value systems' and norms learned to work together. We moved from being a collection of individuals with very different interests, to a group of researchers, and then a productive, if diverse, scholarly team whose liveliness as an interdisciplinary collective was recognized in a case study (Scott 2009). But 'partnership' and 'collaboration' are also major overheads on projects, in effort and time, as well as being *opportunities* for intellectual capital and added value. We kept a record of our academic/HE working lives during the period, which we draw on reflexively here:

> 'A short secondment has turned my life upside down . . . What am I doing this for?';
> 'Lonely in a new environment, two lots of email [to read] . . .'
> 'I'm feeling under attack from all sides' (WL reflexive discussions, 2009).

The team also became a support group. All of the team experienced illness, accidents, caring roles, grief, loss and emotional traumas. These included a broken foot, pneumonia, a series of falls, sudden deaths (a husband, a niece, four parents) which had to be coped with alongside everyday workloads – the dilemmas as well as the highlights of working life familiar to everyone:

> I am off sick at the moment but I am still answering my emails – I never stop because I fear I will miss something and drop the ball (2009).

The ways of working that evolved in the WL group apply to many if not most professionals. We felt that they were worth recording here, however, in reflecting on and putting into a wider connected narrative a discourse about team and collaborative working. That this publication arises some five years after research and data analysis, and six years after initial funding, is we suggest the effect of typical working and eventful lives across five careers and three HE institutions. We contend that this is *normal* and record it in order to *support the longer timescales that collegial bids and proposals for collaborative work may need, and to inform policy-makers.*

Teams, partnership and collaboration

Much contemporary research today is undertaken by teams, including multi-disciplinary groupings (Woods *et al.* 2000; Presser 1980). This is exemplified by several of the contributions to this volume (Nakabugo *et al*; Ylijoki *et al*; Laugharne *et al.*). While large research teams have been common in the sciences (Richards this volume), cross-institutional and sector-funded partnerships have made teamwork more common in education and social/human sciences in recent years too (Musselin 2012; Delanty 2008; Mauthner and Doucet 2008, 2003). This trend for larger research team formation, and the factors around emergent forms of working that collaboration can produce, has received relatively little attention from academics to date (but see Yanez and Altopiedi 2012; Fanghanel 2012; Gundry and Slater 2005; Tett *et al.* 2003; Fox and Faver 1984).

A new collegiality

Writers from Becher (1989), Trowler (1998), Henkel (2000) and Fanghanel (2012) onwards have focused on 'academic identity' as allegiance to disciplines, subject group and affiliation networks. We argue that it was the nature of the group and group working in the WL case that conferred a cultural identity. As one WL team observer (in 2012) pointed out,

> It would have been easy to let the work [project] go . . . you had to constantly work to keep it going, keep it together, problematizing the "binding" that kept things going.

Wider studies suggest that lecturers in HE and FE feel that the 'collegial' ethos of their sector has been significantly eroded or even fatally damaged by the changes of the last two or three decades (Clegg 2008; Winter 1995; Burke 1988). The WL team argued that research revealing some of the more fine-textured aspects of contemporary occupational life was needed, studies that asked academics, in addition, what they *enjoy* about their work (see Fincher 2012; Walker 2001; Usher 2000) and how they relate to others. We wanted to provide a way of representing and denoting newer forms of academic working, that are cross-organizational and instantiated by collaborations such as our own. For this, we propose the term *inter-collegiality*. In other contexts, this may simply be thought of as a mode of professional working. However, in the *efforts* involved in group working in our environment – especially across the 'boundaries' of discipline and institution – the processes of communication, of surmounting barriers and achieving mutual goals are so significant that we feel they are worth a term and consideration of their own.

Inter-professional work and multi-professional learning

As a team and a network of people in different spaces and places, WL members had to actively create and establish the group ethos and culture while working in separate institutional contexts. It is worth recording that we were located variously in a research-intensive 'Russell Group' university, a 'modern' former polytechnic HEI, and a college of the Federal University of Wales, a former college of HE. We were also in five different departments of these HEIs, in different roles, all experiencing change, and with 'extended' professional landscapes (Hoyle and John 1995) at work.

Our starting points in research varied too. We were embarking without further preparation on a demanding new project in which there were high expectations. Because we had 'won' funding and were successful in being re-awarded a further competitive funding allocation, the stakes were raised:

> [It was] a rapid learning curve and led to me deciding to embark on a doctorate (so even more to do!). Before the project, I had not presented at a conference ... and felt like the 'junior member' of the group to start with ... (also the youngest) [but] I was also meeting and being introduced to stimulating people who were interested in our work.
>
> (2008)

We found that the more people there were to be involved, the longer the decision-to-outcome processes were, and because of time pressures, the less likely we were able to act collaboratively or work in an inclusive and capacity-building way and reach targets. Good and frequent communication and the stimulation of interpersonal contact was important, but did not just happen on its own: inter-collegiality had to be actively created through discourse, interaction and focus, which in turn helped to sustain relationships. But this too is a *workload* (Gornall and Salisbury 2012). There were small but significant constraints too:

> [on writing] It would probably take other people four or five minutes. I've got to write it, then I've got to ... do something else, then revisit it. Sure enough, when I re-read it, I've missed a word ...
>
> (2009)

I don't type you see. So I think I've pressed [the keyboard] and it's actually the letter next door. And I think, well can she understand that, it should be *calm*, but it looks like calmber.

(2009)

Alongside unfamiliar paradigms and differential research experience, there were also unequal status and career positionings. But 'difference' was also an heuristic, a source of ideas and varied perspectives – and 'movement' when work hit a block – so individual backgrounds and capabilities came into focus at different stages and times of the project. Theoretical orientations across the team also had a wide span; they included art, education, business, science, anthropology, media, organizational and leadership studies, enterprise, psychology and the management. Members contributed skills in management, project working, publishing, editing, chairing, problem-solving, literature searching – talents not obvious at the outset. But this was also a source of complexity: determining directions and the framing of research design in short timescales was far from easy. We began to adopt approaches that 'research aware' members had used successfully before, for example, but this meant less 'airtime' for other possibilities and perspectives. And whilst our collective expertise and diverse backgrounds offered intellectual 'capital' and resources to draw upon, issues of competing perspectives also came into play: 'Two of us work in the field of "organizational studies", leadership, management and employee relations, and so [absorbing] the work on "ethnography" was new and challenging . . .' (2011).

The role of 'change' was important here too: we were *learning from each other*. This took many different forms and included in-bid writing, project organization, inter-institutional negotiations (working with the micro-politics!), research processes, qualitative studies and so on. We were also trying to innovate, exchanging ideas on working methods as well as on methodologies (see Salisbury and Gornall 2011: 52). In networking externally, we learned too from wider colleagues and shared openly our own work. Many colleagues and network members are included, acknowledged and referenced in this volume and their conference spaces and events provided important objectives for us, in thinking, analysing, writing, framing narratives for this work.

Inter-collegiality

'Inter-collegiality' is thus not simply an 'added' form of collegial relationship but may be seen as part of a wider '*working together and apart*' paradigm. 'Working together apart' is a metonym for the 'dual' components of academic professionalism, working effectively and equally in both the 'solo' and 'collegial' modes, discussed in our Introduction. The term 'communitas' used by the anthropologist Victor Turner (1969), seems appropriate to apply here: thus we argue that when 'familial' types of relationships are replicated across and between institutions, in the same way as those that inhere within them – ones we call our 'colleagues' or as 'collegial' – then the term '*inter*-collegiality' should apply. Some of the character or features of 'inter-collegiality' are discussed below and are laid out in Figure 29.1.

- A high value on 'lateral' non-hierarchical relations

- The give and take of forms of 'anti-structure' or communitas described (Turner 1969), including the work to establish and maintain this

- The need for active discourse and interaction to sustain working relationships

- An affective content or emotional commitment to working together which may contrast with organizational or sector norms in the host institutions

- Relationships formed, sustained and conducted 'face-to-face' at a distance

- Where 'reflexivity' and awareness of process actively operates

Figure 29.1   Features of inter-collegiality

It is a post-modern, pluralist, 'mode 2', kind of working (Gibbons *et al.* 1994) and thus through the WL project we were able to create a 'micro-world' of lateral relationships rather than vertical ones around the work. This was sustained by such basic routines as rotating the chairing and convening of meetings and campus venues for these, discussing explicit aspects of mutual and personal learning, and describing the wider occupational 'hinterland' and challenges we each faced, as recorded here. The 'equity' was not total: there was a leaderly vision and support, and there were also strong disagreements. The team did have its 'forming, norming and performing' phases (Tuckman and Jensen 1977) – which meant that there were 'storming' ones too. Most of the struggle was about the nature of doing academic work itself, research perspectives, differences of values or practice, and perhaps pressures of the external competitive environment:

> I'm taking all the rubbish from everyone and no one even answers an email!
> My work [written contribution] has got lost in all the (document) changes and authors . . .
> I don't recall when that [decision] was discussed . . .
> Let's focus on the project and not the workload.
> Can we keep 'track changes' *on*, everyone please!!
> Stop quantifying your work!
> Calm down and get some sleep . . .
> I'm just watching and keeping quiet . . .
> Did I lose some emails recently?
>   Extracts from WL email correspondence and meeting notes 2009, 2011–2012

Yet the spirit was that everyone made the whole thing work – 'we were best when we were five'. It was a structure and dynamic that was in complete contrast to the organizational hierarchies around us. And while we sometimes competed for who was 'more ill, overworked and most under siege', colleagues' actual well-being was discreetly monitored, often with kind and practical interventions. Frequently, individuals expressed the need to 'steal or borrow time' from other areas of work, had to get 'buy-in' and sometimes formal consent, in order to be involved in the project. This implied sometimes disguising the scale or intensity from managers or colleagues of involvement at particular stages: 'I have never felt so managed'; 'There have been tensions over my use of time . . . however my experience with the group has been very positive'.

There was also an enormous amount of what one member called 'gifted time' to the research, the project and the team. And while institutions, managers, colleagues and friends were pleased about the collaboration, its profile, and intrigued by the research, this still left the work to be done:

> It was fine so long as we didn't ask for anything and we absorbed the extra activity
> (WL reflexive discussions 2009, 2012).

Struggles in writing and working collectively as 'WL'

Co-writing, multiple authorship and editing worked reasonably well in the team but could sometimes be a 'sticky issue' because of the multiple layers of drafting, the long cycles of writing turnover across the group. The different inputs, writing styles, edits and methods of individuals all made it difficult to sustain working attention and coherent arguments. Sometimes, the 'thread' of contribution(s) or authorial inputs was disputed or debated, and the textual structure could likewise be difficult to maintain for readers, with so much engagement across authors. We considered, in response to some of these dilemmas, writing under a 'collective' name, *'Working Lives'*. This idea was inspired by a group of Italian writers who, in a creative gesture arising from similar considerations, resolved to erase the 'star' system of individual authorship: 'People think each author has his or her own voice, one voice. We think that each author has many voices' (*wu ming*, a collective name, quoted in Tayler 2009).

The term *wu ming* signifies 'anonymous' or may also connote 'five people', so it was particularly appropriate for us. We diverge from the official group in that our photographs *do* contain our faces and we also eschew such designations as WL1– WL5, in favour of retaining personal name identities! But the pressures and drivers of the academy and HE world are in entirely the opposite direction to this. Thus the team were working against national and professional norms in a number of ways: 'multiple authorship' is less valued, 'journal articles are better than book chapters', conference presentations are of 'lower value than anything written (unless major keynotes)', the view that 'collaboration dilutes external value' or 'capacity-building is a poor deal for more experienced participants', that any 'output' is prized over even 'good' process. There was also considerable encouragement to individuals in the team to 'go solo', write up themselves, to write up early, get published.

So, whilst 'collaborative research' and/or 'partnership working' are celebrated and pointed to by institutions and governments as 'the way forward' (Tett *et al.* 2003), they can often be poorly understood or supported in practice. And alternative writing strategies or practices would seem radical indeed in the universities of the present.

Review: autoethnography for reflexive inter-professional inter-collegial work

Autoethnography as a methodology has been used in disciplines such as anthropology, sociology and education (Roth 2009; McIlveen 2008; Anderson 2006) to study and write about one's own group. In our case, we were researcher-practitioners (Muncey 2010) and found authoethnographic methods helpful in the group process generally, where we ran reflexive team sessions in autoethnographic mode, sometimes with a facilitator. These were audio-recorded and written up, the recordings providing the basis for the team's 'voices' quoted across this chapter. 'Autoethnography' is not the same as group autobiography, though it has a documentary function, and takes the form of a critical enquiry which is embedded in theory as well as practice. Here, it was the 'practice' of being part of a collaborative cross-disciplinary entity, learning and writing together, producing output (see May 2011; Davies and Salisbury 2009), and thinking reflexively about this.

Using autoethnography reflexively also enabled us as a team to experiment and innovate in a 'safe' environment. In this way, we did not put untried emotional pressures onto study participants, already often under strain (see Parts I and II this volume): our data had been provocative, some sessions were emotionally charged, as interviewees talked about the impact of policy and changes on their lives, work and careers: 'Insulted; only one word. There is only one word I can say. Insulted. Totally insulted' (HE informant, male, new university, commenting on the 'HERA' role analysis system for job evaluation, 2008).

Aware of the *affective* dimension of research (Albion 2012; Salisbury this volume) and in our work, we therefore tried things as a team where we could take risks, give and take informant 'voice', in a reflexive variant of 'anthropology at home'. This sometimes led to sessions that one research member described as 'teary sharings' (2009):

[In my own HEI] I don't fit in, my skills are not valued, I am viewed as part of the old crowd.

Teaching [for me, even more than research] is a high, a real fix and a powerful feeling of reaffirmation.

A valueless treadmill [I'm on].

A very uncertain environment . . . every day is different . . . new uncertainties.

Crazy . . . open office with constant interruptions; I don't take a lunch break and if [staff] are out of the office, undergraduates just come in and stare at me. I need to move.

I have had to learn not to fester . . .

WL reflexive team discussions, 2008–9

The WL team thus developed a *reflexive* version of the 'autoethnographic' methodology of Meneley and Young (2005). We were looking for a language of description for notions such as 'inter-collegiality', to describe relationships in ways that reflected and represented the difficulties and the benefits of cross-working collaboration. There were important and clearly emergent signifiers along this intellectual journey, and one in particular resulted in a very memorable, affirmative, session based on Turkle's (2008) ideas. In a facilitated event, items or ideas that were important to individuals were brought to a team session. These were artefacts and objects that signified our professional work:

> I love these notebooks . . . [this one] it's got my life, my academic life in here . . .

> These two photographs – a portal and a modern glass entrance . . . sum up the two universities I've been associated with . . . the old and the new, different in every way. There is also a link to my father, who attended the university in the first picture.

> I always carry my camera, to record and document stuff; it's a visual diary, a tool, and an affirmation of what I am doing.

> I suppose it is the 'to do list'. When I forget to keep one, I am all right for a while but get to the stage where I am almost bursting and have to discipline myself to start it again. It helps me sleep.

> There's my 'dragon voice' thingy, voice recognition kit. My family says it makes me look like a hospital DJ, and there I am, sitting talking to myself with the head-set wired into the laptop. It works for me.

WL Reflexive group session 2009, revisited 2012

Concluding remarks

Whilst HE organizations, government, policy-makers, together with various funding bodies, constantly call for greater collaboration and integration (Davies and Salisbury 2009), serious consideration needs to be given to the nature, culture, practices and techniques of working across the boundaries of space, place, identity and team. This should examine processes and buy-in by HEIs, since collaborative types of activities can be of 'low monetary value' to the institutions involved. Indeed, participation *is* an overhead, and commitment can vary, as managers, departments and strategic objectives change. All this can lead to mixed allegiances, conflicts and changes of interest, and dilemmas for the co-operating group to deal with, needing 'inter-disciplinarian' enlightened consideration. Collegiality, and specifically, *inter-collegiality*, it seems to us, creates and sustains commitment and produces productivity and innovation. It is also based firmly in the cultures of educational 'collegial working' that bring people together in the first place, as Barnett discusses, this volume.

'Reflexivity' as part of the team studies allowed us to give time to internal processes, revealing things otherwise hidden in research activity. We also used the opportunity of the project to create a wider network that helped to nurture, sustain and grow the research as well as the writing of the group. This drew in new people, and seeing our own activity refracted back, was also helpful analytically. Collaborative research offered the ability to bring together distinctive *and* specialist perspectives, thus the 'pluralistic' stance of multiple researchers can give 'team' research an epistemological edge over solo work (Walker 2001). We were insiders too, sometimes 'lone rangers', against the grain, and made use of this. It has not all been 'fun, friendship and fast work', but the sort of differences that manifested themselves initially, and could have been stalling points, became something 'worked through', ultimately adding value and insights. As Bruner (2004: 691) says, we became in some ways the autobiographical narratives by which we tell of our lives. In our own summaries:

> Working in stimulating teams – you are always learning . . . all the time.

> The boundary crossing has been great. It's made me think 'out of the box' and do things differently.

> We are trying to move from 'inter-collegiality' to intercollegiality.

> I would describe my experiences and change as part of the group as 'profound'.

> We *are* 'lifelong learning' . . .
>
> WL team comments, 2008–12

At the time of writing, two of our HEIs, from completely freestanding and independent institutions when the team formed in 2007, are about to merge (April 2013). We feel that the collaborative process of WL was a 'fit for the future' one, which in some ways, anticipated the 'imagined future' (Morley 2012) of cooperation between our organizations. As with the new institutional partnerships, it is, as they say, a work in progress for them. But as one research student remarked with an emic 'insider' perspective: 'I've always wondered how groups of authors work effectively together and I understand this now. It has been a remarkable experience . . . I learnt from the group's knowledge'.

WL began as a group of people apart, separated by more disparate features of the working environment and background than united us. The team has been remarkably productive and mutually supportive, and has drawn together a large network. Many of the features reported here should make collaborative work more attractive to others; as a WL research assistant who went on to further study commented, 'And now I love research!'

Acknowledgements

This chapter was presented as a paper to PROPEL Conference (Stirling, 2012) and at a Symposium (SRHE, Newport 2012) convened by Dr Janice Malcolm University of Kent. A paper, 'Reflexive teamwork', was presented to IPED at Coventry University in 2009; see also King 2012; King *et al.* 2006.

30

Researching Changes in Higher Education Occupations

Robert Mears and Eric Harrison

Introduction

A key dimension of the changing roles and responsibilities of academic working lives in recent years has been the growing complexity of the division of labour. During the last two decades, universities have been compelled to respond to a range of pressures that have increased the scope and range of their activities. In addition to the relentless pressure arising from sustained student expansion, the assessment of research output has transformed the working lives of many higher education (HE) academic staff today. In addition, they have been expected to become more 'entrepreneurial', engage with employers, focus on teaching quality (Travers 2007), improve the 'student experience', promote 'internationalization' (Knight 2010) and encourage regional economic development (Harding *et al.* 2007). These wider policy initiatives have generated a more complex occupational structure, and a number of researchers have delineated the emerging landscapes of HE in terms of new occupational groups, particularly in roles related to academic work (Brown 2004; Beetham *et al.* 2001; Gornall 1999) and the development of 'third spaces' between traditional administrators and academics (Whitchurch 2008).

Prior to the recent HE expansion, there was a relatively straightforward split between academic and administrative posts. Writing specifically of an 'emergent new group' associated with the support of learning and teaching, Gornall (1999) draws on social anthropological perspectives to describe how new posts demanding 'hybrid' skills emerged in the sector in the 1990s, roles that crossed established academic and support work boundaries. 'Marginal' in the organizational structures of the sector at the time, they were nevertheless by 2001 becoming more mainstream (Gornall and Thomas 2001). These staff had non-traditional contracts of employment, unusual job titles and worked on projects that traversed disciplinary and departmental divisions. Yet they were also invisible in the sector statistics and had 'fuzzy' lines of contact with senior HE management; it made them a kind of 'other' in the HE system (Gornall 2004; 1999). The hybrid new professionals of teaching and learning described by Gornall appear now to have been in the vanguard in terms of newly emerging employment categories of workers 'in between' previous or traditional job boundaries. Whitchurch (2008) describes the notion of '*third space*' as an emergent territory between academic and professional domains, occupied primarily by 'unbounded' forms of professional work. Posts held by such employees are likely to require conventional postgraduate qualifications, but their remit will often transcend disciplines and departments.

The forecast emergence of self-aware new groups of third space professionals seemed to have been realized when, at the 2010 annual conference of the UK Association of University Administrators (AUA), delegates discussed the growth of these 'third spaces' between professional staff and academics. The AUA chair predicted that the future would see administrators and managers taking on roles that overlap with, or were hitherto held by, academics. No longer content with being identified as purveyors of 'support services', this occupational group identifies itself as playing a more central place in the development of the twenty-first century university (Morgan 2011).

The changing nature of HE work, workforce and job market

The transformation of UK HE from an elite to a mass system is well documented (Halsey 1995; Scott 2000; Burrage 2010) and today the university bundles together a range of responsibilities, including the production and dissemination of technical knowledge, academic training and preparation of professionals, and the transmission, interpretation and development of cultural knowledge to enlighten the public sphere as a 'public good' (Fisher 2005). Given such expectations, it is perhaps inevitable that there are tensions and ambiguities about the purposes of the modern university today.

For many years, data produced by the Higher Education Statistics Agency (HESA) showed only 'full time' staff in academic roles; other groups, such as, 'in between', hybrid, or types of 'third space' post-holders were missing from the employment data at that time. Thus, official sources offer no simple answer to the question of the balance between 'academic' and 'support' jobs, while the term 'administrator' remains vague and open to different interpretations.

It can be seen (Table 30.1) that in 2009–10, there were 181,595 staff in the 'academic' category in UK HE, and, with 205,835 'non-academic' staff indicated, there was a total workforce of some 387,436.

Table 30.1:   Split between types of employees in higher education 2009–2010

Staff category	Number of staff (previous year 2008-9)
Academic	181,595 (179,040)
Non-academic: *of which*	205,835 (203,720)
Professional	*29, 005 (27,615)*
Managers	*16, 065 (15,960)*
ALL	387, 436 (382,760)

Source: HESA 2011.

HESA offers a further breakdown of 'non-academic' posts, two of which we extract and show in Table 30.1, as they are relevant to the discussion. In the category of 'manager', HESA data for the previous period showed that 15,960 posts were recorded in 2008–2009, which increased by 105 in 2009–2010. The figure for non-academic posts also increased by 1,390 (from 27,615 to 29,005), while academic posts increased from 179,040 to 181,595. Critics of the governance and management of UK universities (Deem *et al.* 2007) allude to the 'managerial revolution' in UK HE and the impact of managerialism on the academy. Figures indeed show that the number of 'managers, professional staff and technicians' employed in the HE sector as a whole rose by 17 per cent between 2003–4 and 2008–9, whereas the rise in academic numbers was only 11 per cent, while student numbers rose by 7 per cent over the same period (HESA 2005, 2010a, 2010b). For some critics, these trends are clear evidence of the declining status of the academic, in favour of a takeover of the academy by other groups (Morgan 2010).

To explore this further, we decided to examine advertised posts for 'third space' jobs in UK HE, through one main media channel, *Times Higher Education* (*THE*), throughout two years, 20 years apart.

Collecting data on new jobs: methods

Data were drawn from HE vacancies advertised in all editions of *THE* in 1990 and 2010. *THE* is the leading UK magazine for HE and the main vehicle for job advertisements in the recent past. Posts in the recruitment pages were scrutinized, to provide two 'snapshots' of a labour market 20 years apart. We excluded research posts, vacancies at specialist research centres and private sector employment. The posts of interest were advertised alongside conventional academic posts, and typically these required similar academic qualifications but they also demanded the 'flexibility' to help (re)make the modern university (Barnett 2003).

Posts advertised were classified and logged in the following way. **Senior** included vice chancellors, deputy and pro-vice chancellors and executive deans. **Academic** included all full-time posts from lecturer to professor (excluding fixed term research posts, postdoctoral, etc.). **Managerial** posts included registrars, human resource directors, finance directors and planning managers. This left the critical category of hybrid 'in between' posts (Gornall 1999), also categorized as in the '**third space**' (Whitchurch 2008). The *THE* posts that we categorized as 'cross-role' embraced three main areas: 'research', 'teaching and learning', and 'external', usually relating to employer engagement.

It is accepted that there are limitations. It cannot be assumed, for example, that all posts available are advertised, and nor can it be assumed that sampling from one mainstream periodical will capture all HE posts. This is certainly the case for management appointments such as those in human resources (HR), finance, planning, IT/computing and estates, where specialist publications and websites are much more likely to be used now. In 2010, there were also competing outlets for university advertisements of all kinds, and the dominance of one outlet cannot now be taken for granted. Also, these data show only recruitment – that is, new or replacement positions – and do not indicate standing posts or the current establishment of staffing in the various categories of posts across the HE sector. Nevertheless, the data generated from *THE* offer an intriguing insight into the changing occupational landscape of universities.

Findings

The purpose of this data-gathering exercise therefore was to examine the proportion of job opportunities taken up by 'third space' 'new' posts. Table 30.2 shows the number of posts advertised in the identified categories for the years 1990 and 2010.

Broadly speaking, the number of academic posts advertised remained flat. This was also true of managerial (i.e. administrative) opportunities. By contrast, the number of 'senior' opportunities rose by more than 50 per cent between 1990 and 2010, while those posts we categorized as 'third space' rose by 200 per cent.

So our questions were: what exactly are these 2010 posts, what are they about, and what broad functions do they serve? Our analysis generated three categories: 'teaching enhancement and quality assurance', 'research' and 'employer engagement'. Examples from *THE* of such new job titles and roles are presented in Figure 30.1.

Dean of learning, teaching enhancement developer, dean for quality enhancement, director of curriculum, head of education & learning, dean of learning enhancement and innovation, dean for quality enhancement, director of academic delivery; research:director of performance, **dean for research**, research & network development officer, research manager, head of learning & research support, research development manager, business manager, director of research funding, centre for research communication, director of research and innovation, head of impact and innovation, director of REF and doctoral programmes; **employer engagement:** business engagement manager, employability and internship manager, student destination manager, employer engagement manager.

Figure 30.1 Examples of 'third space' job titles from *THE* 2010

Discussion: academics and changing roles and posts in HE

As Gornall and Thomas (2001) and Beetham *et al.* (2001) noted more than a decade ago, something significant is happening in the academic job market, and the surge in new job titles is indicative of a much broader structural change. These changes manifest themselves in contradictory ways. On the one hand, academics may be losing some of their traditional 'gatekeeping' (controlling student admissions) and pastoral roles. On the other hand, they are increasingly required to produce more visible and impressive course material and learning outcomes documentation, as well as spending more time assessing larger numbers of students. In the sphere of scholarship, the time constraints are obvious: the imperative for more and better publications

Table 30.2 HE job advertisements in *THE*, 1990 and 2010

	Senior		Academic		Managerial		'Third space'	
	1990	2010	1990	2010	1990	2010	1990	2010
Jan	13	25	228	207	25	11	18	28
Feb	19	16	243	205	19	28	8	13
March	13	15	338	221	24	22	6	18
April	7	11	209	198	13	15	5	24
May	8	22	142	178	7	14	3	21
June	8	7	254	188	11	12	7	18
July	8	12	163	191	21	16	3	26
Aug	2	0	57	64	10	6	1	5
Sept	4	9	170	136	19	9	6	16
Oct	3	12	123	187	12	8	1	10
Nov	3	1	120	163	10	10	11	19
Dec	1	8	54	76	6	4	2	15
TOTAL	**89**	**138**	**2101**	**2014**	**177**	**155**	**71**	**213**

requires (more often than not) concentrated data analysis and writing time. Similarly, greater numbers of applications for funding will consume significant amounts of academics' time.

A recent *THE* article (Morgan 2011) drew together the views of several contributors. Whitchurch (2008), a former HE senior manager, argued that new post-holders 'often do things that academics used to do, such as developing new modes of learning and delivering student support and pastoral care, which releases academics to focus on mainstream teaching and research'. Relatedly, Christopher Hallas, chair of the University Administrators Association (AUA) asked rhetorically:

> Who will be driving these changes? Will it be academic members of staff? No, I don't think it will be . . . they have to continue to deliver on academic quality and academic programmes. But in terms of students, the concept of 'student experience' as simply being an academic experience – I don't think that is going to hold up and stand the test of time.
>
> Morgan 2011

It seems that the 'administrators' of yesterday are no longer content to play merely a backroom role in supporting the academy. Below, we consider some of the questions raised for lecturers and academics in this context.

Impacts of expansion of HE posts on academics

One strand of the literature on work and academic life is dominated by a narrative in which the shift to a mass HE system has left lecturers overwhelmed by the additional responsibilities expected of them, in some ways unprepared for changing demands, and with a strong sense of being 'undervalued'. According to a study reported by Edwards *et al.* (2009), HE employees in the sample were often 'dissatisfied with their jobs and careers ... generally dissatisfied with working conditions and control at work', and 'stressed' at work'. In a similar vein, Morgan (2010) comments that:

> University staff in the UK tend to report that demands are increasing, while support and a sense of having control at work have fallen. Many complain about the rushed pace of work, the lack of respect and esteem, having too much to do, inadequate support and lack of opportunity for promotion. The psychological stress among university employees appears to be much higher than in other professional groups and the general population.
>
> Easton, cited in Morgan 2010: 9

Similarly the University and College Union (UCU 2007) claim that:

> Provisional findings from new research into the experiences of over 1000 staff in universities, further education colleges and adult education, reveal high levels of stress as workloads increase. But only 16% of staff thought their institution was addressing the causes of stress.

Surveys conducted among a range of different employees confirm the extent to which the discourse of 'work stress' has been assimilated more generally (Wainwright and Calnan 2002). Sims offers a compelling argument about the appeal of what he describes as 'narratives of indignation', in which workers in different kinds of organization engage in a systematic (and often enjoyable) 'demonization' of their more senior colleagues and revel in the 'joy of denunciation' (2005: 1625–40). Dystopian views of work in the contemporary university abound, with a claim that we work in the 'commodified', 'marketized', 'audited', 'neoliberal' and 'managerialized', university in which everything is getting worse! Such misery is tempered by the results of a survey of 100 staff (Amoah 2007) – academics and others – covering different types of institution and broken down by age, role and characteristics (Watson 2009). It offers a more nuanced view: 57 per cent agreed (9 per cent strongly) that the UK system was 'improving in teaching', 61 per cent felt that the quality of research was 'improving' (16 per cent strongly), 63 per cent thought the same about 'services to business' (11 per cent strongly), 50 per cent thought that there were improvements in terms of 'service to society' (11 per cent strongly), 58 per cent thought HE institutions were 'well managed' (6 per cent strongly) and 64 per cent agreed that the sector was 'still significant' (23 per cent strongly) (Watson 2009: 53). While we cannot claim that these results are generally representative, they do provide a counter-narrative to some of the more despairing accounts of working life in the modern university. In their studies of HE 'hyperprofessional' academics, and 'compulsive' as well as 'compulsory' aspects of HE working, Salisbury and Gornall (2011) have reported the pleasures and fascination (as well as the stresses) of the job, described by informants.

Response to third spaces and the 'bureaucratization' of academic life

Gornall (2009) noted a growing but cautious confidence, arising out of the deep commitment of learning and teaching staff to pedagogic innovation and student development. There is sometimes an expectation that the rise of so-called 'third space professionals' will be met with gratitude by academics because of their potential to relieve academic workload pressures (Whitchurch 2008). Faced with the relentless pressures on academics to 'do more', described earlier, the emergence of 'third space professionals' could be viewed as more of a blessing than a threat. But far from being universally welcomed, this phenomenon is sometimes presented as a disturbing and thoroughly unwanted expansion of bureaucracy into the academy. Such objections are located in what du Gay (2005) describes as the romantic objection to bureaucracy. He argues that popular views of the bureaucrat – meddling, interfering and obstructing useful work – are mistaken. He urges us to take a more benign view:

> The non-sectarian bureaucratic comportment of the person, against which so many critics have railed, can ... be seen as a positive ethical and political achievement rather than its opposite. Max Weber was simply among the earliest and most eloquent of human scientists to draw attention to the ethical discipline and rigour required by the conduct of bureaucratic office.
>
> du Gay 2005: 51

The so-called bureaucratization of universities should come as no surprise, given the rise of 'management' roles throughout the wider economy and the expansion of organizations, their finances and community. As public and private sector organizations have grown over the last century, management occupations have been the fastest growing occupations in advanced industrial societies (Salaman 1995; Pearson 2012). The only thing that is surprising about this trend is that it took so long to reach the academy (Mears 2000).

Historically, occupational groups have had a tendency to seek opportunities to extend their domain, and it is highly likely that such ambitions will trigger suspicion and even resentment from neighbouring groups. Bolton *et al.* (2011: 683) maintain that the whole concept of 'professionalism' is under transformation, via 'a performative discourse and rhetorical reform from above, by employers and managers to reframe professional identities around new corporate and managerial priorities'. These 'new' professionals are unlikely to remain passive 'support' workers, however. Like many occupational groups, they will attempt to extend their domain, enhance their rewards and status and use their professional associations to mobilize their collective power (Freidson 1986). A more detailed and longitudinal (cf. Gornall 2009; 1999) analysis would, we suggest, show further examples of the process of professional identity formation in these ways.

Further questions

There are a number of additional questions about the future of 'third space' posts. Whitchurch (2008) takes the view that, far from becoming marginalized, new types of 'third space' professionals are likely to continue to emerge. It is plausible to speculate that the ability of such groups to generate income and prestige for their universities will make them *more*, not less, secure. Their ability to *blend* activities, work across disciplines, departments and traditional divisions of labour, may make them more resilient in turbulent times. We know less about the detailed expectations and requirements of such posts, though it is highly likely that they enjoy far less autonomy than has been the case for traditional academics (see also Hudson this volume). Whilst lecturers have relatively vague job descriptions around teaching, research and administration, many of these 'third space' posts will have very specific targets and thus will need to work to much tighter, target-driven job descriptions (Gornall 2004).

The Dearing Report of 1997 noted the rise of a new group of 'support staff' in HE, but the trends have turned out to be more complex, and several important research questions are generated by the shifts described here. The reorganization of expertise in universities is consistent with trends identified by those who have analysed the redrawing of boundaries and relationships between and among contemporary professions (Ackroyd *et al.* 2007). To what extent 'third space', 'blended' or 'in between' roles take root in HE in different economic and political contexts remains to be studied. Will the people who come to occupy these new professional roles develop a distinct occupational culture and generate a sense of a 'tribe' akin to those academic groups famously identified by Becher (1989), or will they remain in a 'liminal' area (Gornall 1999) and 'between categories' in the organizational chart, subject to wider shifts? Are such spaces – especially if they are perceived as temporary – being occupied disproportionately by women?

The ongoing process of change in the HE sector has been accompanied by an increase in the numbers of managers and 'third space' professionals. The increasing visibility of these new kinds of public space/service sector professionals is challenging existing divisions of labour. This is in turn calling into question the boundaries – and associated identities – of existing, competing professional tribes.

Acknowledgements

An earlier version of this chapter was presented at the 'Work, Employment and Society' conference at the University of Brighton, in September 2010. We are grateful to the participants in that session for their comments as well as involvement in the WL seminars (2010).

31

Ongoing Practice in Researching Academic and Higher Education Life

Martin Gough

Introduction

One of the key principles underpinning the ethos of this book is 'inclusion' and an openness to multidisciplinarity and plurality. This applies in particular to methodological approaches of inquiry. Working with the editors of this volume to convene a chapter of research and studies 'in progress' – imagined, unpublished or merely unreported – this chapter provides an opportunity to record some current research interests, or to describe future, ongoing and potential areas of higher education (HE) research. The editors asked: what are you studying now or writing proposals for; what would you like to be researching? I consider, first, those methodologically more concerned with understanding academic work viewed 'from the outside'. In other words, where the vantage point of the inquiring action is outwith, looking down onto a process (this does not preclude that the individual researchers may well be themselves HE 'insiders'). I turn gradually to approaches concerned more directly with individuals writing about academic lives and work 'from the inside' (Shoemaker 1984: 19), aiming to capture the experience itself.

The broad reach of educational research

Contracted-out research in Scotland

Chris Holligan, professor in the Faculty of Education, Social Science & Health at the University of the West of Scotland, is looking at the decisions of a devolved Scottish administration. He asks what the distribution of government research contracting over the past decade reveals. By means of a content and discourse analysis of contracts awarded, the goal of this research is to provide a 'thick description' (Geertz 1973) of the landscape of the cash nexus, the players involved, and those surrounding the supply of evidence for policy needs.

Holligan discovers that, since 2002, 'third' sector and private companies, and not just within Scotland's borders, have been increasingly successful in winning contracts for educational research. Holligan also explores the role of social, business and political networks that are in play, around tendering and contracting (cf. Ball and Junemann 2012). Holligan's analysis utilizes the notion of 'commodification of knowledge' and Bourdieu's concept of 'social capital' as he reveals the ways in which 'outputs' are increasingly being specified, with an absence of peer review and a preference for *quantitative* research designs. Qualitative investigations are a casualty of policy-informing work, he argues, which is yet not disinterested science but a more partisan one. The result is that the evidence base of the public sector and policy is contracted out, away from the university, education departments and the public sector generally. Determining how the 'free market' actually works here raises a difficult methodological issue, however: the researcher needs access to the bids of those who tendered for the research and to observe the decision-making leading to selection of winning bids (cf. Strathern this volume). Freedom of Information laws do not permit this where commercial sensitivities intervene, so the collection of these data is a key challenge in such research.

New 'enterprise professionalism' in Wales

'Capital' as a theme requires us to consider not just the pursuit of resources coming into universities for academic research, but also what flows out from their knowledge work. Our attention needs to turn to divisions separate from academic departments, those with a remit to create partnerships with mainstream scholars as well as outside agencies. The Commercial Services group at the University of Glamorgan has a well-developed enterprise role, which encompasses support for graduates and local start-ups, facilitating 'knowledge transfer' between the university and external organizations. Traditionally seen as 'industrial liaison', more recently the 'third mission' of HE and now also known as external 'engagement', the business departments of universities are highly significant to HE institutions' (HEIs) activity in the wider community. Much of this involves collaborations and multi-party projects, facilitated by clearly-defined periods of external funding. The imperative from government remains, to link the wealth-creating capacity of both university research and graduate entrepreneurs into regional and national economies (Schmuecker and Cook 2012).

HE business incubation is typically implemented as a graduate enterprise support tool, involving incubation practitioners with graduating students. Posts at UK HEIs that manage and organize this provide often innovative, stimulating work, but with some employment uncertainty. Pam Voisey (Business Incubation Manager within the department of External Services) employs 'stochastic resonance' (Abrahamson and Freedman 2006), a concept used to denote randomness, as part of a methodology for researching aspects of 'new professional' working life. She applies this to the theorization of enterprise collaborations and networking, in an attempt to represent and understand the development of emergent entrepreneurial cultures in HE incubators. Her thoughts and findings to date are included in a number of presentations (Voisey *et al.* 2005) and now a research proposal on innovation and the emergence of 'communities of practice' in UK incubators and management.

Voisey could describe herself as a 'new enterprise professional', the term usefully coined by Gornall (2004) and aimed at capturing the emerging variety of working practices in universities. Many such staff are allies and partners of academic status staff in joint projects (see also Mears and Harrison; Hudson this volume) and their work is integral to and infused by the ongoing purpose and conversation of the academic community in institutions, rather than being generic and merely supporting academic work (cf. Barnett 1993). This is what makes highly problematic the notion of 'outsourcing' of certain university functions (THE 2011), as the work of 'new professionals' as well as conventional 'support' or 'administration', is an integral part of the institution as a whole (Gough 2012).

Accreditation partnerships

Diane Rainsbury (academic registrar at Hull College, one of the largest further education (FE) institutions in the UK with substantial HE course delivery) reminds us that the 'HE sector' contains a variety of working environments. The working situation of her HE lecturers is not the same as for university academics (whether pre- or post-92). There is a well-established tradition of HE provision in the FE sector, with considerable diversity, in terms of organizational and subject profile but colleges today operate in a more deregulated environment. There may be a range of organizations involved in validating collaborative FE/HE partnerships and staff thereby acquire experiences of working with many different validating institutions, multiple regulatory frameworks and with different models of collaboration. However, awarding institutions appear to be becoming increasingly risk-averse. These factors affect the range of curriculum areas that can be validated, limiting new course initiatives by the college and its staff. The development of such an environment suggests some research directions. One is whether there are sufficient opportunities for colleges to collaborate or work in partnership with awarding bodies, particularly where competitive pressures coexist with cooperative ones. The common practice of working within multiple, regulatory and mixed internal and external quality frameworks and reporting modes may not be sustainable. Among other things, the issue of workload looms large, and all changes in accreditation or partnerships involve lecturers in substantial additional work, including the rewriting of courses. That aside, to complete any picture of what is going on, it is important to explore how lecturing and administrative staff in the college sector perceive working with universities and other awarding bodies, and the extent to which these relationships genuinely support lecturers' individual development as scholars and advanced practitioners. Rainsbury's research background, on comparative HE systems, is now reflected in these new interests, around the policies informing collaborative provision and the nature of inter-institutional links.

From consensus and difference to conflict management

Howard Stevenson (University of Nottingham) and Justine Mercer (University of Warwick Institute of Education) explain the importance of analysing structural change to an understanding of working life, in what we might term the 'established' academic workplace. Their research project (supported by the Society for Research into Higher Education) is called 'Challenging times: an analysis of current developments and future prospects for industrial relations in the UK higher education sector', and maps employee relations structures in UK HE. This takes place at a time of unprecedented turbulence in the sector, exemplified by the tripling of tuition fees and the removal of many forms of state funding.

The employment relationship in universities is framed in part by traditions of collective bargaining, in which trade unions represent employees' collective interests. This study seeks to identify how formal and informal processes and structures currently operate, and whether they may be 'fit for purpose' for the future. As marketization of the sector intensifies, HEIs will be driven to contain labour costs and increase 'productivity', whilst often also reconfiguring their workforces to align with changing organizational objectives. The research investigates whether these intended outcomes can be successfully 'managed' within the current employee relations structures. The scoping study seeks to capture views from key players, using interviews with high-ranking officials at UCEA (the national employers' organization), national officials and institution-based lay officers and officials of UCU (the principal union representing academic staff), as well as vice-chancellors and human resources directors of both older and newer universities. The research data thus far identify very considerable challenges ahead, with substantial labour conflict, including formal workplace and national disputes, a distinct possibility (Stevenson and Mercer 2011).

Bullying in the workplace

In the light of the prospect of labour relations breaking down, and with continuous organizational change otherwise in the background, Michael Sheehan (former professor of organizational behaviour at Glamorgan University) is now working as an adviser on workplace behaviours in Australia. He reminds us of the relentless demands made upon managers, both academic and administrative, over a sustained period of time in HE. Those holding positions of authority over others in the workplace, he argues, often find that the pressures of the environment invite them to cut corners in their interpersonal behaviours. They may focus only on particular facts that take their attention, or value those things that can readily be ordered, analysed, defined, dealt with, and contained, ignoring subtleties and the more complex elements of situations. They may start to treat colleagues as means to ends at the expense of, in Kantian terms, making the effort to respect them, listening to and respecting their advice or judgement.

Within such a framework, an HE manager or authority figure may bully staff within their sphere of influence. 'Bullying is offensive, intimidating, malicious or insulting behaviour ... can include spreading rumours, demeaning others ... overbearing supervision or deliberately undermining a competent worker by overloading them' (UCU 2012). Such action is debilitating and degrading for the staff concerned, but also for witnesses, people implicated (complicit or otherwise) and drawn in. Workplace bullying has negative outcomes for organizations (Sheehan 2010). So it is important to extrapolate the research plan to explore not only the conditions and effects within staff working environments, but also to explore whether there are negative consequences for the student body too (Keashly and Neuman 2010). HE managers must act in accordance with the principles of professionalism befitting their position, under the terms of their work that is shared with all colleagues in the organization. (Sheehan 2013, 2010).

The obvious strategy to counter bullying is the development of 'soft skill' provision with managers, authority figures, and perhaps all staff within HE. The concept of 'skill' is sometimes regarded as a polar opposite to the stuff of academic work, and more debate and evidence is needed to develop the concept more robustly (cf. Gough 2011; Gough and Denicolo 2007: 16–19). Some academics have been critical when 'skills' initiatives have emanated from senior management or human resources departments, so research on workplace behaviours needs to give attention to the structural as well as policy elements of the environment. Most effort, Sheehan argues, should be directed towards collection of qualitative data about the lived experiences of the parties involved. The 'bullied rank and file worker' is the obvious focus here. Not only would interviewing them uncover their experiential data, but the use of diaries, for example, could also serve as a fruitful methodological tool. This is a method championed by the 'Sharing Practice Day Surveys' project, in investigating how, why and with what evidence educators change their teaching practice (Fincher 2010–11). Perhaps even more important is the need to understand the protagonists' experience: why they are doing what they are doing? That may be difficult to achieve: the demand of respect towards research participants (Kantianism, in the context of research ethics) will mean they should be informed of the purpose of an interview and they may be wary of exposing their misdeeds and failings. But important work is often difficult and the challenge demands to be taken up.

Resources for resilient working

Even though it might be a key to successful fostering of practices that avoid workplace conflicts of which bullying is a symptom, 'creative leadership' is something that poses opportunities but also dilemmas for academic staff acting in management and leadership roles in HE (see also Floyd this volume). Soyinka is an academic with a filmmaking background in a head of department role, who often feels less like a scholar than a general manager. She asks how we can both stretch and take care of the imagination. As teachers and artists, we shift people's attention, she argues, but in doing this, there is also a responsibility. For this reason, Soyinka's interest is in researching the sort of leadership in HE that takes responsibility for producing 'rounded' creative people who are also resilient as part of the economy.

It can be problematic, she identifies, when the pedagogic or organizational leader must prime students for 'employability' while at the same time seeing their own creative work more as a vocation, a life choice that requires resilience and sustainability. In her research (Coffey *et al.* 2005), Soyinka explores the application of traditional ethnographic notions, such as that of the 'trickster', to modern situations. This is illustrated through writing and performance, storytelling and discussion of cultural translations (www.hodcha.com). Yet all of this must take place in a context of performance quantification and returnability for the Research Assessment Exercise/ Research Excellence Framework (RAE/REF), always more challenging for academics in non-text areas of work. There is also in the workplace a new 'unitization' of everyday academic working life, where teaching, research, support and administrative areas of activity are classified separately and accounted for as bundles of time. To be a good leader today means being on site all the time, reviving the problem of how to reconcile 'presenteeism' with fieldwork research, external partnership meetings and productive working from home (cf Gornall *et al.* this volume).

Soyinka is working on bids for funding activities to examine forms of HE leadership by arts practitioners, exploring the attractiveness of the academy for them. There would be some synergy here with the recent work of Linda Evans (professor of leadership and professional learning at the University of Leeds School of Education) whose recent projects focus on academic leadership. Initially, these have been studies of the 'led' (Evans *et al.* forthcoming), and more recently of the leaders themselves. This is research on 'Professorial academic leadership in turbulent times: the professoriate's perspective' (funded by the Leadership Foundation for Higher Education) and 'Leadership preparation and development for UK-based university professors' (funded by the British Educational Leadership, Management and Administration Society).

Reaching the 'inside'

Longitudinal study of early research careers

The methodological spectrum, 'from the outside' to 'from the inside', mapped in this chapter arrives at the latter end with the established and ongoing work of Lynn McAlpine (Oxford, McGill) and her colleagues: Cheryl Amundsen, Greg Hum and Esma Emmioglu (Simon Fraser), Shuhua Chen (McGill), Jean Rath (Canberra), Gill Turner, Julia Horn and Mahima Mitra (Oxford). The research is supported by the Social Sciences and Humanities Research Council of Canada, the Higher Education Funding Council of England and the Oxford John Fell Fund. The team describe their work as a longitudinal qualitative examination of the experiences of more than 150 early career researchers – doctoral students, post-PhD researchers and new lecturers – that began in 2006 in the social sciences and, since early 2010, has extended also to the sciences. What has become increasingly evident here is the influence of personal lives and goals in navigating careers and seeking employment, whether within or beyond the academy. In common with others, this research is framed within an 'identity' perspective (see also O'Byrne this volume). However, much previous work (a) foregrounds the 'reproductive' features of society thus downplaying the agency individuals bring to pursuing their intentions; (b) frames experience within a particular role, as doctoral students, whereas this research examines how individuals transition through them; (c) draws on evidence collected at only one point in time. McAlpine and colleagues' approaches to the study of identity, by contrast, bring successive narratives (individual's accounts of the meaning and purpose of their experiences) across time and thus role, demonstrating individuals' constructions of their identities in response to shifting circumstances. The construct emerging from this research, *identity-trajectory*, highlights how individual intentions and personal lives (as much as academic work) play an important role in their shifting views of their futures (cf. McAlpine and Amundsen 2011: 173–84).

Clearly, methodological decisions influence findings. The contrast between 'from the outside' and 'from the inside' reports used in this chapter is perhaps captured in the distinction between 'third-person' and 'first-person' accounts of phenomena, a terminology in common use in philosophical discourse. The distinction is echoed in Marton's (1981: 188) 'first-order perspective of statements-about-reality' and 'second-order perspective of statements-about-perceived-reality'. What it is like (cf. Nagel 1979) for someone to experience such situations is excluded from third-person accounts, those that describe what has happened at the merely observational level: the first-person viewpoint is surplus to the requirements of explanation according to scientific objectivity. The contrast, for purposes of researching academic work and life, is brought out well by a writer like Fanghanel (2012: 1) for example, in considering roles as both 'reified descriptions of practice' and as 'instantiations of academic identity'. She, not unlike McAlpine, takes the latter to be of primary importance in understanding the 'being' of an academic. The ideological contrast is between this 'educationist' stance and a sociological stance. The latter is necessarily entirely third-person initially, discovering the 'black box' (e.g. a profession as a whole) and observing how it interacts with other social objects, for example, in terms of relations of power.

Christine Musselin (2012) and others recognize well the methodological problems for sociology in researching these areas. Rather than a 'sociology of the academic profession' taken as a primary unit of inquiry then, she advocates a 'sociology of academic work,' to include an investigation of the myriad of activities and career trajectories potentially involved. This allows for a much more fine-grained analysis and is reflected in the work, for instance, of Janice Malcolm (University of Kent) and Miriam Zukas (Birkbeck, University of London) in their new research 'Discipline and workplace learning in practice: an exploratory study of academic work' (funded by the Society for Research into Higher Education) whereby the latter's 'sociomaterialist' (Fenwick *et al.* 2012) methodology draws innovatively on actor-network theory.

Moving out: the Free University of Melbourne

The final contribution in this 'curated' set of future research studies illustrates the potential of the particular, through the personal story of bringing to our attention pedagogical environments beyond the standard university campus (as Barnett does in his concluding chapter) and strongly hints that we should consider these more in research on academic working lives. Stephen Knight explores possibilities for an alternative politics of inquiry, after finding new circumstances and opportunities offered – and some closed off – on returning to Australia following an academic career in the UK. Now honorary professorial fellow in the School of Culture and

Communication at the University of Melbourne, Knight began by contacting his former department in the University, to offer a lecture course or two on his specialist area, which had gone well in the UK. Several emails later – 'Oh thanks, generous, but we don't do that any more' – he realized that something different was needed. Organized by young staff and postgraduate students from La Trobe University (a c. 1970 creation in the north-east of that spread-eagled city), and with almost no call on funding, 'Melbourne Free University' (counterpart to the 'very expensive university') is offering an idea and discussion-based educational experience that is hardly available in the 'mass training sites' that Knight says we currently describe as 'universities' today. A six-week programme on 'The politics of myth' attracted some 30 people a week – mostly in their late twenties – the semi-employed, those interrupted out of poverty or boredom, a few elderly, altogether a cheerful, talkative group of thinking citizens out for a concept-driven good time.

The sessions were so popular that they were soon upgraded from a radical bookshop to a trendy inner-urban bar. 'You don't get this on campus these days', they said. To Stephen Knight, it seems like old times, and good times, and the experience calls upon us to look at the character of such alternatives to the 'fees, funding and private providers' discourse of conventional education systems. It is certainly unlike learning on the internet, a late capitalist medium, expensive and without much capacity, perhaps, for facilitating concept development. How these new forms of grass-roots organization might affect the mainstream in turn is ripe for consideration. Perhaps, we might speculate, they will follow successfully in the footsteps of Robin Hood (Knight 2003), although things have been quiet around the UK's 'Really Open University' for a while.

For a view of the future then, Knight invites us: 'let us explore and participate in the thriving, and for myself and others, rather fulfilling, Melbourne Free University!'

Conclusion: Academia as Workplace: A Natural Pessimism and a Due Optimism

Ronald Barnett

Introduction

It is easy enough to be pessimistic about the character of academic life in the twenty-first century, for there is much to be pessimistic about; and many *are* pessimistic. Its super-saturated character, being dense with tasks and expectations; its extending into the life-world and so affecting the life-work balance; its audit and surveillance regimes; the 'commodification' of student learning; and its sheer instrumentalism, as every activity in academic life is required to have an outcome or impact beyond itself: these are just some of the sources of pessimism. Writing those scripts of pessimism is relatively easy. The much more interesting and challenging task is that of searching for sources of optimism. Are there spaces available in which there can be sightings that give hope of positive possibilities? Such spaces cannot be spaces of yesteryear; and anyway, those spaces were probably rare if indeed they ever existed. Spaces for optimism in the twenty-first century must surely be new spaces. Or perhaps it is misconceived to be thinking of spaces in this situation; perhaps the adoption of more optimistic outlooks is primarily one of disposition than sightings as such. And perhaps there are always grounds for optimism for those of an optimistic frame of mind.

Doubtful categories

In a turbulent age, the very categories through which we comprehend the academic life are often problematic. One problematic category is that of work. In the past, *was* academia a place of work? For work stands outside of oneself, placing its disciplines on one. Work is work to be *done*, and within set time-frames, monitored for its quality adjudged by others (usually those who own the means of production). Academia is now all of this; but was it so in the past? In the past, in an era of 'donnish dominion' (Halsey 1992), it was the academics who owned the means of production. The academy was in their hands, under their direction; though to speak of 'direction' itself implies a management ethos that would have been otiose. Senates were both powerful and declined to exercise that power; now, courts and governors exercise power, ousting vice-chancellors. No one is safe any longer.

And so the academy has become a workplace, with its disciplinary regimes (in a Foucauldian 1972 sense). Academics are subject to surveillance procedures, to bureaucratic processes, to performance audits, to judgements by quasi-state authorities (or perhaps the 'quasi' is not so quasi), to representation in marketing ploys as if they were themselves objects for consumption, to assessments of their own work for its impact, judged not in the delight it affords or in the growth of human understanding but in its contribution to the 'global knowledge economy', and to the claims of students who exert their wants as customers of education.

In attempting to legitimize this entire dispensation, recourse is frequently had to the idea of accountability: academics, we are told, should be accountable. To whom should they be accountable? To stakeholders, comes the reply. All this begs the questions as to what it is to be accountable, and who is to count as stakeholders. That academics might feel accountable to the academic community as well as the wider civic society and that academics might also count as a body of stakeholders themselves is seldom countenanced. Even less comprehended is the idea that academics might or should work with an integrity of their own, and within a horizon of values sustained by the academic community itself (cf. Macfarlane 2007). And, in the UK at least, the academics are now outnumbered by other staff in universities (Salisbury and Gornall 2011). Are academics an endangered species? Are they heading towards extinction?

Of course, the very category of 'academic' is now a fraught category. As universities become more complex, undertaking many outward-oriented functions (marketing, outreach, knowledge transfer, spinout, income generation as such), 'third space' professionals emerge (Whitchurch 2006), injecting creative dynamism in driving the university, now become 'the entrepreneurial university' (Clark 1998). Whereas academics are devoted to their disciplines, these new professionals can devote themselves to the fortunes of their universities. And so universities become organizations, enterprises that are managed as such, with a level of being (of being a university – Barnett 2011b) separate from and even above that of the disciplines.

At the same time, as universities engage with the world (in widening participation, in learning developments, in securing patents, and in extending their international reach), the boundaries between the 'academic' and the 'non-academic' become fuzzy (Gornall 1999); even liquid (Bauman 2005). At the same time too, dislocations are to be seen among the academics themselves, such that some of those being paid academic salaries (such as those working in some of the professional areas, or in promoting students' academic literacy, or working on post-experience courses where the participants may be advanced not only in age but seniority and educational qualifications or even those who have heavy teaching loads) may hesitate to categorize themselves as 'academics'. The ascription comes with too much baggage (perhaps of scholarliness, of an over-concern with research, or of a remoteness from the wider world). And so other terms are found, of 'researcher', 'facilitator', 'coordinator', 'mentor' and so forth. The vocabulary of the university world moves on.

Responses

In the wake of these movements, academics evince different reactions. Some hanker for a golden age of the past, in which academics were free to pursue their inclinations (a time of 'academic freedom'); others throw themselves into the new milieu, taking on its required entrepreneurial and managed disciplines with alacrity; others try to negotiate a *modus vivendi*, trying to hold onto their own value position while seeming to comply with the new order; others 'flee' from the scene, unwilling to pay the psychic and social and even intellectual cost of 'staying put'. Each person will form her or his own response, weaving a psycho/socio/ethico tapestry, in a personal endeavour to form some pattern, permitting an accommodation between one's personal values and professional aspirations, and the configuration of a university's claims on its individual academics. Perhaps no pattern can be found and then, perhaps too, the disjunction between the personal and the organizational pulls and pushes becomes too much to bear, and 'early retirement' suddenly seems a welcome space.

In such a situation, it is hardly surprising if stress, morale and the quality of working life become matters of significance. But note that stress here becomes as much a social matter as a psychological matter, for it can be understood as the outcome of a disjunction between values held widely within a community and the options presented by the 'real world'. Today, all academics are obliged to become critical realists; very aware of the structure and character of the academic world, as it is being reshaped before themselves, and at the same time adopting critical stances towards it. For some, this perceived disjunction – between the real and the imagined – exerts a heavy toll and reveals itself in occupational stress.

Here, talk of the relationships between 'structure' and 'agency' (Archer 2003, 2000) can carry us only so far. For such abstractions can barely do justice to the turmoil that many academics must be undergoing, as familiar landscapes change on a daily basis. The injunction that students' essays should be not merely marked online but even read online ('to save paper') may become the proverbial straw breaking the camel's back. Of course, as stated, some relish the new order. The spaces that it opens for creative entrepreneurialism, to set up a new course in another country or to find 'real-life' commercial applications for one's research, may open doors to new identities that are very readily taken on. Academics will respond in different ways to the presenting and changing landscapes; that much is obvious. But this is in turn to indicate that the structure-agency relationship takes a particular form for each individual academic; it is not 'given' in any sense. Both the possibilities for agency *and* for the structures are different, even for 'colleagues' in the same department at the same university.

Such differences and complexities at the micro-level are inevitable in 'the schizophrenic university' (Shore 2010), for the university itself is far from being a unitary organization. It faces in several directions, producing different spaces for different academic personas. But even then, individuals – with their differing research, teaching, administrative and outreach profiles – will feel the 'same' spaces alternatively opening and closing. It is as if those individuals were in different institutions, even though their rooms may be adjacent on the one corridor. The fine grain of the agency-structure and their inter-relationships in academic life has yet, I think, to be fully understood.

Resources for the journey

How is it that some individuals seem to thrive amid such academic transformation while others feel the need to make alternative arrangements? Some speak of a 'psychological contract' (Watson 2009; Cook and Daunton this volume) in which the individual comes to form an inward accommodation with the organizational circumstances in which they find themselves. As stated, this idea hardly goes far enough: instead, we should rather speak of a psycho/socio/ethico accommodation (admittedly awkward as such a construction may seem). But how such an accommodation, whatever it may be, is possible, and with whatever degree of identification (by the individual) with the newly unfolding 'mission' of the university, is an open matter.

Drawing on a tradition in German philosophy, Habermas (1984, 1987) writes of the 'lifeworld' that sustains individuals in social settings, especially when confronted with large instrumental forces set over against them. But this lifeworld is being constructed daily by each academic her or himself. How does she or he see themselves in the medium term? Are there others who see the (academic) world in a similar way? Are there external academics with whom one can form alliances? Are there networks that offer hospitality (cf. Derrida 2000) and emotional support? Are there even financial resources opening up that offer new prospects for realizing one's values and goals anew? Layers, boundaries, spaces, journeying: a language of travel beckons, but it is 'travel' without any clear destination; or even any kind of destination. Rocks, winds and currents all threaten; but perhaps some islands can be glimpsed for some respite; or perhaps a new wind or current can impart quite new impetus to the journey.

Delight can be found in small spaces, in the chance meeting walking across the campus or – perhaps more typically these days – in a warm note within an email. This is a form of hospitality, a greeting that offers a recognition and affirmation. Sources of conviviality and renewal are here. Derrida's (2000) cautionary notes about hospitality are all very well (Dufourmantelle 2000) – is there really any hospitality without conditions attached? – but these can surely be overdone. For in such small spaces, the potential generosity of academic life is recaptured and endorsed. If such graciousness has a hope of its return from the other, is that not a better form of life than the dominant instrumentalism that now abounds in the university?

This 'working life', then, is a complex of moments and movements, some of them experienced happily and others where ill-at-ease is a more apt description. Even timeframes vary for individuals. Some have more or less determinate rhythms, especially perhaps those who are focused on teaching. Others, more focused on research, find themselves having to respond immediately to tight deadlines while, at the same time, a paper being just started may – with a fair wind – see the light of day in an international journal in two to three years' time. Yet others intent on seizing the main chance, and exploiting opportunities for outreach and development, may straddle several timeframes and time-zones all at once, as they travel the world, even as they work in cyberspace from their desks.

These multiple time-zones, however, are far from equally distributed. 'Fast-time' crowds out 'slow-time' (courses are provided for speed-reading but not for deep, slow reading; deep understanding gives way to the processing of data; reports that are themselves the result of rapidly-conducted projects are fronted by excessively brief 'executive summaries') and long-term horizons are overtaken by short, urgent and even of-the-moment horizons. Time spent browsing in a library or even reading a book in one's room on the campus is seen as downtime, inefficient time, by a management mode intent on securing the maximum revenue return on its expensive real estate.

All these phenomena of speeded-up comprehension and understanding are, of course, made more stark by the onward march of interactive digital technologies, in the slide towards new forms of the university, now attracting such epithets as 'the borderless university' (Cunningham *et al.* 1998), the 'edgeless university' (Bradwell 2009) and the 'virtual university' (Cornford 2000; Ryan *et al.* 2000; Carswell 1998). The rhythms, and the time-space complexes of the university are changing utterly (Mason 1998, 1999). In the process, the humanities – which rather march to old-fashioned beats of slow-time, of time across centuries and even millennia – face difficulties in securing their survival.

For today's academic, this is a multimodal world (Kress and van Leuuwen 2001), where the modes of communication themselves are several and where individuals can choose from a palette of voices. Yes, academics know a lot; they are paid to do so; and they are ever more adept at communicating in different ways with multiple audiences; Habermassian frames of knowing and of communication may seem adequate here. But for today's academics, we need surely to summon up a Heideggerian (1927) concept of 'being'. Being is only sustainable if it is also 'being-possible', if it contains possibilities for its own authentic 'becoming' (and here Deleuze and Guattari's 1972 brilliant philosophy of 'becoming' amid 'multiplicities' beckons).

Structures of communication change profoundly. In the refurbishment of buildings, one of the spaces to be surrendered is that of the room at the end of the corridor that served as a meeting place for coffee, mid-morning or afternoon. Such space, after all, is unproductive. And, anyway, perhaps the academics themselves have been making less of it, intent as they are in producing yet another paper for the academic journals so as to bolster their publications lists. Convivial spaces vanish, as new spaces open up on the internet. New conversations spring up, even across global distances.

Accordingly, an old academic habitus is not sustainable these days (except for a very few, but even then the old reinvents itself: the philosophy don becomes a media-savvy public intellectual with his/her own website). At least, the academic habitus is now plural: there are many habituses emerging; and much is dependent on the resourcefulness of individuals and their imaginative and bargaining powers. Many, of course, feel relatively powerless.

Optimists and pessimists

The matter of power is a matter of brutal fact, in a way; there are real asymmetries of power in academic life. For all the talk of 'flat' structures, for many – especially for the more junior staff – the structures of academic life seem ever more monolithic, ever more hierarchical. But yet, in all of this, there are the pessimists and the optimists. The pessimism and optimism in question is not a matter of metaphysical thinking about the future of 'the university' but is a matter of personal hope. Here, personal temperament comes into play as well as absolute structure. Some can glimpse ways forward, a new route, that with a fair wind may bring a good landfall; others sense only rocks and tempests and so retreat.

Pessimism is not lightly to be dismissed as a purely negative stance. It harbours, of course, two components: a factual component and a value component. On the factual side, it may contain – indeed, it probably does contain – a rugged realism. Indeed, it starts from here, from a serious understanding of the deep structures of the world. And it sets that understanding against a horizon of values. So informed, it doesn't much like what it sees. From its perspective, the world is nasty and brutish and very short (for everything has a short life in this milieu). Given the features of academic life identified here, and given a perspective informed, say, by values of care, concern for the other, criticality, open dialogue, deep understanding, outspokenness, integrity and authenticity and responsibility, it is understandable that pessimism will arise.

This is a pessimism that has an obvious legitimacy. It is a form of critical realism (Bhaskar 2002), albeit only one form. It is thoroughly realist, being sensitive to and comprehending of the deep structures that are shaping the new academic order. And it is critical of them. It believes that the academic order could have been other than it is. However, it is inclined to leave matters there. It is perhaps over-sensitive to the deep structures of the age. And it perhaps is not so critical of them as it imagines itself to be. Deep in its bones, it actually believes that there is no alternative, even though it is deeply unhappy with the present reshaping of the university.

Note the character of our pessimist's beliefs. His or her belief that there is no alternative is, of course, an empirical belief. It considers that the forces of neoliberalism, of instrumental management, of audit, of consumerism and of the knowledge economy are so overwhelming that there is little or no prospect of this empirical state of affairs being overturned. This belief is not short on conceptual alternatives. On the contrary, the pessimism arises precisely out of a disjunction between its inner ideas of the university and the perceived actual character of academic life and the possibilities that it apparently affords. This pessimism is rich in conceptual alternatives. Its difficulty is that it sees no prospect of them being realized, given the structure of the conditions of, and the forces at work that are shaping, the contemporary university.

The optimist has a different outlook. The optimist starts from a belief not that things will go well in the world but that things *could* go well in the world. Being of this disposition, the optimist looks for spaces that afford a glimpse of positive possibilities. Perhaps the optimist has his or her gaze diverted from the character of the 'real world', being intent on ushering in a new order. For those of this more positive disposition, there *is* an alternative, not only as an idea but as a matter of practical possibility. The university could be other than it is, not just conceptually but in its practices and in its institutional form.

Is optimism a kind of false consciousness, an ideological formation that in effect legitimizes the status quo? Not necessarily at all. An optimism of this persuasion may have its feet firmly on the ground. It may be just as 'realist' as our pessimist's stance. It may well understand the pernicious aspects of the contemporary university and have a clear perception of the forces at work in bringing about the university's reshaping.

But, in being of an optimistic persuasion, it has two strong features that are noteworthy here. First, as stated, it actively seeks out moments, spaces and opportunities that lend themselves to more progressive forms of the university. And secondly, it works to put them into practice. On the old principle that oak trees grow from acorns, this optimism works – in the first place – in the interstices of academic life. At every level of the university, in convivial collegial relationships, in curricula construction, in the pedagogical relationship, in the forming of teaching strategies and of research strategies, and in a myriad of other ways, micro-spaces and even not so micro-spaces, are seized in which different ideas of the university might be subtly advanced and given the makings of an institutional form.

This is still a critical realism in action but it is a critical realism with a smile on its face; a critical realism that believes that matters could go better. It is still realist, since it takes serious account of the world as it is; and it is still critical, in forming its evaluations of the world. But now it is seized with a sense of the possibilities of agency, and of responsible action. The world is not just out-there but is now also in-here. For those of this disposition, the concept of responsibility has existential force, prompting an openness to glimpsing spaces for new positive possibilities and identifying and feeling an obligation to act, so as to realize those positive possibilities, howsoever small they may be.

There may well be a suspicion that such optimists are liable to fall prey to fanciful ideas. There is no sure boundary between a due optimism and an undue optimism, after all. An optimistic outlook may lead to a 'castles-in-the-air' syndrome. Illusions rather than grounded projects are likely to result from this form of optimism. A due optimism will therefore be willing to bring its ideas for the renewal of the university before a tribunal comprised both of fact and value, both of understandings about the world and of principles for well-being. In reconceiving the university and its practices, imagination is a necessary but not a sufficient condition of such a project. Realism, critique and a worked-out value position are also necessary: are the imagined possibilities *really* feasible? The imaginative reconstruction of the university is necessarily a hard-headed enterprise, intellectually and practically (Barnett 2013).

Concluding remarks

As stated, in taking up a stance in the contemporary university, both pessimism and optimism are options. It is understandable if there is much pessimism about the university as a workplace; indeed, that is part of the problem, for the university has become a place of work rather than of vocation. Now, those involved in the activities of universities are governed by rules and regulations beyond themselves, rather than those activities being organically connected to virtues inherent in a form of life (of an academic community). Pessimism, it may seem, has to carry the day. After all, under such conditions, pessimism is understandable, likely and justifiable. Pessimism is simply *natural*.

However, it is the optimists who have to take the prizes. For they carry within themselves a sense that things can go forward, that the university can yet be reborn and still bear honourably the title of 'university'. They are the poets of the university, imaginatively creating new forms and new spaces that yet live out the emancipatory and humane hopes buried deep in the idea of the university.

Certainly, as we have seen, optimism on campus may take various forms, being more or less realistic, and more or less illusory, and more or less ideological. Accordingly, optimism, especially imaginative optimism, has to be put to work, being tested against the severest criteria of feasibility, value principles and deep realism. In this evaluation of such optimism and its imaginative possibilities, we see real 'academic work' taking place, real hard work that may just yet see a 'new' university arise, that is even metaphysical in its association with the largest themes of life, culture, sociality and well-being. It is just possible, accordingly, that a due optimism may emerge.

Note

This chapter is based on a talk given at the Working Lives (WL) Seminar, held at the University of Wales, Newport on 19 November 2010, and the WL Symposium, CETL conference, University of Oxford, 4–6 April 2011.

Notes on Contributors

Professor Sandra Acker is Professor Emerita in the Department of Humanities, Social Sciences and Social Justice Education, University of Toronto, Canada.

Dr Trevor Austin is a Senior Teaching Fellow at the Hull York Medical School. He also holds a Lectureship in Medical Education at Cardiff University, where he obtained his Doctorate in 2011.

Dr Eimear Barrett is a Public Health Intelligence Officer at the Centre of Excellence for Public Health in Northern Ireland and also coordinates the Northern Ireland Public Health Research Network.

Professor Ronald Barnett is Emeritus Professor of Higher Education and Consultant in the Faculty of Policy and Society at the Institute of Education's Department of International and Lifelong Education, Lodnon. His publications and contributions to the understanding of higher education systems are acknowledged worldwide.

Maria Bertani Tress, originally from Mexico, is currently a Doctoral Student in Education at the University of Leeds, exploring Latin American academics' experiences in UK higher education.

Professor Rebecca Boden is Professor of Critical Management at the University of Roehampton, London, where she is currently involved in a major European Union project on 'Universities in the Knowledge Economy'.

Dr Mary Carter is an Academic Associate at the School of Education, Cardiff Metropolitan University, where she obtained her Doctorate in 2013.

Christine Chapman, AM was first elected to the National Assembly for Wales as Assembly Member for the Cynon Valley in 1999, and has twice served as a Deputy Minister. She currently chairs the Assembly's Communities, Equalities and Local Government Committee, and the Women and Democracy Group.

Dr Ming Cheng is a Lecturer at the Learning and Teaching Centre at the University of Glasgow. She obtained her Doctorate at the University of Bristol in 2008.

Caryn Cook is a Senior Lecturer at the University of South Wales (Newport), in the Business School. Her research interests are employee relations and the field of international human resources management.

Dr Paul Conway is a Senior Lecturer in the School of Education, University College Cork, and represents Ireland at the World Educational Research Association (WERA).

Lyn Daunton is a Principal Lecturer and Deputy Head of the Glamorgan Business School, and a member of the Working Lives team.

Philippa Dixey is a former Lecturer in Psychology and Sociology in further education colleges and community education.

Nigel Ecclesfield is Manager for Technology, Research and Evaluation at the Learning and Skills Improvement Service of JISC, and a Visiting Research Fellow at Coventry University.

Dr Seán Farren is Visiting Professor at the School of Education, University of Ulster, and a former Government Minister for Higher Education in the Northern Ireland Executive.

Dr Alan Floyd is Associate Professor in Educational Leadership and Management at the University of Reading, with particular interests in the role of the 'middle manager' in higher education, the subject of his Doctorate.

Fred Garnett is a visiting research associate at the London Knowledge Lab and Theme Leader for the Digital Literacies TLRP-TEL programme.

Dr Lynne Gornall is Leader of the Working Lives research team and has held academic and interdisciplinary leadership posts in two higher education insitutions in England and Wales.

Dr Martin Gough's career has combined academic development with academic roles. He is currently Lecturer in Education Studies at De Montfort University, UK, and Convenor for the Society for Research into Higher Education (SRHE) Postgraduate Issues Network.

Lynette ('Lyn') Harbottle was Lecturer in Health and Social Care in the FE sector, following several years working as a psychiatric nurse. She was undertaking doctoral research at Cardiff University's School of Social Sciences where she was an Associate Lecturer. Sadly, Lynette died in November 2013 as this book was in press.

Dr Eric Harrison is a Senior Research Fellow in the Centre for Comparative Social Surveys at City University London, and a Fellow of the Higher Education Academy.

Dr Lea Henriksson is Adjunct Professor, with a double degree in sociology and social policy, and a Senior Researcher at the Finnish Institute of Occupational Health.

Johanna Hokka is a Doctoral Student in Sociology and also Secretary for the Research Centre for Knowledge, Science, Technology and Innovation Studies (TaSTI) at the University of Tampere, Finland.

Dr Alison Hudson is a Senior Lecturer in Education and Research and Programme Director for the MEd in the School of Education, Social Work and Community Education, University of Dundee.

Dr Jan Huyton is a Senior Lecturer and Personal Development Planning (PDP)/Personal Tutoring Co-ordinator at Cardiff School of Education, Cardiff Metropolitan University.

Professor Martin Jephcote is Deputy Director of the University of Cardiff School of Social Sciences, with particular interests in post-16 further education.

Professor Eleri Jones is a Professor and Associate Dean (Research) at Cardiff Metropolitan University, and Director of the Professional Doctorate programme.

Dr Virve Kallioniemi-Chambers is a Research Fellow in the School of Education at the University of Tampere, Finland.

Dr Rod Kelly is Head of Accounting and Financial Markets at the University of Derby, with a background in local government as well as higher education.

Judith Larsen teaches part time on the PGCE (PCET) programmes at Cardiff University, which prepare teachers for the further education sector. Previously she was a college teacher of history and sociology.

Professor Janet Laugharne is a Professor Emerita of Language in Education. Janet is on the Executive of the Welsh Education Research Network (WERN), and was formerly Director of Research in the Cardiff School of Education.

Professor Robert Mears is Professor of Sociology and Dean of the School of Society, Enterprise and Environment at Bath Spa University, and a former Chair of the British Sociological Association (BSA).

Dr Mary Goretti Nakabugo is Senior Lecturer in Higher Education Studies and Coordinator of the PhD in the Higher Education Cohort Programme at the University of KwaZulu-Natal (UKZN), South Africa.

Jon Nixon has held chairs at four UK universities and currently holds a senior research fellowship at the Hong Kong Institute of Education. He is widely published, with three recent new books on higher education.

Dr Carol O'Byrne is a Lecturer at the Waterford Institute of Technology, and completed doctoral studies in higher education at the University of Sheffield in 2009.

Dr Sarah-Jane Richards is currently a solicitor at Secure Law, Cardiff, and Assistant Coroner for Bridgend, Glamorgan Valleys and Powys. For many years, she led university-based clinical research teams.

Dr Susy Rogers is an independent tutor in maths and sciences. Her recent Doctorate at the University of Glamorgan explored the pedagogy of online learning and teaching.

Dr Andrew Rothwell is Research Associate in the School of Business and Economics at Loughborough University, with interests in academic professional development.

Frances Rothwell is a Senior Lecturer in Business Education at the School of Education, Nottingham Trent University, with interests in the challenges facing part-time academics in further and higher education.

Dr Jane Salisbury is the Course Director for the PGCE (PCET) teacher education programmes in the School of Social Sciences at Cardiff University.

Dr Machi Sato is Associate Professor, Research Institute for Higher Education, Hiroshima University, Japan. She gained her Doctorate from the University of Oxford in 2012.

Professor Marilyn Strathern, DBE, is now Professor Emerita and a distinguished anthropologist with a worldwide reputation for scholarly writing as well as policy contributions to government committees. She has held chairs in social anthropology, alongside departmental leadership roles, at the University of Cambridge and the University of Manchester. Marilyn is a Fellow of the British Academy.

Dr Brychan Thomas is a Doctoral Supervisor at the University of Gloucester Business School and Visiting Professor of the University of South Wales Business School.

Val Walsh is a poet and educationalist based in Liverpool. She was formerly a Senior Lecturer in Higher Education and has co-edited three collections of writing on women's studies.

Dr Matthew Waring is a Senior Lecturer in the Cardiff School of Management, Cardiff Metropolitan University, specializing in strategic human resources management, the subject of his recent Doctorate.

Dr Michelle Webber is Associate Professor in the Department of Sociology at Brock University, Canada, where she is also Director of the MA in Critical Sociology.

Dr Oili-Helena Ylijoki is Adjunct Professor of Social Psychology and Academy Research Fellow at the Centre for Knowledge, Science, Technology and Innovation Studies (TaSTI) at the School of Social Sciences and Humanities, University of Tampere, Finland.

Working Lives team

The Working Lives group involves a collaboration between the Universities of Glamorgan, Cardiff and Newport, UK, and the (five) team members have been highly proactive in forming collegial networks around these interests, as well as in disseminating and developing the research. Formed in 2007 following research interests and a successful funding bid to the ESRC/Welsh Education Research Network (WERN), there are entries for members of the Working Lives team under Brychan Thomas, Jane Salisbury, Lyn Daunton, Lynne Gornall and Caryn Cook.

Bibliography

Note: author entries are shown with latest date **first**

Abrahamson, E and Freedman, D H (2006) *A perfect mess: the hidden benefits of disorder – how crammed closets, cluttered offices and on-the-fly planning make the world a better place.* London: Weidenfeld & Nicolson.

Acker, S Webber, M and Smyth, E (2012) 'Tenure troubles and equity matters in Canadian academe', *British Journal of Sociology of Education*, 33 (5), pp.743–761.

Acker, S and Webber, M (2006) 'Women working in academe: approach with care'. In C Skelton B Francis and L Smulyan (eds) *Handbook on gender and education.* London: Sage, pp.483–496.

Acker, S and Armenti, C (2004) 'Sleepless in academia', *Gender and Education*, 16 (1), pp.3–24.

Acker, S and Feuerverger, G (1996) 'Doing good and feeling bad: the work of women university teachers', *Cambridge Journal of Education*, 26 (3), pp.17–18.

Ackers, H L and Oliver, E A (2007) 'From Flexicurity to Flexsequality? The impact of the fixed–term contract provisions on employment in science research', *International Studies of Management and Organization*, 37 (1), pp.53–79.

Ackroyd, S, Kirkpatrick, I and Walker, R M (2007) 'Public management reform in the UK and its consequences for professional organization: A comparative analysis', *Public Administration*, 85 (1), pp.9–26.

Adam, B (1995) *Timewatch.* Cambridge: Polity Press.

Adelman, C (ed) (1981) *Uttering, muttering: collecting, using and reporting talk for social and educational research.* London: McIntyre.

Afonso, A (2004) 'New graphics for old stores: representations of local memories through drawings', in S Pink, L Kurti and A Alfonso (eds) *Working images.* London: Routledge, pp.72–89.

Agasisti, T, Catalano, G, Landoni, P and Verganti, R (2012) 'Evaluating the performance of academic departments: an analysis of research-related output efficiency', *Research Evaluation*, 21, pp.2–14.

AGCAS (2012) *What do graduates do?* London: Association of Graduate Careers Advisory Services/Higher Education Careers Service Unit.

Agre, P (2002) 'Infrastructure and institutional change in the networked university'. In W H Dutton and B Loader (eds) *Digital academe: the new media and institutions of higher education and learning.* London: Routledge.

Ainsworth, I (2002) *Higher education in a re-constituted state: the experience of Wales.* Doctoral thesis. Cardiff: Cardiff University of Social Sciences.

Aisenberg, N and Harrington, M (1988) *Women of academe: outsiders in the sacred grove.* Amherst, MA: University of Massachusetts Press.

Albion, C (2012) 'Down the rabbit hole – "curiouser and curiouser": using autoethnography as a mode to writing to re-call, re-tell and reveal bodily embodiment as self-reflexive inquiry', *Journal of Organisation Ethnography*, 1 (1), pp.62–71.

Allegretto, S A, Corcoran, S P and Mishel, L (2004) *How does teacher pay compare? methodological challenges and answers*. Washington, DC: Economic Policy Institute.

Allen-Collinson, J (2006) 'Just 'non-academics'?: research administrators and contested occupational identity', *Work, Employment & Society*, 20 (2) pp.267–288.

Altbach, P G and Musselin, C (2008) 'The worst academic careers – world wide', *Inside Higher Education*, September.

Altbach, P G (1996) *The international academic profession: portraits from fourteen countries*. Princeton, NJ: Carnegie Foundation for the Advancement of Teaching.

Ambler, T and Barrow, S (1996) 'The employer brand', *The Journal of Brand Management*, 4, pp.185–206.

Amoah, M (2007) '100 voices': the state of the HE nation. In D watson and M Amoah (eds) *The Dearing Report Ten years on*. London: Bedford Way Papers.

Anderson, G (2008) 'Mapping academic resistance in the managerial university', *Organization*, 15 (2), pp.251–270.

Anderson, L (2006) 'Analytic auto-ethnography', *Journal of Contemporary Ethnography*, 35 (4), pp.373–395.

Andrusyszyn, M, Iwasiw, C and Goldenberg, D (1999) 'Computer conferencing in graduate nursing education: perceptions of students and faculty', *The Journal of Continuing Education in Nursing*, 30 (6), pp.272–278.

Archer, L (2008) 'The new neoliberal subjects? Young/er academics' constructions of professional identity', *Journal of Education Policy*, 23 (2), pp.265–285.

Archer, L (2002) *Higher education and social class: Issues of inclusion and exclusion*. London: RoutledgeFalmer.

Archer, M S (2007) *Making our way through the world: human reflexivity and social mobility*. Cambridge: Cambridge University Press.

Archer, M S (2003) *Structure, agency and the internal conversation*. Cambridge: Cambridge University Press.

Archer, M S (2000) *Being human: the problem of agency*. Cambridge: Cambridge University Press.

Archer, M S (1995) *Realist social theory: the morphogenetic approach*. Cambridge: Cambridge University Press.

Argyris, C P (1960) *Understanding organizational behaviour*. Homewood, IL: Dorsey Press.

Arimoto, A (2005) *Academic profession and faculty development in USA and Japan*. Tokyo: Toshindo Publishing.

Arimoto, A (ed) (2004) *Study of the institutionalization of faculty development part 1: report of the nationwide survey on university presidents in 2003*. Hiroshima, Japan: Research Institute for Higher Education Hiroshima University.

Armellini, A. and Aiyegbayo, O (2010) 'Learning design and assessment with E–tivities', *British Journal of Educational Technology*, 41 (6), pp.922–935.

Armellini, A and Jones, S (2008) 'Carpe diem: seizing each day to foster change in e-learning design', *Reflecting Education*, 4 (1), pp.17–29.

Armstrong, M (2006) *A handbook of human resource management* (10th edition). London: Kogan Page.

Ashforth, B and Humphrey, R (1993) 'Emotional labour in service roles: the influence of identity', *Academy of Management Review*, 18 (1), pp.88–115.

Atkinson, P and Delamont, S (eds) (2005) *Narrative methods*. London: Sage.

Atkinson, P and Coffey, A (1997) 'Analysing documentary realities', in D Silverman (ed.) *Qualitative research: theory, method, and practice*. Thousand Oaks, CA: Sage, pp.45–62.

Atkinson, P, Davies, B and Delamont, S (eds) (1995) *Discourse and reproduction: essays in honor of Basil Bernstein*. Cresskill, NJ: Hampton Press.

Auster, C (1996) *Sociology of work: concepts and cases*. Thousand Oaks, CA: Pine Forge Press.

Austin, T (2011) 'Transition, perspectives and strategies: the process of becoming a teacher'. Unpublished Ed.D thesis, Cardiff University.

Avis, J, Kendell, A and Bathmaker, A-M (2003) 'The politics of care – emotional labour and trainee FE teachers', paper presented at the British Educational Research Association annual conference, Heriot Watt University, Edinburgh, 11–13 September.

Avolio, B J, Bass, B M and Jung, D I (1999) 'Re-examining the components of transactional and transformational leadership using the Multifactor Leadership Questionnaire', *Journal of Occupational and Organizational Psychology*, 72, pp.441–462.

Baker, B, Brown, B and Fazey, J (2006) 'Individualization in the widening participation debate', *London Review of Education*, 4 (2), pp.169–182.

Bakker, A, Demerouti, E and Verbeke, W (2004) 'Using the job demands resources model to predict burnout and performance', *Human Resources Management*, 43, pp.83–104.

Ball, S and Junemann, C (2012) *Networks, new governance and education*. Bristol: Polity Press.

Ball, S (2008a) *The education debate*. Bristol: The Policy Press.

Ball, S (2008b) 'Performativity, privatization, professionals and the state', In B Cunningham (ed.) *Exploring professionalism*. London: Institute of Education.

Ball, S (2007) *Education Plc: understanding private sector participation in public sector education*. Abingdon: Routledge.

Ball, S (2005) 'Education reform as social barbarism: economism and the end of authenticity', *Scottish Educational Review*, 37 (1), pp.4–16.

Ball, S (2003) 'The teacher's soul and the terrors of performativity', *Journal of Education Policy*, 18 (2), pp.215–228.

Ball, S (2000) 'Performativities and fabrications in the education economy: towards the performative society', *Australian Educational Researcher*, 27 (2), pp.21–24.

Ball, S (1994) *Education reform: a critical and post–structural approach*. Buckingham: Open University Press.

Banwell, L, Ray, K, and Coulson (2004) 'Providing access to electronic information resources in further education', *British Journal of Educational Technology*, 35 (5), pp.607–616.

Baptiste, N R (2007) 'Tightening the link between employee wellbeing at work and performance, a new dimension for HRM', *Management Decision*, 46 (2), pp.284–309.

Barber, M, Donnelly, K and Rizvi, S (2013) *An avalanche is coming: higher education and the revolution ahead*. London: Institute for Public Policy Research (IPPR).

Barbezet, D A (1987) 'Salary differentials by sex in the academic labour market', *Journal of Human Resources*, 22 (3), pp.422–428.

Barnett, R (2013) *Imagining the university*. Abingdon: Routledge.

Barnett, R (ed) (2012) *The future university: ideas and possibilities*. New York: Routledge.

Barnett, R (2011a) 'The coming of the ecological university', *Oxford Review of Education*, 37 (4), pp.439–455.

Barnett, R (2011b) *Being a university*. Abingdon: Routledge

Barnett, R (2010) 'Academic working lives', concluding keynote presentation at the Working Lives in Further and Higher Education Seminar, University of Wales, Newport, 8 October.

Barnett, R (2008) 'Critical professionalism in an age of supercomplexity', In B Cunningham (ed) *Exploring professionalism*. London: Institute of Education.

Barnett, R and Di Napoli, R (eds) (2008) *Changing identities in higher education: voicing perspectives*. Abingdon: Routledge.

Barnett, R (2003) *Beyond all reason: living with ideology in the university*. Buckingham: SRHE/Open University Press.

Barnett, R (2000) *Realising the university in an age of supercomplexity*. Buckingham: Open University Press.

Barnett, R (1993) 'The idea of academic administration', *Journal of Philosophy of Education*, 27 (2), pp.79–92.

Barney, J B (1991) 'Firm resources and sustained competitive advantage', *Journal of Management*, 17 (1), pp.99–120.

Barry, B, Berg, E and Chandler, J (2006) 'Academic shape shifting: gender, management and identities in Sweden and England', *Organization*, 13 (2), pp.275–298.

Barton, J (2008) 'The UK academic system: hierarchy, students, grants, fellowships and all that', School of Life Sciences, University of Dundee.

Bartunek, J M, Crosta, T E, Dame, R F and LeLacheur, D F (2000) 'Managers and project leaders conducting their own action research interventions', in R T Golembiewski (ed.) *Handbook of organizational consultation*. New York: Marcel Dekker, pp.59–70.

Baruch, Y and Hall, D T (2004) 'The academic career: A model for future careers in other sectors?' *Journal of Vocational Behaviour*, 64, pp.241–262.

Bass, B M and Avolio, B J (1997) *Full range leadership development: manual for the Multifactor Leadership Questionnaire*, Palo Alto, CA: Mind Garden.

Bauman, Z (2005) *Liquid life*. Cambridge: Polity Press.

Bauman, Z (2000) *Liquid modernity*. Cambridge: Polity Press.

Baume, D (2002) 'Scholarship, academic development and the future', *International Journal for Academic Development*, 7 (2), pp.109–111.

Bayer, A E and Astin, H S (1968) 'Sex differences in academic rank and salary amongst science doctorates in teaching', *Journal of Human Resources*, 2 (2), pp.191–200.

Beard, K M and Edwards, J R (1995) 'Employees at risk: contingent work and the psychological experience of contingent workers', in C L Cooper and D M Rousseau (eds) (2005) *Trends in organizational behaviour*. Hoboken, NJ: John Wiley, pp.109–126.

Becher, T and Trowler, P (2001) *Academic tribes and territories* (2nd edition). Buckingham: SRHE/Open University Press.

Becher, T (1994) 'The significance of disciplinary differences', *Studies in Higher Education*, 19 pp.151–161.

Becher, T (1989) *Academic tribes and territories*. Buckingham: Open University Press.

Beck, J and Young, M (2005) 'The assault on the professions and the restructuring of academic and professional identities: a Bersteinian analysis', *British Journal of Sociology of Education*, 26 (2), pp.183–197.

Beck, J (2002) 'The sacred and the profane in recent struggles to promote official pedagogic identities', *British Journal of Sociology of Education*, 23 (4), pp.617–625.

Beck, U and Beck-Gernsheim, E (2002) *Individualization: institutionalized individualism and its social and political consequences*. London: Sage.

Beck, J (1999) 'Makeover or takeover? The strange death of educational autonomy in neo-liberal England', *British Journal of Sociology of Education*, 20 (2), pp.223–238.

BECTA (2006) *The BECTA review 2006: Evidence on the progress of ICT in education*, British Educational Technology Association, available at: http://dera.ioe.ac.uk/1427/1/becta_2006_bectareview_report.pdf, accessed 7 June 2011.

Beetham, H, Jones, S and Gornall, L (2001) *Career development of learning technology staff: scoping study final report for the JISC JCALT*. Bristol: University of Plymouth, University of Bristol.

Bekhradnia, B and Bailey, N (2009) *Demand for higher education to 2029*. Higher Education Policy Institute report. Oxford: Hepi.

Bellard, E (2005) 'Information literacy needs of non-traditional graduate students in social work', *Research Strategies*, 20 (4), pp.494–505.

Bellas, M (1999) 'Emotional labor in academia: the case of professors', *Annals of Political and Social Science*, 561 pp.96–110.

Berg, E, Barry, J and Chandler, J (2004) 'The new public management and higher education: a human cost?' in M Dent, J Chandler and J Barry, *Questioning the new public management*. Aldershot: Ashgate Publishing.

Berge, Z L and Collins, M P (2000) 'Perceptions of e–moderators about their roles and functions in moderating electronic mailing lists', *Distance Education: An International Journal*, 21(1), pp.81–100.

Berge, Z L (1997) 'Characteristics of on-line teaching in post-secondary, formal education', *Educational Technology*, 37(3), pp.35–47.

Berger, P L and Luckmann, T (1976) *The social construction of reality*. Harmondsworth: Penguin.

Berker, T (2006) *Domestication of media and technology*. Maidenhead: Open University Press.

Berlach, R G (2011) 'The Cyclical Integration Model as a way of managing major educational change', *Education Research International*, article ID 963237, http://downloads.hindawi.com/journals/edu/2011/963237.pdf, accessed 22 July 2011.

Bernstein, B (2000) *Pedagogy, symbolic control and identity: theory, research, critique* (revised edition). Lanham: Bowman & Littlefield.

Bernstein, B (1997) 'Class and pedagogies: visible and invisible', in A H Halsey, H Lauder, P Brown and A S Wells (eds) *Education for economic survival*. London: Routledge, pp.117–143.

Bernstein, B (1996) *Pedagogy, symbolic control and identity: theory, research, critique*. London: Taylor & Francis.

Berthiaume, D (2007) *Une étude empirique du savoir pédagogique disciplinaire des professeur-e-s d'université*. Paper presented at the 24ème Congrès de l'Association Internationale de Pédagogie Universitaire, 16–18 May, Montréal, Canada.

Bhaskar, R (2002) *From science to emancipation*. New Delhi: Sage.

Biesta, G (2005) 'The role of educational ideals in teachers' professional work'. Paper presented at C–TRIP Seminar 1: Identity, agency and policy in teachers' professional lives. King's College London, 20 January.

Biggs, J and Tang, C (2011) *Teaching for quality learning at university* (4th edition). New York: Open University Press.

Birdwell, J, Grist, M and Margo, J (2011) *The forgotten half*. A Demos and Private Equity Foundation Report. London: Demos.

Bissett, A (2009) 'Academics as entrepreneurs: the changing nature of academic professionalism', In IPED (eds) *Academic futures*. Newcastle: Cambridge Scholars Publishing, pp.111–126.

Blackaby, D, Booth, A and Frank, J (2005) 'Outside offers and the pay gap: empirical evidence from the UK academic labour market', *The Economic Journal*, 155, pp.81–107.

Blackmore, P and Kandiko, C B (2011) 'Motivation in academic life: a prestige economy', *Research in post-compulsory education*, 16 (4), pp.399–411.

Blackmore, P and Blackwell, R (2006) 'Strategic leadership in academic development', *Studies in Higher Education*, 31 (3), pp.373–387.

Blanton, J E, Watson, H J and Moody, J (1992) 'Toward a better understanding of information technology organisations: a comparative case study', *MIS Quarterly*, 16 (4), pp.531–555.

Bloomer, M and Hodkinson, P (2000) 'Learning careers: continuity and change in young people's dispositions to learning', *British Education Research Journal*, 26 (5), pp. 583–597.

Blunkett, D (2000) 'Greenwich speech'. London: DfEE, http://cms1.gre.ac.uk/dfee/, accessed 26 April 2012.

Bocock, J (1994) 'Curriculum change and professional identity: the role of the university lecturer'. In J Bocock and D Watson (eds) *Managing the university curriculum: making common cause*. Buckingham: SRHE/Open University Press, pp.116–126.

Boden, R and Epstein, D (2011) 'A flat earth society? Imagining academic freedom', *Sociological Review*, 59 (3), pp.476–495.

Boden, R and Epstein, D (2006) 'Managing the research imagination', *Globalisation and Research in Higher Education, Globalisation, Societies and Education*, 4 (2), pp.223–236.

Bolden, R, Gosling, J, O'Brien, A, Peters, K, Ryan, M and Haslam, A (2012) *Academic leadership: changing conceptions, identities and experiences in UK higher education – final report*. London: Leadership Foundation for Higher Education.

Bolden, R, Petrov, G and Gosling, J (2008) *Developing collective leadership in higher education – final report*. London, Leadership Foundation for Higher Education.

Bolton, S, Muzio, D and Boyd-Quin, C (2011) 'Making sense of modern medical careers: the case of the UK's National Health Service', *Sociology*, 45 (4), pp.682–699.

Bonanno, G A (2004) 'Loss, trauma, and human resilience: have we underestimated the human capacity to thrive after extremely aversive events?' *American Psychologist*, 59, pp.20–28.

Boonstra, J J and Bennebroek Gravenhorst, K M (1998) 'Power dynamics and organizational change: a comparison of perspectives', *European Journal of Work and Organizational Psychology*, 7 (2), pp.97–120.

Boston Women's Health Collective (1973) *Our bodies ourselves*. Boston, MA: Simon & Schuster.

Bottery, M (2000) *Education, policy and ethics*. New York: Continuum.

Bottery, M (1996) 'The challenge to professionals from the new public management', *Oxford Review of Education*, 22, pp.179–197.

Bourdieu, P (2003) 'Participant objectivation', *Journal of the Royal Anthropological Institute*, 9 (2) pp.281–291.

Bourdieu, P (1992) 'A radical doubt', in P Bourdieu and L J D Wacquant, *An invitation to reflexive sociology*. Cambridge: Polity Press.

Bourdieu, P and Wacquant, L (1992) *An invitation to reflexive sociology*. Oxford: Polity Press.

Bourdieu, P (1986) 'The forms of capital', in J G Richardson (ed.) *Handbook of theory and research for the sociology of education*. New York: Greenwood Press, p.241.

Boxall, P and Macky, K (2009) 'Research and theory on high-performance work systems: progressing the high-involvement stream', *Human Resource Management Journal*, 19 (1), pp.3–23.

Boyd, P and Smith, C (2010) 'Becoming an academic: the reconstruction of identity by recently appointed lecturers in nursing, midwifery and the allied health professions', paper presented at the Academic Identities Conference, Strathclyde University, Glasgow, 16–18 June.

Boyers, J (1988) *Interactive video in industry and education: a study commissioned by industrialists*. London: National Interactive Video Centre.

Boyle, D and Wambach, K (2001) 'Interaction in graduate nursing web-based instruction', *Journal of Professional Nursing*, 17 pp.128–134.

Boyle, G (2006) 'Pay peanuts get monkeys? Evidence from Academia', *The B.E. Journal of Economic Analysis and Policy*, 8 (1), pp.art.21.

Bradley, S, Crawford, K, Cope, S and Rothwell, A (2008) 'CPD: Who is it for, what is it for, why bother?' SEDA 2008 conference, 'Changing educational development: whose values? whose agendas? whose future?' Aston Business School Conference Centre, Birmingham, 18–19 November.

Bradshaw, A (2008) 'How to enhance wellbeing at work: six positive evidence–based interventions', http://www.quowl.co.uk.qowl_articles.html.

Bradwell, P (2009) *The edgeless university*. London: Demos and JISC.

Bransford, J D and Schwartz, D L (1999) 'Rethinking transfer: a simple proposal with multiple implications'. In A Iran-Nejad, A and P D Pearson (eds) *Review of Research in Education*, 24, pp.61–100. Washington, DC: American Educational Research Association.

Braverman, H (1998 [1974]) *Labour and monopoly capital*. New York: Monthly Review Press.

Brooks, S and ap Gareth, O (2013) *Welsh Power Repair Women in Public Life*. Wales: Electoral Reform Society, March 2013.

Brown, J (2012) 'Public-sector salary cuts "will widen pay gap between men and women"', *The Independent*, 26 March.

Brown, P and Hesketh, A (2004) *The mismanagement of talent: employability and jobs in the knowledge economy*. Oxford: Oxford University Press.

Brown, P and Lauder, H (2003) *Education for economic survival: from Fordism to postFordism*. London: Routledge.

Brown, P, Green, A and Lauder, H (2001) *High skills – globalisation, competitiveness and skill formation*. Oxford: Oxford University Press.

Brown, R (2013) *Everything for sale: the marketization of UK higher education*. London: Routledge/SRHE.

Brown, R (2004) *Quality assurance in higher education, the uk experience since 1992*. London: Taylor & Francis.

Browne, J (2010) 'Securing a sustainable future for higher education', *An Independent Review of Higher Education Funding and Student Finance*, 12 October, www.independent.gov.uk/browne–report.

Browne, T and Beetham, H (2009) *The positioning of educational technologists in enhancing the student experience*. Report funded by the Higher Education Academy under their Call4: Enhancing Learning and Teaching through the use of Technology. York: HEA.

Bruner, J (2004) 'Life as a narrative', *Social Research*, 71 (3), pp.691–710.

Bryman, A (2009) *Effective leadership in higher education – final report*. London: Leadership Foundation for Higher Education.

Bryman, A (2008) *Social research methods*. Oxford: Oxford University Press.

Burke, D L (1988) *A new academic marketplace*. New York: Greenwood Press.

Burke, P J and Stets, J E (2009) *Identity theory*. Oxford: Oxford University Press.

Burrage, R (ed) (2010) *Martin Trow – twentieth century higher education: elite to mass to universal*. New York: Johns Hopkins University Press.

Burton, G (2008) 'The open scholar', http://www.academicevolution.com/2009/08/the-open–scholar.html, accessed 20 February 2013.

Butterwick, S and Dawson, J (2005) 'Undone business: examining the production of academic labour', *Women's Studies International Forum*, 28, pp.51–65.

CAUT (Canadian Association of University Teachers) (2011) 'The persistent gap: understanding male–female salary differentials amongst Canadian academic staff', *CAUT Education Review*, 5.

Cannon, R J (2004) *Organisation and Assessment in the e-learning environment: a case study of innovation*. Doctor of Education thesis (unpublished). School of Social Sciences, Cardiff University.

Caproni, P (1997) 'Work/life balance: you can't get there from here', *The Journal of Applied Behavioural Science*, 1(33), p.46–56.

Carew, A L, Lefoe, G, Bell, M and Armour, L (2008) 'Elastic practice in academic developers', *International Journal for Academic Development*, 13 (1), pp.51–66.

Carr, D (2006) 'Professional and personal values and virtues in education and teaching', *Oxford Review of Education*, 32 (2), pp.171–183.

Carr, D (2000) *Professionalism and ethics in teaching*. London: Routledge.

Carswell, L (1998) 'The "virtual university": toward an internet paradigm?' Proceedings of 6th annual conference on the 'Teaching of Computing'/3rd annual conference on 'Integrating Technology into Computer Science Education on Changing the Delivery of Computer Science Education', Dublin City University: Ireland, August, pp.46–50.

Carusetta, E (2001) 'Evaluating teaching through teaching awards', *New Directions for Teaching and Learning*, 88, pp.31–40.

Castells, M (2010) *Communication Power*. Oxford: Oxford University Press.

Castells, M (1997) *The Power of Identity*. Oxford: Blackwell.

Chaney, P, Mackay, F and McAllister, L (2007) *Women, politics and constitutional change: The first years of the National Assembly for Wales*. Cardiff: University of Wales Press.

Chaney, P (2006) 'Women in democracy: critical mass, deliberation and the engendering of public policy in post–devolution Wales', lecture to the National Assembly's Cross Party Women in Democracy Group, November.

Chaney, P, Hall, T and Pithouse, A (eds) (2001) *New governance – new democracy? post-devolution Wales*. Cardiff: University of Wales Press.

Chapman, V (2011) 'Appreciative Inquiry as evaluation: enhancing and developing academic practice'. In M Saunders, P Trowler and V Bamber (eds) *Reconceptualising evaluative practices in higher education: the practice turn*. London: OUP/SRHE, Chapter 22.

Chapman, V and Bowen-Jones W (2008) 'From elitism to inclusion – developing an inclusive curriculum through an appreciative inquiry approach'. University of Worcester Annual Learning and Teaching Conference, University of Worcester.

Charmaz, K (1995) 'Grounded theory'. In J A Smith, R Harre and L Van Langenhove (eds) *Rethinking methods in psychology*. London: Sage, pp.27–49.

Chase, N M (2008) 'An exploration of the culture of information technology: focus on unrelenting change', *Journal of Information, Information Technology and Organisations*, 3, pp.135–150.

Chevalier, A, Doulton, P and McIntosh, S (2002) 'Recruiting and retaining teachers in the uk: an analysis of graduate occupation choice from 1960s to 1990s'. Centre for the Economics of Education Discussion Paper, University of London, London School of Economics.

Chevallier, T (2002) 'Higher education and its clients: institutional responses to changes in demand and in environment', *Higher Education*, 44 (3/4), pp.303–308.

Chitty, C (2009) *Education policy in Britain* (2nd edition). Basingstoke: Palgrave Macmillan.

Chriss, J (1999) 'Introduction'. In J Chriss (ed.) *Counseling and the therapeutic state*. New York: Aldine de Gruyter.

Chu, Hui-Chin and Kuo, Tsiu-Yank (2012) 'Exploring faculty psychological contract through leadership style and institutional climate in a higher education setting', *International Journal of Business and Social Science*, 3 (4), pp.159–164.

Churchman, D (2006) 'Institutional commitments, individual compromises: identity-related responses to compromise in an Australian university', *Journal of Higher Education Policy and Management*, 28 (1), pp.3–15.

Clandinin, D J and Connelly, F M (2000) *Narrative inquiry – experience and story in qualitative research*. San Francisco: Jossey-Bass.

Clark, B R (2004) *Sustaining change in universities: continuities in case studies and concepts*. Maidenhead: Open University Press/SRHE.

Clark, B R (1998) *Creating entrepreneurial universities: organisational pathways of transformation*. Oxford: Elsevier.

Clark, B R (1987) *Academic life: small worlds, different worlds*. A Carnegie Foundation Special Report. Lawrenceville, NJ: Princeton University Press and Carnegie Foundation for the Advancement of Teaching.

Clark, M S (ed) (1992) 'Emotion', *Review of Personality and Social Psychology*, 13, pp.25–59.

Clarke, J, Gewirtz, S and McLaughlin, E (eds) (2000) *New Managerialism, new welfare?* London: Sage.

Clarke, M (2009) 'Plodders, pragmatists, visionaries and opportunists: career patterns and employability', *Career Development International*, 14, pp.8–28.

Clegg, S (2008) 'Academic identities under threat?' *British Educational Research Journal*, 34 (3), pp.329–345.

Clifford, J (1986) 'Partial truths'. In J Clifford and G Marcus (eds) ([1986] 2005) *Writing culture: the poetics and politics of ethnography*. Berkeley, CA: University of California Press, pp.1–26.

Clifford, J and Marcus, G E (eds) ([1986] 2005) *Writing culture: the poetics and politics of ethnography*. Berkeley, CA: University of California Press.

Clow, R (2005) 'Just teachers: the work carried out by full-time further education teachers', *Research in Post-Compulsory Education*, 10 (1), pp.63–81.

Cobley, R S (2001) 'A comparative investigation into the issues affecting IT Directors in UK HE', unpublished DBA thesis, Henley Management at Brunel University.

Cochrane, T D (2010a) 'Exploring mobile learning success factors', *ALT-J Research in Learning Technology*, 18 (2), pp.133–148.

Cochrane, T D (2010b) 'Beyond the Yellow Brick Road: mobile Web 2.0 informing a new institutional e-learning strategy', *ALT-J*,18 (3), pp.221–231.

Coffey, A, Dicks, B, Renold, E, Soyinka, B, William's, M (2005) *Ethnography for the Digital Age* Methods Briefing (8) Cardiff: School of Social Sciences, Cardiff University.

Coffield, F, Steer, R, Hodgson, A, Spours, K, Edward, S and Finlay, I (2005) 'A new learning and skills landscape? The central role of the Learning and Skills Council', *Journal of Education Policy*, 20 (5), pp.631–656.

Cohen, A (ed) (1986) *Symbolising boundaries: identity and diversity in British cultures*. Manchester: Manchester University Press.

Colleges Wales (2011) '*Colleges welcome stability but challenges remain*', http://www.colegaucymru.ac.uk/cy GB/colleges_welcome_stability_but_challenges_remain-211.aspx, accessed 12 April 2012.

Colley, H (2012) 'What (a) to do about impact: a Boudiesian critique'. Paper presented at the ECER Conference, University of Cadiz, 19 September.

Colley, H, James, D and Diment, K (2007) 'Unbecoming teachers: towards a more dynamic notion of professional participation', *Journal of Education Policy*, 22 (2), pp.173–193.

Collins, M, Vignoles, A and Walker, J (2007) *Higher education academic salaries in the UK*. London: London School of Economics, pp.1–27.

Condrey, S C, Decker, I M and McCoy, C L (2011) *Human resource management, encyclopedia of public administration and public policy* (2nd edition). London, Taylor & Francis.

Conrad, D (2007) 'The plain hard work of teaching online'. In M Bullen and D P Janes (eds) *Making the transition to e-learning: strategies and issues*. Hershey, PA: Idea Group Inc.

Conrad, D (2004) 'University instructor's reflections on their first online teaching experiences', *JALN*, 8 (2), p.11.

Constanti, P and Gibbs, P (2004) 'Higher education teachers and emotional labour', *The International Journal of Education Management*, 18 (4), pp.243–249.

Conway, P F (2001) 'Anticipatory reflection while learning to teach: from a temporally truncated to a temporally distributed model of reflection in teacher education', *Teaching and Teacher Education*, 17 (1), pp.89–106.

Cook, C and Daunton, L (2010) 'Human resource management implications of "Working Lives" findings on working practices of academics in higher education'. Society for Research into Higher Education Conference Proceedings, December.

Cook, C and Gornall, L (2010) 'Working together and working apart: academic life, contemporary work and some issues for research', Working Lives Seminar series, No.4, University of Glamorgan, 19 November.

Cook, C (2009) 'Narratives of the new researcher within a WERN Group bursary project'. Paper to the NEXUS HE Conference 15, 16 June, Newport, UK.

Cook, C, Gornall, L, Daunton, L, Salisbury, J and Thomas, B C (2009) 'The "Working Lives" research report on narratives of occupational change in further and higher education in post-devolution Wales', *Welsh Journal of Education*, 14 (2), pp.97–103.

Cooper, C (2004) Cited in Curtis P and Crace, J, 'Cracks in the ivory tower', *The Guardian*, 16 November.

Cooper, K and Olson, M R (1996) 'The multiple "i"s of teacher identity'. In M Kompf, W R Bond, D Dworet and R T Boak (eds) *Changing research and practice: teachers' professionalism, identities and knowledge*. London: The Falmer Press, pp.78–89.

Cooperrider, D, Whitney, D and Stavros, J M (2008) *Appreciative inquiry handbook for leaders of change* (2nd edition). San Francisco: Crown Custom and Berrett-Koehler.

Cooperrider, D (1986) *Appreciative inquiry: toward a methodology for understanding and enhancing organizational innovation*. Doctoral dissertation, Western Reserve University, Cleveland, OH.

Cornford, J and Pollock, N (eds) (2003) *Putting the university online: information, technology, and organisational change*. Maidenhead: SRHE/Open University Press.

Cornford, J (2000) 'The virtual university is . . . the university made concrete?', *Information, Communication and Society*, 3 (4) pp.508–52.

Coughlan, D (2001) 'Insider action research projects – implications for practising managers', *Management Learning*, 32 (1), pp.49–60.

Court, S (2004) 'Hands on, hands off! The state and higher education relationship in the UK in the 20th century'. Presentation on behalf of AUT to Society for Research into Higher Education, University of Bristol, 14–16 December.

Covey, S (1989) *The seven habits of highly effective people*. New York: Simon & Schuster.

Coyle-Shapiro, J (2010) 'The London School of Economics and Political Science, LSE research online', December, http://eprints.lse.ac.uk/26866/.

Crawley, A L (1995) 'Critical tensions in faculty development: a transformative agenda', *Innovative Higher Education*, 20 (2), pp.65–70.

Cribb, A (2005) 'Education and health: professional roles and the division of ethical labour'. Paper presented at C–TRIP Seminar 2: 'Professional Identities and Teacher Careers' King's College London, 15 March.

Cromford, J and Pollok, N (2003) *Putting the university online: information, technology and organisational change*. Maidenhead: SRHE/Open University Press.

Crozier, G, Reay, D, Clayton, J and Colliander, L (2008) *The socio cultural and learning experiences of working class students in higher education*. London: ESRC/TLRP.

Cullinane, N and Dundon, T (2006) 'The psychological contract: a critical review', *International Journal of Management Reviews*, 8 (2), pp.113–129.

Cunningham, S (ed) (2008) *Exploring professionalism*. London: Institute of Education.

Cunningham, S, Ryan, Y, Stedman, L, Tapsall, S, Bagdon, K, Flew, T and Coaldrake, P (1998) *New media and borderless education: a review of the convergence of global media networks and higher education provision*. Canberra: Department of Employment, Education Training and Youth Affairs.

Currie, J and Eveline, J (2011) 'E-technology and work/life balance for academics with young children', *Higher Education*, 62 (4), pp.533–550.

Curtis, M, Luchini, K, Bobrowsky, B, Quintana, C and Soloway, E (2002) 'Handheld use in K-12: a descriptive account'. In *Proceedings of the IEEE International Workshop on Wireless and Mobile Technologies in Education*. Los Alamitos, CA: IEEE Computer Society.

Curtis, P and Crace, J (2004) 'Cracks in the ivory towers', *The Guardian*, 16 November.

Cuthbert, R (1996) 'Working in higher education'. In R Cuthbert (ed.) *Working in higher education*. Proceedings of the SRHE annual conference. Buckingham: SRHE/Open University Press, pp.3–20.

CVCP (1996) *Concordat and research careers initiative*. London: Committee of Vice-Chancellors and Principals (CVCP). CVCP, pp.1–10.

CVCP (1985) *Report of the steering committee for efficiency studies in universities* (Jarratt Report). London: CVCP.

Dacre Pool, L and Qualter, P (2012) 'Improving emotional intelligence and emotional self–efficacy through a teaching intervention for university students', *Learning and Individual Differences*, 22 (3), pp.306–312.

Daunton, L, Gornall, L, Cook, C and Salisbury, J (2008) 'Starting the day fresh: hidden work and discourse in contemporary academic practice'. Paper presented at SRHE, Liverpool, December.

David, M E (2011) 'Overview of researching global higher education: challenge, change or crisis', *Contemporary Social Science: Journal of the Academy of Social Sciences*, 6 (2), pp.147–163.

Davies, S M B and Salisbury, J (2009) 'Building educational research capacity through institutional collaboration: an evaluation of the first year of the Welsh Education Research Network (WERN)', *Welsh Journal of Education*, 14 (2), pp.78–94.

Dawson, D, Britnell, J and Hitchcock, A (2010) 'Developing competency models of faculty developers – using World Cafe to foster dialogue', *To Improve the Academy*, 28, pp.3–24.

Day, C (2005) 'Conceptualising the role of identity in variations in teachers' work, lives and effectiveness'. Paper presented at C–TRIP seminar 2: 'Professional Identities and Teacher Careers', King's College London, 15 March.

Day, C (2004) *A passion for teaching*. London: Routledge Falmer.

DBIS (Department for Business Innovation and Skills) (2012) 'Priorities for 2012 to 2013', Department for Business Innovation and Skills, website www.gov.uk.

DBIS (Department for Business Innovation and Skills) (2011) *Putting students at the heart of the system*, CM8122. London: Stationery Office, http://stats.bis.gov.uk/UKSA/he/sa20110331.htm.

DBIS (Department for Business Innovation and Skills) (2009) *High ambitions: the future of universities in a knowledge economy*. London: DBIS.

Dean, M (2007) *Governing societies: political perspectives on domestic and international rule*. Maidenhead: Open University Press.

Dean, M (1999) *Governmentality, power and rule in modern society*. London: Sage.

Dearing, R (1997) See: NCIHE 1997.

Deem, R, Hillyard, S and Reed, M (2007) *Knowledge, higher education and the new managerialism: the changing management of uk universities*. Oxford: Oxford University Press.

Deem, R and Brehony, K J (2005) 'Management as ideology: the case of "new managerialism" in higher education', *Oxford Review of Education*, 31 (2), pp.217–235.

Deem, R and Johnson, R (2003) 'Risking the university? learning to be a manager-academic in uk universities', *Sociological Research Online*, 8 (3), http://www.socresonline.org/8/3/deem.html, accessed 25 August 2006.

Deem, R (2001) 'Globalisation, new managerialism, academic capitalism and entrepreneurialism in universities: Is the local dimension still important?' *Comparative Education*, 37 (1), pp.7–20.

Deem, R (2000) *'New managerialism' and the management of UK universities*. End of award report on the findings of an Economic and Social Research Council funded Project, October 1998 to November 2000, ESRC award number R000 237661, Lancaster University.

Deem, R (1998) 'New managerialism' and higher education: the management of performances and cultures in universities in the United Kingdom', *International Studies in Sociology of Education*, 8 (3), pp.47–70.

Delamont, S (2002) *Fieldwork in educational settings: methods, pitfalls and perspectives*. London: Routledge Falmer.

Delamont, S (1996) *A women's place in education*. Aldershot: Avesbury.

Delanty, G (2008) 'Academic identities and institutional change'. In R Barnett and R Di Napoli (eds) *Changing identities in Higher Education: Voicing Perspectives*. Abingdon: Routledge, pp.124–133.

Delanty, G (2001) 'The university in the knowledge society', *Organization*, 8 (2), pp.149–153.

Deleuze, G and Guattari, F (1972) *Anti-Oedipus*, trans. R Hurley, M Seem and H R Lane. London: Continuum.

Denzin, N (1989) *Interpretive biography*. London: Sage.

Denzin, N (1970) *The research act: a theoretical introduction to sociological methods*. Chicago: Aldine Publishing Company.

DES (Department of Education and Science) (1992) *Further and higher education act 1992*. London: HMSO.

DfE (Department for Education) (2011) *Education and training statistics for the United Kingdom*, London: DfE, http://www.education.gov.uk/rsgateway/DB/VOL/v001045/v02-2011v2.pdf, accessed 12 December 2012.

DfES (Department for Education and Skills) (2003) *Towards a unified e-learning strategy*. London: DfES, http://www.dfes.gov.uk/elearningstrategy/downloads/e-learningstrategypdffinal.pdf, accessed 30 July 2003.

Department of Enterprise, Trade and Employment (2009) *Science, engineering and technology: delivering the smart economy.* Dublin: Government Stationery Office.

DTI (Department of Trade and Industry) (2002) *Full and fulfilling work.* London: DTI.

DWP (Department of Work and Pensions) (2001) *Britain in 2010.* London: DWP.

Derrida, J (2000) *Of hospitality,* trans. R. Bowlby. Stanford, CA: Stanford University Press.

Dijk, D-J and von Schantz, M (2005) 'Timing and consolidation of human sleep, wakefulness, and performance by a symphony of oscillators', *Journal of BioRhythms,* 20 (4), pp.279–290.

Doherty, L and Manfredi, S (2010) 'Improving women's representation in senior positions in universities', *Employee Relations,* 32 (2), pp.138–155.

Doherty, L and Manfredi, S (2006) 'Action research to develop work-life balance in a UK university', *Women in Management Review,* 21 (3), pp.241–259.

Doherty, N (1996) 'Surviving in an era of insecurity', *European Journal of Work and Organizational Psychology,* 5, pp.471–478.

Donkin, R (1995) 'Happy workers can generate high profits, review of J Pfeffer, Competitive advantage through people', Harvard Business School, *Financial Times,* 8 February, p.10.

Douglas, M (ed) (1973) *Rules and meanings: the anthropology of everyday knowledge – selected readings.* Harmondsworth: Penguin Education.

Douglas, M (1966) *Purity and danger.* London: Routledge & Kegan Paul.

Drucker, P (1969) *The age of discontinuity.* New York: Harper & Row.

Du Gay, P (2009) 'In defence of mandarins: recovering the "core business" of public management', *Management and Organizational History,* 4 (4), pp.359–84.

Du Gay, P (ed) (2005) *The values of bureaucracy.* Oxford: Oxford University Press.

Du Gay, P (2000) *In praise of bureaucracy.* London: Sage.

Dufourmantelle, A (2000) *Of hospitality: Anne Dufourmantelle invites Jacques Derrida to respond.* Stanford, CA: Stanford University Press.

Duke, C (2002) *Managing the learning university.* Buckingham: SRGE/Open University Press.

Dunn, A, Jenkins, L, Kop, R, Von Rothkirch, A and Trotman, C (2007) *Evaluation of the appropriateness of access to higher education programmes in Wales for progression to higher education.* Report commissioned by Open College Network Wales. Cardiff: OCN.

Earwaker, J (1992) *Helping and supporting students.* Buckingham: SRHE/Open University Press.

Easton, S and Van Laar, D (1995) 'Experiences of lecturers helping distressed students in higher education', *British Journal of Guidance and Counselling,* 23 (2), pp.173–178.

Ecclesfield, N, Rebbeck, G and Garnett, F (2012) 'The case of the curious and the confident – the untold story of changing teacher attitudes to e-learning in the further education sector', *Compass 5,* University of Greenwich, London, pp.45–56.

Ecclesfield, N, Rebbeck, G and Garnett, F (2011) 'The digital practitioner when digital natives grow up', presentation to ALT–C 2011, http://www.slideshare.net/fredgarnett/digital–practitioner–2011, accessed 30 April 2012.

Ecclesfield, N and Garnett F (2010) 'The open context model of learning and the craft of teaching', presentation to iPED 2010, http://wwwm.coventry.ac.uk/researchnet/iped2010/Pages/IPED2010.aspx, accessed 30 April 2012.

Ecclesfield, N and Garnett, F (2009) 'Learning from the learners experience: policy perspectives'. In S Walker M Ryan and R Teed (eds) *Learning from the learners' experience,* post-conference reflections, University of Greenwich, London, learning@greenwich.

Ecclestone, K and Hayes, D (2009) *The dangerous rise of therapeutic education.* Abingdon: Routledge.

Ecclestone, K (2004) 'Learning or therapy? The demoralisation of education', *British Journal of Educational Studies*, 52 (2), pp.112–137.

Ecclestone, K and Pryor, J (2003) ' "Learning careers" or "assessment careers"?: the impact of assessment systems on learning', *British Educational Research Journal*, 29, pp.471–488.

Ecclestone, K (2002) *Learning autonomy in post-compulsory education: the politics and practice of formative assessment.* London: Routledge Falmer.

Economic and Social Research Council (ESRC) (2006) *Health and well-being at work of working age people.* Seminar series, 'Mapping the Public Policy Landscape'. Swindon: ESRC.

Edwards, J, Van Laar, D, Easton, S and Kinman, G (2009) 'The work–related quality of life scale for higher education employees', *Quality in Higher Education*, 15 (3), pp.207–219.

Eggins, H and Macdonald, R E (2003) *The scholarship of academic development.* Philadelphia, PA: SRHE/Open University Press.

Electoral Reform Society Wales (2012) *Women and Local Government.* Cardiff: ERSW.

Electoral Reform Society/Centre for Women and Democracy (2011) *Women's representation in Scotland and Wales.* London: Electoral Reform Society.

Elizabeth, V and Grant, B (2013) 'The spirit of research has changed: reverberations from researcher identities in managerial times', *Higher Education Research and Development*, 32 (1), pp.122–135.

Ellaway, R, Dewhurst, D and McLeod, H (2004) 'Evaluating a virtual learning environment in the context of its community of practice', *ALT-J*, 12(2), pp.125–145.

Elliott, A and Urry, J (2010) *Mobile lives.* London: Routledge.

Ellis, C and Bochner, A P (2000) 'Autoethnography, intimacy and ethnorgraphy'. In N K Denzin and Y S Lincoln (eds) *Handbook of qualitative research.* Thousand Oaks, CA: Sage.

Ellis, S (1999) 'The patient–centred care model: holistic, multi–professional and reflective', *British Journal of Nursing*, 8 (5), pp.296–301.

Elton, L (2009) 'Continuing professional development in higher education – the role of the scholarship of teaching and learning'. In M Laycock and L Shrives (eds) *Embedding CPD in higher education.* London: Staff and Educational Development Association.

Enders, J and de Weert, E (eds) (2009) *The changing face of academic work.* New York: Palgrave Macmillan.

Enders, J and Kaulisch, M (2006) 'The binding and unbinding of academic careers'. In U Teichler, *The formative years of scholars.* London: Portland Press.

Enders, J (2005) 'Border crossings: research training, knowledge dissemination and the transformation of academic work', *Journal of Higher Education*, 49 (1–2), pp.119–133.

Enders, J and Fulton, O (eds) (2002) *Higher education in a globalising world: international trends and mutual observation. A Festschrift in honour of Ulrich Teichler.* Dordrecht: Kluwer Academic Publishers.

Enders, J (ed.) (2001) *Academic staff in Europe.* Westport, CT: Greenwood.

Equality and Human Rights Commission (2012) *Who run Wales?* 2012 update. European Commission, http://ec.europa.eu/research/horizon2020/index_en.cfm?pg=h2020, accessed 24 October 2012.

Erickson, F (1986) 'Qualitative methods in research on teaching', in M Wittrock (ed.) *Handbook of research on teaching.* New York: Macmillan, pp.119–161.

Eriksen, T H (2001) *Tyranny of the moment*. London: Pluto Press.

Erikson, R J and Wharton, A S (1997) 'Inauthenticity and depression: assessing the consequences of interactive service work', *Work and Occupations*, 24 (2), pp.188–213.

ESRC/TLRP (2008) *Inside further education: the social context of learning*. Teaching and Learning Research Programme (TLRP) Research Briefing no.52. Swindon: ESRC.

EU (European Union) (2002) *Fixed term employees (prevention of less favourable treatment) regulations*, SI 2002No. 2034. London: HMSO.

Evans, K and O'Connor, B (eds) (2011) *The Sage handbook of workplace learning*. London: Sage, pp.149–161.

Evans, K, Guile, D and Harris, J (2011) 'Re-thinking work-based learning: for education professionals and professionals who educate'. In M Malloch, L Cairns, Evans and B O'Connor (eds) *The SAGE Handbook of work place learning* London: Sage .

Evans, L, Homer, M S and Rayner S G (forthcoming) 'Professors as academic leaders: the perspectives of "the led" ', *Educational Management Administration and Leadership*.

Evans, L and Mercer, J (2012) 'Professors, leaders and led'. Paper to SRHE conference December 2012, Newport.

Evans, L. (2011) 'Location, location, location: proximity theory and the ideal job'. Paper and symposium, Cetl conference, 8 April, University of Oxford.

Evans, L and Abbott, I (1998) *Teaching and learning in higher education*. London: Cassell.

Fairclough, N (1989) *Language and power*. London: Longman.

Fanghanel, J (2012) *Being an academic*. New York: Routledge.

Fanghanel, J and Trowler, P (2008) 'Exploring academic identities and practices in a competitive enhancement context: a UK–based case study', *European Journal of Education*, 43 (3), pp.301–313.

Fanghanel, J (2004) 'Capturing dissonance in university education departments', *Studies in Higher Education*, 29 (5), pp.575–590.

Farnham, D (1999) 'Managing universities and regulating academic labour markets'. In D Farnham, *Managing academic staff in changing university systems: international trends and comparisons*. Buckingham: SRHE/Open University Press, pp.3–31.

Fawcett Society (2012) *The impact of austerity on women*, Fawcett Society, http://www.fawcettsociety.org.uk/index.asp?PageID=1208, accessed 22 August 2012.

Felstead, A (2008) *Detaching work from place: charting the progress of change and its implications for learning*. Draft discussion paper, October. Cardiff: Cardiff University.

Felstead, A, Jewson, N and Walters, S (2005) *Changing places of work*. London: Palgrave.

Feltham, C (2000) 'Counselling supervision: baselines, problems and possibilities'. In B Lawton and C Feltham (eds) *Taking supervision forward: enquiries and trends in counselling and psychotherapy*. London: Sage.

Fenwick, T, Nerland, M and Jensen, K (2012) 'Sociomaterial approaches to conceptualising professional learning and practice', *Journal of Education and Work*, 25 (1), pp.1–13.

Fern, E (2001) *Advanced focus group research*. Thousand Oaks, CA: Sage.

Field, K (2011) 'Reflection at the heart of effective continuing professional development', *Professional Development in Education*, 37 (2), pp.171–175.

Filippakou, O and Tapper, T (2008) 'Quality assurance and quality enhancement in higher education: contested territories?', *Higher Education Quarterly*, 62 (1/2), pp.84–100.

Finch, J (1984) ' "It's great to have someone to talk to": the ethics and politics of interviewing women'. In C Bell and H Roberts (eds) *Social researching: politics, problems, practice*. London: Routledge & Kegan Paul, pp.71–78.

Fincher, S (2012) The Sharing Practice Day Surveys project 2010–2011, www.sharingpractice.ac.uk, accessed 8 March 2013.

Fincher, S (2010–11) 'The Sharing Practice Day Surveys project', http://www. sharingpractice.ac.uk, accessed 8 March 2013.

Fineman, S (2003) *Understanding emotion at work*. London: Sage.

Fineman, S (1993) *Emotion in organisations*. London: Sage.

Finkelstein, M J (2012) 'The power of institutional and disciplinary markets: academic salaries in the United States'. In P G Altbach, L Reisberg, M Yudkevich, G Androushchak and I F Pacheco (eds) *Paying the professoriate: a global comparison of compensation and contracts*. New York: Routledge, pp.308–328.

Finkelstein, S and Hambrick, D (1996) *Strategic leadership*. St Paul, MN: West Publishing Co.

Fischer, M J (2003) *Emergent forms of life and the anthropological voice*. Durham, NC: Duke University Press.

Fisher, S (2005) 'Is there a need to debate the role of higher education and the public good?' Dublin: Dublin Institute of Technology, arrow@dit.

Fitzgerald, T, White, J and Gunter, H (2012) *Hard labour? academic work and the changing landscape of higher education*. Bingley: Emerald.

Flaherty, M G and Seipp-Williams, L (2005) 'Sociotemporal rhythms in e-mail: a case study', *Time and Society*, 14 (39), pp.39–49.

Floyd, A (2012a) 'Narrative and life history'. In A Briggs, M Coleman and M Morrison (eds) *Research methods in educational leadership and management*. London: Sage, pp.223–235.

Floyd, A (2012b) ' "Turning points": the personal and professional circumstances that lead academics to become middle managers', *Educational Managemen Administration and Leadership*, 40 (2), pp.272–284.

Floyd, A and Dimmock, C (2011) ' "Jugglers", "copers" and "strugglers": academics' perceptions of being a HoD in a post-1992 UK university and how it influences their future careers', *Journal of Higher Education Policy and Management*, 33 (4), pp.387–399.

Flynn, N (2000) 'Managerialsim and public services: some international trends'. In J Clarke, S Gewirtz and E McLaughlan (eds) *New managererialism, new welfare?*. London: Sage, pp.27–44.

Foster, A (2005) *Realising the potential: a review of the future role of further education colleges*. London: DfES.

Foucault, M (1977) *Discipline and punish: the birth of the prison*. New York: Vintage Books.

Foucault, M (1972) *The archaeology of knowledge*. London: Tavistock.

Fox, A (1974) *Beyond contract: work, power and trust relations*.London: Faber.

Fox, A (1966) 'Industrial sociology and industrial relations', *Royal Commission Research Paper no. 3*. London: HMSO.

Fox, M F and Faver, C A (1984) 'Independence and co–operation in research: the motivations and costs of collaboration', *The Journal of Higher Education*, 55 (3), pp.347–359.

Frant, F, Lee, A, Clegg, S, Manathunga, C, Barrow, M, Kadibinder, P, Brailsford, I, Gosling, D and Hicks, J (2009) 'Why history? Why now? Multiple accounts of the emergence of academic development', *International Journal for Academic Development*, 14 (1), pp.83–86.

Freedman, E (2009) 'The 2008 "BERA" charter for research staff', *Research Intelligence*, 108, August, p.11.

Freidson, E (2001) *Professionalism, the third logic*. Cambridge: Polity Press.

Freidson, E (1986) *Professional powers: a study of the institutionalization of formal knowledge*. Chicago: University of Chicago Press.

Friedberg, E and Musselin, C (1987) 'The academic profession in France'. In B.R. Clarke (ed) *The academic profession: national, disciplinary and institutional settings*. Berkeley, CA: University of California Press, pp.93–122.

Frith, U and Frith, C (2010) 'The social brain: allowing humans to boldly go where no other species has been', *Philosophical Transactions of the Royal Society B: Biological Sciences*, 365, 12 January, pp.165–176.

Fulton, O (2002) 'Higher education governance in the UK: change and continuity'. In A Amaral, G Jones and B Karseth (eds) *Governing higher education: comparing national perspectives*. Dordrecht: Kluwer Academic Publishers, pp.205–229.

Fulton, O (1998) 'Unity or fragmentation, convergence or diversity? the academic profession in comparative perspective in the era of mass higher education'. In W G Bowen and H Shapiro (eds) *Universities and their leadership*. Princeton, NJ: Princeton University Press.

Fulton, O, Fitz, J, Hesketh, A and Rees, G (1991) 'Slouching towards a mass system: society, government and institutions in the UK', *Higher Education*, 21, pp.589–605.

Gale, H (2011) 'The reluctant academic: early career academics in a teaching orientated university', *International Journal for Academic Development*, 16 (3), pp.215–227.

Gappa, J M and Austin, A E (2010) 'Rethinking academic traditions for twenty-first century faculty', *AAUP Journal of Academic Freedom*, 1, pp.1–20.

Garmezy, N (1971) 'Vulnerability research and the issue of primary prevention', *American Journal of Orthopsychiatry*, 41, pp.101–116.

Garnett, F and Ecclesfield, N (2011) 'Towards a framework for co–creating open scholarship', Proceedings of ALT–C 2011, ALT, Oxford, http://repository.alt.ac.uk/2177/7/RLT_A_007795_O.html, ccessed 30 April 2012.

Garnett, F and Ecclesfield, N (2008) 'Colloquium: Developing an organisational architecture of participation', *British Journal of Educational Technology*, 39 (3), pp.468–474.

Garrison, D R and Anderson, T (2003/2007) *E–learning in the 21st century: a framework for research and practice*. London: Routledge Falmer.

Geertz, G (1988) *'Work and lives': the anthropologist as author*. Stanford, CA: Stanford University Press.

Geertz, G (1973) *The interpretation of cultures: selected essays*. London: Fontana Press.

Gennard, J and Judge, G (2005) *Employee relations* (4th edition). London: Chartered Institute of Personnel and Development.

Gergen, K and Gergen, M (1988) 'Narrative and self as relationship'. In L Berkowitz (ed.) *Advances in experimental social psychology*. New York: Academic Press.

Gergen, K (1982) *Towards transformation in social knowledge*. New York: Springer-Verlag.

Gershuny, J (1978) *After industrial society: the emerging self-economy*. London: Macmillian.

Gewirtz, S, Cribb, A, Mahony, P and Hextell, I (2006) 'A review of key themes from the ESRC seminar series on "Changing Teacher Roles, Identities and Professionalism" (C-TRIP), King's College London, 26 June.

Gibb, S (2001) 'The state of human resource management: evidence from employees' views of HRM systems and staff', *Employee Relations*, 23 (4), pp.318–336.

Gibbons, M, Limoges, C, Nowotny, H, Schwartzman, S, Scott, P and Trow, M (1994) *The new production of knowledge: the dynamics of science and research in contemporary societies*. London: Sage.

Gibbs, G (2000) 'Are the pedagogies of the disciplines really different?' In C Rust (ed.) *Improving student learning through the disciplines*. Oxford: Oxford Centre for Staff and Learning Development.

Giddens, A (1991) *Modernity and self–identity: self and society in the late modern age*. Cambridge: Polity Press.

Gill, J (2011) 'New scheme offers hope in the uncertain world of postdoctoral despair', *Times Higher Education*, 2 June.

Ginns, P, Kitay, J and Prosser, M (2010) 'Transfer of academic staff learning in a research-intensive university', *Teaching in Higher Education*, 15 (3), pp.235–246.

Ginther, D and Hayes, K J (1999) 'Gender differences in salary and promotion in the humanities', *The American Economic Review*, 89 (2), pp. 445–460.

Glaser, B G (ed) (1993) *Examples of grounded theory: a reader*. Mill Valley, CA: Sociology Press.

Gleeson, D (2005) 'Learning for a change in Further education: a project review', *Journal of Vocational Education and Training*, 57 (2), pp.239–46.

Gleeson, D, Davies, J and Wheeler, E (2005) 'On the making and taking of professionalism in further education workplace', *British Journal of Sociology of Education*, 26 (4), pp.445–460.

Gleeson, D and Shain, F (1999) 'Managing ambiguity: between markets and managerialism', *Sociological Review*, 57 (3), pp.461–490.

Goodall, A (2009) *Socrates in the boardroom: why research universities should be led by top scholars*. Princeton, NJ: Princeton University Press.

Goodrham, M (2006) *Using research to enhance professionalism in further education (fe), professional lifelong learning: beyond reflective practice*. Paper to ESRC Teaching and Learning Research Programme seminar 'Changing teacher roles, identities and professionalism': the impact of research on professional practice and identity', King's College, 26 April 2006.

Goodrham, M and Hodkinson, P (2004) 'Professionalism and the educational practioner – continuity and change'. Paper presented to annual conference of the British Educational Research Association, UMIST, 16–18 September.

Goodson, I (2003) *Professional knowledge, professional lives: studies in education and change*. Philadelphia, PA: Open University Press.

Goodson, I and Sikes, P (2001) *Life history research in educational settings: learning from lives*. Buckingham: Open University Press.

Goodson, I (ed) (1992) *Studying teachers' lives*. London: Routledge.

Goody, J (1977) *Domestication of the savage mind*. Cambridge: Cambridge University Press.

Gordon, G and Whitchurch, C (2010) *Academic and professional identities in higher education: the challenges of a diversifying workforce*. New York: Routledge.

Gornall, L and Hudson A (2013) 'New professionals in teaching and learning and in educational development: a joint case study and comparison'. Working paper, Working Lives and University of Dundee.

Gornall, L (2012) 'Working together and working apart: HE working lives'. Presentation to the Professional Practice, Education and Learning (ProPel) international conference, University of Stirling, 10 May.

Gornall, L and Salisbury, J (2012) 'Compulsive working, "hyperprofessionality" and the unseen pleasures of academic work', *Higher Educational Quarterly*, 66 (2), pp.135–154.

Gornall, L (2009) 'Our careers, ourselves: new professionals ten years on'. Paper presented at Association for Learning Technology (ALT) Conference, Manchester, September.

Gornall, L, Thomas, B and Salisbury, J (2008) 'Working Lives: narratives of occupational change from further and higher education in post-devolution Wales'. BERA Conference, September.

Gornall, L (2004) ' "New professionals": academic work and occupational change in higher education'. Doctoral thesis, School of Social Sciences, Cardiff University.

Gornall, L. and Thomas, B (2001) ' "New professionals" – mainstreaming or marginlisation?' *International Journal of Applied HRM*, 2 (3), pp.45–58.

Gornall, L (1999) ' "New professionals": change and occupational roles in higher education', *Perspectives: Policy and Practice in Higher Education*, 3(2), pp.44–49.

Gosling, D (2008) *Educational development in the United Kingdom*. Report for the Heads of Educational Development Group (HEDG). London: HEDG.

Gough, M (2012) 'The problem of identity for academic practice in terms of definition', *Studies in Higher Education*, DOI: http://dx.doi.org/10.1080/03075079.2012.711219.

Gough, M (2011) 'Education as philosophy, philosophy as education and the concept of practice: considerations of disciplinarity arising out of learning and teaching development work', *Discourse: Learning and Teaching in Philosophical and Religious Studies*, 10 (3), http://prs.heacademy.ac.uk/publications/discourse/10_3.html.

Gough, M and Denicolo, P (2007) *Research supervisors and the skills agenda: learning needs analysis and personal development profiling*. London: SRHE.

Gouldner, A (1957) 'Cosmopolitans and Locals: towards an analysis of latent roles', *Administrative Science Quarterly*, 2 (3), pp.281–306.

Grant, B *et al.* (2009) 'Why history? Why now? Multiple accounts of the emergence of academic development', *International Journal For Academic Development*, 14 (1), pp.83–86.

Grey, C (2009) *A very short, fairly interesting and reasonably cheap book about studying organizations* (2nd edition). Thousand Oaks, CA: Sage.

Grindle, M (1997) *Getting good government: capacity building in the public sectors of developing countries*. Cambridge, MA: Harvard University Press.

Grint, K (1997) *Fuzzy management: contemporary ideas and practices at work*. New York: Oxford University Press.

Grint, K and Woolgar, S (1997) *The machine at work: technology, work and organisation*. Cambridge: Polity Press.

Grint, K (1991) *The sociology of work: an introduction*. Cambridge: Polity Press.

Grow, G O (1991) 'Teaching learners to be self–directed learning', *Adult Education Quarterly*, 41(3), pp.125–149.

Gu, Q and Day, C (2007) 'Teachers' resilience: a necessary condition for effectiveness', *Teaching and Teacher Education*, 23 (8), pp.1302–1316.

Guest, D E (2011) 'Human resource management and performance: still searching for some answers', *Human Resource Management Journal*, 21 (1), January, pp.3–13.

Guest, D E, Michie, J, Conway, N and Sheehan, M (2003) 'Human resource management and corporate performance in the UK', *British Journal of Industrial Relations*, 41 (2), pp.291–314.

Guest, D (1997) 'Human resource management and performance: a review and research agenda', *International Journal of Human Resource Management*, 8 (3), pp.263–276.

Guile, D and Lucas, N (1999) 'Rethinking initial teacher education and professional development'. In A Green and N Lucas (eds) *FE and lifelong learning: realigning the sector for the twenty-first century*. London: Institute of Education, University of London, pp.113–118.

Gundry, J and Slater, S (2005) *Flexible working: can home workers and their managers make it work? A knowledge ability white paper*. Malmesbury: Knowledge Ability Ltd.

Guzman, C (2012) 'Two kinds of academic fragility: the marketized university in Chile'. Presentation to the European Council for Educational Research (ECER) conference, Cadiz, Spain, October.

Habermas, J (1987a) *Lifeworld and system: a critique of functionalist reason*, vol. 2 of *The theory of communicative action*, trans. T McCarthy. Boston, MA: Beacon Press.

Habermas, J (1987b) *The theory of communicative action: a critique of functionalist reason*, vol. 2, *Lifeworld and system*, trans. T McCarthy. London: Polity Press.

Habermas, J (1984) *The theory of communicative action, vol. 1: reason and the rationalization of society*, trans. T McCarthy. Boston, MA: Beacon Press.

Hall, J (2009) 'Time to develop my career? That's a fantasy! UK professional standards framework and ethical staff and educational development'. In M Laycock and L Shrives (eds) *Embedding CPD in higher education*. London: Staff and Educational Development Association.

Halsey, A H (1995) 'Dons' decline reviewed'. In F Coffield (ed.) *Higher education in a learning society*, papers presented at St Edmund Hall, Oxford University, October. Durham: Durham University Press, pp.29–44.

Halsey, A H (1992) *The decline of donnish dominion*. Oxford: Clarendon Press.

Halsey, A H Trow, M A, with Fulton O (1971) *The British academics*. London: Faber & Faber.

Handel, M J (2003) *Complex picture of information technology and employment emerges*. Arlington, VA: SRI.

Hannan, A and Silver, H (2000) *Innovating in higher education: teaching, learning and institutional cultures*. Buckingham: SRHE/Open University Press.

Harding, A, Scott, A, Laske, S and Burtscher, C (eds) (2007) *Bright satanic mills: universities, regional development and the knowledge economy*. Aldershot: Ashgate.

Hargreaves, A and Fullan, M (2012) *Professional capital: transforming teaching in every school*. New York: Teachers' College Press.

Hargreaves, A (2000) 'Four ages of professionalism and professional learning', *Teachers and Teaching: History and Practice*, 6 (2), pp.151–182.

Hargreaves, A (1999) 'The psychic rewards (and annoyances) of classroom teaching'. In M Hammersley (ed.) *Researching school experience: ethnographic studies of teaching and learning*. London: Falmer Press, pp.87–106.

Hargreaves, A (1998) 'The emotional practice of teaching', *Teaching and Teacher Education*, 14 (8), pp.835–854.

Hargreaves, A (1994) *Changing teachers, changing times: teachers' work and culture in the post modern age*. New York: Teachers' College Press.

Harland, T and Staniforth, D (2003) 'Academic development as academic work', *International Journal of Academic Development*, 8 (1/2), pp.25–35.

Harris, L (2003) 'Home-based teleworking and the employment relationship, managerial challenges and dilemmas', *Personnel Review*, 32 (4), pp.422–437.

Harris, S (2005) 'Rethinking academic identities in neo-liberal times', *Teaching in Higher Education*, 10 (4), pp.421–433.

Haskel, J E and Slaughter, M J (2002) 'Does the sector bias of skill–biased technical change explain changing skill premia?' *European Economic Review*, 46, pp.1757–1783.

Hata, T (2009) 'Daigaku kyouiku kaikaku to fakaruthī diberoppumento' ['University education reform and faculty development']. In Center for Advancement of Higher Education, *Fakaruthī diberoppumento wo koete [Beyond faculty development]*. Sendai: Tohoku University Press, pp.3–22.

Hawkins, P and Shohet, R (2007) *Supervision in the helping professions* (3rd edition). Maidenhead: Open University Press.

Haynes, K (2011) 'Tensions in (re) presenting the self in reflexive autoethnographical research', *Qualitative Research in Organizations and Management: An International Journal*, 6 (2), pp.134–149.

Haythornthwaite, C and Andrews, R (2011) *E-learning theory and practice*. London: SAGE.

Haythornthwaite, C (2010) Leverhulme trust public lectures, http://newdoctorates. blogspot.com/2009/10/leverhulme-trust-public-lectures.html, accessed 30 April 2012.

HEA (Higher Education Academy) (2008a) 'Quality enhancement and assurance – a changing picture', Higher Education Academy, http://www.heacademy.ac.uk/assets/ documents/events/QualityEnhancement_report.pdf, accessed 11 February 2013.

HEA (Higher Education Academy) (2008b) National Teaching Fellowship Scheme, Higher Education Academy, http://www.heacademy.ac.uk/ourwork/professional/ntfs, accessed 11 February 2013.

Healey, M (2000) 'Developing the scholarship of teaching in higher education: a discipline-based approach', *Higher Education Research and Development*, 19, pp.169–189.

HEFCE (2012) *Panel criteria and working methods*. London: Higher Education Funding Council for England (HEFCE).

HEFCE (2001) *Rewarding and developing staff in higher education*. London: Higher Education Funding Council for England (HEFCE), pp.1–24.

Heidegger, M (1927) *Being and time*, trans. J. Macquarrie and E. Robinson. London: SCM Press.

Held, D (2005) *Debating globalization*. Cambridge: Polity Press.

Hendry, C (1995) *Human resource management: a strategic approach to employment*. Oxford: Butterworth Heinemann.

Henkel, M (2005) 'Academic identity and autonomy in a changing policy environment', *Higher Education*, 49 pp.155–176.

Henkel, M (2002) 'Emerging concepts of academic leadership and their implications for intra-institutional roles and relationships in higher education', *European Journal of Education*, 3 (1), pp.29–41.

Henkel, M (2000) *Academic identities and policy changes in higher education*, HE policy series 46. London: Jessica Kinglsey.

Henkel, M and Little, B (1999) 'Introduction'. In M Henkel and B Little (eds) *Changing relationships between higher education and the state*. London: Jessica Kingsley, pp.9–21.

HEQCO (Higher Education Quality Council of Ontario) (2013) *Quality: shifting the focus. A report from the Expert Panel to assess the strategic mandate agreement submissions*. Toronto: HEQCO, www.heqco.ca/SiteCollectionDocuments/FINAL%20 SMA%20Report.pdf.

Herzfeld, M (1992) *The Social production of indifference. Exploring the symbolic roots of western bureaucracy*. Chicago: University of Chicago Press.

HESA (2012) *Resources of higher education institutions 2010/11*. SFR 170. Cheltenham: Higher Education Statistics Authority (HESA).

HESA (2011a) *Staff at higher education institutions in the UK 2009/10*. SFR 154. Cheltenham: HESA.

HESA (2011b) *Staff in higher education institutions 2009/10*. Cheltenham: HESA.

HESA (2010a) *Staff in higher education institutions 2009/10*. Cheltenham: HESA.

HESA (2010b) *Resources of higher education institutions 2008/09*. Press release 147, http:// www.hesa.ac.uk/content/view/1730/161/.

HESA (2009) *Resources of higher education institutions 2007/08*. Cheltenham: HESA.

HESA (2008) 'Student numbers by HE institution', http://www.hesa.ac.uk/content/ view/1897/239/, accessed 23 January 2009.

HESA (2005) *Staff in higher education institutions 2003/04*. Cheltenham: HESA.

HESA (2002) *Resources of higher education institutions 2001/2002*. Cheltenham: HESA.

Higham, J and Yeomans, D (2007) 'Policy memory and policy amnesia in 14–19 education: learning from the past'. In D Raffe and K Spours (eds) *Policy learning in 14–19 education and training: learning from the past*. London: Bedford Way.

Higher Education Strategy Group (2010) *National strategy for higher education to 2030: report of the National Strategy Group*. Dublin: Department of Education and Skills.

Hillage, J and Pollard, E (1998) *Employability, developing a framework for policy analysis*, research report RR85. Brighton: Institute for Employment Studies.

Hilsdon, J (2011) 'What is learning development?' In P Hartley, J Hilsdon, C Keenan, S Sinfield and M Verity (eds) *Learning development in higher education*. Basingstoke: Palgrave Macmillan.

Hiltz, S R and Wellman, B (1997) 'Asynchronous learning networks as a virtual classroom', *Communications of the ACM*, 40 (9), pp.44–49.

Hiltz, S R (1986) 'The virtual classroom: using computer-mediated communication for university teaching', *Journal of Communication*, 36 (2), pp.95–104.

Himanen, P (2001) *The Hacker ethic and the spirit of the information age*. Harmondsworth: Vintage.

Hochschild, A (2003) *The managed heart* (20th anniversary edition). London: University of California Press.

Hochschild, A (1983) *The managed heart: commercialisation of human feeling*. Berkley, CA: University of California Press.

Hochschild, A (1979) 'Emotion work, feeling rules, and social structure', *American Journal of Sociology*, 85 (3), pp.551–575.

Hodgson, A and Spours, K (1999) *New Labour's educational agenda*. London: Kogan Page.

Hodkinson, S and Taylor, A (2002) 'Initiation rites: the case of new university lecturers', *Innovations in Education and Teaching International*, 39 (4), pp.256–264.

Holdsworth, C (2006) 'Don't you think you're missing out, living at home? Student experiences and residential transitions', *Sociological Review*, 54 (3), pp. 95–519.

Holmes, G and McElwee, G (1995) 'Total quality management in higher education, how to approach human resource management', *TQM Magazine*, 7 (6), p.6.

Hong, K-S, Ridzuan, A and Kuek, M-K (2003) 'Students' attitudes toward the use of the internet for learning: a study at a university in Malaysia', *Educational Technology and Society*, 6 (2) pp.45–49.

Hope-Hailey, V, Farndale, E and Truss, C (2005) 'The HR department's role in organisational performance', *Human Resource Management Journal*, 15 (3), pp.49–66.

Hoskin, K (1996) 'The "awful idea of accountability": Inscribing people into the measurement of objects'. In R Munro and J Mouritsen (eds) *Accountability: power, ethos and technologies of managing*. London: International Thomson Business Press, https://www.gov.uk/government/speeches/david-willetts-university-challenge, accessed 18 March 2013.

Hoyle, E and John, P (1995) *Professional knowledge and professional practice*. London: Cassell.

Hoyle, E (1974) 'Professionality, professionalism and control in teaching', *London Educational Review*, 3 (2), pp.13–19.

Huberman, M (1991) 'Surviving the first phase of the teaching career', *Cahiers Pedagogiques*, 290, pp.15–17.

Hudson, A (2009) 'New professionals and new technologies in new higher education? conceptualising struggles in the field'. Unpublished doctoral thesis, Umeå University, Stockholm Department of Interactive Media and Learning (IML).

Hughes, L W (2005) 'Developing transparent relationships through humour in the authentic leader-follower relationship'. In J W Gardner, B J Avolio and F Walumbwa (eds) *Authentic leadership theory and practice: origins, effects and development monographs in leadership and management*. San Diego, CA: Elsevier, pp.83–106.

Humphrys, N (2005) 'Values and student support'. In *Values in Higher Education*. Leeds: St Bride's Major/Aureus/University of Leeds.

Hunt, L, Bromage, A and Tomkinson, B (2006) *The realities of change in higher education: interventions to promote learning and teaching*. Abingdon: Routledge.

Huselid, M A (1995) 'The impact of human resource management practices on turnover, productivity, and corporate financial performance', *Academy of Management Journal*, 38, pp.635–672.

Hyland, T and Merrill, B (2003) *The changing face of further education*. Falmer: Routledge.

Illes, L (1999) 'Ecosystems and villages: using transformational metaphors to build community in higher education institutions', *Journal of Higher Education Policy and Management*, 21 (1), pp.57–69.

Illich, I (1971) *Deschooling society*. London: Marion Boyars.

Inkson, K, Gunz, H, Ganesh, S and Roper, J (2012) 'Boundaryless careers: bringing back the boundaries', *Organizaton Studies*, 33 (3), pp.323–340.

Inman, M (2009) 'Learning to lead: development for middle-level leaders in higher education in England and Wales', *Professional Development in Education*, 35 (3), pp.417–432.

Inoshita, O (2008) 'FD no dagisei to katsudo no kadai' ['Multivocality of FD and issues with practices'], *IDE gendai no koto kyoiku* [*IDE Current Higher Education*], 8/9, pp.10–16.

Isenbarger L and Zembylas, M (2006) 'The emotional labour of caring in teaching', *Teacher and Teacher Education*, 22, pp.120–134.

Jackson, A (ed.) (1987) *Anthropology at home*. London: Tavistock.

Jackson, J C, Hart, R P, Gordon, S M, Hopkins, R O, Girard, T D and Ely, E W (2008) 'Post-traumatic stress disorder and post-traumatic stress symptoms following critical illness in medical intensive care unit patients: assessing the magnitude of the problem', *Nurse Critical Care*, 13 (4), pp.215–226.

James, A (1986) 'Learning to belong: the boundaries of adolescence'. In A P Cohen (ed.) *Symbolising boundaries: identity and diversity in British cultures, anthropological studies of Britain No.2*. Manchester: Manchester University Press, pp.155–170.

James, D and Biesta, G (2007) *Improving learning cultures in further education*. London: Routledge Falmer.

Jameson, J (2012) 'Leadership values, trust and negative capability: managing the uncertainties of future English higher education', *Higher Education Quarterly*, 66 (4), pp.391–414.

Jenkins, R (2008) *Social identity*. Abingdon: Routledge.

Jenkins, S and Conley, H (2006) 'Living with the contradictions of modernisation? Emotional management in the teaching profession', *Public Administration*, 85 (4), pp.979–1001.

Jephcote, M (2011) 'The unintended consequences of funding policies on student achievement at colleges of further education in Wales and England'. In E Sutin, D Derrico, R Raby and E Valeau (eds) *Increasing effectiveness of community college financial models: a global perspective for the global economy*. New York: Palgrave Macmillan, pp.265–275.

Jephcote, M and Salisbury, J (2009) 'Further education teachers' accounts of their professional identities', *Teaching and Teacher Education*, 25 (7), pp.966–972.

Jephcote, M and Salisbury, J (2008) 'Being a teacher in further education in changing times', *Research in Post Compulsory Education*, 13 (2), pp.163–172.

Jephcote, M, Salisbury, J and Rees, G (2008) 'Being a further education teacher in changing times', *Research in Post Compulsory Education*, 13 (2), pp.163–172.

Jephcote, M and Salisbury, J (2007) 'The long shadow of incorporation: the further education sector in devolved Wales', *The Welsh Journal of Education*, 14 (1), pp.100–116.

Jephcote, M, Salisbury, J, Roberts, J and Rees, G (2006) 'Locality, learning and identity: teachers' constructs of students and their learning', Working Paper No.6: *Learning and Working in Further Education in Wales*, www.FurtherEducationResearch.org, accessed 29 January 2013.

Jephcote, M and Salisbury, J (2005) 'Entering the field: researching further education'. Paper presented at British Educational Research Association annual conference, University of Glamorgan, 14–17 September.

JISC (Joint Information Systems Committee) (2011a) 'Retaining students', http://www.jisc.ac.uk/supportingyourinstitution/studentjourney/retainingstudents.aspx, accessed 11 June 2011.

JISC (2011b) 'How can we improve the way students are assessed?' http://www.jisc.ac.uk/supportingyourinstitution/studentjourney/studentassessment.aspx, accessed on 17 June 2011.

JISC Joint information systems Committee (JISC) (2010a) 'Effective assessment in a digital age: a guide to technology-enhanced assessment and feedback', http://www.jisc.ac.uk/supportingyourinstitution/studentjourney/~/media/documents/programmes/elearning/digiassess_eada.ashx, accessed: 19 June 2011.

JISC (2010b) 'Learning literacies in a digital age (LLiDA)', http://www.jisc.ac.uk/whatwedo/projects/elearningllida.aspx, accessed 30 April 2012.

Johnson, T J (1972) *Professions and power: studies in sociology.* London: Macmillan.

Jones, G (2012) 'Ontario higher education's year of living dangerously', *University World News*, 253, http://www.universityworldnews.com/article.php?story=20121230140612586.

Jones, N (2004) 'From here to e-ternity: a learning journey, professorial inaugural lecture', University of Glamorgan, Pontypridd, UK, March.

Jones, R W and Scully, R (2012) *Wales says yes: devolution and the 2011 Welsh referendum.* Cardiff: University of Wales Press.

Josselson, R and Lieblich, A (eds) (1993) *The narrative study of lives.* Thousand Oaks, CA: Sage.

Kahai, S S, Sosik, J J and Avolio, B J (2004) 'Effects of participative and directive leadership in electronic groups', *Group and Organization Management*, pp.67–105.

Kallioniemi-Chambers, V (2010) *Kulttuuriset ajan mallit yliopiston pedagogisessa projektitoiminnassa acta universitatis tamperensis: cultural models of time in educational projects at the university*, 1496. Tampere: Tampere University Press.

Keashly, L and Neuman, J H (2010) 'Faculty experiences with bullying in higher education', *Administrative Theory and Praxis*, 32 (1), pp.48–70.

Keenoy, T (2007) 'Chasing the shadows of HRM'. Paper given to the fifth Annual Critical Management Studies Conference ('Where is Critical HRM?'), Manchester Business School, Manchester University, 11–13 July.

Kelly, G A ([1955] 1991) *The psychology of personal constructs.* New York: Norton.

Kerr, C (1994) *Higher education cannot escape history: issues for the twenty-first century.* Albany, NY: State University of New York Press.

Kerr, C (1963) *The uses of the university.* Cambridge, MA: Harvard University Press.

Kersley, B, Alpin, C, Forth, J, Bryson, A, Bewley, H, Dix, G, and Oxenbridge, S (2006) *Inside the workplace: findings from the 2004 workplace employment relations survey*, London: Taylor & Francis Group.

King, K and McGrath, S A (2005) *Knowledge for development?: comparing British, Japanese, Swedish and World Bank aid*. London: Zed Books.

King, V (2012) 'Novel readings: the history of a writing community by a partial, prejudiced and ignorant historian', *Arts and Humanities in Higher Education*, 1–11, published online 12 December 2012.

King, V, Clouder, L, Dean, M, Deepwell, F, and Ganobcsik-Williams, L (2006) 'Reflections on the first international iPED conference', Coventry TechnoCentre, UK, 10–11 September, 'Teaching in Higher Education'. London: Taylor & Francis.

Kinukawa, M (1999) 'FD towa nanika' ['What is FD?']. In University Seminar House, *Daigakuryoku wo tsukuru* [*Handbook of Faculty Development*. Tokyo: Toshindo.

Kitagawa, F (2012) 'Academic salary in the United Kingdom: marketization and national policy development'. In P G Altbach, L Reisberg, M Yudkevich, G Androushchak and I F Pacheco *Paying the professoriate: a global comparison of compensation and contracts*. New York: Routledge, pp.308–328.

Knight, J (2010) 'Higher education crossing borders'. In *International Encyclopedia of Education* (3rd edition). Oxford: Elsevier.

Knight, P (2006) *The effects of post graduate certificates in teaching and learning in higher education. Report to sponsor*. Milton Keynes: Open University Institute of Technology.

Knight, S (2003) *Robin Hood: a mythic biography*. Ithaca, NY: Cornell University Press.

Kodner, D (2002) 'Integrated care: meaning, logic, applications, and implications – a discussion paper', *International Journal of Integrated Care*, 2 (12), http://www.ncbi.nlm. nih.gov/pmc/articles/PMC1480401/?tool=pubmed, accessed 26 January 2011.

Kogan, M and Hanney, S (2000) *Reforming higher education*. London: Jessica Kingsley.

Kogan, M, Bauer, M, Bleiklie, I and Henkel, M (2000) *Transforming higher education: a comparative study*. London: Jessica Kingsley.

Kogan, M (1999) 'Academic and administrative interface'. In M Henkel and B Little (eds) *Changing relationships between higher education and the state*. London: Jessica Kingsley, pp.263–279.

Kogan, M (1984) 'The political view'. In B R Clark (ed.) *Perspectives on higher education*. Berkeley, CA: University of California Press, pp.56–75.

Kogan, M (1983) *The attack on higher education*. London: Kogan Page.

Kolsaker, A (2008) 'Academic professionalism in the managerialist era: a study of English universities', *Studies in Higher Education*, 33 (5), pp.513–525.

Kreber, C (2000) 'How university teaching award winners conceptualise academic work: some further thoughts on the meaning of scholarship', *Teaching in Higher Education*, 5 pp.61–78.

Kress, G and van Leeuwen, T (2001) *Multimodal discourse: the modes and media of contemporary communication*. London: Arnold.

Kristeva, J (1991) *Strangers to ourselves*. New York: Columbia University Press.

Kusterer, K (1978) *Know-how on the job: the important working knowledge of 'unskilled' workers*. Boulder, CO: West View Press.

Kyvik, S (2000) 'Academic work in Norwegian higher education'. In M Tight (ed.) *Academic Life and Work*, Oxford: Elsevier Press, pp.33–72.

Lacey, C (1977) *The socialization of teachers*. London: Taylor & Francis.

Laffin, M (1998) *Beyond bureaucracy? The professions in the contemporary public sector*. Aldershot: Ashgate.

Lamont, M (2009) *How professors think: inside the curious world of academic judgement*. Cambridge, MA: Harvard University Press.

Land, R (2004) *Educational development. Discourse, identity and practice.* Maidenhead: Open University Press.

Lane, J E (1993) *The public sector: concepts, models and approaches.* London: Sage.

Lau, A, Blackey, H and Jones, N (2006) 'Embedding blended learning in a higher education institution', Proceedings of 6th international conference on 'The Scholarship of Teaching and Learning' (SoTL), London.

Laurillard, D (2002) *Design tools for e-learning.* London: DfES.

Lave, J and Wenger, E (1991) *Situated learning: legitimate, peripheral participation.* Cambridge: Cambridge University Press.

Lawton, W and Katsomitros, K (2012) *MOOCs and disruptive Innovation: the challenge to HE business models.* London: Observatory on Borderless Higher Education (OBHE).

Laycock, M (2009a) 'CPD and critical learning communities: you can't have one without the other'. In M Laycock and L Shrives (eds) *Embedding CPD in higher education.* London: Staff and Educational Development Association.

Laycock, M (2009b) *Personal tutoring in higher education – where now and where next?* London: SEDA.

Le Cornu, R (2009) 'Crossing boundaries: challenges of academics working in professional experiences', refereed paper presented at 'Teacher Education Crossing Borders: Cultures, Contexts, Communities And Curriculum' the annual conference of the Australian Teacher Education Association (ATEA), Albury, 28 June–1 July.

Lea, M and Stierer, B (2009) 'Lecturers' everyday writing as professional practice in the university as a workplace: new insights into academic identities', *Studies in Higher Education*, 34 (4), pp.417–428.

Lea, T (2008) *Bureaucrats and bleeding hearts: indigenous health in Northern Australia.* Sydney: UNSW Press.

Leach, E (1976) *Culture and communication the logic by which symbols are connected.* Cambridge: Cambridge University Press.

Leathwood, C and Hey, V (2009) 'Gender/ed discourses and emotional sub-texts: theorising emotion in UK higher education', *Teaching in Higher Education*, 14 (4), pp.429–440.

Leathwood, C and O' Connell, P (2003) ' "It's a struggle": constructing the new student in HE', *Journal of Education Policy*, 18 (6), pp.597–615.

Leccardi, C (2007) 'New temporal perspectives in the "high-speed society" '. In R Hassan and P Ronald (eds) *24/7: Time and temporality in the network society.* Stanford, CA: Stanford University Press, pp.25–36.

Lee, A and McWilliam, E (2008) 'What game are we in? Living with academic development', *International Journal for Academic Development*, 13 (1), pp.67–77.

Lee, D M S, Trauth, E M and Farwell, D (1995) 'Critical skills and knowledge requirements of IS professionals: a joint academic/industry investigation', *MIS Quarterly*, 9 (3), pp.313–340.

Legge, K (2005) *Human resource management – rhetorics and realities.* Basingstoke: Palgrave Macmillan.

Leitch, A (2006) *Prosperity for all in the global economy– world class skills: the Leitch Review of Skills.* London: HMSO.

Leithwood, C and O' Connell, P (2003) ' "It's a struggle": constructing the new student in HE', *Journal of Education Policy*, 18 (6), pp.597–615.

Lepak, D P and Snell, S A (1999) 'The human resource architecture: towards a theory of human capital allocation and development', *Academy of Management Review*, 24 (1), pp.31–48.

Levie, J and Hart, M (2012) *Global enterpreneurship monitor: United Kingdom 2011 monitoring report*. Strathclyde: University of Strathclyde and Aston Business School.

Levine, R B, Lin F, Kern, D E, Wright, S M and Carrese, J (2011) 'Stories from early-career women physicians who have left academic medicine: A qualitative study at a single institution', *Academic Medicine*, 86 (6), pp.752–758.

Levine, R B and Mechaber, H F (2006) 'Opting in: part–time careers in academic medicine', *American Journal of Medicine*, 119, pp.450–453.

Lewig, K and Dollard, M (2003) 'Emotional dissonance, emotional exhaustion and job satisfaction in call centre workers', *European Journal of Work and Organizational Psychology*, 12 (4), pp.366–392.

Liamputtong, P and Ezzy, D (2005) *Qualitative research methods*. Oxford: Oxford University Press.

Liberman, M (2011) 'Translated phrase-list jokes', http://languagelog.ldc.upenn.edu/nll/?p=3154, accessed 20 June 2011.

Lichtman, M (2010) *Qualitative research in education: a user's guide*. Thousand Oaks, CA: Sage.

Lipsett, A and Demopoulos, K (2005) 'Star staff cosseted in bid to up RAE rating', *Times Higher Educational Supplement*, 13 May.

Locke, W and Bennion, A (2010) *The changing academic profession in the UK and beyond*. London: UUK.

Lortie, D (1975) *School teacher: a sociological study*. Chicago: University of Chicago Press.

Lucas, N (2007) 'Rethinking initial teacher education for further education teachers: from a standards-led to a knowledge-based approach', *Teaching Education*, 18 (2), pp.93–106.

Luckin, R, Clark, W, Garnett, F, Whitworth, A, Akass, J and Cook, J (2010) 'Learner generated contexts: a framework to support the effective use of technology for learning'. In M Lee, C Sturt, and C McLoughlin, (eds) *Web 2.0–based e-learning: applying social informatics for tertiary teaching*. Sydney: IGI Global.

Lumby, J and Foskett N (2005) *14–19 education policy, leadership and learning*. London: Sage.

Lynch, K (1989) 'Solidary Labour: its nature and marginalisation', *The Sociological Review*, 37 (1), pp.1–14.

Macdonald, L (1998) 'Points mean prizes: reflections on awards for teaching excellence', *Innovations in Education and Training International*, 35 (2), pp.130–132.

MacDonald, L A C (2005) *Wellness at work: protecting and promoting employee well-being*. London: Chartered Institute of Personnel and Development.

Macdonald, R (2003) 'Developing a scholarship of academic development: setting the context'. In H Eggins and R Macdonald (eds) *The scholarship of academic development*. Philadelphia, PA: SRHE/Open University Press, pp.1–10.

Macfarlane, B (2007) *The academic citizen: the virtue of service in university life*. Abingdon: Routledge.

Macfarlane, B (2005) 'The disengaged academic: the retreat from citizenship', *Higher Education Quarterly*, 59 (4), pp.296–312.

Macfarlane, B (2004) *Teaching with integrity: the ethics of academic practice*. London: Routledge Falmer.

Machlup, F (1962) *Knowledge production and distribution in the United States*. Princeton, NJ: Princeton University Press.

MacNeil, M (1997) 'From nurse to teacher: Recognizing a status passage', *Journal of Advanced Nursing*, 25 (3), pp.634–642.

Macpherson, C B (1962) *The political theory of possessive individualism: Hobbes to Locke*. Oxford: Clarendon Press.

Madden, A (2008) 'The researchers the RAE forgot', *The Guardian*, 18 December.

Malcolm, J and Zukas, M (2009) 'Making a mess of academic work: experience, purpose and identity', *Teaching in Higher Education*, 14 (5), pp.495–506.

Malloch, M, Cairns, L, Evans, K and O'Connor, B (eds) (2011) *The SAGE handbook of workplace Learning*. London: Sage.

Manathunga, C (2007) '"Unhomely" academic developer identities: more post–colonial explorations', *International Journal for Academic Development*, 12 (1), pp.25–34.

Markham, A N (2004) 'The internet as research context'. In C Seale, G Giampietro, J F Bubrium and D Silvermen (eds) *Qualitative research practice*. London: Sage.

Martin, S B (1999) 'Employment in the information age: information technology and information work', *Journal of Policy, Regulation and Strategy for Telecommunications Information and Media*,1 (3), June, pp.271–283.

Martinez, P and Munday, F (1998) *9,000 voices: student persistence and drop-out in further education*. Report commissioned by Further Education Development Agency. London: FEDA.

Marton, F (1981) 'Phenomenography – describing conceptions of the world around us', *Instructional Science*, 10, pp.177–200.

Masino, G (1999) 'Information technology and dilemmas in organizational learning', *Journal of Organizational Change Management*, 12 (5), pp.360–376.

Mason, R (1999) 'European trends in the virtual delivery of education'. In G Farrell (ed.) *The development of virtual education: a global perspective*. Vancouver: Commonwealth of Learning, pp.77–87.

Mason, R (1998) *Globalising education: trends and applications*. London: Routledge.

Mauthner, N S and Doucet, A (2008) 'Knowledge once divided can be hard to put together again: an epistemological critique of collaborative and team-based research practices', *Sociology*, 42 (5), pp.971–985.

Mauthner, N S and Doucet, A (2003) 'Reflexive accounts and accounts of reflexivity in qualitative data analysis', *Sociology*, 37 (3), pp.413–431.

May, H and Bridger, K (2010) *Developing and embedding inclusive policy and practice in higher education*. York: Higher Education Academy.

May, T (2011) *Social research, issues, methods and process* (4th edition). Maidenhead: Open University Press/McGraw-Hill Education.

McAlpine, L and C Amundsen (eds) (2011) *Doctoral education: research-based strategies for doctoral students, supervisors and administrators*. Amsterdam: Springer.

McAlpine, L and Åkerlind, G S (2010) *Becoming an academic: international perspectives*. Basingstoke: Palgrave Macmillan.

McCaffery, P (2004) *The higher education manager's handbook*. London: Routledge Falmer.

McCloskey, D W, Antonucci, Y L S and Schug, J (1998) 'Web-based vs. traditional course development: identifying differences in user characteristics and performance outcomes'. In: *Proceedings of the International Business Schools Computing Association Annual Conference. Denver, Colorado, 1998.*

McDowell, L (2009) *Working bodies: interactive service employment and workplace*. Oxford: Wiley-Blackwell.

McGettigan, A (2011) '"New providers": the creation of a market in higher education', *Radical Philosophy*, 167, pp.2–8.

McGivney, V (2004) *Men earn, women learn: bridging the gender divide in adult education and training*. Leicester: NIACE.

McGivney, V (1999) *Excluded men: men who are missing from education and training*. Leicester, UK: NIACE.

Bibliography

337

McGregor, F (1960) *The human side of enterprise*. New York: McGraw-Hill.

Mcllveen, P (2008) 'Autoethnography as a method for reflexive research and practice in vocational psychology', *Australian Journal of Career Development*, 17 (2), pp.13–20.

McInnis, C (2000) 'Towards new balance or new divides? The changing work roles of academics in Australia'. In M Tight (ed.) *Academic work and life: what it is to be an academic and how this is changing*. Oxford: Elsevier Press.

McLaughlan (ed) *New Managerialism, new welfare?* London: Sage, pp. 45–61.

McNally, J (2006) 'From informal learning to identity formation: a conceptual journey in early teacher development', *Scottish Educational Review*, 37, pp.79–89.

McNamara, O, Roberts, L, Basit, T and Brown, T (2002) 'Rites of passage in initial teacher training: ritual, performance, ordeal and numeracy skills test', *British Educational Research Journal*, 28 (6), pp.863–878.

McNay, I (1998) 'The paradoxes of research assessment and funding'. In M Henkel and B Little (eds) *Changing relationships between higher education and the state*. London: Jessica Kingsley, pp.191–203.

McNay, I (1992) 'Structure, restructuring and resourcing'. In I McNay (ed). *Visions of post-compulsory education*. Birmingham: SRHE/Open University, pp.143–151.

Mears, R (2000) 'Called to account, the last autonomous profession?' In E Harrison and R Mears (eds) *Assessing sociologists in higher education*. Aldershot: Ashgate.

Meneley, A and Young, D J (eds) (2005) *Auto-ethnographies: the anthropology of academic practices*. Peterborough, ON: Broadview Press.

Menzies, H and Newson, J (2008) 'Time, stress and intellectual engagement in academic work: exploring gender difference', *Gender, Work and Organization*,15 (5), pp.504–505.

Merrill, B and McKie, J (1998) 'Money and the mature student', *Adults Learning*, 9 (6), pp.6–7

Metcalf, H, Rolfe, H, Stevens, P and Weale, M (2005) *Recruitment and retention of academic staff in Higher Education*. London: DfES, p.55.

Metcalfe, A S (2010) 'Revising academic capitalism in Canada: no longer the exception', *Journal of Higher Education*, 81 (4), pp.489–514.

MEXT (2009) *Chishiki kiban shakai wo kenin suru jinzai no ikusei to katuyaku no sokushin ni mukete* [*Educating future leaders of knowledge based society*]. Tokyo: Ministry of Education, Culture, Sport, Science and Technology.

MEXT (2008) *Gakushi katei kyōikuno kouchiku ni mukete* [*Establishing undergraduate education*]. Tokyo: Ministry of Education, Culture, Sport, Science and Technology, http://www.mext.go.jp/b_menu/shingi/chukyo/chukyo0/toushin/1217067.htm, accessed 7 February 2013.

MEXT University Council (1998) *A vision for the university of the 21st century and future reform measures: to be distinctive universities in a competitive environment*. Tokyo: Ministry of Education, Culture, Sport, Science and Technology, http://www.mext.go.jp/b_menu/shingi/12/daigaku/toushin/981002.htm, accessed 8 February 2013.

Miller, H (1995) 'States, economies and the changing labour process of academics: Australia, Canada and the United Kingdom'. In J Smyth (ed.) *Academic work: the changing labour process in higher education*. Buckingham: SRHE/Open University Press.

Minchington, B (2010) *Employer Brand Leadership – A Global Perspective*. Australia: Collective Learning Australia.

Mitra, S and Dangwal, R (2010) 'Limits to self-organising systems of learning – the Kalikuppam experiment', *British Journal of Educational Technology*, 41 (5), pp.672–688.

Mitwa (2007) 'Technology for teaching and learning in higher education contexts: Activity theory and actor network theory analytical perspectives', *International Journal of Education and Development using Information and Communication Technology*, 3 (4), pp.54–70.

Moore, W J, Newman, R J and Turnball, G K (1998) 'Do academic wages decrease with seniority?', *Journal of Labour Economics*, 16 (2), pp.352–366.

Morelli, N (2001) 'The space of telework physical and virtual configurations for remote work'. In D Holmes (ed.) *Virtual globalization: virtual spaces/tourist spaces*. London: Routledge.

Morgan, J (2011) 'A Starring role beckons', *The Times Higher*, 14 April.

Morgan, J (2010) 'Stressed staff can't get no satisfaction', *The Times Higher*, 13 May.

Morley, L (2012) 'Imagining the university of the future'. In: R Barnett (ed.) *The future university: ideas and possibilities*. New York: Routledge, pp.26–35.

Morley, L (2010) 'Imagining the university of the future', keynote lecture to Society for Educational Studies conference, November 2010, London, http://www.sussex.ac.uk/newsandevents/sussexlectures/louisemorley.php.

Morley, L (2008) 'The micropolitics of professionalism: power and collective identities in higher education'. In B Cunningham (ed.) *Exploring Professionalism*. London: Institute of Education, pp.99–120.

Morley, L (2005) 'Opportunity or exploitation? Women and quality assurance in higher education', *Gender and Education*, 17 (4), pp.411–429.

Morley, L (2003) *Quality and power in higher education*. Buckingham: Open University Press.

Morley, L (1998) 'All You need is love: feminist pedagogy for empowerment and emotional labour in the academy', *International Journal of Inclusive Education*, 2 (1), pp.15–27.

Morley, M (2005) 'Gender equity in Commonwealth higher education', *Women's Studies International Forum*, 28, pp.209–221.

Morris, J and Feldman, D (1996) 'The dimensions, antecedents, and consequences of emotional labour', *Academy of Management Review*, 21 (4), pp.986–1010.

Mottl, J N (2000) 'Money matters, but not that much', *Information Week*, 816, pp.223–228.

Moule, P (2007) 'Challenging the five-stage model for e-learning: a new approach', *ALT-J, Research in Learning Technology*, 15 (1), pp.37–50, March.

MRC (2011a) 'Supporting scientists'. In *Annual Report 2011/12*. London: MRC.

MRC (2011b) 'Next destination'. In *Annual Report 2011/12*. London: MRC.

MRC (2010) 'Supporting staff'. In *Annual Report 2009/10*. London: MRC.

MRC (2009) *Outputs, outcomes and impacts of medical research: analysis of MRC e-val data*. London: MRC.

MRC (2006) *A review of UK health research funding* (Cooksey Review). London: MRC.

Muncey, T (2010) *Creating authoethnographies*. London: Sage.

Murray, J (2005) 'Re-addressing the priorities: new teacher educators and induction into higher education', *European Journal of Teacher Education*, 28 (1), pp.67–85.

Musselin, C (2012) 'Revisiting academic work and academic trajectories: why? how?' Presentation to the University of Kent Centre for the Study of Higher Education Research Seminar, Canterbury, UK, 16 October 2012.

Musselin, C (2007) 'The transformation of academic work: facts and analysis', *Research and occasional paper series*, CHSE 4.07. Berkeley, CA: Centre for Studies in Higher Education, University of California.

Nadeem, S and Hendry, C (2003) 'Power dynamics in the long-term development of employee-friendly flexible working', *Women in Management Review*, 18 (1/2), pp.32–49.

Nagel, T (1979) 'What is it like to be a bat?' In T Nagel, *Mortal questions*. Cambridge: Cambridge University Press, pp.165–180.

NATFHE (2006) *Professional development and the academic role: a discussion paper*. London: NATFHE, pp.1–4.

Naidoo, S (2004) 'Bourdieu, the concept of "capital" and academic knowledge', paper presented to Society for Research into Higher Education annual conference, University of Bristol, December.

National Assembly for Wales (2012a) http://assemblywales.org/abthome/about_us-assembly_history_buildings.htm, accessed 23 August 2012.

National Assembly for Wales (2012b), http://www.assemblywales.org/bus–home/bus-comm-expert.htm, accessed 23 August 2012.

National Assembly for Wales Enterprise and Learning Committee (2009) *Final Report on the Economic Contribution of Higher Education in Wales*. Cardiff: NAFW.

NCIHE (National Committee of Inquiry into Higher Education) (1997a) *Higher education in the learning society*. London: HMSO.

NCIHE (1997b) *Academic staff in higher education: their experiences and expectations*, Report 3, National Commission of Inquiry into Higher Education, NCIHE ('Dearing'). London: HMSO.

Ncinda, T (2002) 'Research capacity strengthening in the south', *Social Science and Medicine*, 54, pp.1699–1711.

Nedeva, M and Boden, R (2006) 'Changing science: the advent of neo-liberalism', *Prometheus*. 24 (3), pp.269–281.

Neumann, A (2009) *Professing to learn: creating tenured lives and careers in the american research university*. Baltimore, MD: The Johns Hopkins University.

Newman, J (2000) 'Beyond the new public management? modernising public services'. In J Clarke, S Gewintz, and E McLaughlin (eds) *New managerialism, new welfare?* London: Sage, pp.45–61.

Newman, M (2009) 'HR report on staff stress dismissed "valueless"', *Times Higher Education*, 15 January.

Newman, M (2008) 'The UCEA [universities and colleges employers' association] poll says life is good on campus', *Times Higher Education*, 19 June.

Newson, J (2012) 'Academic feminism's entanglements with university corporatization', *Topia: Canadian Journal of Cultural Studies*, 28, pp.41–63.

Nias, J (1999) 'Teaching as a culture of care'. In J Prosser (ed.) *School culture*. London: Paul Chapman, pp.66–81.

Nickel, S and Quintini, G (2002) 'The consequences of the decline in public sector pay in Britain: a little bit of evidence', *The Economic Journal*, 112, F107–F118.

Nieminen, M (2005) *Academic research in change. transformation of Finnish university policies and university research during the 1990s*. Helsinki: The Finnish Society of Sciences and Letters.

Nixon, I, Smith, K, Stafford, R and Camm, S (2006) *Work-based learning: illuminating the higher education landscape (final report)*. York: Higher Education Academy.

Nixon, J (2012) 'Universities and the common good'. In R Barnett (ed.) *The future university: ideas and possibilities*. New York: Routledge, pp.141–151.

Nixon, J (2011) *Higher education and the public good: imagining the university*. London: Continuum.

Nixon, J (2003) 'Professional renewal as a condition of institutional change: rethinking academic work', *International Studies in Sociology of Education*, 13 (1), pp.3–15.

Nixon, J, Marks, A, Rowland, S and Walker, M (2001) 'Towards a new academic professionalism: a manifesto of hope', *British Journal of Sociology of Education*, 22 (2), pp.227–244.

Nixon, J (1996) 'Professional Identity and the restructuring of higher education', *Studies in Higher Education*, 21 (1), pp.5–16.

Noddings, N (1992) *The challenge to care in school*. New York: Teachers' College Press.

Norton, K, Longley, MJ and Ponton, M (2012) *The Best configuration of hospital services for Wales: a review of the evidence summary*. Pontypridd: University of Glamorgan and welsh NHS Confederation.

O'Connor, K E (2008) 'You choose to care: teachers, emotions and professional identity', *Teaching and Teacher Education*, 24 (1), pp.117–126.

O'Reilly, T (2005) 'What is Web 2.0?' http://oreilly.com/pub/a/web2/archive/what-is-web-20.html?page=1, accessed 30 April 2012.

Oades, L G, Caputi, P, Robinson, P M and Partridge, B (2005) 'A contemporary coaching theory to integrate work and life in changing times'. In M Cavanagh, A and T Kemp (eds) *Evidence-based coaching: volume-1, theory, research and practice from the behavioural sciences*. Queensland: Australian Academic Press.

Oancea, A (2009) 'Fixed-term employment in research: questions and experiences', *Research Intelligence*, 108, August, p.10.

OECD (2004) *Review of national policies for education – higher education in Ireland*. Paris: Organisation for Economic Cooperation and Development (OECD).

Office for National Statistics (2012) 'Measuring national well-being: education and skills'. London: ONS, http://www.ons.gov.uk/ons/dcp171766_268091.pdf, accessed 12 December 2012.

Ogbonna, E and Harris, L (2004) 'Work intensification and emotional labour amongst UK university lecturers: an exploratory study', *Organization Studies*, 25 (7), pp.1185–1203.

Oliver, L and Hooley, T (2010) *Researchers, fixed-term contracts and universities: understanding law in context, Vitae: realising the potential of researchers*. Cambridge: Careers Research and Advisory Centre (CRAC).

Oliver, L (2009) 'Researchers, fixed-term employment and the law', *Research Intelligence*, 108, August, p.12.

Oliver, M, Sharpe, R, Duggleby, D, Jennings and Kay, D (2004) 'Accrediting learning technologists: a review of the literature, schemes and programmes', ALT Accreditation project report no. 1.

Oliver, M (2002) 'What do learning technologists do?' *Innovations in Education and Teaching International*, 39 (4), pp.245–252.

Olssen, M and Peters, M (2005) 'Neoliberalism, higher education and the knowledge economy: from the free market to knowledge capitalism', *Journal of Education Policy*, 20 (3), pp.313–345.

Ong, L L and Mitchell, J D (2000) 'Professors and hamburgers: an international comparison of relative academic salaries', *Applied Economics*, 32 (7), pp.869–876.

Open University (2012) *History of the Open University*, http://www8.open.ac.uk/about/main/the-ou-explained/history-the-ou, accessed 3 April 2012.

Ornstein, M, Stewart, P and Drakich, J (1998) 'The status of women faculty in Canadian universities', *Education Quarterly Review*, 5 (2), pp.9–29.

Owen, M (2002) 'Sometimes you feel you're in niche time': the personal tutor system, a case study', *Active Learning in Higher Education*, 3 (1), pp.7–23.

Palloff, R M and Pratt, K (2007) *Building online learning communities: effective strategies for the virtual classroom*. Oxford: John Wiley.

Parliamentary Office of Science and Technology (2005) 'The 24-hour society', *Postnote*, 250, p.2.

Parsons, J, Avis, J and Bathmaker, A (2001) 'Now we look through the glass darkly: a comparative study of the perceptions of those working in FE with trainee teachers'. Paper presented at the Fourth International Conference on Vocational Education and Training Research, University of Wolverhampton, 16–18 July 2001.

Paton, N. (2009) 'Stress levels too high among university staff', *Personnel Today*, 20, 14 February, p.35.

Pears, I (2010) 'Universities are not businesses', *Times Higher Education*, 1 April.

Pearson, G (2012) *The rise and fall of management*. Farnham: Gower Press.

Peccei, R (2004) *Human resource management and the search for the happy workplace*. Rotterdam: Erasmus Research Institute of management, Rotterdam School of Management, Rotterdam School of Economics.

Peirce, G L, Desselle, S P, Draugalis, J R, Spies, A R, Davies, T S and Bolino, M (2012) 'Identifying psychological contract breaches to guide improvements in faculty recruitment, retention and development', *American Journal of Pharmaceutical Education*, 76 (6), p.108.

Pennings, J M, Lee, K and Van Witteloostuijin, A (1998) 'Human capital, social capital and firm dissolution', *Academy of Management Journal*, 41, pp.425–440.

Pennington, G (2003) *Guidelines for promoting and facilitating change*. York: Learning and Teaching Support Network.

Perutz, M (2000) 'A science video interview with molecular biologist, Max Perutz', 13 October.

Pfeffer, J (1998) *The human equation*. Boston, MA: Harvard Business School Press.

Phillips, D (1996) 'Campus support services'. In D Warner and D Palfreyman (eds) *Higher education management: the key elements*. Buckingham: SRHE/Open University Press, pp.155–165.

Phillips, S (1986) 'Natives and incomers: the symbolism of belonging in Muker parish, North Yorkshire'. In A Cohen (ed) *Symbolising boundaries: identity and diversity in British cultures*. Manchester: Manchester University Press, pp.141–154.

Polster, C (2012) 'Reconfiguring the academic dance: a critique of faculty's responses to administrative practices in Canadian universities', *Topia: Canadian Journal of Cultural Studies*, 28, pp.115–141.

Power, S (2008) 'The imaginative professional'. In B Cunningham (ed.) *Exploring Professionalism*. London: Institute of Education.

Pratt, D *et al.* (1998) *Five perspectives on teaching in adult and higher education*. Malabar, FL: Krieger.

Pratt, M L (1996) 'Fieldwork in common places'. In J Clifford and GE Marcus (eds) *Writing culture: the poetics and politics of ethnography*. Berkeley, CA: University of California Press, pp.27–50.

Prensky, M (2001) 'Digital natives, digital immigrants, part 1', *On the Horizon*, September/October, 9 (5), pp.1–6.

Presser, S (1980) 'Collaboration and the quality of research', *Social Studies of Science*, 10 (1), pp.95–101.

Prosser, M and Trigwell, K (1999) *Understanding learning and teaching*. Buckingham: SRHE/Open University Press, pp.15–18.

Punch, K F (2009) *Introduction to research methods in education*. London: Sage.

Pyoria, P (2005) 'Information technology, human relations and knowledge work teams', *Team Performance Management*, 11 (3/4), pp.104–112.

QAA (2010) *Celebrating 20 years of access to HE.* London: Quality Assurance Agency (QAA).

QAA (2003) 'Key statistics', www.accesstohe.ac.uk/partners/statistics/2003/key_stats_2003asp, accessed 16 July 2011.

Quinn, J (2010) *Learning communities and imagined social capital: learning to belong.* London: Continuum.

Quinlan, K and Akerlind, G (2000) 'Factors affecting departmental peer collaboration for faculty development: two cases in context', *Higher Education*, 40, pp.23–52.

Radin, B (2006) *Challenging the performance movement: accountability, complexity and democratic values.* Washington, DC: Georgetown University Press.

Rafaelli, A (1989) 'When cashiers meet customers: an analysis of the role of supermarket cashiers', *Academy of Management Journal*, 32, pp.245–273.

Rajaratnam, S M W and Arendt, J (2001) 'Health in a 24-h society', *The Lancet*, 358 (22), September.

Raman, S (2000) 'From industrial feudalism to industrial capitalism: putting labour back into knowledge politics'. In M Jacob and T Hellstrom (eds) *The future of knowledge.* Buckingham: SRHE/Open University Press, pp.109–124.

Ramsden, P (1991) *Learning to teach in higher education.* London: Routledge.

Rana, R (2000) *Counselling students: a psychodynamic perspective.* Basingstoke: Macmillan.

Randle, K and Brady, N (1997) 'Managerialism and professionalism in the Cinderella service', *Journal of Vocational Education and Training*, 49, pp.121–139.

Ranson, S (1994) *Towards the Learning Society.* London: Cassell Education.

Rayner, S, Fuller, M, McEwen, L and Roberts, H (2010) 'Managing leadership in the uk university: a case for researching the missing professoriate?' *Studies in Higher Education and the Social Sciences*, 35 (6), pp.617–631.

Reed, J (2007) *Appreciative inquiry research for change.* London: Sage.

Reed-Danahay, D (2001) 'Autoethnography, intimacy and ethnography'. In P Atkinson, A Coffey, S Delamont, J. Lofland and L Lofland (eds) *Handbook of contemporary ethnography.* London: Sage, pp.407–426.

Rees, C and Monrouxe, L (2011) 'Narrative enquiry research and case studies of identity and emotion in medical education'. Paper to special seminar, 'Narrative Enquiry: Making Meaning in Educational Research', 19 May, University of Dundee.

Reijerse, C and von Domberg, R (2010) 'Team and group development the AI way', *AI Practitioner*, 12 (4), pp.4–9.

Remmik, M, Karm, M, Haamer, A and Lepp, L (2011) 'Early-career academics learning in academic communities', *International Journal for Academic Development*, 16 (3), pp.187–199.

Research Councils UK (RCUK) and UUK (2008) *The Concordat to support the career development of researchers, an agreement between the funders and employers of researchers in the UK.* London: Research Councils UK and Universities UK.

Research Councils UK (RCUK) (2004) *International partnerships in action.* London: RCUK.

Reynolds, S (1994) 'Welsh credit developments', *Access Networking*, 1, pp.9–10.

Rhoades, G (1998) *Managed professionals.* Albany, NY: State University of New York Press.

Richardson, G E (2002) 'The metatheory of resilience and resiliency', *Journal of Clinical Psychology*, 58 (3), pp.307–332.

Ricoeur, P (1992) *Oneself as another*, trans. K. Blamey. Chicago: University of Chicago Press.

Ritchie, S M and Rigano, D L (2007) 'Solidarity through collaborative research', *International Journal of Qualitative Studies in Education*, 20 (2), pp.129–150.

Roberts, G (2003) *Review of research assessment.* Report by Sir Gareth Roberts to the UK Funding Bodies. Bristol: HEFCE.

Roberts, G (2002) *Set for success: the supply of people with science, technology, engineering and mathematical skills*, London: HM Treasury, pp.143–152.

Roberts, J, Salisbury, J, Jephcote, M and Rees, G (2006) 'Secondary schools and "last chance saloons": critical voices from further education on the deficits of secondary schooling'. Paper presented at British Educational Research Association annual conference, University of Warwick, 6–9 September.

Rogers, M S (2011) 'Online pedagogy: developing a model for online teachers from the pedagogical implications emerging from e-moderator perceptions of their online roles in asynchronous learning networks', doctoral thesis submitted August 2011, University of Glamorgan, Pontypridd.

Rogers, M S (2004) 'Investigating e-moderator perceptions of their online roles in asynchronous discussion forums through a leadership paradigm lens'. Unpublished MSc thesis, University of Glamorgan, Pontypridd.

Rolfe, G (2013) *The university in dissent: scholarship in the corporate university*. Abingdon: Routledge/SRHE.

Rosa, H (2010) *Alienation and acceleration*. Malmö: NSU Press.

Rosaldo, R (1996) 'From the door of his tent: the fieldworker and the inquisitor'. In J Clifford and G E Marcus (eds) ([1986] 2009) *Writing culture: the poetics and politics of ethnography*. Berkeley, CA: University of California Press, pp.77–97.

Rose, N (1996) 'Governing "advanced" liberal democracies'. In A Barry, T Osbourne and N Rose, *Foucault and political reason*. Abingdon: Routledge.

Roth, P (2009) 'Teamworking: an anathema to academics?' *Leadership for Higher Education in Practice: Engaging with Leaders in Higher Education*, 21, pp.3–4.

Rothman, R A and Perrucci, R (1971) 'Vulnerability to knowledge obsolescence among professionals', *The Sociological Quarterly*, 12 (2), pp.147–158.

Rothwell, A, Herbert, I and Seal, W (2011) 'Shared service centers and professional employability', *Journal of Vocational Behavior*, 79, pp.241–252.

Rothwell, A and Arnold, J (2007) 'Self perceived employability, development and validation of a scale', *Personnel Review*, 36 (1), pp.23–41.

Roxå, T and Mårtensson, K (2005) 'Educational developers: a strategic community', *Higher Education Research and Development Society of Australia Conference Proceedings* 2005, pp.447–454.

Rutter, M (1979) 'Protective factors in children's response to stress and disadvantage'. In M. W. Kent and J. E. Rolf (eds) *Primary prevention of psychopathology: vol. 3, social competence in children*. Hanover, NH: University Press of New England, pp.49–74.

Ryan, S, Scott, B, Freeman, H and Patel, D (2000) *The virtual university*. London: Kogan Page.

Sabelis, I (2007) 'The clock-time paradox: time regimes in the network society'. In R Hassan and P Ronald (eds) *24/7: time and temporality in the network society*. Stanford, CA: Stanford University Press, pp.254–277.

Salaman, G (1995) *Managing*. Buckingham: Open University Press.

Salisbury, J and Gornall, L (2011) 'Compulsive working and the pleasures of academic work'. Paper and symposium, CETL conference, 8 April, University of Oxford.

Salisbury, J, Jephcote, M and Roberts, J (2009) 'FE teachers talking about learning: outcomes, contexts and methodologies', *Research Papers in Education*, 24 (4), pp.421–438.

Salisbury, J (2008) 'Martini working – a metaphor for academic working any time any place any where'. Personal correspondence, analytic memo to Working Lives team, 1 March.

Salisbury, J and Jephcote, M (2008) 'Initial encounters of an FE kind', *Research in Post Compulsory Education*, 13 (2), pp.149–162.

Salisbury, J (2004) 'Clients, claimants, learners? Exploring the tailored approaches of New Deal for 18 to 24 year olds', *Journal of Education Policy*, 19 (1), pp.81–104.

Salisbury, J (1994) 'Becoming qualified: an ethnography of a post-experience teacher training course'. Unpublished PhD thesis, University of Wales, Cardiff.

Salmon, G (2011) *E-moderating – The Key to Teaching and Learning Online* (3rd edition). Abingdon: Routledge.

Salmon, G and Lawless, N (2006) 'Management education for the twenty-first century'. In C J Bonk and C R Graham (eds) *The Handbook of Blended Learning*. NJ: Pfeiffer/John Wiley.

Salmon, G (2002) *E-tivities: the key to active on-line learning*. London: Kogan Page.

Samara, D and Luce-Kaplar, R (1996) 'Becoming a teacher: negotiating identities while learning to teach', *Canadian Journal of Education*, 21 (1), pp.65–83.

Sato, M (2010) 'Discussions about the specialization, role and identity of faculty development practitioners: review of research papers by faculty development practitioners in English speaking countries', *NIER Research Bulletin*, 139, pp.63–72.

Saunders, M, Lewis, P and Thornhill, A (2007) *Research methods for business students* (4th edition). Harlow: Pearson Education.

Savin-Baden, M (2008) 'Liquid learning and troublesome spaces: journeys from the threshold?' In R Land J Mayer and J Smith (eds) *Threshold concepts within the discipline*. Rotterdam: Sense Publishers, pp.75–90.

Sawyerr, A (2004) 'African universities and the challenge of research capacity development', *JHEA/RESA*, 2 (1), pp.213–242.

Scarborough, H (ed) (1996) *The management of expertise*. Basingstoke: Macmillan.

Schein, E (1996) 'Career anchors revisited: implications for career development in the 21st century', *Academy of Management Executive*, 10 (4), pp.80–88.

Schein, E (1978) *Career dynamics*. Reading, MA: Addison-Wesley.

Schmuecker, K and Cook, W (2012) *Beyond bricks and mortar boards, universities and the future of the regional economic development*. Report to IPPR North and UUK, Newcastle/London, February 2012.

Schön, D (1987) *Educating the reflective practitioner*. San Francisco: Jossey-Bass.

Schön, D (1967) *Technology and change: the new Heraclitus*. New York: Pergamon Press.

Scott, P (2010) 'Higher education: an overview', *International Encyclopaedia of Education* (3rd edition). Oxford: Elsevier.

Scott, P (2009) 'Markets and new modes of knowledge production', in J Enders and E de Weert (eds) *The Changing face of academic life: analytical and comparative perspectives*, pp. 58–77. Baskinstoke: Palgrave Macmillan.

Scott, P (ed) (2000) *Higher education re-formed*. London: Falmer Press.

Scott, P (ed) (1998) *The globalisation of higher education*. Buckingham: Open University Press.

Scott, P (1995) *The meanings of mass higher education*. Buckingham: SRHE/Open University Press.

Sebalj, D, Holbrook, A and Bourke, S (2012) 'Supporting research in Australian universities: a model of engagement'. Paper presented at the 2012 AARE/APERA Joint International Conference, Sydney 2–6 December 2012.

Seddon, T, Henriksson, L and Niemeyer, B (2010) 'Disturbing academic work'. In T Seddon, L Henriksson and B Niemeyer (eds) *Learning and work and the politics of working life*. London: Routledge: pp.16–29.

Seidman, I (2006) *Interviewing as qualitative research – a guide for researchers in education and the social sciences*. New York: Teachers' College Press.

Seldin, P (1999) *Changing practices in evaluating teaching*. Boulton, MA: Anker.

Selwyn, N (2012) *Education in a digital world: global perspectives on technology and education*. London: Routledge.

Sennett, R (2008) *The craftsman*. London: Allen Lane.

Shaffer, D W, Squire, K R, Halverson, R and Gee, J P (2004) 'Video games and the future of learning', http://citeseerx.ist.psu.edu/viewdoc/download?doi=10.1.1.134.9102&rep=rep1&type=pdf, accessed 30 April 2011.

Shain, F and Gleeson, D (1999) 'Under new management: changing conceptions of teacher professionalism and policy in the further education sector', *Journal of Education Policy*, 14 (4), pp.445–462.

Sharma, V K (2003) 'Adaptive significance of circadian clocks', *Chronobiology International*, 20 (6), pp.901–919.

Sharpe, L J (ed.) (1993) *Rise of meso government in Europe*. London: Sage.

Shaw, W (2001) 'The use of the internet by academics in the discipline of English literature: a quantitative and qualitative approach', *Information Research*, 6 (2), pp.1–10.

Sheehan, M (2013 in press) *Sustainability and the Small and Medium Enterprise (SME): becoming more professional*. Sydney: Xlibris.

Sheehan, M (2010) 'Bullying in the (HE) workplace'. Presentation given to the second Working Lives seminar event, Cardiff University, 14 May.

Shepherd J (2009) 'Humanities research threatened by demands for "economic impact"', *The Guardian*, 13 October.

Shoemaker, S (1984) *Identity, cause, and mind*. Cambridge: Cambridge University Press.

Shore, C (2010) 'Beyond the multiversity: neoliberalism and the rise of the schizophrenic university', *Social Anthropology: European Association of Social Anthropologists*, special issue: *Anthropologies of University Reform*, 18 (1), February, pp.15–29.

Shore, C and Wright, S (2000) 'Coercive accountability: the rise of audit culture in higher education'. In M Strathern (ed), *Audit cultures: anthropological studies in accountability, ethics and the academy*. New York: Routledge.

Shortland, S (2010) 'Feedback within peer observation: continuing professional development and unexpected consequences', *Innovations in Education and Teaching International*, 47 (3), pp.295–304.

Shurville, S, Browne, T and Whitaker, M (2009) 'Accommodating the newfound strategic importance of educational technologists within higher education: a critical literature review', *Campus-wide Information Systems*, 26 (3), pp.201–231.

Sikes, P (2006) 'Working in a "new" university: in the shadow of the Research Assessment Exercise', *Studies in Higher Education*, 31 (5), pp.555–568.

Sims, D (2005) 'You bastard: a narrative exploration of the experience of indignation within organizations', *Organization Studies*, 26 (11), pp.1625–1640.

Skelton, A (2012) 'Teacher identities in a research – led institution: in the ascendancy or on the retreat?' *British Education Research Journal*, 38 (1), pp.23–39.

Skelton, A (2005) *Understanding teaching excellence in higher education: towards a critical approach*. Abingdon: Routledge.

Skelton, A (2004) 'Understanding "teaching excellence" in higher education: a critical evaluation of the National Teaching Fellowships scheme', *Studies in Higher Education*, 29 (4), pp.451–468.

Skocpol, T (1992) *Protecting soldiers and mothers: the political origins of social policy in the United States*. Cambridge, MA: Harvard University Press.

Slaughter, S and Leslie, L (1997) *Academic capitalism: politics, policies and the entrepreneurial university*. Baltimore, MD: Johns Hopkins University Press.

Smith, B and Sparkes, A (2008) 'Contrasting perspectives on narrating selves and identities: an invitation to dialogue', *Qualitative Research*, 8 (1), pp.5–35.

Smith, B (2005) 'Departmental leadership and management in chartered and statutory universities: a case of diversity', *Educational Management Administration and Leadership*, 33 (4), pp.449–464.

Smith, B (2002) 'The role of the university head of department – a survey of two British universities', *Educational Management and Administration*, 30 (3), pp.293–312.

Smith, B W, Dalen, J, Wiggins, K, Tooley, E, Paulette, C and Bernard, J (2008) 'The brief resilience scale: assessing the ability to bounce back', *International Journal of Behavioral Medicine*, 15, pp.194–200.

Smith, J (2008) 'Quality assurance and gender discrimination in English universities: an investigation', *British Journal of Sociology of Education*, 29 (6), pp.623–638.

Social Exclusion Unit (1999) *Bridging the gap: new opportunities for 16–18 year olds not in education, employment or training*. London: Stationery Office.

Sosik, I J, Avolio, B J and Kahai, S S (1997) 'Effects of leadership style and anonymity on group potency and effectiveness in a group decision support system environment', *Journal of Applied Psychology*, 82, pp.89–103.

Sparkes, A (2007) 'Embodiment, academics, and the audit culture: a story seeking consideration', *Qualitative Research*, 7 (4), pp.521–550.

Spours, K, Coffield, F and Gregson, M (2007) 'Mediation, translation and local ecologies: understanding the impact of policy levers on FE colleges', *Journal of Vocational Education and Training*, 59 (2), pp.193–211.

Spradley, J (1979) *The ethnographic interview*. New York: Holt, Reinhart & Winston.

Squire, K D and Johnson, C B (2000) 'Supporting distributed communities of practice with interactive television', *Educational Technology Research and Development*, 48 (1), pp.23–43.

Stanczak, G (ed) (2007) *Visual research methods*. Thousand Oaks, CA: Sage.

Stanley, N and Manthorpe, J (2001) 'Responding to students' mental health needs: impermeable systems and diverse users', *Journal of Mental Health*, 10 (1), pp.41–52.

Statistics Canada (2012) *Salaries and salary scales of full-time teaching staff at Canadian universities, 2010/2011: final report*, http://www.statcan.gc.ca/pub/81-595-m/81-595-m2012097-eng.pdf.

Stephens, D (2009) *Higher education and international capacity building: twenty five years of higher education links*. London: Symposium.

Stevenson, H and Mercer, J (2012) 'Industrial relations in transition – an analysis of employer-union relations in the UK higher education sector'. Presentation to the American Educational Research Association (AERA) Annual Conference, Vancouver, Canada.

Stevenson, H and Mercer, J (2011) 'Challenging times: an analysis of current developments and future prospects for industrial relations in the UK HE sector'. Presentation to the Society for Research into Higher Education Annual Conference, University of Wales, Newport.

Stevens, P A (2004) 'Academic salaries in the UK and US', *National Institute Economic Review*, 24, pp.323–339.

Stoddard, C (2005) 'Adjusting researcher salaries for the cost of living: the affect on salary comparisons and policy conclusions', *Economics of Education Review*, 24, pp.323–339.

Storey, J (2001) *Human resource management: a critical text* (2nd edition). London: Thomson Learning.

Storey, J (1992) *Developments in the management of human resources*. Oxford: Blackwell.

Strathern, M *et al.* (2010) 'Writing across boundaries/writing on writing', ESRC project, Department of Anthropology, Universities of Durham and Newcastle (initiated by B Simpson and R Humphrey), www.dur.ac.uk/writingacrossboundaries.

Strathern, M (ed.) (2000) *Audit cultures: anthropological studies in accountability, ethics and the academy.* New York: Routledge.

Strathern, M (1999) 'The ethnographic effect'. In M Strathern (ed.) *Property, substance and effect.* London: Athlone Press.

Strathern, M (ed) (1995) *Shifting contexts: transformations in anthropological knowledge.* London: Routledge.

Strathern, M (1984) 'Localism displaced: a "vanishing village" in rural England?' *Ethnos*, 49, pp.43–61.

Strathern M (1981) *Kinship at the core: an anthropology of Elmdon, a village in north-west Essex in the nineteen-sixties.* Cambridge: Cambridge University Press.

Strauss, A and Corbin, J (eds) (1997) *Grounded theory: practice.* Thousand Oaks, CA: Sage.

Stronach, I (2009) 'A research charter based on research: taking educational research forward at LJMU', *Research Intelligence*, British Educational Research Association, 108, August, p.20.

Stroud, D (2012) 'Organising training for union renewal', *Economic and Industrial Democracy*, 33 (2), pp.225–244.

Stroud, D (2001) 'The independent investigation of student hardship', *Welsh Journal of Education*, 10 (2), pp.123–142.

Stroud, D (2000) 'The social construction of labour markets by students of higher education'. Unpublished PhD thesis, Cardiff University.

Sutherland, G (1994) 'Emily Davies, the Sidgwicks and the education of women in Cambridge'. In R Mason (ed.) *Cambridge minds.* Cambridge: Cambridge University Press.

Tayler, C (2009) 'A life in writing: Wu Ming', *The Guardian*, 14 November.

Taylor F W ([1911] 1998) *The principles of scientific management.* Mineola: Dover Publications.

Taylor, J A and Wilson, G (2011) *Continuing professional learning of teachers: is this concept more valid for current higher education?* Gold Coast: Higher Education Research and Development Society of Australasia (HERDSA).

Taylor, L (2009) 'Educational development practice and scholarship: an evolving discourse', *International Journal of Academic Development*, 14 (1), pp.1–3.

Taylor, L L (2005) 'Comparing teacher salaries: insights from the US census'. Bush School Working Paper 581.

Taylor, P G (1999) *Making Sense of academic life: academics, universities and change.* Buckingham: SRHE/Open University Press.

Taylor, S and Tyler, M (2000) 'Emotional labour and sexual difference in the airline industry', *Work, Employment and Society*, 14 (1), pp.77–95.

Tehrani, N, Humpage, S, Willmott, B and Haslam, I (2007) *What's happening with well-being at work? Change agenda.* London: Chartered Institute of Personnel Development.

Terasaki, M. (2006) *Daigaku wa Rekishi no shisō de kawaru [University reform: a historical perspective].* Tokyo: Toshindo Publishing.

Tett, L, Crowther, J and O'Hara, P (2003) 'Collaborative partnerships in community education', *Journal of Education Policy*, 18 (1), pp.37–51.

THE (Times Higher Education) (2011) 'The week in higher education', 30 June, http://www.timeshighereducation.co.uk/news/the-week-in-higher-education/416657 accessed 8 March 2013.

THE (Times Higher Education) (2004) 'Academic pay rises lag behind teachers', 15 October.

THE (Times Higher Education) (2001) 'London faces mass academic job losses', June (online).

Thomas, B, Gornall, L and Cook, C (2010) 'The admin that they do'. Paper to the launch of Working Lives seminar series, 26 February, University of Glamorgan, Cardiff.

Thomas, L (2006) 'Widening participation and the increased need for personal tutoring.' In L Thomas and P Hixenbaugh (eds) *Personal tutoring in higher education*. Stoke-on-Trent: Trentham Books.

Thomas, W L with Park, R E and Miller, H A (1921) *Old world traits transplanted*. London: Harper.

Thorpe, M (2009) 'Technology-mediated learning contexts'. In R Edwards, G Biesta and M Thorpe (eds) *Rethinking contexts for learning and teaching: communities, activities and network*. London: Routledge.

Tietze, S and Musson, G (2005) 'Recasting the home-work relationship: a case of mutual adjustment?' *Organisation Studies*, 26 (9), pp.1331–1352.

Tight, M (2010) 'Are academic workloads increasing? The post-war survey evidence in the UK', *Higher Education Quarterly*, 64 (2), pp.200–215.

Tight, M (ed) (2004) *The Routledge Falmer reader in higher education*. London: Routledge.

Tight, M (ed) (2000) *Academic life and work*. Oxford: Elsevier Press.

TLRP (Teaching Learning and Research Programme) (2005) 'Challenge and change in further education: a commentary by the Teaching and Learning Research Programme', http://www.tlrp.org/pub/documents/FEcommentary.pdf, accessed 12 June 2011.

Tolsby, J (2000) 'Taylorism given a helping hand: how an IT system changes employees' flexibility and personal involvement in their work', *Journal of Organizational Change Management*, 13 (5), pp.482–492.

Townley, B (2002) 'Managing with modernity', *Organization*, 9 (4), pp.549–573.

Trainor, J (2011) 'University to offer widespread redundancies', *Varsity Online*, January.

Travers, M (2007) *The new bureaucracy: quality assurance and its critics*. Bristol: Policy Press.

Trigwell, K (2000) 'Phenomenography: variation and discernment'. In C Rust (ed.) *Improving student learning, proceedings of the 1–3 september, 1999 7th international symposium*. Oxford: Oxford Centre for Staff and Learning Development.

Trigwell, K and Prosser, M (1997) 'Towards an understanding of individual acts of teaching and learning', *Higher Education Research and Development*, 16, pp.241–252.

Trigwell, K (1995) 'Increasing faculty understanding of teaching'. In W A Wright (ed.) *Teaching improvement practices: successful strategies for higher education*. Bolton: MA, Anker.

Tripp, D (1993) *Critical incidents in teaching*. London: Routledge.

Trow, M (2004) 'An American perspective on British higher education: the decline of diversity, autonomy and trust in post-war British higher education'. Paper presented for the Symposium on Funding of and Access to US and UK HE, Oxford, Oxford Centre for Higher Education Policy Studies (OxCheps), also in *Perspectives*, 9 (1), pp.7–11.

Trow, M (1975) 'The public and private lives of higher education', *Daedalus*, 104 (1), winter, pp.113–127.

Trowler, P (2008) *Cultures and change in higher education: theories and practice*. Basingstoke: Palgrave.

Trowler, P, Fanghanel, J and Wareham, T (2005) 'Freeing the chi of change: the higher education academy and enhancing teaching and learning in higher education', *Studies in Higher Education*, 30, pp.427–444.

Trowler, P (1998) *Academics responding to change: new higher education frameworks and academic cultures.* Buckingham: SRHE/Open University Press.

TRSE (The Royal Society of Edinburgh) (2012) *Tapping all our talents – women in science, technology, engineering and mathematics: a strategy for Scotland.* Edinburgh: The Royal Society of Edinburgh.

Tuchman, G (2009) *Wannabe U: Inside the corporate university.* Chicago: University of Chicago Press.

Tuckman, B W and Jensen, M A C (1977) 'Stages of small group development revisited', *Group and Organizational Studies,* 2 (4), pp.419–427.

Tunstall, J (1974) *The Open University opens.* London Routledge.

Turkle, S (2011) *Alone together: why we expect more from technology and less from each other.* New York: Basic Books.

Turkle, S (2008) *The inner history of devices.* Cambridge, MA: MIT Press.

Turkle, S (2007) *Can you hear me now?* Special report, Forbes.com, pp.1–4, ttp://www.forbes.com/forbes/2007/0507/176.html, accessed 11 May 2011.

Turkle, S (1995) *Life on the screen: identity in the age of the internet.* London: Simon & Schuster.

Turner, R and Gosling, D (2012) 'Rewarding excellent teaching: the translation of a policy initiative in the UK', *Higher Education Quarterly,* 66 (4), pp.415–430.

Turner, V (1969) *The ritual process, structure and anti-structure.* New York: Aldine de Guyer.

Turoff, M (1995) 'Designing a virtual classroom', paper at International Conference on Computer Assisted Instruction, 7–10 March 1995, National Chiao Tung University, Hsinchu, Taiwan.

UCU (Universities & Colleges Union) (2012) 'How choice has declined in higher education', http://www.ucu.org.uk/media/pdf/c/h/Choice_cuts_report_Feb12.pdf, accessed 12 December 2012.

UCU (Universities & Colleges Union) (2011a) *The impact of the science and research budget allocations for 2011/12 to 2014/15.* Submission to the House of Commons Science and Technology Committee Inquiry. London: UCU.

UCU (Universities & Colleges Union) (2011b) *University and college union submissions to the science and technology committee inquiry into international policies and activities of the research councils.* London: UCU.

UCU (Universities & Colleges Union) (2010) *Universities at risk.* London: UCU.

UCU (Universities & Colleges Union) (2009) *Challenging redundancies in higher education: a UCU briefing document* (appendix 3 revised June 2009). London: UCU.

UCU (Universities & Colleges Union) (2008) *Consultation on the assessment and funding of higher education research post-2008, response to the Research Excellence Framework.* London: UCU.

UCU (Universities & Colleges Union) (2007) *Use of fixed-term contracts in the employment of UK academic staff 1995-6 to 2005-6.* London: UCU.

UCU (Universities & Colleges Union) (1995-2006) *Higher education employment data: academic staff.* London: UCU.

Uddin, S and Hopper, T (2001) 'A Bangladesh soap opera: privatisation, accounting and regimes of control in a less developed country', *Accounting, Organisations and Society,* 26, pp.643–672.

Universitas 21 (2008) Universitas 21 symposium: Strategic Partnerships with the Developing World: A new direction for Universitas 21 in Research and Education. Dublin: University College Dublin [Universitas 21 is a global network of research universities].

University of Wales Institute, Cardiff (2010) *Professional doctorate handbook*. Cardiff: UWIC.

Uschi, F (2005) 'E-learning pedagogy in the third millennium: the need for combining social and cognitive constructivist approaches', *ReCALL*, 17, pp. 85–100.

Usher, R (2000) 'Imposing structure, enabling play: new knowledge production and the "real world" university'. In C Symes and J McIntyre (eds) *Working knowledge – the new vocationalism and higher education*. Buckingham: SRHE/Open University Press, pp.98–110.

UUK (Universities UK) (2013) *The Funding environment for Universities: an assessment*. Report, May. London: UUK.

UUK (Universities UK) (2010) *The competency of the workforce*. London: UUK.

UUK (Universities UK) (2006) *The changing academic profession in the UK: setting the scene*. Research Report, June 2007. London: UUK/Centre for Higher Education Research and Information (CHERI).

Van Dijk, P and Kirk Brown, A (2006) 'Emotional labour and negative job outcomes: an evaluation of the mediating role of emotional dissonance', *Journal of Management and Organisation*, 12 (2), pp.101–115.

Van Driel, J H, Beijaard, D and Verloop, N (2009) 'Experienced science teachers' learning in the context of educational innovation', *Journal of Teacher Education*, 60 (2), pp.184–219.

Van Maanen, J (1992) 'The smile factory work at Disneyland'. In P Frost, L F Moore, C C Louis, E Lundberg and J Martin, (eds) *Reframing organisational culture*. Thousand Oaks, CA: Sage, pp.58–76.

Van Maanen, J and Barley, S (1984) 'Occupational communities: culture and control in organisations', in B M Straw and L O Cummings (eds) *Research in organisational behaviour*, 6, pp.287–365.

Voisey, P, Gornall, L, Jones, P and Thomas, B (2005) 'Developing a model for a "ladder of incubation" linked to higher and further education institutions in Wales', *Industry and Higher Education*, 19 (6), pp.445–456.

Vygotsky, L S (1978) *Mind and society: the development of higher mental processes*. Cambridge, MA: Harvard University Press.

Waddell, G and Burton K (2006) 'Is work good for your health and well-being?' Report commissioned by the Department of Work and Pensions. London: The Stationery Office.

Wainwright, D and Calnan, M (2002) *Work stress the making of a modern epidemic*. Buckingham: Open University Press.

Walker, M (2006) *Higher education pedagogies*. Maidenhead: SRHE/Open University Press.

Walker, M (2004) 'Beyond the impossibly good place: research and scholarship.' In M Walker and J Nixon (eds) *Reclaiming universities from a runaway world*. Maidenhead: Open University Press, pp. 178–194.

Walker, M and Nixon, J (eds) (2004) *Reclaiming universities from a runaway world*. Maidenhead. SRHE/Open University Press.

Walker. M (ed) (2001a) *Reconstructing professionalism in university teaching: teachers and learners in action*. Buckingham: SRHE/Open University Press.

Walker, M (2001b) 'Collaboration with/in a critical community of practice'. In M Walker (ed) *Reconstructing professionalism in university teaching: teachers and learners in action*. Buckingham: SRHE/Open University Press, pp.39–58.

Walker, M (1998) 'Academic Identities: women on a South African Landscape', *British Journal of Sociology of Education*, 19 (3), pp.335–354.

Wallace, M (2005) 'Towards effective management of a reformed teaching profession'. Paper presented at C–TRIP Seminar 4 'Enactments of Professionalism: Classrooms and Pedagogies', King's College, London, 5 July.

Waller, P (1987) *Spinning room*. Documentary film, former Royal Dockyard at Chatham.

Wallman, S (1986) 'The boundaries of household'. In A Cohen (ed.) *Symbolising boundaries: identity and diversity in British cultures*. Manchester: Manchester University Press, pp.50–70.

Wallman, S (ed) (1979) *Social anthropology of work*, ASA Monograph 19. London: Academic Press.

Walters, S and Watters, K (2001) 'Lifelong learning, higher education and active citizenship: from rhetoric to action', *International Journal of Lifelong Education*, 20 (6), pp.471–478.

Waring, M A (2010) 'Moments of vision: HRM and the individualization of academic workers'. Unpublished PhD thesis, University of Wales.

Waring, M A (2009) 'Labouring in the Augean stables', *International Journal of Management Concepts and Philosophy*, 3 (3), pp.257–274.

Warr, P (2002) *Psychology at work*. Pakefield: Penguin Group.

Warren, R and Plumb, E (1999) 'Survey of "Distinguished Teacher" award schemes in higher education', *Journal of Further and Higher Education*, 23 (2), pp.245–255.

Watkins, J M and Mohr, B J (2001) *Appreciative inquiry: change at the speed of imagination*. San Francisco: Jossey-Bass.

Watson, D (2009) *The question of morale, managing happiness and unhappiness in university life*. Maidenhead: Open University Press, p. 285.

Watson, T (1987) *Sociology, work and industry* (2nd edition). London: Routledge.

Webb, A (2008) *Promise and performance*. The Webb Report of the Independent Review of the Mission and Purpose of Further Education in Wales in the context of the Learning Country: Vision in to Action. Cardiff: Wales Assembly Government.

Webster, L and Mertova, P (2007) *Using narrative inquiry as a research method – an introduction to using critical event narrative analysis in research on learning and teaching*. Abingdon: Routledge.

Wellin, M (2007) *Managing the psychological contract: using the personal deal to increase business performance*. Aldershot: Gower.

Welsh Assembly Government (WAG) (2012a) *Micro-business task and finish group report*. January 2012, Cardiff: Welsh Government.

Welsh Assembly Government (2012b) *Further and Higher Education (Wales) Bill*. July 2012, Cardiff: Welsh Government.

Welsh Assembly Government (2012c) *Science for Wales: A strategic agenda for science and innovation in Wales*. March 2012, Cardiff: Welsh Government.

Welsh Assembly Government (2012d) *Wales and the European Union: The Welsh Government's EU strategy*. May 2012, Cardiff: Welsh Government.

Welsh Assembly Government (2012e) *Consultation paper – Further and Higher Education (Wales) Bill*, http://wales.gov.uk/consultations/education/feandhebill/?lang=en, accessed 4 January 2013.

Welsh Assembly Government (2010) *Securing a sustainable future for higher education: an independent review of higher education funding and student finance*. October 2010, Cardiff: Welsh Government.

Welsh Assembly Government (2009) *For our future: the 21st century higher education strategy and plan for Wales*. November 2009, Cardiff: Welsh Government.

Welsh Assembly Government (2008) *Skills that work for Wales*. Cardiff: DELLS.

Welsh Assembly Government (2006a) *The Learning Country 2: delivering the promise.* A consultative Document, April 2006. Cardiff: Dept of Education, Lifelong Learning and Skills.

Welsh Assembly Government (2006b) *The Learning Country 3: vision into action.* Cardiff: Department of Education, Lifelong Learning and Skills.

Welsh Assembly Government (2002) *Reaching higher: higher education and the learning country.* March 2002, Cardiff: Welsh Government.

Welsh Assembly Government (2001) *The Learning Country 1: a comprehensive education and life long learning programme to 2010 in Wales.* Cardiff: Dept. of Education, Lifelong Learning and skills.

Welsh Assembly Government (October 2000) *Putting Wales first: a partnership for the people of Wales.* Cardiff: Welsh Government.

Welsh Labour Party (2011) *Standing up For Wales: Welsh Labour manifesto 2011.* Cardiff: Welsh Labour Party.

Wenger, E, White, N and Smith, J D (2009) *Digital habitats: stewarding technology for communities.* Portland: CP Square.

Wenger, E (1998) *Communities of practice: learning, meaning and identity.* Cambridge: Cambridge University Press.

Werner, E and Smith, R (1982) *Vulnerable but invincible: a longitudinal study of resilient children and youth.* New York: Adams, Bannister & Cox.

Wertsch, J V (1985) *Vygotsky and the Social Formation of Mind.* Cambridge, MA: Harvard University Press.

WFEPC (Welsh Further Education Purchasing Consortium) (2010) 'Further education funding briefing paper (2010–2011)', collegeswales.ac.uk/download.aspx?r=90, accessed 12 April 2010.

Whitchurch, C (2013) *Reconstructing identities in higher education: the rise of third space professionals.* London: Routledge.

Whitchurch, C (2008) 'Shifting identities and blurring boundaries: the emergence of third space professionals in UK higher education', *Higher Education Quarterly*, 62 (4), pp.377–396.

Whitchurch, C M (2006) *Professional managers in UK higher education: preparing for complex futures.* Interim report, July. London: Leadership Foundation.

White, J (2012) 'Turning a scholarly blind eye'. In T Fitzgerald, J White and H Gunter, *Hard Labour? Academic Work and the Changing Landscape of Higher Education.* Bingley: Emerald, pp.87–111.

White, J and Beswick, J (2003) *Working long hours.* Sheffield: Health and Safety laboratory (HSL/2003/02).

Wilcox, P, Winn, S and Fyvie–Gauld, M (2005) ' "It was nothing to do with the university, it was just the people": the role of social support in the first-year experience of higher education', *Studies in Higher Education*, 30 (6), pp.707–722.

Wilkins, P (1997) *Personal and professional development for counsellors.* London: Sage.

Wilkinson, R and Pickett, K (2010) *The Spirit level: why equality is better for everyone in Great Britain.* Harmondsworth: Penguin.

Willmott, H (1995) 'Managing the academics: commodification and control in the development of university education in the UK', *Human Relations*, 48 (9), pp.993–1027.

Wilson, T (2012) *A review of business-university collaboration.* London: BIS.

Winter, R and O'Donohue, W (2012) 'Understanding academic identity conflicts in the public university: importance of work ideologies', *Research and Development in Higher Education*, 35, pp.340–351.

Winter, R (2009) 'Academic manager or managed academic? Academic identity schisms in higher education', *Journal of Higher Education Policy and Management*, 31 (2), pp.121–131.

Winter, R and Sarros, J (2002) 'The academic work environment in Australian universities: a motivating place to work?' *Higher Education Research and Development*, 21 (3), pp.241–242.

Winter, R (1995) 'The University of Life plc: the "industrialisation" of higher education?' In J Smyth (ed) *Academic work*. Buckingham: SRHE/Open University Press.

WJEC (1992) *Modularisation: towards a flexible further education system in Wales*. Cardiff: Welsh Joint Education Committee (WJEC).

Wolf Report (2009) *An adult approach to further education*. London: The Institute of Economic Affairs, http://www.iea.org.uk/sites/default/files/publications/files/upldbook498pdf.pdf, accessed 8 August 2012.

Wolf Report (2011) *Review Of Vocational Education*. London: UK Department For Education.

Woods, P, Boyle, M, Jeffrey, B and Troman, G (2000) ' A research team in ethnography', *Qualitative Studies in Education*, 13 (1), pp.85–98.

Woods, P (1981) Strategies, commitment and identity: making and breaking the teacher. In L Barton and S Walker (eds) *Schools, Teachers and Training*. London: Falmer.

Woolgar, S (2002) *Virtual society? Technology, cyberbole, reality*. Oxford: Oxford University Press, pp.302–313.

Woolgar, S (ed) (1988) *Knowledge and reflexivity: new frontiers in the sociology of knowledge*. London: Sage.

Woodward, K (ed) (1980) *The myths of information: technology and postindustrial culture*. London: Routledge.

Wozniak, H, Mahony, M J, Lever, T and Pizzica, J (2009) 'Stepping through the orientation looking glass: a staged approach for postgraduate students', *Australasian Journal of Educational Technology*, 25 (2), pp.221–234.

Wozniak, H (2007) 'Empowering learners to interact effectively in asynchronous discussion activities', in M Bullen and D Janes (eds) *Making the transition to e-learning: strategies and issues*. Hershey, PA: Idea Group Publishing, pp.208–228.

Wozniak, H, Silveira, S, Brew, A and Sachs, J (2007) *Transforming learning using structured online discussions to engage learners*. Sydney: University of Sydney Press.

Wright, A W (1995) *Teaching improvement practices: successful strategies for higher education*. Boulton, MA: Anker.

Wright, P M, Gardner, T M and Moynihan L M (2003) 'The impact of HR practices on the performance of business units', *Human Resource Management Journal*, 13(3), pp.21–36.

Wright, P M, Smart, D L and McMahan, G C (1995) 'Matches between human resources and strategy among NCAA basketball teams', *Academy of Management Journal*, 38, pp.1052–1074.

Wright, S and Ørberg, J W (2008) 'Autonomy and control: Danish university reform in the context of modern governance', *Learning and Teaching: International Journal of Higher Education in the Social Sciences*, 1 (1), pp.27–57.

Wright, S (ed) (1994) *Anthropology of organisations*. London: Routledge.

Wright Mills, C (1940) 'Situated actions and vocabularies of motive', *American Sociological Review*, 6, pp.904–913.

Yanez, J L and Altopiedi, M (2012) 'Outstanding research groups in HE organisations'. Presentation to the European Council for Educational Research (ECER) conference, Cadiz, Spain, October 2012.

Yeomans, D (2002) *Constructing vocational education: from TVEI to GNVQ*. Leeds: School of Education, University of Leeds, www.leeds.ac.uk/educo/documents/00002214.htm, accessed 11 September 2012.

Ylijoki, O-H (2013) 'Boundary-work between work and life in the high-speed university', *Studies in Higher Education*, 38 (2), pp.242–255.

Ylijoki O-H and Mäntylä, H (2003) 'Conflicting time perspectives in academic work', *Time and Society*, 12 (1), pp.55–78.

Yorke, M and Thomas, L (2003) 'Improving the retention of students from lower socio-economic groups', *Journal of Higher Education Policy and Management*, 25 (1), pp.63–74.

Young, P (2010) 'The loneliness of the long distance doctoral student: a personal reflection on process and outcomes'. In T Brown (ed.) *The doctorate: stories of knowledge, power and becoming*. Bristol: ESCalate, pp.53–59.

Young, P (2006) 'Out of balance: lecturers' perceptions of differential status and rewards in relation to teaching and research', *Teaching in Higher Education*, 11 (2), pp.191–202.

Zembylas, M (2013) 'Transnationalism, migration and emotions: implications for education', *Globalisation, Societies and Education*, 10 (2), pp.163–179.

Zhang, D (2003) 'Powering e–learning in the new millennium: an overview of e-learning and enabling technology', *Information Systems Frontiers*, 5 (2), pp.201–221.

Index

Internet 116, 232, 238, 239, 295, 300
Ireland (North and South)/Irish 13, 15–19, 69, 119, 121–8; (North only) 125, 126, 163

Japan 141, 170–9
JISC (Joint Information Systems Committee) 238
  library facilities and growing demand 243
Job market 281
  'Ice Age of the Job Market' (Japan) 175
Job titles
  e-learning posts 246
  educational developer 243
  educational research co-ordinator 244
  emerging in workplaces using new teaching and learning technologies 243
  hybrid roles to support teaching and learning 243
  job descriptions for new posts 244
  learning 282
  learning technologist 243, 244
  'lecturer' 134
  new professionals 'servicing the needs of re-formed institutions' 243
  non-traditional 249
  research 282
  teaching 282
  'third space' 284, 287
Job satisfaction 81
  journey 91
Jobs 24, 29, 37, 51, 54, 55, 74, 79, 110, 114, 117
  'brain-drain' into industry 191
  full-time HE staff appointments given to 'outsiders', mostly from EU 192
  high competition for science jobs 192
  internal and external job markets for science research staff 196
  job creation (RCB4D chairs) 127
  job dissatisfaction 285
  job evaluation sheets 148
  job insecurity 261
  job prospects for late-career staff problematic 192
  job redundancies 261
  job security factors in science 189
  opportunities for permanent assistant lectureships 192

research appointments in HE 192
  serial fixed-contracts underpin full-time – pyramid structure of fixed-term awards 194
  target-driven 287
  'third space' 28, 259
Journey
  of becoming a teacher in HE 57, 61
Judgement 85, 111, 112
  interpersonal behaviour 291
  of work monetarily 98
  professional 114

Knowledge 111
  'change project' (ProfDoc) as contribution to knowledge 266
  commodification of 289
  construction ability (online) 230
  creation 9
  cultural 281
  factors affecting academic research in generating new knowledge 101
  'half-life' knowledge 133
  intersubjective knowledge for understanding how colleagues work with ICT 225
  knowledge 'capital' 196
  lack of knowledge about personal tutoring 155
  multidisciplinary knowledge generation versus individual knowledge 120
  'obsolescence' 133
  pursuit of 82
  scholarly 163
  sharing 251
  technical 281
  work 289
  workers 102
Knowledge-base practitioners 170
Knowledge based economy (*see* Economy)
Knowledge development (*see* Development) knowledge economy 29
Knowledge transfer 297

Labour Party Women's Education Group 40
Language
  'beyond language': what British say, what the British means, what others understand 184